LAW AND THE QUEST FOR GENDER EQUALITY

MARGARET THORNTON

LAW AND THE QUEST FOR GENDER EQUALITY

MARGARET THORNTON

Australian
National
University

ANU PRESS

GLOBAL THINKERS SERIES

For Lizzie and Luke

Australian
National
University

ANU PRESS

Published by ANU Press
The Australian National University
Canberra ACT 2600, Australia
Email: anupress@anu.edu.au

Available to download for free at press.anu.edu.au

ISBN (print): 9781760465490
ISBN (online): 9781760465506

WorldCat (print): 1348911047
WorldCat (online): 1348910574

DOI: 10.22459/LQGE.2022

Cover design and layout by ANU Press

Cover illustration: David Boyd, *Cockatoos Watching Europa's Attempt to Fly* (detail), 1995. Oil on board, 30.5 x 25.5 cm. Reproduced with permission of the estate of David Boyd.

This book is published under the aegis of the Public Policy editorial board of ANU Press.

Contents

Part VII: The Corporatised Academy

Abbreviations

AA	affirmative action
AA Act	*Affirmative Action (Equal Employment Opportunity for Women) Act 1986*
AHRC	Australian Human Rights Commission
ANU	The Australian National University
CEDAW	Convention on the Elimination of All Forms of Discrimination against Women
EEO	equal employment opportunity
EO	equal opportunity
EOA	*Equal Opportunity Act 1984* (Vic.)
EOT	Equal Opportunity Tribunal
GFC	Global Financial Crisis
HREOC	Human Rights and Equal Opportunity Commission
ILO	International Labour Organization
LPA	*Legal Practitioners Act 1893* (WA)
NSW	New South Wales
OECD	Organisation for Economic Co-operation and Development
SA	South Australia
SDA	*Sex Discrimination Act 1984* (Cth)
UK	United Kingdom
US	United States
WA	Western Australia
WGEA	*Workplace Gender Equality Act 2012* (Cth)
WLB	work–life balance

Acknowledgements

The author and the publisher thank the following for permission to reproduce copyright material:

Elsevier for Thornton, 'Feminism and the Contradictions of Law Reform' (1991) 19 *International Journal of the Sociology of Law* 453–74. Taylor & Francis for Thornton, 'Feminism and the Changing State: The Case of Sex Discrimination' (2006) 21(50) *Australian Feminist Studies* 151–72; Thornton, 'The Mirage of Merit: Reconstituting the "Ideal Academic"' (2013) 28(76) *Australian Feminist Studies* 127–43; Thornton, 'Hypercompetitiveness or a Balanced Life? Gendered Discourses in the Globalisation of Australian Law Firms' (2014) 17(2) *Legal Ethics* 153–76. The *Federal Law Review* for Thornton, 'Sex Discrimination, Courts and Corporate Power' (2008) 36(1) *Federal Law Review* 31–56. *Melbourne University Law Review* for Thornton, 'Sexual Harassment Losing Sight of Sex Discrimination' (2002) 26 *Melbourne University Law Review* 422–44. The *Sydney Law Review* for Thornton, 'The Flexible Cyborg: Work–Life Balance in Legal Practice' (2016) 38(1) *Sydney Law Review* 1–21; and Thornton, '"Otherness" on the Bench: How Merit is Gendered' (2007) 29(3) *Sydney Law Review* 391–413. The University of New South Wales Law Journal for Thornton, 'Who Cares? The Conundrum for Gender Equality in Legal Practice' (2020) 43(4) *UNSW Law Journal* 1473–93. And the University of Western Australia Law Review for Thornton, 'Challenging the Legal Profession a Century On: The Case of Edith Haynes' (2018) 44(1) *UWA Law Review* 1–20.

The following publications are in the public domain: Thornton, *Portia Lost in the Groves of Academe Wondering What to Do about Legal Education* (Inaugural Lecture, La Trobe University Press, 1991); Thornton, 'Technocentrism in the Law School: Why the Gender and Colour of

Law Remain the Same' (1998) 36(2) *Osgoode Hall Law Journal* 369–98; Thornton, 'Universities Upside Down: The Impact of the New Knowledge Economy' (2009) 21(2) *Canadian Journal of Women and the Law* 375–93.

The essays are based on presentations made in various parts of the world in pre-Covid times, when travel was possible. The author thanks the following institutions for providing a platform on which to present draft papers and receive valuable comments from colleagues: American Law & Society; ANU College of Law; ANU Gender Institute; The Australian National University; Australian Law and Society Conference; Columbia University Law School; Equal Opportunity Commission, Melbourne; Griffith University; ILS Law College, Pune, India; La Trobe University; Macquarie University; Open Embodiments Conference, Tucson, Arizona; Research Committee on the Sociology of Law Conference, Bonn; University of Melbourne; University of Vienna; Women's Studies Centre, University of Sydney; Osgoode Hall Law School, York University, Toronto.

For organising visits and visitorships, as well as for their generous hospitality, I would like to thank Martha Fineman of Columbia Law School, New York, and Emory University School of Law, Atlanta, GA; Alix Frank-Thomasser and Franz Heidinger of the University of Vienna; Nicola Lacey of New College, Oxford, and the London School of Economics; Mary Jane Mossman of Osgoode Hall Law School, Toronto; and Hilary Sommerlad of Leeds Law School.

I acknowledge the institutional support of Macquarie University Law School, the former School of Law and Legal Studies at La Trobe University and the ANU College of Law at The Australian National University. I also acknowledge and thank the Australian Research Council for financial support.

For their helpful comments on chapters, I thank Tony Blackshield, Judy Fudge, Narrelle Morris, Susan Priest and Judith Resnik, as well as a host of anonymous referees. For research assistance and valuable discussion, I thank Chris Atmore, Renee Burns, Trish Luker, Harry McLaurin, William Mudford, Lucinda Shannon and Margot Stubbs. A special debt is owed to Richard Collier for his support and challenging questions. Above all, I thank Ann Genovese for her unremitting faith in the feminist jurisprudential project and for writing the Foreword.

Not to be forgotten are my former (mostly male) colleagues at Macquarie Law School who challenged me with their scepticism about feminist legal scholarship (Drew Fraser suggested that if women wished to engage in critique from a feminist perspective, they should establish their own university!). I thank my former colleagues at La Trobe Law School, particularly Sandy Cook, Sue Davies, Judy Grbich, Adrian Howe and Andrea Rhodes-Little, who, in contrast, had already accepted new ways of seeing. I also acknowledge the support of present and past colleagues at the ANU College of Law, including Dorota Gozdecka, Anne Macduff, Heather Roberts and Kim Rubenstein, and I would particularly like to thank the former dean, the late Michael Coper, for encouraging me to come to The Australian National University and for his ongoing support. I also acknowledge many former students—undergraduate and postgraduate—for their engaging and stimulating exchanges.

I am most grateful to the Boyd estate, particularly Lucinda Boyd, for permission to reproduce the cover image of David Boyd's painting *Cockatoos Watching Europa's Attempt to Fly* (1995).

Finally, I thank ANU Press for inviting me to contribute to its Global Thinkers series. I am particularly grateful to Andrew Kennedy, chair of the Public Policy editorial board, for his support and encouragement and to Jan Borrie for her eagle eye and superior copyediting skills.

Margaret Thornton
ANU College of Law
The Australian National University
Canberra
March 2023

Foreword

I have been a close reader of Margaret Thornton's scholarship since the early 1990s, when I began my own life as a scholar. The institutional conditions in which feminist postgraduate students could do our work back then were still relatively new and precarious. But as students we were encouraged to think it was possible to do feminist, critical and interdisciplinary research because of the intellectual example and advocacy of scholars like Margaret Thornton. We learned that taking up a role as a feminist in legal institutions took courage and had many forms: as advisor to government, as empirical researcher, as advocate. But being 'a feminist at law' was also capacious enough to enable the invention of the role of the feminist scholar who was responsible for the care of legal knowledge as an intellectual task. Margaret's work exemplified all these possibilities with an unflinching attitude. She captured a moment of institutional self-determination in her writing that was deeply important then, and her body of work has continued to be influential ever since.

Margaret's single-authored books, for example, are rightly understood as classics and forerunners in their fields and genre: *The Liberal Promise: Anti-Discrimination Legislation in Australia* (1990); *Dissonance and Distrust: Women in the Legal Profession* (1996); *Privatising the Public University: The Case of Law* (2011). Her numerous edited collections, which include *Public and Private: Feminist Legal Debates* (1996), *Romancing the Tomes: Popular Culture, Law and Feminism* (2002), *Sex Discrimination in Uncertain Times* (2010) and *Gender and Careers in the Legal Academy* (2021, with Ulrike Schultz, Gisela Shaw and Rosemary Auchmuty), have brought together the work of other feminists at law, creating community and renewing projects for change. However, there are other works by Margaret—essays and journal articles written over the course of her career that are dispersed and have been much harder to access. For many years, I have sought them out, putting together a cumbersome set of PDFs for students, which I call 'the Thornton essential' reading list. Or, I have referred to them in my own writing, item by item, to cite effectively both the breadth and the overarching argument of Margaret's contributions. It is a selection of these essays that fortunately, finally, is presented in *Law and the Quest for Gender Equality*; and for me (and I think for many others) to have the body of work joined together in one volume is timely and valued.

For those not previously familiar with Margaret Thornton's work, the essays you are about to read are a great introduction to an important Australian legal scholar. This book spans work produced between 1986 and 2020, but Margaret has also written a new introductory essay to orient *Law and the Quest for Gender Equality* as a collection. The Introduction begins: 'While sometimes reformist and occasionally transformative, engagement with law poses a challenge for those pursuing the path of social change.' From this opening sentence, Margaret is inviting any reader, new or old, to understand the relationship between the selected essays, how they fit into a career project as whole, as well as what work they do jurisprudentially and politically in each instance. Margaret Thornton's authorial voice is resolute and constant in this Introduction, as it is in all her work. She does not write with hubris or accept the promise of law reform as easy or a tool for change if it is unfounded, untested and unsupported by a realist's appraisal of social, historical and doctrinal evidence. Her project is to provide readers with a community, to show them they are not alone and to equip them with techniques they can use to foster clear analysis, demonstrated as a prerequisite for adaptive and targeted change for gender recognition in law and justice before it. That attitude and tone are important compass points, as is the clarity with which Margaret explains and exemplifies in the pages that follow her own unique methodological framing and her long-term political commitments.

To give an example: a hallmark of Margaret's work is her ability to lead in the articulation of a feminist jurisprudential praxis in Australia. The cross-disciplinarity of her work, in which she joined often distinct modes of engagement and spoke between them, offered something new in 1986, when she wrote 'Feminist jurisprudence: Illusion or reality?'—the first article in Australia to join the words 'feminist' and 'jurisprudence' in title or subject matter. This positioning is now taken for granted in the international feminist and critical legal landscape, so it is timely that Margaret's leadership is reprinted and centralised in this collection. The innovation of Margaret's approach was, and is, to begin with philosophically informed attention to liberalism and its project, and its inviolability in law. This activity, if undertaken from a feminist perspective, exposes and problematises how law works in real-life situations that effect diverse constituencies of marginalised subjects of law. Margaret repeatedly uses that investigation to then propose action, to build resistant sites for engagement. This produces a unique foundation for a sociolegal scholarship, a basis for public engagement and a career-sustained argument for committed political change. These are essential tools for feminists working as lawyers today, be it as students, researchers, advocates or institutional officials. The Introduction makes these achievements plain, and the book as it is then described and arranged opens space for discussion by all these different participants.

The other current in Margaret's work that is clearly articulated across *Law and the Quest for Gender Equality* is her historical framing of practice and reformist projects. Margaret trained as an ancient historian before coming to law and this gives all her work a clear eye and a viewpoint that contextualises the conditions and situation of the here and now, and what might be required to attend to the entrenched everyday injustice experienced by subjects of law excluded from the liberal promise. Margaret's historical approach is not directed to a transcendent overcoming by law reform and a false sense that the present is teleologically an improvement on the past (a liberal promise in itself). She instead uses history to show how that project is never over and changes over time. Material and political events at the time of writing each essay are signposted, to show markers of ebb and flow, how perennial problems of discrimination re-create themselves in courts, parliaments, workplaces, homes and streets. Importantly, Margaret's essays demonstrate that these are systemic problems, not individualised causes (as orthodox legal form and philosophy would like us to accept).

The value and power of these collected essays are that they show how and why people's difficult, exclusionary and problematic experiences with law can be reframed by *feminists*, using the tools we have at our collective disposal to fight problems for our own time. *Law and the Quest for Gender Equality* reminds all of us as readers to watch what is unfolding before us in everyday life with acute attention and to marshal our resources to renew the quest for gender justice in law and as lawyers.

Ann Genovese
Professor of Law
Melbourne Law School
June 2022

Introduction

While sometimes reformist and occasionally transformative, engagement with law poses a challenge for those pursuing the path of social change. It is easy to cling to the liberal progressivist myth that things are always getting better and to overlook the past, even when the seeds of invidiousness linger. This is apparent when we turn to feminist engagement with law, particularly as law was long a means of entrenching the subordination of women. To expect law to change instantaneously and become the primary means of effecting gender equality must inevitably produce uncertainty and ambivalence.

The common law—that is, law made by judges, all of whom were men until very recently—is replete with misogyny. A startling illustration was the doctrine of coverture by which a woman entered what amounted to a state of civil death on marriage. While she had few rights when single, she had none when she married, as her persona merged with that of her husband. To paraphrase the noted eighteenth-century English jurist Sir William Blackstone, 'the husband and wife are one person in law and that one is the husband'.[1]

The heritage of coverture, or what Thomas Hobbes referred to as 'domesticated command',[2] long shaped marital relations. Even in terms of entry into the marriage contract, the bride was merely an object of exchange; the arrangement was a fraternal contract effected between the father or guardian of the bride and the prospective husband.[3] The metaphysical ramifications of this were profound, for it meant the wife had no right to refuse sexual relations with her husband. Her consent was implied as her will had been vitiated on marriage. The fiction that

---

1   William Blackstone, *Commentaries* (University of Chicago Press, 1979 [1765–69]) 442.
2   Thomas Hobbes, *De Cive: Or The Citizen*, edited & introduced by Sterling Lamprecht (Appleton-Century-Crofts, 1949 [1642]) IX, 6.
3   Carole Pateman, *The Sexual Contract* (Polity Press, 1988).

the wife was incapable of withholding consent prevented a husband from being prosecuted for the rape of his wife and was only formally abandoned by superior courts in 1991 in both the United Kingdom and Australia,[4] thereby pointing to the deeply patriarchal nature of the common law.[5] The recent abandonment of the rape immunity also underscores just how novel is reform in the history of gender relations.

Marriage generally has been slow to shed elements of its premodern status and to transition 'from status to contract' in accordance with Maine's famous aphorism that marked the shift from feudalism to contractualism in areas such as employment and commerce.[6] Nevertheless, marriage was regarded as a perfect form of contract in nineteenth-century law textbooks because of the assumed indivisibility of the wills of the husband and wife, as well as being a religious sacrament.[7] The premodern status element in the marriage contract meant the parties were not free to negotiate its terms like other contracting parties, which included being able to choose the sex of one's partner.[8] Thus, marriage could occur only between a man and a woman; the right to marry a partner of the same sex is a very recent development,[9] although some relationships, such as polygamy, are still prohibited.

The philosophical separation between public and private life that disproportionately impacted women and long contributed to their status as nonpersons remains a structural impediment at the heart of the equality/inequality conundrum, and the private sphere continues to be largely immunised against legal regulation. The private sphere was historically regarded as a sphere of inequality because of the 'domesticated command' exercised by the male head of the household over subordinates—that is, the wife, children and servants. The 'law of the father' prevailed in the home rather than the law of the state, which was largely confined to the public sphere.

---

4   *R v R* (1991) 3 WLR 767; *R v L* (1991) 174 CLR 379.
5   For a detailed study of this issue, see Ngaire Naffine, *Criminal Law and the Man Problem* (Hart, 2019).
6   Sir Henry Sumner Maine, *Ancient Law: Its Connection with the Early History of Society and its Relation to Modern Ideas* (J. Murray, 1917 [1861]), n2t.net/ark:/13960/t7cr67j5g.
7   For example, Theophilus Parsons, *Law of Contracts* (Little, Brown, 1980 [1853]) 556–57.
8   Margaret Thornton, 'Intention to Contract: Public Act or Private Sentiment' in Ngaire Naffine, Rosemary Owens & John Williams (eds), *Intention in Law and Philosophy* (Ashgate, 2001), doi.org/10.4324/9781315187136-10.
9   For example, *Marriage Amendment Act 2017* (Cth).

In the public sphere, male citizens alone were able to participate in the governance of the democratic polity and promulgate whatever laws they thought fit. Furthermore, formal equality was attainable only in public life where it was the prerogative of free men. Women were permanently confined to the private sphere and the status of inequality. First-Wave Feminism—associated with the nineteenth and early twentieth centuries—entailed the struggle by women to enter the public sphere and the 'community of equals', which included attending universities and gaining admission to the professions, as well as securing the right to vote.

Inroads have undoubtedly been made into the idea that there is a strict line of demarcation between the public and the private spheres, particularly through the endeavours of Second-Wave Feminism since the late twentieth century. The insistence that the polity pay attention to the injustices of private life—symbolised by the catchphrase 'the personal is political'—changed the notion that what occurs in the home is largely beyond the jurisdiction of the state. Nevertheless, contemporary liberalism remains resistant to the regulation of the private sphere and lukewarm about radically reforming seemingly intractable gendered harms, such as domestic violence, which continue to be treated differently from assaults in the public realm. The echoes of 'domesticated command' may still be discerned in the policing of domestic violence, which remains a highly gendered phenomenon in which men are overwhelmingly the perpetrators.

While sexual assault is no longer formally gender-specific, it has also been unable to slough off its misogynistic history of male sex right, which has been sustained through the law of rape. Hence, the antifeminist myths surrounding the act of sexual penetration and the notion of consent linger. Furthermore, the criminal law remains fixated on the accused, who is deemed to be 'innocent until proven guilty'—a factor that deflects attention from the harm to the victim, who becomes merely a witness for the prosecution if a trial takes place. The individualised perspective that is central to legal form causes law to lose sight of the systemic nature of gendered violence that inhibits substantive reform. Historically, liberal legalism has preferred to treat each instance of criminality as the aberrant act of an individual perpetrator and to slough off the harm to victims generally, although this paradigm is very much a contemporary site of context.

The public/private dichotomy constitutes an ongoing impediment not just to the operation of the criminal law, but also to the efficacy of the civil law. Thus, the promise of antidiscrimination legislation, which was an important initiative of Second-Wave Feminism in the late twentieth century, is undermined by the fact that its operation is restricted to the public sphere, paying scant regard to what occurs in the home. This is even though the private sphere continues to be a primary source of inequality for women, whose disadvantage may be compounded by having a disability or being Indigenous, aged or LGBTIQ+. Women are generally still expected to assume the major responsibility for caring for children, the sick and the elderly, as well as performing the preponderance of unpaid domestic labour, which disproportionately impacts on their ability to participate as equals in the public sphere. As a result, the commitment to the non-discrimination principle fails to live up to its legislative promise of promoting the 'principle of the equality of men and women'.[10]

Rather than engaging in thoroughgoing social change, this is a matter that liberal legalism prefers to leave to chance. Unlike medicine, law is resistant to taking preventative or prophylactic action and chooses to provide a course of action for affected individuals to assume the burden of pursuing a remedy themselves. Any ripples that flow from individual action to civil society more broadly are merely a matter of chance. Accordingly, social change is likely to be slow and uneven. There is resistance to imposing ongoing obligations on employers or other institutions as a means of foreclosing legal action by individuals, even though preventative action is a far more effective mechanism for securing substantive equality. Indeed, proactive measures are wont to be trenchantly attacked by conservatives as a misguided form of reverse discrimination. This was the fate of affirmative action (AA) initiatives designed to promote sexual and racial equality in the United States in the more progressive context of the 1970s.[11] In Australia, the life of very weak AA legislation on the ground of sex[12] was haunted by specious claims that AA would entail the appointment of unqualified women and the legislation reduced men to 'victims'.[13] Liberal legalism favours a formal understanding of equality, or equality before the law, where everyone is

---

10   For example, *Sex Discrimination Act 1984* (Cth), s. 3(d).
11   For example, *Regents of University of California v Bakke* 438 US 165 (1978).
12   *Affirmative Action (Equal Opportunity for Women in the Workplace) Act 1986* (Cth).
13   Gabriël Moens, *Affirmative Action: The New Discrimination* (Centre for Independent Studies, 1985).

treated the same regardless of how historically disadvantaged they are or how different their personal circumstances might be. Liberal legalism is generally opposed to mechanisms for achieving substantive equality.

While the rhetoric that justice is blind has been a familiar trope associated with law since antiquity, recourse to the courts as a means of achieving a modicum of equality is all too often available only to those who can afford to pay. The myth of equality before the law nevertheless assumes that the impoverished individual and the multinational corporation will be treated the same when confronting each other in the courtroom. Our legal system tends to be silent when it comes to economic disparities, although class represents a profound source of injustice and is compounded by the fact that it is all too often invisible and ineffable in our society. Most notably, class is not included as a proscribed ground in antidiscrimination legislation, although it may intersect with and exacerbate the impact of the proscribed grounds of sex, race, sexuality, disability and/or age.

Despite the rhetoric, the swing from social liberalism to neoliberalism in the late twentieth century caused support even for formal equality to recede. The centrality of the market to governance of the state resulted in Keynesianism, with its modest support for public goods and progressive taxation, being abandoned in the interests of economic elites and the generation of wealth. Entrepreneurialism, competition, promotion of the self and regressive taxation became the central tenets of neoliberal governmentality. Antidiscrimination legislation was not repealed, but it became more difficult to use. Not only did human rights bodies receive reduced funding to enable them to undertake their basic legislative functions, but also the erosion of workers' rights through the gig economy and new forms of contractualism precluded operation of the typical individualised model of antidiscrimination legislation—for example, a single employer could not be held responsible for a systemic harm that arose from government policy. The emphasis on profit maximisation and competition policy meant *inequality* had become a social norm that was extolled by the state, which exacerbated the tension with the elusive equality ideal.

Women struggled to be admitted to the practice of law from the late nineteenth century in the belief that this would equip them with the means to rectify some of the injustices in women's lives. Despite the inauspicious beginnings, as discussed in the case of Edith Haynes, women are now most of both law students and legal practitioners. Numerosity, however, cannot be equated with substantive equality, the quest for which is ongoing, as discussed in Parts IV and V, regarding the contradictions arising from authority, affectivity and care.

Law schools have been overcome with a sense of cognitive dissonance ever since the teaching of law for practice moved into universities in the nineteenth century. They were uncertain as to whether they were merely another branch of the legal profession where their role was to teach law *as it is* or whether they were free to critique the presuppositions of legal doctrine in the same way as a faculty of humanities or social sciences. The impact of the modernisation of law schools in conjunction with the increasing proportion of women over the past 50 years has been dramatic. The move away from a focus on the *is* of law to what it *ought* to be in the 1970s and 1980s provided a green light for feminist legal scholars not only to agitate for the repeal of the misogynistic laws of the past,[14] but also to articulate their concern about the persistence of the masculine bias in the law curriculum. A noted example arose when Justice Derek Bollen, during the course of a rape in marriage case in the early 1990s, stated that a little 'rougher than usual handling' was acceptable on the part of a husband towards his wife who was less than willing to engage in sexual intercourse.[15] This resulted in a public outcry, which showed how society was changing from the masculinist 'domesticated command' that had prevailed only a short time before. As a result of the adverse publicity, feminist legal scholars, with the support of the Commonwealth attorney-general, prepared gender-sensitive materials for inclusion in the 11 compulsory core subjects of the law curriculum specified throughout Australia. Materials were sent to all law schools, as well as being made available on the internet.[16] Law students, legal practitioners and judges were no longer expected to blindly pay obeisance to law as it *is*, but to approach it as a dynamic entity appropriate for contemporary society.

---

14   Loss of consortium is one such anachronistic example. This enabled a husband to bring an action for the loss of household and sexual services against a third party when the man's wife was injured; no comparable action was available to the wife. See Ann C. Riseley, 'Sex, Housework and the Law' (1981) 7 *Adelaide Law Review* 421; Margaret Thornton, 'Loss of Consortium: Inequality before the Law' (1984) 10 *Sydney Law Review* 259.
15   *R v Johns*, Supreme Court of South Australia, Bollen J, 26 August 1992 (unreported).
16   Regina Graycar & Jenny Morgan, 'Legal Categories, Women's Lives and the Law Curriculum— Or, Making Gender Examinable' (1996) 18 *Sydney Law Review* 431.

However, one of the themes I have sought to highlight in this collection is the uneven and often contradictory nature of social change. Thus, immediately after completion of the Gender Issues in the Law Curriculum Project, the Howard government was elected to office and cut the budgets for public goods, including universities. While the commodification of higher education has undoubtedly been one of the downsides of neoliberalism, the encouragement of research as a dimension of competition policy nevertheless proved to be beneficial for feminist legal research. The production of a rich body of legal scholarship has enabled the concept of gender equality to be interrogated and imagined in novel ways. Indeed, law reform, whether it takes place through legislation or through adjudication, has often been instigated and supported by creative feminist scholars. This is even though the admitting authorities, dominated by members of the judiciary, continue to specify familiarity with traditional areas of legal practice as a prerequisite for admission to legal practice.[17]

The essays in this collection explore the struggle for gender justice in a sociolegal context that adopts both theoretical and applied perspectives. The issues are considered against a dynamic backdrop of social change, which underscores the fact that change does not occur in a linear fashion. The essays put paid to the liberal progressivist assumption that things are always getting better, although many things have undoubtedly improved since Edith Haynes sought to sit for her intermediate examination as a prerequisite to qualifying for admission to legal practice at the beginning of the twentieth century. Subsequent chapters address ongoing questions pertaining to public and private life, taking into consideration aspects of the criminal law, antidiscrimination legislation, sexual harassment, the practice of law and what it means to be a judge, together with legal education and the nature of scholarly life in the corporatised academy. The essays were selected because they were believed to capture a sense of the struggle for gender equality in the history of Second-Wave Feminism of the late twentieth and early twenty-first centuries. The essays have been minimally edited, such as adapting a consistent form of citation and including updated references.

---

17   Law Admissions Consultative Committee, *Prescribed Areas of Knowledge* (Law Council of Australia, 18 October 2019), available from: www.lawcouncil.asn.au/files/web-pdf/LACC%20docs/Redrafting%20the%20Academic%20Requirements%20for%20Admission%20-%20Subs/657475579_1_657475579.01%20Prescribed%20Areas%20of%20Knowledge.pdf.

The chapters

Chapter 1: Edith Haynes Challenges the Legal Profession

The claimed objectivity of judging is thrown into high relief by a series of cases at the turn of the twentieth century, known as the 'Persons' Cases', in which women challenged their exclusion from the legal profession, but courts held that they were not 'persons' for the purposes of admission. This chapter considers the case of Edith Haynes, who challenged the refusal of the Western Australian Barristers' Board to permit her to sit for her intermediate examination when enrolled as an articled clerk—the only route to admission at that time in Western Australia. The decision was upheld by a unanimous decision of the Full Court of the WA Supreme Court in 1904. The judges took no cognisance of the fact that recent legislation had been enacted by both the WA legislature (1899) and the federal parliament (1902) conferring the franchise on (white) women and recognising them as full citizens. The chapter goes on to imagine what the outcome might have been had Edith Haynes appealed to the recently established High Court of Australia.

Chapter 2: Feminist Jurisprudence: Illusion or Reality?

This essay was the first to be written on feminist jurisprudence in Australia. It elaborates on the public/private dichotomy underpinning liberal theory, equality and access to law. Despite the claims of liberal legalism to universality and objectivity, the harms endured in the private sphere continue to be fraught. The chapter considers the resistance of liberal equality theory to corporeal specificity, such as pregnancy, as well as some of the ways that gender equality might be conceptualised. However, if feminists are too assiduous in compressing feminist perspectives into prevailing understandings of jurisprudence, particularly analytical jurisprudence, they could lose sight of the possibility of a transformative approach. In view of the skewed nature of law towards the feminine, the chapter questions whether the idea of feminist jurisprudence is in fact viable.

Chapter 3: The Contradictions of Law Reform

This chapter goes to the heart of the problem posed by the public/private dichotomy as the gendered harms of domestic violence and sexual assault occur largely in the private sphere—the sphere historically regarded as beyond the reach of the law of the state. It is argued that the seeds of invidiousness associated with the historical privatisation of these harms complicate their reform. Sexual harassment is a little different as its proscription was an innovative illustration of law reform in the early 1980s. It is nevertheless suggested that the reason it was supported with alacrity was because sexual activity had the potential to detract from productivity in the workplace, rather than because its proscription was an innovative feminist-inspired reform that benefited working women.

Chapter 4: Feminism and the Changing State

Although the enactment of sex discrimination legislation initially met with trenchant opposition from conservative forces, it quickly became an accepted fixture of the cultural landscape. The character of the state is nevertheless shown to have changed as a site of reform due to the neoliberal embrace and the focus on global competitiveness and profit maximisation. Even though employment is traditionally the major focus of complaints of sex discrimination, deterioration in the conditions of work, including its intensification and casualisation, has rendered the legislation problematic. It is also argued that the individualised model of antidiscrimination legislation does not sit well with the possibility of addressing systemic harms.

Chapter 5: Sexual Harassment Losing Sight of Sex Discrimination

This chapter argues that the separation of sexual harassment from sex discrimination within antidiscrimination legislation is an effective means of deflecting attention from systemic discrimination. It examines a range of instances of harassing conduct that might be conceptualised as occupying positions on a continuum. Beginning with heterosex, moving to sex-based harassment in sexually permeated workplaces and then to work rage, it is argued that the closer to heterosex the conduct is, the more likely it is to be comprehended as sexual harassment. Despite the invidiousness and prevalence of multiple sex-based harms, their systemic nature means they are less likely to be cognisable as acts of unlawful discrimination. The chapter argues that the unremitting focus on the sexual in sexual harassment thereby serves a convenient political and ideological role within a neoliberal climate by privileging employer prerogative over workers' rights.

Chapter 6: Hypercompetitiveness or a Balanced Life?

Although women make up more than 50 per cent of the practising legal profession in Australia and elsewhere, numerosity is insufficient to overcome the 'otherness' of the feminine in corporate law firms. Despite measures to recognise the ethic of a balanced life for those with caring responsibilities, these initiatives are undermined by the contemporary imperative in favour of competition. This chapter argues that there was a hyper-masculinist subtext invoked by the media reporting of a flurry of mergers between super-elite London-based global law firms and Australian firms with an eye to expansion in the Asia-Pacific. It is suggested that the incommensurability of the discourses of flexible work and hypercompetition symbolically served to revive and sustain the masculinity of super-elite law firms just as the gender tipping point had been reached. To illustrate the thesis, the representation of the two discourses in the print media is considered—namely, in *The Times* (London) and *The Australian* (Sydney).

Chapter 7: The Flexible Cyborg

Flexible work was regarded as particularly appealing for women in law because it was thought that if a balance could be effected between work and private life, satisfying careers and the raising of children could be combined. Technology facilitated this flexibility as all that was required was a device with an internet connection and a mobile phone. Provided the employer was agreeable, the lawyer also had a degree of autonomy in determining *when* and *where* the work was carried out. The chapter nevertheless argues that the shift from face time to virtual time blurs the boundary between work and life, insidiously extending the hours of work and impinging on the realm of intimacy.

Chapter 8: Who Cares? The Conundrum for Gender Equality

As women seek equality in the public sphere, the challenge of caring for children and those unable to care for themselves has become more acute. As the 'ideal worker' is regarded as one who is unencumbered, this ideal has assumed a male persona. It is argued that gender equality is attainable only if men share in parenting responsibilities. Even though the norms of fatherhood are changing, professional men are nevertheless resistant to sustained absences from work because they believe their careers will be negatively impacted. Drawing on studies from Scandinavia, the chapter considers the feasibility of shared parenting regimes. The competing narratives of the 'new father' (the 'good dad') and the unencumbered worker who devotes himself to work nevertheless produce a paradox that underscores the ongoing elusiveness of gender equality in the professional workplace.

Chapter 9: Sex Discrimination, Courts and Corporate Power

This chapter draws on Robert Cover's idea that judges rely on two distinct models of adjudication: the paideic, or 'world creating', model, and the imperial, or 'world maintaining', model. The sex discrimination cases heard by the High Court of Australia can be conceptualised in respect of these models, although only three sex discrimination cases have been heard by the High Court in 40 years: *Wardley*, *Banovic* and *Amery*. The first two involved the entry of women into non-traditional areas of employment and could be described as paideic. It is argued that the imperial model, which is represented by *Amery*, is preferred by more conservative courts as the potential for disruption to the traditional gender order is likely to be less and it can be seen when the political mood moves to the right. This model is also apparent in the application of the familiar legal test of reasonableness in two Federal Court and state Supreme Court decisions.

Chapter 10: The High Court and Judicial Activism

This chapter takes issue with the detractors of judicial activism, such as former Australian High Court judge Dyson Heydon, who claimed that it undermines the rule of law. It is argued that all judging necessarily involves an activist element because of the choices judges make. Their reliance on values is starkly illustrated in discrimination law, where there may be no precedents and judges find themselves facing interpretative crossroads. The neoliberal turn and a change in the political composition of the Australian High Court following the controversial race cases of *Mabo* and *Wik* underscore the activist role. With reference to a tranche of disability discrimination decisions handed down by the court, it is argued that it is not so much the progressive judges as the conservatives who are the rogue activists engaged in corroding the rule of law because they consistently subvert legislative intent.

Chapter 11: 'Otherness' on the Bench

This chapter argues that merit, which is arguably the key selection criterion for the appointment of a judge, is constructed in terms of benchmark masculinity, which militates against the acceptance of women and 'Others'. The social construction of the feminine in terms of disorder in the public sphere long fanned doubts that women were appointable as judges. This essay argues that merit—far from being an objective variable as commonly claimed—operates as a rhetorical device shaped by power. The argument is illustrated by reference to the media representations of women judges in three scenarios: an appointment to the Australian High Court, the appointment of women to almost 50 per cent of positions in Victorian courts and the scapegoating of a woman chief magistrate (resulting in imprisonment) in Queensland.

Chapter 12: Wondering What to Do about Legal Education

This chapter is the author's inaugural lecture following appointment to a chair in legal studies. To better equip students for an uncertain future, they need to understand law in its social context rather than as a system of rules privileging property and profits. This is even though earlier examples of innovation at Yale and Columbia universities that sought to integrate law and the social sciences were unsuccessful. To overcome the resistance and educate the 'compleat lawyer', a transdisciplinary model, comparable to that espoused by feminist scholarship, was recommended in which law would be taught by humanities scholars and social scientists, as well as by lawyers. The hope was that locating the teaching of law in a school of social sciences rather than a separate law school would assist in the success of the project.

Chapter 13: Why the Gender and Colour of Law Remain the Same

Despite valiant endeavours by feminist, critical race and LGBTQI+ scholars to transform the legal culture, the transformative project has been limited because of the power of corporatism that emerged from the neoliberal turn. Postmodern as well as liberal scholars have preferred to downplay the ramifications of the 'new economy' with its marked shift to the right, the contraction of the public sphere, the privatisation of public goods, globalisation and a preoccupation with efficiency, economic rationalism and profits. It is argued that the predominance of technical reasoning, or 'technocentrism', in the teaching of law has enabled the injustices of corporatism and discrimination to evade scrutiny. The chapter shows how the diffused nature of corporate power impacts legal education from outside as well as from within the legal academy in an endeavour to maintain the status quo. As a result, the innovative reforms discussed in Chapter 12 are likely to fail.

Chapter 14: Universities Upside-Down

This chapter considers the knowledge revolution that is presently occurring in the academy. Instead of pursuing knowledge for its own sake, à la Newman, universities everywhere are playing a key role in the production of 'new knowledge', which has replaced land in the struggle between nation-states. It is suggested that the commodification of knowledge and knowledge transfer is profound. The key question considering these phenomena is what space is there within the new paradigm for the pursuit of feminist, critical and theoretical knowledge that lacks use value in the market? The chapter suggests that the contraction of the critical space is insidiously allowing a remasculinisation of the academy.

Chapter 15: The Mirage of Merit

As with the legal profession, within universities, a fear of feminisation has emerged because women occupy almost half of all full-time and fractional appointments. I suggest that male flight has been allayed by the neoliberal turn and the corporatisation of the university. The benchmark men of the academy have remained because of academic capitalism, the commodification of education and competition policy. As a result, the ideal academic is now conceptualised as a 'technopreneur' who combines techno-scientific knowledge with business acumen and is increasingly assuming a masculinist persona. 'He' undertakes little teaching, which tends to be assigned to the 'less than ideal' academic, who is invariably female. The masculinisation of research and the feminisation of teaching, which is increasingly casualised, show how the academy is once again in danger of bifurcation along gender lines.

Part I: Women as Nonpersons

1

Edith Haynes Challenges the Legal Profession

Introduction

The struggle by women to enter the legal profession in many parts of the world was a notable manifestation of the internationalisation of First-Wave Feminism in the late nineteenth and early twentieth centuries. It represented one piece of the mosaic relating to the desire to be treated as the equals of men in public life, but corporeality, emotion and eroticism had been indelibly imprinted on the feminine psyche throughout the Western intellectual tradition[1] and endlessly repeated as a justification for the exclusion of women from public life.[2] Opponents argued that the admission of women would not only corrupt the rationality of the public sphere but, bizarrely, also exercise a deleterious impact on the private sphere as intellectual activity had the potential to 'unsex' women and induce sterility.[3] The endless repetition of such myths, particularly under

---

1   For example, Aristotle, *Politics*, translated by John Warrington (Dent, 1959) §1260a.
2   For example, Genevieve Lloyd, *The Man of Reason: 'Male' and 'Female' in Western Philosophy* (Methuen, 1984); Lyn Hunt (ed.), *Eroticism and the Body Politic* (Johns Hopkins University Press, 1991); Margaret Thornton, *Dissonance and Distrust: Women in the Legal Profession* (Oxford University Press, 1996) 41 ff.
3   For example, Herbert Spencer, *The Principles of Biology. Volume II* (Williams & Norgate, 1899) 512–13. In 1903–04, a report by the NSW Royal Commission on the Decline of the Birth Rate and on the Mortality of Infants in New South Wales gave weight to the fantasy by blaming the falling birthrate on the women's movement. See Audrey Oldfield, *Woman Suffrage in Australia: A Gift or a Struggle?* (Cambridge University Press, 1992) 200.

the imprimatur of official reports, deflected attention from the economic threat posed to masculine hegemony if women were permitted to enter professions such as law.[4]

Perhaps it is unsurprising that the earnest pronouncements of judges legitimised the exclusion of women from the public sphere in a spate of cases known as the 'Persons' Cases' that occurred throughout the English common-law world in a reaction to First-Wave Feminism. Women who sought entry to universities, the professions and public office were consistently found not to be 'persons' for the purposes of admission, even though the relevant legislation was expressed in gender-neutral terms.[5] Julius Stone noted that the exercise of 'leeways of choice' by judges was an inevitable dimension of the interpretative role,[6] but when subjectively opposed to a particular outcome, judges claimed to be 'inexorably bound' to reach a particular determination. In the Persons' Cases, judges sought authority in the ancient common law to support a finding that the gender-neutral word 'person' did not include women. This was despite the existence of interpretation Acts from the middle of the nineteenth century that expressly stated that words importing the masculine should include the feminine.[7] Judges nevertheless argued that no legislature could have *intended* to refer to women as potential legal practitioners because they had *never* been admitted in the past. Judges invariably cite Lord Coke's view of 300 years before as authoritative.[8]

While sharing a common-law heritage with other parts of the British Empire, Australasia was to the fore in terms of the enfranchisement of women and, in some jurisdictions,[9] the admission of women to legal

---

4   In the parliamentary debate on the admission of women to legal practice in Western Australia, Mr Marshall argued that admitting women would be 'cutting all the [male] solicitors and barristers out of their jobs'. See *WA Parliamentary Debates (Hansard)*, Legislative Assembly, Women's Legal Status Bill 1923 (WA), Second Reading, 5 September 1923, Vol. 69, 593. Cf. Thornton (n. 2) 45–46; Albie Sachs & Joan Hoff Wilson, *Sexism and the Law: A Study of Male Beliefs and Judicial Bias* (Martin Robertson, 1978) 170.

5   For a thoroughgoing treatment of the leading cases, see Sachs & Wilson (n. 4).

6   Julius Stone, *Legal System and Lawyers' Reasonings* (Maitland Publications, 1968) 319.

7   The *Interpretation Act 1850* (13 & 14 Vict c 21) (Lord Brougham's Act) was the first of such Acts.

8   For example, *Bebb v Law Society* [1914] 1 Ch. 286. A rare example of a progressive interpretation of legislative intent led to the admission of Arabella Mansfield by an Iowa Court in 1869. The court held that the gender-specific phrase 'white male persons' should be interpreted to include females in accordance with the interpretation statute. However, this decision was not accepted by courts elsewhere. See Mary Jane Mossman, *The First Women Lawyers: A Comparative Study of Gender, Law and the Legal Professions* (Hart, 2006) 41.

9   Australia retained its six separate state jurisdictions even after Federation in 1901, which accounts for the variable dates for the admission of women. A *Uniform Law Application Act 2014* has been developed but, by mid 2022, only New South Wales, Victoria and Western Australia had endorsed it.

practice.[10] Despite this seeming progressiveness, the animus towards women seeking to enter the public sphere in Australia echoed the experience elsewhere. The legal profession was the most intransigent, being described by Theobald as even 'more misogynist' than the medical profession.[11]

While the Persons' Cases are a curious anomaly in the history of jurisprudence, the Australian examples are striking because they occurred *after* enfranchisement. Women were enfranchised in South Australia in 1894, white women in Western Australia in 1899 and, after Federation, all Australian women (other than Aboriginal women in Queensland and Western Australia) in 1902.[12] Citizenship, however, includes civil as well as political elements.[13] Thus, in addition to the right to vote and the right to be elected to parliament to represent others, citizenship implies a cluster of rights associated with active participation in civil life. This necessarily included a right to engage in the professions, entailing practising as a lawyer and assuming leadership positions in civil society. Equality between all citizens of the polity in the exercise of civil rights is a norm of the liberal state.[14] Hence, once women were enfranchised, they were theoretically entitled to exercise the full panoply of political and civil rights in the same way as men. While this factor was recognised by numerous politicians in the enfranchisement debates,[15] it seems to have eluded the judges.

---

10   Ethel Benjamin was admitted to legal practice in New Zealand in 1897. The *Female Law Practitioners Act 1895* (NZ) and *Women's Disabilities Act 1895* (NZ) were passed following the enfranchisement of New Zealand women in 1893. See Gill Gatfield, *Without Prejudice: Women in the Law* (Brookers, 1996) 30. Benjamin's admission occurred in the same year as that of Clara Brett Martin in Ontario. For detailed discussion of the admission of Canadian women, see Mossman (n. 8) 67–112.

11   Marjorie Theobald, *Knowing Women: Origins of Women's Education in Nineteenth-Century Australia* (Cambridge University Press, 1996) 71.

12   *Commonwealth Franchise Act 1902* (Cth). For a thoroughgoing study of the campaigns in the states and the Commonwealth, see Oldfield (n. 3) 64–67.

13   T.H. Marshall, *Citizenship and Social Class and Other Essays* (Cambridge University Press, 1950) 74.

14   Jean Bethke Elshtain, *Power Trips and Other Journeys: Essays in Feminism in Civic Discourse* (University of Wisconsin Press, 1990) 49.

15   For example, Mr Walter James, Assembly, *Parliamentary Debates on Parliamentary Franchise (WA)*, 1 December 1897, 738 ff.; Hon R.S. Haynes, Legislative Council, *Parliamentary Debates on Legal Practitioners Bill 1900 (WA)*, 18 September 1900, 451; Hon A. Jameson, Legislative Council, *Parliamentary Debates on Legal Practitioners Bill 1900 (WA)*, 18 September 1900, 453; The Colonial Secretary, Hon G. Randell, Legislative Council, *Parliamentary Debates on Legal Practitioners Bill 1900 (WA)*, 18 September 1900, 453; Senator O'Connor (NSW, Protectionist Party), *Parliamentary Debates on Commonwealth Franchise Act 1902 (Cth)*, Senate, Hansard, 9 April 1902, 11451.

In this chapter, I address *In re Haynes*,[16] a case that arose when Edith Haynes was refused permission by the WA Barristers' Board to sit her intermediate examination in 1903, even though the board had approved her articles in 1900. The Supreme Court of Western Australia took no cognisance whatsoever of the issue of enfranchisement, which begs the question as to its meaning in the Australian context, other than placing a ballot in a ballot box. In addition to interrogating the philosophical underpinnings of citizenship, I speculate as to what might have happened had Edith Haynes appealed the decision to the newly created High Court of Australia. Would the neonate judges, one of whom strongly supported the enfranchisement of women, have adopted a more enlightened view than the judges of the WA Supreme Court?

Edith Haynes, 1876–1963

Biographical details relating to the entry of women to the legal profession are scant and law reports are notorious for their lack of detail, which compel the scholar to search for other clues, as Rosemary Auchmuty points out.[17] Male historians have also largely ignored the early women of law as their contributions to the legal profession have tended to be seen as unimportant.[18] Lloyd Davies states, for example, that the WA Barristers' Board 'expunged Edith Haynes from its records'[19]—a fact that was confirmed by an officer of the WA Legal Practice Board (the successor of the Barristers' Board) when, in preparing this chapter, I sought permission to peruse the minutes of the Barristers' Board for the period 1900–04. Nevertheless, there is a little sketchy information about Haynes, some of which came to light from family members on the centenary of her unsuccessful Supreme Court action.[20]

---

16   *In re Haynes* (1904) 6 WAR 209. Cf. *In re Kitson* (1920) SALR 230, in which Mary Kitson had already been admitted to legal practice and was a partner in a law firm when she applied in 1920 to be appointed as a notary public. However, the Supreme Court of South Australia interpreted the phrase 'every person' in the *Public Notaries Act 1859* (SA) in similarly narrow terms even though the *Constitutional Amendment Act 1894* (SA) not only enfranchised women, but also bestowed on them the right to be elected to parliament.

17   Rosemary Auchmuty, 'Recovering Lost Lives: Researching Women in Legal History' (2015) 42(1) *Journal of Law and Society* 34, 35, doi.org/10.1111/j.1467-6478.2015.00697.x.

18   ibid., 52.

19   Lloyd Davies, *Sheila: A Biography of Sheila Mary McClemans* (Desert Pea Press, 2000) 9.

20   David K. Malcolm, 'Centenary of *Edith Haynes* Decision' (2004) 31(9) *Brief* 16.

Edith Ann Mary Haynes was born in Sydney, New South Wales, the eldest of six children to Edward James Ambrose Haynes and Theresa Mooney. Edward Haynes was a doctor, which signifies the middle-class status typical of early women lawyers.[21] While the family moved to Perth, Western Australia, in 1891, it appears Edith stayed in Sydney to complete her schooling at a private girls' school.[22] Her uncle's law firm in Perth subsequently employed her. Her uncle Richard Septimus Haynes was a member of the WA Barristers' Board and was described as a 'radical'.[23] He was also a member of the WA Legislative Council (1896–1902). He not only supported the enfranchisement of women in Western Australia in 1899, but also proposed a Bill in 1900 amending the *Legal Practitioners Act 1893* (WA) (hereinafter *LPA*) by including the words 'any person of the female sex' to overcome the 'problem' in the United Kingdom and elsewhere caused by the supposed ambiguity inhering in the word 'person'.[24]

While Edith lived for another 60 years after the unsuccessful attempt to sit for her intermediate examination, there is no evidence of what she thought about her rejection, or whether she contemplated appealing the decision or moving to another state. There is also no evidence of whether she campaigned for a change to the law in Western Australia or how she reacted to the passage of the *Women's Legal Status Act 1923* (WA). In fact, we know little of Edith Haynes after her abortive attempt to enter the legal profession, as she seems to have abandoned altogether her youthful aspiration of becoming a lawyer. Indeed, there is no further sign of the spirit she displayed in standing up to the Barristers' Board. Based on archival material held by the National Bank of Australia, Malcolm ascertained that she worked for the bank between 1916 and 1931. She then cared for her brother's children following the death of her sister-in-law.[25] Family members described Edith, in contrast to her politically radical uncle, as conservative and straitlaced, but with a weakness for a flutter on the horses![26]

---

21   Mossman (n. 8); Elizabeth Cruikshank, '"Follow the Money": The First Women Who Qualified as Solicitors 1922–1930' in Judith Bourne (ed.), *First Women Lawyers in Great Britain and the Empire Record. Volume 1* (St Mary's University, 2016) 48.
22   St Vincent's College, Potts Point, run by the Sisters of Charity.
23   Tom Stannage, 'Haynes, Richard Septimus (1857–1922)', *Australian Dictionary of Biography* (National Centre of Biography, The Australian National University, published first in hardcopy 1983), available from: adb.anu.edu.au/biography/haynes-richard-septimus-6615/text11389.
24   *WA Parliamentary Debates (Hansard)*, Legislative Council, *Legal Practitioners Act Amendment Bill*, Second Reading, 18 September 1900, Vol. 17, 450.
25   Malcolm suggests Edith's work must have been valued as she was not required to relinquish her position after the war. See Malcolm (n. 20) 18.
26   ibid.

In re Haynes

Unlike the eastern states, there was no law school in Western Australia when Edith contemplated entering the profession. Nevertheless, as was common at the time, the path of apprenticeship—which entailed five years of articles, the completion of prescribed examinations and the payment of a fee (12 guineas)—was open to those wishing to practise law. Edith Haynes' uncle Richard Haynes wrote to the Barristers' Board in 1900 seeking to article his niece to himself. The board approved Edith's articles and exempted her from sitting the preliminary examination.

While accepting her registration as a student-at-law, the board nevertheless advised her in writing that it could not guarantee the court would admit her to practice and she would have to bear the risk of ultimately being refused admission. However, long before Edith was eligible to be admitted, the board refused her permission to sit her intermediate examination. The initial doubt expressed by the board regarding the admission of women had crystallised into opposition, but the reason for the change of heart is unknown.[27] Edith Haynes then issued a writ of mandamus directing the board to show cause why she should not be admitted to the examination.[28]

Richard Haynes, now a King's Counsel (1902), appeared for Edith before the WA Supreme Court, arguing that the word 'person' in the *LPA*, supported by the *Interpretation Act 1898* (WA), included women. Haynes KC pointed out that Edith Haynes was seeking permission to sit for the intermediate examination—not admission to practice, for which she would not have been eligible for another two or three years. By a certain sleight of hand, however, the full bench of the Supreme Court did not confine itself to the issue of whether she should be permitted to sit for the examination but focused almost exclusively on the question of whether women were eligible to be admitted as legal practitioners under the *LPA*. It is nevertheless unclear why Haynes KC did not make more of

---

27   Davies (n. 19, 7) suggests it could have been because of the refusal of the NSW authorities to admit Ada Evans, Australia's first female law graduate, in 1902. The rejection of Bertha Cave by Gray's Inn in London in 1903 and the Lord Chancellor soon afterwards may have been determinative. See Judith Bourne, *Helena Normanton and the Opening of the Bar to Women* (Waterside Press, 2016) 60–62.
28   In the leading British case, Gwyneth Bebb, who wished to present herself for the preliminary examination with a view to becoming bound by articles, unsuccessfully sought a declaration that she was a 'person' within the meaning of the *Solicitors Act 1843*. See *Bebb v Law Society* [1914] 1 Ch. 286; see also Rosemary Auchmuty, 'Whatever Happened to Miss Bebb? *Bebb v The Law Society* and Women's Legal History' (2011) 31(2) *Legal Studies* 199, doi.org/10.1111/j.1748-121x.2010.00180.x.

the representation contained in the letter from the board to Edith Haynes in 1900, which had noted there was some doubt regarding the eligibility of women to be admitted.

The three judges in *In re Haynes* were unanimous in finding that women had no right to be admitted to legal practice and, accordingly, no right to be registered as articled clerks under the *LPA*. In focusing on the interpretation of the word 'person', the judges were less concerned with the recently enacted *LPA* than with its antecedents, the *Supreme Court Ordinance 1861* (WA) and the imperial statute of 1831:

> I think that one must first bear in mind what was the law at the time the Statute was passed, and if one takes the trouble to go back to the earlier Statutes of this Colony it will be found that the first references to admissions to the Court go back to 2 Wm IV, No 1 ... There is nothing there conferring a right on women to be admitted as solicitors.[29]

The judicial manipulation of legislative intent is a familiar device invoked by judges 'as an escape from avowing judicial policy choices'.[30] Hence, the judges in *In re Haynes* were able to find that in enacting the *LPA*, the legislature could not have *intended* the word 'person' to apply to women because they had *never* been lawyers. As Burnside J expressed it, legal practice had been confined to the male sex 'from almost time immemorial'[31]—a sentiment unequivocally supported by his fellow judges:

> The idea of women practising in the Supreme Court seems to me quite foreign to the legislation which has prevailed for years past, not only here but in the mother country.[32]

> It is not for us whatever our opinions may be to depart from what has always been the established practice both in England and in all the Colonies and in the United States, which have originally derived their law from England.[33]

---

29 *In re Haynes* (1904) 213 (Burnside J). Cf. *In re French* (1905) 37 New Brunswick Reports 359 (SC); *Re French* (1910–12) 17 *British Columbia Law Reports* 1 (CA). For discussion, see Mossman (n. 8) 89–99 ff.

30 Julius Stone, *Precedent and Law: Dynamics of Common Law Growth* (Butterworths, 1985) 113. Cf. J.M. Balkin, 'Ideology as Constraint' (1991) 43(5) *Stanford Law Review* 1133, 1153, doi.org/10.2307/1228897.

31 *In re Haynes* 214.

32 ibid., 211 (Parker J). Cf. *Bebb v Law Society*, in which the judges similarly relied on inveterate usage. Swinfen-Eady LJ 295 cites Coke and the statue of 1402 in support, with no evidence of a woman attorney in 500 years. Cf. *Bebb* 298 (Phillimore LJ).

33 *In re Haynes* 212 (McMillan J).

The inveterate practice of the English common law was unquestioningly accepted to apply in what was no longer a colony, but a state within a newly federated nation.[34] As Grata Flos Greig, the first Australian woman to be admitted to legal practice, drily observed a few years later: 'I notice that most men, when it comes to an argument as to what women could or could not do, generally argue "You have not, ergo, you cannot".'[35]

Despite the existence of the *Interpretation Act 1898* (WA), the judges were of the view that 'every person' did not apply to both men and women in the context of admission to legal practice. If women were to be included, express words to that effect were deemed necessary. Burnside J referred to the wording in the *Medical Act*: 'Every person, *male and female* may be a doctor.'[36] The judges were insistent that they did not make law; the prerogative resided with the legislature:

> I am not prepared myself to create a precedent by allowing the admission of a woman to the Bar of this Court … [I]f the legislature desired that a woman should be capable of being admitted as a practitioner of this Court, or indeed if the Legislature intended to make women eligible for admission to the Court, that they should have said so in express language, as I believe has been done in New Zealand.[37]

Burnside J referred to the English case of Miss Cave and the decision of the Lord Chancellor to rule against her admission because it would similarly 'create a precedent'.[38] The rejection of Miss Cave undoubtedly carried weight with the court and Burnside J went on to state that 'we have not been able to ascertain any instances under the Common Law in the United States, England or [any] British-speaking colony where the right of women to be admitted to the Bar has ever been suggested'.[39]

---

34 'Inveterate usage' to resolve the supposed 'ambiguity' of the word 'person' was also used by the Scottish Court of Session in a case comparable to that of Edith Haynes, which denied a woman access to the Law-Agents' examinations: *Hall v Incorporated Society of Law-Agents in Scotland* (1901) 3F 1059. Although not enfranchised, Scottish women could be medical practitioners, parish councillors and factory inspectors.

35 Grata Flos Greig, 'The Law as a Profession for Women' (1909) 6 *Commonwealth Law Review* 145.

36 *In re Haynes* 214. Emphasis added.

37 ibid., 211 (Parker J). Cf. *In re Haynes* 212 (McMillan J).

38 Bertha Cave sent a letter to the Benchers of Gray's Inn to be admitted as a student of the society for the purpose of being called to the bar in 1903. Her application was rejected and she appealed unsuccessfully to the Lord Chancellor and a group of Law Lords. See Bourne (n. 27) 60–61; Daniel F. Gosling, 'Women & the Law: Bertha Cave's Application to Join Gray's Inn', *Gray's Inn*, 27 June 2017, available from: www.graysinn.org.uk/the-inn/history/women-of-the-inn/bertha-cave/application/.

39 *In re Haynes* 213 (Burnside J); cf. *In re Haynes* 212 (McMillan J).

Strictly speaking, however, this was not the case, as lower courts had admitted women in multiple US states by the 1880s,[40] even though the US Supreme Court in 1873 had rejected the idea that women, especially married women, could be lawyers.[41]

Despite Edith Haynes' completion of three years of articles, the WA Supreme Court determined that nothing would be gained by making the rule absolute. As Parker J said, somewhat patronisingly: 'In my opinion this lady is not qualified to be an articled clerk, and consequently it seems to me that the time and money which would be expended would be quite wasted.'[42] The time and money already expended, to say nothing of Edith Haynes' abilities or her wish to enter the profession, were accorded short shrift.

In the case of the absence of a binding precedent, the judiciary has the power to adapt the common law in accordance with changing social mores by exercising the leeways of choice open to it; a specific Act of Parliament is unnecessary.[43] In this case, however, it is difficult to disagree with Auchmuty that the reasoning 'camouflaged the underlying "prejudice and fear" … of the majority of the legal men who did not want women intruding upon their professional space'.[44]

The citizenship conundrum

Apart from the antipathy towards women as lawyers, the Haynes case reveals the parlous and contingent status of citizenship for women. In construing the meaning of 'any person' in the *LPA*, the judges failed to take judicial notice of the fact that (white) women not only had been enfranchised in Western Australia in 1899 and federally in 1902,[45] but

---

40 Virginia G. Drachman, *Sisters in Law: Women Lawyers in Modern American History* (Harvard University Press, 1998), 151–53; Mossman (n. 8) 50–51.

41 *Bradwell v Illinois* 83 US130 (1873).

42 *In re Haynes* 212.

43 It was many years before an Anglo-Australian court was prepared to take the initiative and admit women to public office without the benefit of express legislation. This was *Edwards v Attorney-General for Canada* (1930) AC 124, the last of the Persons' Cases, when the Privy Council decided that women were eligible to sit in the Canadian Senate.

44 Auchmuty (n. 28).

45 Only Western Australia and Queensland expressly excluded Aboriginal persons, although exclusion undoubtedly occurred informally in other states.

also were eligible to stand for election to parliament.[46] Furthermore, the judges would have been aware that numerous women's groups all over the country were actively campaigning not only for the suffrage, but also for improvement in the status of women more generally. The Karrakatta Club in Perth, for example, pursued political, legal and educational aims on behalf of women for many years.[47] Indeed, there had been an attempt to enact legislation that would enfranchise women in Western Australia as early as 1893,[48] but the WA Supreme Court ignored all such activity.[49]

What is even more surprising is the fact that Edith Haynes' counsel, her uncle R.S. Haynes KC,[50] failed to advert to the crucial fact of enfranchisement. Not only had he employed his niece and supported her application for articles, but also he had been a member of parliament (MP) at the time of the passage of the 1899 legislation when he spoke strongly in favour of the vote for women, as well as their right to stand for parliament and their right to enter universities and the professions.[51] In the Second Reading Speech on the LPA Amendment Bill in 1900, in which he advocated clarifying the meaning of the word 'person', R.S. Haynes, in his capacity as a member of the legislative council (MLC), noted that extension of the franchise to women in Western Australia 'on exactly the same footing as men' had made the country better.[52]

Davies suggests the narrow approach adopted by Haynes in arguing the case as counsel for Edith Haynes was determined by the fact he was addressing the full court on a question of law.[53] This may have been the case, but an application for a writ of mandamus constituted a hearing *de novo*, not an appeal. Enfranchisement for some, however, seemed to have a limited substantive meaning, which, Oldfield suggests, appears to

---

46 Vida Goldstein was the first woman to stand for election to a national parliament, when she stood in 1903, albeit unsuccessfully. See Janette M. Bomford, *That Dangerous and Persuasive Woman: Vida Goldstein* (Melbourne University Press, 1993) 55.

47 Peter Cowan, *A Unique Position: A Biography of Edith Dircksey Cowan 1861–1932* (University of WA Press, 1978) 65 ff.

48 ibid., 73 ff.

49 The struggle for the enfranchisement of women had been on the feminist agenda for much of the nineteenth century. See, for example, Harriet Taylor Mill, 'Enfranchisement of Women' (1851) in John Stuart Mill & Harriet Taylor Mill, *Essays on Sex Equality*, edited with an introductory essay by Alice S. Rossi (University of Chicago Press, 1970).

50 Not 'QC' as Davies describes him. See Davies (n. 19) 2–4.

51 Hon R.S. Haynes, Legislative Council, *Parliamentary Debates on Electoral Act 1899 (WA)*, Hansard, 17 August 1899, 952.

52 Hon R.S. Haynes, Legislative Council, *Parliamentary Debates on Legal Practitioners Bill 1900 (WA)*, 18 September 1900, 451.

53 Davies (n. 19) 7.

have had more to do with the preservation of the power of conservatives in the legislature than with equal political rights for men and women.[54] While such a view might have animated some of the men in the WA Parliament, it does not detract from the import of Haynes KC's speeches in parliament or the support he otherwise gave his niece.

In making an argument in respect of citizenship, I stress I am focusing not on the question of nationality, as Edith Haynes was a British subject,[55] but the philosophical meaning of citizenship. In this regard, Kant recognised enfranchisement as the mark of an active citizen,[56] whose attributes were freedom, equality and independence. The active category of citizenship was distinguishable from the passive category to which Kant assigned women, children, domestic servants and apprentices. Whereas male children and apprentices were eventually able to make the transition from passive to active citizens, women and domestic servants were not. Instead, they remained permanently confined to the passive category. Although members of a legally cognisable political community, they were 'mere underlings [*Handlanger*] of the Commonwealth' who lacked 'civil independence'.[57] While Kant was writing in the eighteenth century, long before women's enfranchisement, his schema nevertheless should have sufficed to enable women to move into the active category once enfranchised and to exercise the qualities of freedom, equality and independence like adult men. This would include being able to choose whether to enter a profession. What we see, however, is that enfranchisement did not have this substantive meaning for women because the judicial gatekeepers of civil society sought to confine women to the passive category.

Hence, just as the word 'person' was read down in *Haynes*, the concept of enfranchisement was also implicitly read down to ensure that women were denied the entire complement of rights enjoyed by men arising from the basic assumption that formal equality prevails between and among citizens.[58] Decisions such as *In re Haynes* therefore played an important ideological role in legitimising the ongoing subordination of women. In no country in the world could the vote be anything *but* a gift from

54   Oldfield (n. 3) 47.
55   The *Australian Citizenship Act* was not enacted until 1948.
56   Immanuel Kant, *The Metaphysics of Morals*, translated by Mary Gregor (Cambridge University Press, 1991) 126.
57   ibid.
58   Elshtain (n. 14) 49.

male parliamentarians.[59] However, once gifted, *In re Haynes* suggests, the donors, who included the powerful men of law, could circumscribe the value of the gift.

In re Haynes implies that the freedom, equality and independence associated with enfranchisement were lesser rights than the autonomy associated with legal practice. The position appears to have been the converse in some US states where admission to legal practice commonly preceded enfranchisement. When Mary Hall was admitted in Connecticut in 1882, the role of an attorney was characterised as a 'lower' kind of public officer.[60] Nevertheless, there was a clear connection between enfranchisement and admission to legal practice in most jurisdictions, with the former opening the door to the latter, albeit with the assistance of specific legislation.[61] It is apparent that the freedom, equality and independence associated with enfranchisement and active citizenship were deemed to be vitiated by femaleness. In the judges' view, women, like children, remained in the passive category.

The judges also failed to take judicial notice of the steps recognising women as active citizens that were occurring in other Australian states. For example, there was no advertence to the fact that Victoria had already enacted legislation to admit women to legal practice,[62] Tasmania was in the process of doing so[63] and Queensland was about to do so.[64] New South Wales was reluctant to admit women but there had been significant activity since the early 1890s.[65] Ada Evans graduated from the University of Sydney in 1902—the first Australian woman to graduate in law—but

---

59 Oldfield (n. 3) 213.

60 *In re Hall*, 50 Connecticut Reports 131 (1882); cf. *In re Ricker*, 66 New Hampshire Reports 207 (1890). See also Mossman (n. 8) 50–51.

61 Two Acts, the *Female Law Practitioners Act 1895* (NZ) and *Women's Disabilities Act 1895* (NZ), followed the enfranchisement of New Zealand women in 1893. See Gatfield (n. 10) 30. The enfranchisement of women in the United Kingdom in 1918 led immediately to legislation that admitted them to legal practice. See *Sex Disqualification (Removal) Act 1919* (UK).

62 The *Women's Disabilities Removal Act 1903* (Vic.) was known colloquially as the 'Flos Greig Enabling Bill' as it was enacted to allow Grata Flos Greig, who graduated from the University of Melbourne in 1903, to be admitted to practice. See Ruth Campbell, *A History of the Melbourne Law School 1857–1973* (Faculty of Law, University of Melbourne, 1977) 28.

63 *The Legal Practitioners Act 1904* (Tas.).

64 *Legal Practitioners Act 1905* (Qld), although Agnes McWhinney, the first woman to be admitted to practice in Queensland, was not admitted until 1915.

65 Rose Scott and the Womanhood Suffrage League were among the most prominent. See Judith A. Allen, *Rose Scott: Vision and Revision in Feminism* (Oxford University Press, 1994).

she was refused admission to practice.[66] Unlike Edith Haynes, Ada Evans did not formally challenge the interpretation of the gender-neutral word 'person' in the *Legal Practitioners Act 1898* (NSW). However, a bill to admit women, supported by the Women's Progressive Association, was unsuccessfully introduced into the NSW Parliament in 1902—the year of Ada Evans' graduation, as well as the year of the enfranchisement for women at both the NSW and the federal levels.

The history of women as active citizens as manifested by the admission of women to legal practice in most Australian states suggests that Western Australia lagged in the rear.[67] In fact, Western Australia should have been the first state to admit women to legal practice, as R.S. Haynes' LPA Amendment Bill of 1900, which was designed to clear up any doubt about the meaning of the word 'person', passed the Legislative Council with strong support from members, 13 votes to eight. Hon A. Jameson exhorted members to support the Bill to show how liberal-minded the House was. The Colonial Secretary, Hon G. Randell, also spoke strongly in favour, stating his belief in the equality of women with men, as well as appealing to the grounds of justice and equity;[68] none of the members spoke in opposition. Western Australia lost the opportunity to be the trailblazer in the admission of women to legal practice, however, when the Bill was discharged by the assembly. It was withdrawn because '[t]he member who was in charge of it did not wish to proceed with it, as his main contention had been conceded by the Barristers' Board admitting ladies to practise'.[69]

In speculating as to why R.S. Haynes persuaded his niece to apply to the board before securing his amendment to the *LPA*, Davies suggests Haynes might have thought that rejection would have supported his argument.[70] However, the withdrawal, which occurred two days *after* Edith Haynes received her letter of acceptance from the board, was premature. It appears R.S. Haynes paid insufficient attention to the qualification in the letter expressing doubt regarding the admission of women to legal practice.

---

66   Ada Evans was not admitted until 1921 following enactment of the *Women's Legal Status Act 1918* (NSW). By that time, she declined to practise as she thought too much time had elapsed since her graduation.
67   Cf. Cowan (n. 47) 211.
68   *WA Parliamentary Debates (Hansard)*, Legislative Council, Legal Practitioners Act Amendment Bill, Second Reading, 18 September 1900, Vol. 17, 453–54.
69   *WA Parliamentary Debates (Hansard)*, Legislative Assembly, Legal Practitioners Act Amendment Bill, Discharge of Order, 29 November 1900, Vol. 17, 2052–53.
70   Davies (n. 19) 5.

Of course, we do not know for sure how the House of Assembly would have decided the issue had it gone to the vote, but Haynes may have been worried that the Bill did not have the numbers to pass, despite the positive support from the Legislative Council. Mr Illingworth, the only member to speak apart from the attorney-general, pointed out that the amendment 'was of great importance to a few people, and he hoped the Government would take steps to amend the small difficulty in the existing law'.[71] On its face, this statement appears to be supportive of the admission of women, but Davies points out that the ambiguity in 'the small difficulty in the existing law' might have had the opposite meaning and Illingworth wanted it made clear that the word 'person' meant 'man'.[72] This is because Illingworth had opposed suffrage for women in 1897,[73] but such an interpretation would have been at odds with the *Acts Interpretation Act 1898* (WA) and similar legislation enacted since Lord Brougham's Act.

Although it transpired that Western Australia was the last state to admit women to legal practice, the enabling legislation was secured by Edith Cowan,[74] the first woman elected to an Australian parliament.[75] It would have been worthwhile to have had the benefit of her analysis on the *Haynes* case or that of Grata Flos Greig, who graduated from the University of Melbourne in 1903 and was admitted to legal practice in 1905—the first Australian woman to be admitted. In 1909, Flos Greig wrote an article dismissing the '"heaps of twaddle" that surrounded women's unsuitability to legal practice',[76] pointing out that it was '[l]aw itself [that] prevented women from entering its precincts'.[77]

Contemporary commentary is sketchy when we venture beyond the official law reports. There is no extant record of support for Edith Haynes' Supreme Court action or criticism of the outcome from women's groups, although Edith Cowan was active in the Karrakatta Club at the time.[78]

---

71   *WA Parliamentary Debates (Hansard)*, Legislative Assembly, Legal Practitioners Act Amendment Bill, Discharge of Order, 29 November 1900, Vol. 17, 2053.

72   Davies (n. 19) 6.

73   *WA Parliamentary Debates (Hansard)*, Legislative Assembly, Women's Franchise, 1 December 1897, Vol. 11, 749–50.

74   *Women's Legal Status Act 1923* (WA). Alice May Cummins was the first woman to be admitted, in 1931.

75   Edith Cowan was elected in 1921. See Cowan (n. 47) 210 ff.

76   Grata Flos Greig, 'The Law as a Profession for Women' (1909) 6 *Commonwealth Law Review* 145, 149.

77   ibid., 147.

78   Cowan (n. 47) 105.

A critical editorial, however, appeared in *The West Australian* four days after the *Haynes* decision, although there is no record of it having been followed up:

> But the reign of prejudice is to come to an end, and, if abstract justice is to carry the day, it is hard to see how one sex can for ever be debarred from following whatever occupation nature and inclination will permit, however incongruous to modern ideas the occupation may seem.[79]

Imagining an appeal

Edith Haynes did not appeal the WA Supreme Court decision but, in this section, I imagine her chances of success had she done so. Theoretically, she could have appealed to the Privy Council in London, although the idea of a young woman travelling to London from Western Australia with a legal team to assert a questionable 'right' at the dawn of the twentieth century is virtually unimaginable.[80] In any case, the record of the Persons' Cases in the United Kingdom since the nineteenth century was not promising.[81]

Alternatively, appealing to the newly established High Court of Australia[82] would have been a far cheaper option as the court established a practice at an early stage of travelling to state capitals, including Perth.[83] Nevertheless, would the fledgling High Court have come to a different conclusion from the Supreme Court of Western Australia? Would the three neonate High Court judges have taken judicial notice of the recent enfranchisement of women and the flurry of activity it engendered to achieve a radically different outcome in the interpretation of 'any person'? After all, two of the judges, Edmund Barton and Richard O'Connor, had been actively involved as politicians in the new federal parliament and had voted in favour of the *Commonwealth Franchise Act* in 1902—Barton as prime minister and O'Connor as leader of the Senate with carriage of the Act.[84]

---

79   Editorial, *The West Australian*, [Perth], 13 August 1904, 6.
80   Burnside J insists in *In re Haynes* (214) that admission to legal practice is a privilege, not a right.
81   Sachs & Wilson (n. 4) Ch. 1. The rejection of Bertha Cave, first by Gray's Inn and second by the Lord Chancellor, could have been determinative (n. 38).
82   Established by the *Judiciary Act 1903* (Cth).
83   The High Court travelled to Perth in both 1905 and 1906. Roger B. Joyce, *Samuel Walker Griffith* (University of Queensland Press, 1984) 266.
84   Jennifer Norberry, 'The Evolution of the Commonwealth Franchise: Tales of Inclusion and Exclusion' in Graeme Orr, Bryan Mercurio & George Williams (eds), *Realising Democracy: Electoral Law in Australia* (The Federation Press, 2003) 81.

Of the three judges of the Griffith Court (1903–05), Barton is reported to have been initially lukewarm about the enfranchisement of women but softened his position when he saw how strongly they supported Federation.[85] Although he did not participate in the House of Representatives debates on the franchise, he is recorded as voting in favour.[86] The progressiveness of Australia-wide suffrage was recognised internationally and, when Prime Minister Barton was in London for the coronation of Edward VII later in the same year (1902), he accepted a formal address of congratulations from the English suffragists.[87] His biographer, Geoffrey Bolton, described him as one who was 'never unwilling to accept congratulations',[88] but would this acceptance have been sufficient to embarrass him into subsequently supporting Edith Haynes had she appealed the Supreme Court decision in 1904? Surely, he would have been unable to ignore women's enfranchisement as was the case with the WA judges.

In contrast to Barton's initial ambivalence regarding women's enfranchisement, O'Connor consistently expressed strong support not just for the vote, but also for women's enhanced role in public life:

> I should like to say that I see no reason in the world why we should continue to impose laws which have to be obeyed by the women of the community without giving them some voice in the election of the members who make those laws. Their capacity for understanding political questions, for thinking over them, and for exercising their influence in regard to public affairs, is certainly of that order and of that level which entitles them to take that part in public affairs which the franchise proposes to give them.[89]

O'Connor's strong advocacy on behalf of women may have dispelled any lingering doubt that Barton had, as the pair are described as having been the closest of friends since boyhood.[90] Both were members of the Sydney School of Arts Debating Club and 'comrades in the struggle for union'

---

85   Geoffrey Bolton, *Edmund Barton* (Allen & Unwin, 2000) 197.

86   Final Vote, *Parliamentary Debates on Commonwealth Franchise Act 1902 (Cth)*, House of Representatives, Hansard, 23 April 1902, 11953.

87   Bolton (n. 85) 262.

88   ibid.

89   Senator O'Connor (NSW, Protectionist Party), *Parliamentary Debates on Commonwealth Franchise Act 1902 (Cth)*, Senate, Hansard, 9 April 1902, 11451.

90   Martha Rutledge, 'O'Connor, Richard Edward' in Tony Blackshield, Michael Coper & George Williams (eds), *The Oxford Companion to the High Court of Australia* (Oxford University Press, 2001) 509.

in the 1890s.[91] O'Connor seems to have possessed considerable strength of character and is described as bringing to the bench 'sound common sense', as well as being able to exercise 'a restraining influence' on Barton.[92] Hence, Edith Haynes would almost certainly have been able to count on one vote and possibly two.

But what of the chief justice? Like his fellow judges, Samuel Griffith also had an extensive political career that included a stint as premier as well as chief justice of Queensland. However, his stance on women's rights is uncertain, although he is described as 'liberal and humanitarian' and, like O'Connor, 'a radical',[93] although this may have been in his younger days. As with O'Connor and Barton, O'Connor and Griffith also shared a common outlook. According to Griffith himself, his and O'Connor's minds 'ran ... in similar grooves'.[94]

Griffith CJ wrote most of the early judgements of the court and it is notable that Barton shared Griffith's views in all 164 cases reported in the first three years,[95] with O'Connor normally concurring. The three judges were therefore exceptionally close. Nevertheless, would their shared outlook have extended to the idea of women becoming legal practitioners—a stance adopted by no other Anglo-Australian court at the time?

While O'Connor did not write any of the joint judgements of the court, he seems to have been the pivotal member of the triumvirate. Not only was he respected for his common sense, but also he was clearly skilled in the art of persuasion. His sway over the NSW Legislative Council as Leader of the Government from 1892 was described as 'supreme and unquestioned'.[96] This is despite his ostensibly radical stance in respect of women and Aboriginal people, to whom he also advocated extending

---

91   Martha Rutledge, 'O'Connor, Richard Edward (1851–1912), Senator for New South Wales, 1901–03 (Protectionist)', *The Biographical Dictionary of the Australian Senate. Volume 1, 1901–1929* (Melbourne University Press, 2000) 27–30, available from: biography.senate.gov.au/richard-edward-oconnor/.

92   Martha Rutledge, 'O'Connor, Richard Edward (Dick) (1851–1912)', *Australian Dictionary of Biography. Volume 11* (Melbourne University Press, 1988).

93   Harry Gibbs, 'Griffith, Samuel Walker' in Blackshield et al. (n. 90) 309.

94   Rutledge (n. 90), 510. Griffith also wrote to Commonwealth attorney-general Josiah Symon and indicated that when the three justices of the High Court were travelling together on circuit, '[i]t has fortunately happened that we are on terms of personal friendship'. See National Library of Australia, Symon Papers MS1736/11/862, Letter from the Chief Justice to the Attorney-General, 14 June 1905.

95   Geoffrey Bolton & John Williams, 'Barton, Edmund' in Blackshield et al. (n. 90) 54.

96   Rutledge (n. 91).

the franchise.[97] Indeed, subsequent scholars, including the noted constitutional lawyer Geoffrey Sawer, are of the view that the 'ability and independence of mind' of O'Connor have been 'grossly undervalued by Australian legal tradition'.[98]

The Griffith Court favoured a purposive construction in the interpretation of statutes,[99] which would also have been in Edith Haynes' favour. This jurisprudential style entails paying particular attention to legislative intention—a concept I have already problematised. Would the court have been able to transcend the ideologically laden interpretation of the WA Supreme Court that the legislature did not *intend* the word 'person' to apply to women in the *LPA* because of the inveterate practice of the common law? Unlike the Supreme Court of Western Australia in 1904, the Griffith Court is described as 'applying scholarly standards to their judgments' and, even more promisingly, we are told that decisions of the state judiciaries were overturned with 'fatal frequency'.[100] Hence, the High Court would not have deferred to some imagined notion of 'states' rights', despite the novelty of Federation. In scanning the early decisions of the Griffith Court, I note there is some regard for the changing status of women, particularly married women, who are persons *sui juris* for all purposes,[101] including having the right to maintain their own banking accounts,[102] to hold their own property,[103] to operate a manufacturing concern[104] and to act as administrators of estates and trustees of infants.[105] These decisions are heartening, albeit not conclusive.

While the jurisprudential nub of *Haynes* was the interpretation of the word 'person' in the WA *LPA*, the issue of women's entry to the legal profession was one of significance Australia-wide—underscored by the *Australian Franchise Act 1902*. It is nevertheless conceded that, by 1904–05, when an

---

97   Senator O'Connor (NSW, Protectionist Party), *Parliamentary Debates on Commonwealth Franchise Act 1902 (Cth)*, Senate, Hansard, 9 April 1902, 11453. See also Marian Sawer, 'Enrolling the People: Electoral Innovation in the New Australian Commonwealth' in Orr et al. (n. 84) 52n.1. The enfranchisement of Aboriginal people did not occur for another 60 years. See *Commonwealth Electoral Act 1962*.

98   Rutledge (n. 90).

99   Sir Anthony Mason, 'The High Court in Sir Samuel Griffith's Time: Contemporary Parallels and Contrasts' (1994) 3 *Griffith Law Review* 179, 191.

100   Rutledge (n. 92).

101   *Paterson v McNaghten* (1905) 2 CLR 615.

102   *Marshall v Colonial Bank of Australia Ltd* (1904) 1 CLR 632.

103   *Jack v Small* [1905] 2 CLR 684.

104   *Beath, Schiess & Co v Martin* (1905) 2 CLR 716.

105   *Holden v Black* (1905) 2 CLR 768.

appeal would have been heard, New Zealand and three Australian states had turned to the legislature to admit women to legal practice. However, rather than remit the case to the WA Supreme Court, the High Court could have grasped the nettle and decided the issue there and then.

At the same time, we cannot ignore the fact that Haynes KC as counsel for his niece in *In re Haynes* did not advert to the citizenship argument before the WA Supreme Court even though, as an MLC, he had strongly supported both the enfranchisement of women in 1899 and the amendment to the *LPA* in 1900. Hence, it is uncertain whether we would have been able to rely on him in the appeal even if he were to have represented his niece. It is also entirely possible that O'Connor, too, might have treated enfranchisement and admission to legal practice as discrete. This would be unlikely, however, as O'Connor introduced the Franchise Bill into parliament—one of the few bills to have emanated from the Senate in the first parliament.[106] His commitment is supported by his rhetoric in the debates espousing a positive role for women in public life. Indeed, it is apparent from his speech that he envisaged the exercise of the vote to be much more than placing a ballot in a ballot box, for he refers to enfranchisement as not only a 'measure of justice', but also a means for women to be able to 'exercise their influence in Australian public affairs'.[107] Such sentiments support the Kantian notion of active citizenship. Furthermore, if O'Connor were prepared to swim against the tide and make international history by taking carriage of an Act to enfranchise women and elect them to parliament in the very first term of the new Australian Parliament, why would he demur about taking an equally daring decision to admit women to legal practice?

Of course, we will never know how the High Court might have determined the hypothetical appeal, such are the vagaries associated with the judicial leeways of choice in the absence of binding precedents. I do not wish to attribute modern sentiments to the legal dramatis personae in the *Haynes* case, but I would like to think that the express support of O'Connor together with the influence he exerted on his two fellow judges would have carried the day and enabled Edith Haynes to sit for her intermediate examination.

---

106 *Parliamentary Debates*, First Parliament First Session, Senate Official Hansard, 9 April 1902.
107 ibid., 11452.

As admission was a state issue, the High Court might have been diffident about deciding whether women should be admitted to legal practice. However, it could have referred the matter back to the WA Supreme Court, upbraiding it for its flawed reasoning regarding its interpretation of the word 'person', its reliance on the inveterate practice of the common law, its failure to take judicial notice of the enfranchisement of women and their admission to and graduation from law schools, to say nothing of their admission to legal practice elsewhere. The High Court also could have pointed out that the Supreme Court of Western Australia had the power either to admit women to legal practice by its own motion or, alternatively, to recommend that the WA Barristers' Board put pressure on the WA Parliament to enact an amendment to the *LPA* along the lines of that originally proposed by R.S. Haynes MLC in 1900.

The words of the WA Colonial Secretary Hon G. Randall in support of amending the *LPA* in 1900 are salutary as far as both Barton and O'Connor are concerned: 'Having voted for female suffrage I do not see how I can consistently do other than further the advance of women in this direction.'[108] If Barton and O'Connor similarly did not resile, Edith Haynes would then have been admitted to practice when she had completed her articles and the course of the history of women and law in Western Australia, Australia generally and possibly the Empire, too, might have been somewhat different.

Conclusion

When women won the vote in the United Kingdom at the end of World War I, the legal profession hoped to retain its masculinist monopoly, but MPs feared losing their seats and supported legislation admitting women to legal practice.[109] Although times had also changed in Australia by the end of the war, there is no evidence that women used the power of the ballot box to vote out of office those MPs opposed to admitting women to legal practice,[110] even though the potential of the vote had been recognised

---

108 *WA Parliamentary Debates (Hansard)*, Legislative Council, Legal Practitioners Act Amendment Bill, Second Reading, 18 September 1900, Vol. 17, 453.

109 Sachs & Wilson (n. 4) 173.

110 Following the 1896 election in South Australia, in which women voted for the first time, Catherine Helen Spence, the prominent SA political reformer, expressed her disappointment that women allowed their interest in public affairs to stop short at the act of voting. Helen Thomson (ed.), *Catherine Helen Spence* (Queensland University Press, 1987) 464.

by influential suffragists in the nineteenth century. In 1892, Rose Scott, for example, observed that enfranchisement meant more than 'merely to drop a paper in a ballot box' and it was 'better for men and better for women that the laws which we must both obey we should have a direct voice in determining'.[111]

The complementarity thesis—a central trope of the Western intellectual tradition—which averred that men were *naturally* suited to the public sphere and women to the private, was endlessly repeated by the opponents of enfranchisement,[112] as well as by judges opposed to the admission of women to legal practice.[113] Despite the passage of legislation and the understanding that 'reasonable people did not condemn the suffrage outright',[114] doubts about women's capacity lingered or were adduced as a convenient fig leaf to disguise the economic threat posed by the entry of women.[115] The vested interests of male lawyers inferentially prevailed in sustaining the complementarity thesis and the construction of women as passive citizens, even after they had been admitted to legal practice. Of course, the sustained resistance to which women had been subjected for decades regarding their acceptance as active citizens in the public sphere was hardly likely to evaporate overnight and, a century later, sites of contestation remain, particularly regarding authoritative positions and the issue of caring for children, as I show in ensuing chapters.

111 'Rose Scott on Womanhood Suffrage (1892)' in James Walter & Margaret MacLeod (eds), *The Citizens' Bargain: A Documentary History of Australian Views Since 1890* (UNSW Press, 2002) 82. Perhaps influenced by Rose Scott, the same sentiment was echoed by Richard O'Connor a decade later.
112 For example, Senator Josiah Symon, SA, *Parliamentary Debates on Commonwealth Franchise Act 1902 (Cth)*, Senate, 9 April 1902, 11463.
113 The concurring opinion of Bradley J in *Bradwell v Illinois* 83 US 130 (1872) at 141 is exemplary: 'The constitution of the family organization, which is founded in the divine ordinance, as well as in the nature of things, indicates the domestic sphere as that which properly belongs to the domain and functions of womanhood … The paramount destiny and mission of woman are to fulfil the noble and benign offices of wife and mother. This is the law of the Creator.'
114 Helen Irving, *To Constitute a Nation: A Cultural History of Australia's Constitution* (Cambridge University Press, 1997) 181–82.
115 The WA Colonial Secretary Hon G. Randell alluded to this in exhorting support for the LPA Amendment Bill in 1900: 'I do hope members of the legal profession will give this Bill careful consideration and will not, from any low motive as to the fear of competition, oppose this further advance of the enfranchisement of women.' See *WA Parliamentary Debates (Hansard)*, Legislative Council, Legal Practitioners Act Amendment Bill, Second Reading, 18 September 1900, Vol. 17, 453–54. Cf. Gosling (n. 38).

Part II: The Limits of Law

2

Feminist Jurisprudence: Illusion or Reality?

Introduction: Public and private worlds

Law is not only a powerful mechanism for social control by the state, but also a powerful conduit for the transmission and reproduction of the dominant ideology. Accordingly, law has been used to maintain a rigid line of demarcation between the two analytically distinct spheres of public and private; the former has been designated the world of men, the latter the world of women. However, far from the two spheres being commensurate, there is a marked asymmetry between them. Hannah Arendt, for example, accepts as axiomatic the existence of an ontological dualism between public and private.[1] Freedom and equality are realisable only among citizens in the public sphere, for the private sphere is perceived to be the locus of domination and inequality.[2] Nevertheless, Arendt has chosen to ignore the fact that the 'society of equals' was traditionally confined to male citizens alone. She has also chosen to ignore the violence emanating from the public sphere, as manifested in foreign policy, for example, to emphasise what she considers to be the noble and ethical intellectualism of the polis, while implicitly denigrating the private sphere's association with nature and nurture. The historical exclusion of women from the society of equals, together with the elevation of the public above the private sphere, is typical of mainstream thought—aphoristically termed 'male-stream' by Mary O'Brien.[3]

---

1   Hannah Arendt, *The Human Condition* (University of Chicago Press, 1958) Part II.
2   ibid.
3   Mary O'Brien, *The Politics of Reproduction* (Routledge & Kegan Paul, 1981).

As a corollary of the ideology underpinning the division between public and private life, women have been subjected to the inescapable stigma of intellectual inferiority. Propped up by pseudo-scientific theories based on biology or nature, the Western intellectual tradition has been bolstered by the antifeminism of Aristotelianism and Judaeo-Christian scholasticism. Indeed, feminist scholarship has demonstrated that the work of Aristotle and other influential philosophers is in fact the study of the male human and not of the human species.[4] The notion of phallocentrism masquerading as universalism is therefore characteristic of the Western intellectual tradition. Any specific reference to women tends to emphasise their marginality to the public sphere.[5]

Tönnies' *Gemeinschaft/Gesellschaft* dichotomy is exemplary, for it seeks to assign men and women to the different spheres on account of what are claimed to be their psychologically different characteristics. Women are associated with *Gemeinschaft* ('community') and the traditional values of the private sphere involving intimacy and family. Men, on the other hand, are associated with *Gesellschaft* ('society'), which embraces those values associated with the public realm, including business, travel and society. The assignation of rational will to one sex only is made clear:

> It is an old truth … that women are usually led by feelings, men more by intellect. Men are more clever. They alone are capable of calculation, of calm (abstract) thinking, of consideration, combination, and logic. As a rule, women follow these pursuits ineffectively. They lack the necessary requirement of rational will.[6]

While feminist scholarship has successfully rebutted asseverations of women's intellectual inferiority,[7] the ideology that indelibly associates women with the private sphere is resistant to change because it is functionally necessary to capitalism. According to Marxist theory, capitalism requires the continued subordination of women to provide a cheap source of labour, to boost the

---

4   For example, Susan Moller Okin, *Women in Western Political Thought* (Virago, 1980); Lynda Lange, 'Woman is Not a Rational Animal: On Aristotle's Biology of Reproduction' in Sandra Harding & Merrill B. Hintikka (eds), *Discovering Reality: Feminist Perspectives on Epistemology, Metaphysics, Methodology and Philosophy of Science* (University of Chicago Press, 1983).

5   For example, Cynthia Fuchs Epstein, 'Women in Sociological Analysis: New Scholarship Versus Old Paradigms' in Elizabeth Langland & Walter Gove (eds), *A Feminist Perspective in the Academy: The Difference it Makes* (University of Chicago Press, 1981) 150.

6   Ferdinand Tönnies, *Community and Association (Gemeinschaft und Gesellschaft)* (Routledge & Kegan Paul, 1955) 151.

7   Eleanor Emmons Maccoby & Carol Nagy Jacklin, *The Psychology of Sex Differences* (Stanford University Press, 1974).

demand for consumption goods and to engage in socially necessary but unpaid housework and childcare in the home.[8] Furthermore, women are assigned a primary role in the guardianship and reproduction of ideology through the family. Inevitably, therefore, the liberal state has responded with some ambivalence to the feminist movement's demands for an end to the subordination of women in the private sphere. While the state has overtly fostered a belief in the idea that regulation of the private sphere is not feasible, it has nevertheless been instrumental in shaping and reinforcing the favoured family form through governmental policies designed to encourage the dependency of women.

The epistemological constraints that a misogynistic intellectual tradition poses for feminist reform of the law cannot be gainsaid, particularly as the dichotomised language of public and private, male and female, is built into the form of law itself. Indeed, in recent years, feminist scholars have shown how the entire corpus of liberal thought is structured around a series of sexualised, hierarchised dualisms.[9] As the Tönnies example suggests, men are identified with one side of the dualism—namely, thought, rationality, reason, culture, power, objectivity and abstract and principled activity. The terms associated with women are the converse: irrationality, feeling, emotion, passivity, nature, subjectivity, sensitivity and contextualised and personalised behaviour. Predictably, law is associated with the male side of the dualism, in that it is supposed to be rational, objective, abstract and principled. Therefore, in constructing difference as a set of binary oppositions, there appears to be no room for authentic difference outside the established system.[10] Thus, the difficulties involved in constructing a feminist model of law reform that takes cognisance of difference are increasingly apparent from a methodological as well as an epistemological perspective.

Rosaldo contrasts the public universalistic world with that of the 'relatively particularistic' domestic sphere. While the former is governed by 'formal norms of relationship and publicly recognised characteristics of roles', the

---

8   Alison Jaggar, 'Political Philosophies of Women's Liberation' in Mary Vetterling-Braggin, Frederick Elliston & Jane English (eds), *Feminism and Philosophy* (Littlefield, Adams & Co., 1977) 10.

9   Nancy C.M. Hartsock, 'The Feminist Standpoint: Developing the Ground for a Specifically Feminist Historical Materialism' in Sandra Harding and Merrill B. Hintikka (eds), *Discovering Reality: Feminist Perspectives on Epistemology, Metaphysics, Methodology, and Philosophy of Science* (Reidel Publishing, 1983); Frances Olsen, 'The sex of law' (Unpublished conference paper, European Conference on Critical Legal Studies, April 1986).

10   Josette Feral, 'The Powers of Difference' in Hester Eisenstein & Alice Jardine (eds), *The Future of Difference* (G.K. Hall, 1980).

latter is 'governed by informal and personal knowledge of individuals'.[11] This conflation of the public sphere with universalism is central to the operation of law within liberal legalism. The objectification of law successfully disguises the fact that it is the product of fallible humans while, at the same time, it promotes the unquestioning acceptance of the rule of law:

> Through objectification, the law achieves an illusory but intimidating authority. It appears to be the embodiment of a neutral or natural ethic, a 'given' structure, rather than a contingent construction. The hierarchies that the law guards, institutionalized in our society, likewise appear to be natural and necessary, rather than the malleable creations of men that they actually are.[12]

Women are necessarily rendered marginal to the operation of the law by virtue of assignation to the private sphere and particularity. This asymmetry between public and private spheres therefore constitutes an impediment to law reform, for it involves a failure to grapple with the inequities within women's domestic lives that drastically affect their public-sphere participation.

Yeatman takes the Rosaldo model somewhat further in explaining how it legitimates the domination of men over women:

> If domestic = particularistic, and public = universalistic, and if domestic : women :: public : men, then men in their capacity as expositors of the public domain must be endowed with legitimate authority over women in their capacity as representatives of the domestic domain.[13]

The equation explains why the universal, as the ubiquitous and superior standard, tends to absorb the particular or inferior variable. This hierarchisation of male and female also renders it unsurprising that the liberal feminist imperative has been to absorb the private into the public.[14] The result has been that either the quotidian realities of women's lives, including domestic violence, incest, marital rape and the drudgery of housework, are repressed and ignored, or a false but rosy vision of

---

11   Michelle Rosaldo, 'Women, Culture and Society: A Theoretical Overview' in Michelle Z. Rosaldo & Louise Lamphere (eds), *Women in Culture and Society* (Stanford University Press, 1974).
12   Christine A. Desan Husson, 'Expanding the Legal Vocabulary: The Challenge Posed by the Deconstruction and Defense of Law' (1986) 95(5) *Yale Law Journal* 969, 971, doi.org/10.2307/796379.
13   Anna Yeatman, 'Gender and Differentiation of Social Life into Public and Domestic Domains' (1984) 15 *Social Analysis* 32, 41.
14   Jean Bethke Elshtain, *Public Man, Private Woman* (Martin Robertson, 1981) 248.

the family as the locus of caring and love is presented. The private has therefore been successfully immunised against state regulation—a factor that underscores the residual right of men to domination in the home.

In the public sphere, the equation of maleness with the universal standard necessarily precludes attempts to transform the prevailing standard, with the result that some attempts at law reform have served to reinforce rather than to redress gender inequalities. Women's participation in the public sphere is contingent on their role in the private sphere, which has shaped the construction of the feminine in conformity with a model that suits capitalism.[15] The sexual segmentation of the labour force is the most dramatic exemplification of this phenomenon.[16] The ancillary nature of these occupations, together with the confinement of women to the lower echelons of the employment hierarchy, has also served to legitimate the authority of men over women in the public sphere.

So successful has been the prevailing ideology of law as a neutral arbiter of disputes and as a positive instrument of social change, rather than as a primary determinant of social relations, that little attention has been directed to the possibility that the form of law might itself be flawed. Thus, the law reform that feminists have sought has necessarily contained a fundamental paradox—that is, how can the use of what must always be a male-defined and superior standard ever achieve any semblance of equality for women unless women become token men in specified fields of public endeavour? In other words, can the woman lawyer in a three-piece, pinstripe suit ever be more than a parody of her male counterpart?

The search for equality

Although the feminist movement has its genesis within liberalism and reflects its contradictions, feminism does seek to transcend its limitations.[17] Given the grossness of the inequalities in the public sphere and the doubts surrounding the amenability of the private sphere to state regulation, it is

---

15 Iris Young, 'Socialist Feminism and the Limits of Dual Systems of Theory' (1980) 10 *Socialist Review* 169, 178.

16 In the twenty-first century, the Australian labour force remains highly gender segregated by both industry and occupation. See Workplace Gender Equality Agency, *Gender Segregation in Australia's Workforce* (Australian Government, 17 April 2019), available from: www.wgea.gov.au/publications/gender-segregation-in-australias-workforce.

17 Miriam Dixson, 'Gender, Class, and the Women's Movements' in Norma Grieve & Alisa Burns (eds), *Australian Women: New Feminist Perspectives* (Oxford University Press, 1986).

not surprising that the energies of both First-Wave and Second-Wave Feminism have been propelled by a desire to ensure women's ability to function as equals in the public realm. First-Wave Feminism, accordingly, directed its energies towards the struggle for emancipation and for entry into universities and the professions.[18]

Political action emanating from the efforts of Second-Wave Feminism secured initiatives such as no-fault divorce, new sexual assault laws and domestic violence legislation. Consequently, considerable energy has been expended in securing a modicum of state regulation within the private sphere. By and large, however, the focus has been on gender neutrality and formal equality, which are perceived to accord with liberal notions of fairness in the public realm. There has been little exploration of the question of the applicable standard; the underlying and unquestioned implication seems to be that the only standard is the androcentric standard. Women, therefore, must be encouraged and assisted to be brought *up* to that standard. Little attention has been paid to female behaviour, believing, perhaps, that it would wither away.[19]

While formal equality is a basic norm of liberalism, it is frequently forgotten in legal discourse that *inequality* is also a norm of liberalism, albeit it is unlikely to feature prominently within the rhetoric. In fact, our society is preoccupied with sorting people out and ranking them according to perceived abilities.[20] Indeed, the concept of merit within liberalism operates as an ideological construct to mask inequitable allocations that preserve established social relations according to sex, race and class.[21] Therefore, the beneficiaries of feminist-initiated law reform, for the most part, have been white, middle-class women. The reforms have had little effect on those women disadvantaged by Aboriginality, disability or class. Accordingly, Elshtain, for example, is dismissive of liberal feminism on account of what she calls its 'self-interested, predatory individualism'.[22] Individualism, however, is central to liberalism. Thus, while the feminist movement for law reform is propelled by a vision of a better society, it is inevitably constrained by the bourgeois predilections of liberal legalism.

---

18   Carol L. Bacchi, 'First-Wave Feminism: History's Judgment' in Grieve & Burns (n. 17).
19   Note, 'Toward a Redefinition of Sexual Equality' (1981) 95(2) *Harvard Law Review* 487, doi.org/10.2307/1340713.
20   Andre Béteille, 'The Idea of Natural Inequality' in Gerald D. Berreman (ed.), *Social Inequality: Comparative and Developmental Approaches* (Academic Press, 1981).
21   Margaret Thornton, 'Affirmative Action, Merit and the Liberal State' (1985) 2(2) *Australian Journal of Law and Society* 28.
22   Elshtain (n. 14).

Therefore, it is necessarily only those individual women who are most like their male comparators who are likely to benefit from the equal treatment model, as their admission to the 'society of equals' will be least destabilising.

A preoccupation with equality dominates the American feminist legal literature—a reflection of the status of the concept in US constitutional law doctrine, although litigation and legal argument also stress the preeminence of equal rights as a means of reform.[23] Feminist strategies identified by Olsen have focused on attacking the sexualisation of the dualisms referred to, attacking their hierarchisation or attacking the ostensible neutrality of law—an approach that rejects the taxonomy.[24] The first strategy has predominated, which allows laws to be challenged because they are not rational, objective and principled. Thus, sex-based classifications that discriminate against women have been successfully attacked on the basis that they are fundamentally irrational,[25] such as a preference for men over women in the administration of a deceased estate.[26] While such cases do question the rigidity of the public/private dichotomy, and successes do permit a few women to enter the society of equals, such challenges do not pose a fundamental threat to the existence of the polarised spheres.

Although Australia has no constitutional guarantee of equality, the idea of equality before the law does constitute a basic principle of the Anglo-Australian legal system.[27] The principle, however, is not sufficient to confer a substantive legal right; it constitutes no more than a procedural standard requiring the application of legal rules in the same way to all regardless of sex, race or class. However, equality of opportunity, with its connotations of individual responsibility for success or failure, is formally acknowledged in antidiscrimination legislation.[28] Again, the focus is on equal treatment, although the theory may permit limited affirmative measures to allow women to be brought up to a point where they may compete equally with men for education and jobs.

---

23 Ann E. Freedman, 'Sex Equality, Sex Differences, and the Supreme Court' (1983) 92(6) *Yale Law Journal* 913, doi.org/10.2307/796279.
24 Olsen (n. 9).
25 Freedman (n. 23).
26 *Reed v Reed* 404 US 71 (1971).
27 Albert Venn Dicey, *Introduction to the Study of the Law of the Constitution* (Macmillan, 10th edn, 1964).
28 For example, *Sex Discrimination Act 1984* (Cth).

Although there was initially some doubt as to whether the absence of male-sex comparability meant that pregnancy could not be subsumed within a general law proscribing sex discrimination, Australian antidiscrimination legislation now includes a specific proscription against discrimination on the ground of pregnancy.[29] There have not been the curious judicial attempts to analogise pregnancy and male-specific medical conditions such as prostatectomy, circumcision, haemophilia and gout, which emerged in the United States in the 1970s.[30] Clearly, the liberal model of sex equality allowed such a comparability requirement to be attacked as irrational. Although the US Supreme Court subsequently conceptualised less favourable treatment arising from pregnancy as a lawful distinction between 'pregnant and non-pregnant persons',[31] determining the relationship between pregnancy and equal treatment continues to be problematic.[32]

Comparability is the doctrine that lies at the heart of sex discrimination legislation and, while the need for a male comparator may have been dispensed with in respect of the unique physiological characteristic of pregnancy, it is otherwise necessary for a female complainant to establish less favourable treatment vis-a-vis a real or hypothetical male in the same or similar circumstances. This continues to be analytically problematic for most women in employment, given the existence of structural impediments, such as the sexual segmentation of labour.

In Australia, it is legislation rather than litigation per se that is viewed as the primary locus of law reform.[33] This perception arises partly from the positivist myth that the judiciary is apolitical and it does not create law; its job is merely to interpret it. In part, however, this negative perception of litigation has a sound empirical basis, for common law adjudication has served to entrench the inferior status of women in society. Consequently, law reform is generally perceived to be a political question for the legislature.[34] However, a specialist tribunal might feel that it has a mandate

29   ibid., s. 7.
30   *Geduldig v Aiello* 417 US 48 (1974) per Brennan J.
31   *General Electric v Gilbert* 429 US 125 (1976).
32   Linda J. Krieger & Patricia N. Cooney, 'The Miller-Wohl Controversy: Equal Treatment, Positive Action and the Meaning of Women's Equality' (1983) 13(3) *Golden Gate University Law Review* 513.
33   Jude Wallace & John Fiocco, 'Recent Criticisms of Formalism in Legal Theory and Legal Education' (1980–81) 7 *Adelaide Law Review* 309.
34   Australian judges long clung to the legal fiction that they lacked the power to alter the common law even when anachronistic, such as the loss of consortium (an action upholding the property interest of a husband in a wife's household and sexual services). Margaret Thornton, 'Loss of Consortium: Inequality before the Law' (1984) 10 *Sydney Law Review* 259.

to make decisions of a more adventurous nature. For example, the NSW Equal Opportunity Tribunal was the first Anglo-Australian judicial body to find that sexual harassment constituted sex discrimination.[35]

Equality, in the formal equal treatment sense, has been the first goal of feminist law reform in the Western world. As a corollary, the move from sex specificity to sex neutrality was perceived by feminist law reformers as desirable because it meant the seeds of invidiousness associated with dependency or with protective legislation, for example, would be discarded. However, the preoccupation with equality has constituted an impediment to the development of feminist theory.

The reforms that have occurred have exposed contradictions inherent within the liberal paradigm. On the one hand, equality discourse has a seductive appeal because it eschews the language of dominance. On the other hand, the application of formal equality has demonstrated that it can create and entrench substantive inequality. For example, an equal division of assets between parties on divorce is very much within the equal treatment model,[36] but it ignores the fact that the former wife is more likely than not to be living in poverty within a short time as a result of her unequal status in the labour market or because of her dependency on welfare.[37] The husband, on the other hand, is likely to be financially better off, advancing in his career and anticipating a substantial superannuation payout on retirement.

It is the combination of the equality prescript and sex neutrality that has had a distorting effect for women, perhaps most marked when there is a conflation of violence and sexuality, as in cases of rape, incest and domestic violence. The sex specificity in respect of both victim and oppressor does not lend itself to compression within the neutrality mould that mandates that both be treated with the same degree of impartiality by the law. The harm suffered by the female victim is likely to be undervalued and trivialised. Indeed, it may be largely incomprehensible to the legal culture in view of the absence of a male benchmark. The history of women's intersection with the law consists of a litany of complaints as to the unresponsiveness

---

35 *O'Callaghan v Loder* (1984) EOC ¶92–103.

36 Jocelynne A. Scutt & Di Graham, *For Richer, For Poorer: Money, Marriage and Property Rights* (Penguin Books, 1984).

37 Martha L. Fineman, 'Implementing Equality: Ideology, Contradiction and Social Change— A Study of Rhetoric and Results in the Regulation of the Consequences of Divorce' (1983) *Wisconsin Law Review* 789.

and lack of comprehension of liberal legalism. For example, it was believed that the move towards 'sexual assault' in lieu of 'rape' would overcome some of the anomalies arising from its limited legal definition and that it would also rid the offence of its pejorative antifeminist connotations, such as the perception of a woman as a false accuser. Law reform resulted in sex neutrality, which means a woman herself can now be convicted of sexual assault. There was also a deflection of attention from the sexual component and a greater focus on physical violence, as reflected in the graduated scale of punishment. The by-product of the latter, however, has been to discount the psychological violence occasioned to victims resulting from a rape. In other words, the focus on physical violence or the threat of physical violence is accentuated, rather than the sexual violation, because it comports with a male model of harm.

The current ambivalence of feminists towards the retention of a sex-neutral standard is underscored by reference to the term 'sexual' in the Canadian case of *R v Chase*.[38] The court held that the word 'ought to be given its natural meaning as limited to the sexual organs of genitalia' and concluded that secondary sexual characteristics, such as breasts, did not fall within the rubric of 'sexual', which was not defined in the relevant legislation. The court determined that, if breasts are sexual, so are men's beards. Christine Boyle has presented a critique of this decision, describing it as the 'antithesis of feminist analysis' because it refuses to recognise that gender is a material fact in sexual assault.[39] As Boyle notes, this is an example of abstracting a proposition to a point where it is gender neutral. Indeed, the question of touching a woman's breast must be, even in the eyes of the 'reasonable man', an unequivocally sex-specific act.

The question is how should women's differences be considered in view of the preeminence accorded to male norms? In the United States, a spirited debate was conducted among feminist legal scholars in the late twentieth century based on variants of the equality prescript—namely, 'equal treatment' versus 'special treatment'. The equal treatment model endorses an androgynous approach on the basis that any acknowledgement of women's differences is counterproductive.[40] The model avers that the discourse of special treatment is demeaning to women, for it is a further

---

38   (1984) 13 CCC (3d) 187 (NBCA).
39   Christine Boyle, 'Sexual Assault and the Feminist Judge' (1985) 1 *Canadian Journal of Women and the Law* 93, 100.
40   Wendy W. Williams, 'The Equality Crisis: Some Reflections on Culture, Courts and Feminism' (1982) 7(3) *Women's Rights Law Reporter* 175.

reminder of otherness and inequality. On the other hand, the special treatment model takes the view that equal treatment in circumstances such as pregnancy results in inequality for women;[41] the model avers that equality can be achieved for women in the workplace only if such differences are considered. The special treatment model also challenges the liberal assimilationist view that maleness is a norm that is neutral. Krieger and Cooney endorse the 'bivalent' view of Wolgast,[42] which allows special measures to be developed for pregnant women based on the analogy with the 'reasonable accommodation' model that permits a ramp to be provided for a person confined to a wheelchair, for example. The conferral of this 'special' right enables the recipient to exercise an 'equal right' in respect of access to education or employment, without which the individual is effectively denied equal treatment. Although the special treatment model adopts a qualified substantive rather than formalistic interpretation of equality, the model is still constrained by the liberal legal view that it is equality with the norm, whether it be in terms of gender, race, ableness or another attribute, that is sought.

The work of psychologist Carol Gilligan, which identifies two gendered voices in moral discourse, has struck a chord with feminist legal scholars. Her vision is a transformative one, for it rejects the constraints of equality and the myth of maleness as universal: 'One voice speaks about equality, reciprocity, fairness, rights; one voice speaks about connection, not hurting, care and response.'[43] Gilligan uses the analogy of the ladder and the web to encapsulate this dualism. On the one hand, men's preoccupation with hierarchy confines women perennially to the lower rungs of the ladder. On the other hand, the web analogy reflects women's perception of a conflict situation as one involving a network of relationships, rather than a contest of rights between opponents.

Gilligan takes the universality problematic a step further: since human equals male, and the female virtue of care equals self-sacrifice, the good woman who values care would sacrifice herself rather than challenge the equation of human with male.[44] Equality has thereby become deformed,

---

41   Krieger & Cooney (n. 32).
42   Elizabeth Wolgast, *Equality and the Rights of Women* (Cornell University Press, 1980).
43   Carol Gilligan, cited in Ellen C. Dubois, Mary C. Dunlap, Carol J. Gilligan, Catharine A. MacKinnon, Carrie J. Menkel-Meadow, Isabel Marcus & Paul J. Spiegelman, 'Feminist Discourse, Moral Values, and the Law—A Conversation' (1985) 34(1) *Buffalo Law Review* 11, 44, available from: digitalcommons.law.buffalo.edu/buffalolawreview/vol34/iss1/4.
44   ibid., 46.

just as attachment is deformed in the equation of care with self-sacrifice.[45] But this does not mean that inequality becomes a human good, since the condition for women has frequently been one that is synonymous with exploitation and violence. According to the Gilligan approach, equality should not necessarily be jettisoned but the discourse needs to be transformed by the caring voice. That is, responsibilities, as well as rights, need to be considered by replacing equality with equity: 'The morality of rights is predicated on equality and centered on the understanding of fairness, while the ethic of responsibility relies on the concept of equity, the recognition of differences in need.'[46]

Menkel-Meadow extrapolates from Gilligan's thesis to make a case that women may make better lawyers, which is illustrated, for example, by their ability to personalise and contextualise problems in relationships with children.[47] Indeed, Epstein, in her thoroughgoing study of women in the legal profession in the United States, notes that many of her female subjects advocated a more 'participatory mode of decision making'.[48] Nevertheless, there would seem to be something of a gap between the advocacy and the realisation. At present, the institutional constraints are such that women who are promoted to partnerships or to professorships are rewarded for acting within the conventional parameters laid down by the organisation, not for startling innovations. Indeed, a challenge to institutional norms is more likely to incur disapprobation manifesting itself in a detriment, such as a refusal to confirm tenure or promotion, if not to bring about outright dismissal.

The psychological contrast between men and women arouses ambivalent feelings in feminists because of its essentialising overtones. The ambivalence is painfully acute for feminist lawyers. Gilligan's thesis suggests that women are likely to be able to deal with family law matters, for example, with greater skill and sensitivity than men and that the assignation of women to this traditional area of practice is appropriate, despite the fact that many women have consciously avoided it to escape being 'typecast'.[49] Women may, in fact, have more to offer in dealing

---

45   ibid., 58.
46   Carol Gilligan, *In a Different Voice: Psychological Theory and Women's Development* (Harvard University Press, 1982) 164.
47   Carrie J. Menkel-Meadow, 'Portia in a Different Voice: Speculations on Women's Lawyering Process' (1985) 1(1) *Berkeley Women's Law Journal* 39.
48   Cynthia Fuchs Epstein, *Women in Law* (Basic Books, 1981) 385.
49   Jane Matthews, 'The Changing Profile of Women in the Law' (1982) 56 *The Australian Law Journal* 634.

with family law because of their private-sphere experiences, although the characterisation of women lawyers in this way not only accentuates their marginality to the profession as a whole, but also reinforces a male mode of practice and exonerates men from any responsibility to develop a more caring style appropriate to family law practice:

> It implies that women have a unique responsibility for bringing the humanistic principles derived from the experience of nurturing and caring in the private world of personal relationships and family to bear on the public sphere. This skirts perilously close to recommending that women shoulder responsibility for humanizing a public arena brutalized by men's neglect. It ignores the potential for transformation of men's consciousness, and far from exploding artificial divisions between public (male) and private (female), it threatens to institutionalize those divisions within the heart of the public sphere itself.[50]

Thus, some feminist lawyers take the view that it is more empowering for women to engage in non-traditional areas of practice than to perpetuate the caring stereotype that operates to militate against the acceptance of women in the public sphere. There is also concern that the assignation of women to private-sphere concerns validates the views of traditional malestream theorists, such as Tönnies, particularly in the way they have sought to exaggerate the extent of difference between women and men.[51]

Gilligan's work can be criticised because it fails to take sufficient cognisance of the sociopolitical reality that has contributed to the emergence of two distinct moral voices. As MacKinnon points out, women are caring because that is the way they have been constructed by men.[52] Indeed, our society values women only when they act in conformity with this caring model in the private domain. Paradoxically, however, this nurturing role is undervalued vis-a-vis the abstract intellectual pursuits of men in the public domain. If preoccupied with careers in non-traditional areas, for example, women are likely to be castigated for acting 'like men' and (unlike men) can expect to be characterised as selfish and ambitious for challenging the bounds of propriety.

---

50   Janet Siltanen & Michelle Stanworth, 'The Politics of Private Woman and Public Man' in Janet Siltanen & Michelle Stanworth (eds), *Women and the Public Sphere* (Hutchinson, 1984) 199.
51   ibid.
52   Catharine A. MacKinnon, cited in Dubois et al. (n. 43) 11.

Women wish to speak with a proliferation of voices and to be heard, but not so that all but the predictable is sifted out. The question is whether legal discourse has been so thoroughly distorted by the straitjackets of acculturation into which men and women have been compressed for so long that there is no scope for the acceptance of difference.

Gunning has been critical of the liberal feminist preoccupation with equality rhetoric and argues that it is the diversity of women that leads to the questioning of the discourse of homogeneity, unity, identity and similarity:

> Equality is merely a condition for recognising the specificity of women, but enunciating likenesses merely fills the gaps in the dominant discourse. Women should be inside and at the edge of the dominant discourse. The difference is in the margin: otherness, multiplicity, heterogeneity.[53]

Thus, rather than seek to compress women into the same mould as men, a feminist theory of law should be the beginning of new legal thinking. This can be achieved only if we escape imprisonment from the dominant discourse, if we untangle the metaphor and the reality presently contributing to women's undervaluation in the public sphere and if we construct a feminist cultural image based on the feminine.

Feminism and the academy

Feminism, with its commitment to antihierarchical values and collective action, attempts to deconstruct the law's facade of neutrality and objectivity, the right of men to domination and the existence of a clear line of demarcation between public and private. The feminist aphorism of the 1960s that 'the personal is political' most dramatically encapsulates the essence of this challenge,[54] for it repudiates the Aristotelian dictum that the political is confined to the public world of men. The private and supposedly apolitical world of women, together with the hitherto sacrosanct family, has been exposed by feminists as a world of violence and inequality—a world that is fundamentally political. Feminism is

---

53   Marjet Gunning, 'A feminist paradigm in legal theory' (Unpublished conference paper, European Conference in Critical Legal Studies, London, 1986).
54   Linda J. Nicholson, 'The Personal is Political: An Analysis in Retrospect' (1981) 7(1) *Social Theory and Practice* 85.

therefore potentially destabilising, not only to the conventional wisdom of male supremacy, but also to the essential architecture of capitalism within the liberal state. A feminist approach transcends any simplistic idea of 'add women and stir', for it demands that the reality and particularity of women's experience be considered; it categorically rejects the notion that women be treated merely as objects.[55]

A feminist approach also strikes at the heart of traditional scholarship within the academy—a scholarship that has been historically masculinist, although masquerading beneath a veneer of neutrality. The exclusion of women from the neutrality prescript has been self-serving and a whole panoply of assumptions emanating from the nature/culture dichotomy has been adduced to justify this exclusion.

The most significant contribution of feminist scholarship to date, across disciplines, has been to demonstrate that the ostensible neutrality of scholarship is indelibly associated with maleness;[56] it has been shown to be culture-bound in its misogyny, just as it is in its classism and racism. However, a feminist deconstruction of the neutrality myth of law and legal theory has been less conspicuous than feminist critiques in the social sciences. This is partly attributable to the fact that the cartography of law is rigorously controlled by the state, for law is the primary custodian of the mores of liberalism. It is also partly attributable to the intellectual gulf between jurisprudence and other kinds of social theory.[57] This is the case even though legal ideology operates through legal positivism as though it were neutral.[58]

The favouring of a narrow, doctrinal, atheoretical approach to legal education, which eschews critical consideration of the wider contextual and ideological role of law, ensures the perpetuation of the myth of the neutrality of liberal legalism. The favoured judicial and pedagogical method also ensures the reproduction of hierarchically and professionally

---

55   Maureen Cain, 'Realism, feminism, methodology and the law' (Conference paper, European Conference in Critical Legal Studies, London, 1986). Catharine MacKinnon takes this subject/object dichotomy further and equates it with the heterosexist male/female paradigm of sexuality. Catharine MacKinnon, 'Feminism, Marxism, Method, and the State: An Agenda for Theory' in Elizabeth Abel & Emily K. Abel (eds), *Women, Gender and Scholarship* (University of Chicago Press, 1983) 250–54.
56   See, for example, Marilyn Strathern, 'Dislodging a World View: Challenge and Counter-Challenge in the Relationship between Feminism and Anthropology' (1985) 1(1) *Australian Feminist Studies* 1, doi.org/10.1080/08164649.1985.10382902.
57   Judith Shklar, *Legalism* (Harvard University Press, 1964) vii.
58   ibid., 34.

oriented values with each class of law students.[59] The curriculum in Australian law schools is largely traditional, with a focus on nineteenth-century private law doctrines of contract, torts and property; public law, social policy and legal theory are generally perceived to be marginal to the primary project of producing conventional legal practitioners. Problems are portrayed as individualistic, with solutions attained by means of an adversarial process in a court setting with its semblance of formal equality between the parties. Thus, the amorality of positivism requires that the battered and the batterer be treated the same; such is the power of equality before the law. Both the pedagogical method and the mode of legal discourse also reflect the competitive, abstract and acontextual values favoured by liberal legalism.

Such a pedagogy can only serve to reinforce law's masculinist bias. This is clearly evinced by the concept of the 'reasonable man'—the ideal and objective personification of law—from whose perspective the failings of ordinary people are judged and who represents the embodiment of wisdom, rationality and good sense. Indeed, the 'reasonable woman' is no more than a figment of the feminist imagination; she is unknown and incomprehensible to the law. The reasonable man most graphically encapsulates the paradigmatic realisation of Simone de Beauvoir's conception of woman as the eternal Other.[60] Consequently, the feminist lawyer herself must always be an aberration, a fringe-dweller, surviving at the edge of the dominant discourse: 'For a woman to be in a man's world is to be objectified, silenced and pacified—to be rendered an object.'[61]

While there has been an increase in the number of women academics in universities, they are likely to be casualised and struggling for survival with heavy teaching loads.[62] Furthermore, the constraints that militate against radical activity are greater for feminist legal scholars, as Cole percipiently notes in discussing the domination of the US critical legal studies movement by white, male professors in elite law schools: 'White

59   Duncan Kennedy, 'Legal Education as Training for Hierarchy' in David Kairys (ed.), *The Politics of Law: A Progressive Critique* (Pantheon Books, 1982).
60   Simone de Beauvoir, *The Second Sex*, translated by Howard M. Parshley (Penguin, 1972).
61   David Cole, 'Getting There: Reflections on Trashing from Feminist Jurisprudence and Critical Theory' (1985) 8 *Harvard Women's Law Journal* 59.
62   Bettina Cass, Madge Dawson, Diana Temple, Sue Wills & Anne Winkler, *Why So Few? Women Academics in Australian Universities* (University of Sydney Press, 1983).

males, especially those with tenure, can afford to appear crazy; members of racial minorities and women, however, have to "prove" themselves in more conventional ways because they are presumed unconventional.'[63]

Homosocial reproduction within the academy further secures the perpetuation of values associated with one sex and is reflected in the institutional preference for men with similar values in appointments, promotions and decision-making positions: 'Homosociability suggests that senior men are more comfortable imparting relevant organisational knowledge and experience to junior men.'[64] The process of homosociability clearly demonstrates how institutional power remains the prerogative of benchmark men. As the arbiters of merit, they can regulate the admission of women to the inner sanctum of the academy. The familiar phenomenon of the successful female 'token' is a conscious act designed to delude us into believing the process is neutral.

Perhaps most devastating for the feminist scholar are the seeds of invidiousness that continue to attach to feminist scholarship so that it is valued even less highly than that of earlier male radicals, as observed by McCormack in discussing women and the scientific community:

> [W]omen bear the burden of a pejorative stereotype which pictures them as lacking qualities of mind which make for outstanding scientific achievement. It is this stereotype and the sexual division of labour within the scientific community which it sanctions that has led to the often-heard condescending reflection: women make good scientists but never great ones.[65]

This male-defined perception of 'inferiority' provides a convenient rationalisation for the rejection and disparagement of innovative feminist scholarship, which may be effectively denied the legitimation that flows from publication in a prestigious journal. Dale Spender has demonstrated how the process of reviewing manuscripts tends to operate in such a way that material that adopts a different political stance from that of the reviewer is likely to be rejected.[66] Since editors and reviewers in the legal academic

---

63   Cole (n. 61) 73.
64   Clare Burton, 'Equal Employment Opportunity Programmes: Issues and Implementation' in Norma Grieve & Alisa Burns (eds), *Australian Women: New Feminist Perspectives* (Oxford University Press, 1986) 301.
65   Thelma McCormack, 'Good Theory or Just Theory? Toward a Feminist Philosophy of Social Science' (1981) 4(1) *Women's Studies International Quarterly* 1, 2, doi.org/10.1016/s0148-0685(81) 96298-9.
66   Dale Spender, 'The Gatekeepers: A Feminist Critique of Academic Publishing' in Helen Roberts (ed.), *Doing Feminist Research* (Routledge & Kegan Paul, 1981).

world are likely to be men unsympathetic to feminism, their significant gatekeeper function in inhibiting the dissemination of radical ideas, or at least confining them to feminist or fringe publications, is apparent.

Feminist scholarship is also treated with suspicion within the academy because the feminist scholar is likely to have invested part of herself in work that may contain a critique of existing society or a vision of the way things might be. On the other hand, the male legal academic who writes about abstract doctrinal questions, such as promissory estoppel or land tenure in feudal England, will be praised for his 'objectivity'. Nevertheless, as de Beauvoir has observed, such men do in fact describe the world from their own point of view, which they confuse with absolute truth.[67] Male academics may find feminist scholarship personally threatening because it highlights the flaws in their own work. It makes them confront the idea that maleness may not be a universal and that legal positivism may not be neutral. Male scholars, for the most part, therefore have good reason to delegitimate feminist scholarship.

Male legal academics have unquestioningly accepted the inevitability of the public/private split that informs legal discourse. For mainstream legal academics, women are unlikely to be worthy of consideration since they do not fit into male paradigms of hierarchy, theory or dogma. Until recently, women were invisible in legal scholarship, making only tentative appearances in stereotypical areas, such as family law or as the victims of crime. Following March,[68] Thiele has described this process as 'pseudo-inclusion', which simultaneously serves to marginalise women and to remind the reader that the norm is male: 'Women become defined as a "special case", as anomalies, exceptions to the rule which can be noted and then forgotten about.'[69] This approach was also commonly adopted by Marxist and Left-oriented scholars who criticised feminism as a bourgeois movement that worked in the interests of the ruling class. As evidence, they point to the feminist movement's composition of largely middle-class, educated women.[70]

---

67   de Beauvoir (n. 60) 175. Cf. Gross: 'Truth, as a correspondence or veridical reflection of reality is a perspectiveless knowledge, a knowledge without a point of view—or what amounts to the same thing, a truth claiming a universal perspective'; in Elizabeth Gross, 'What is Feminist Theory' in Carole Pateman & Elizabeth Gross (eds), *Feminist Challenges: Social and Political Theory* (Allen & Unwin, 1986) 199.

68   Artemis March, 'Female Invisibility in Androcentric Sociological Theory' (1982) 11(2) *Insurgent Sociologist* 99.

69   Beverly Thiele, 'Vanishing Acts in Social and Political Thought: Tricks of the Trade' in Pateman & Gross (n. 67) 33.

70   MacKinnon (n. 55) 229–30.

Although the relationship between gender divisions and the contradictions of capitalism continues to be contentious among feminists,[71] Marxist and socialist feminists believe the nature of contemporary capitalism cannot be understood unless the oppression of women is placed at the centre of any analysis.[72] For some feminist scholars, the dilemma is whether to adopt theories such as Marxism, which display the typical intellectual fallacy of presenting maleness as a universal, or whether such theories should be jettisoned *ad limine* because of the perception that the 'woman question' is auxiliary to the central question of a Marxian theory of society.[73] The utilisation of such theories suggests that innovative feminist scholarship needs to be legitimated by securing the imprimatur of famous men, for it is apparent that the structural differences in women's lives have not yet received the epistemological attention they warrant.[74]

The role of the state constitutes a further problem. While feminists have an ambivalent attitude towards the state as an expression of male ideology and power, there is a recognition that women are forced to resort to it for relief from male violence, but some members of the male Left would eschew state help altogether, as epigrammatically observed by Catharine MacKinnon: 'Liberal strategies entrust women to the state. Left theory abandons us to rapists and batterers.'[75] Fraser, for example, opposed South Australian legislation that abolished the common law immunity for husbands who raped their wives in favour of women engaging in a collective enterprise with other popular groups to resist 'the fragmentation and alienation of capitalist social relations'.[76] The implication of Fraser's stance is deeply misogynistic, for it purports to uphold the right of men to continue to rape women—a form of domination regarded as incidental to the primary socialist project. Plaza has made a similar point regarding Foucault's blindness as to the way male power injures women, despite his innovative contributions to social theory: 'Here we see how

---

71   Suzanne Franzway, 'With Problems of Their Own: Femocrats and the Welfare State' (1986) 1(3) *Australian Feminist Studies* 45.

72   Margaret Benston, 'The Political Economy of Women's Liberation' (1969) 21(4) *Monthly Review* 13; Roisin McDonough & Rachel Harrison, 'Patriarchy and Relations of Production' in Annette Kuhn & AnnMarie Wolpe (eds), *Feminism and Materialism: Women and Modes of Production* (Routledge & Kegan Paul, 1978) 12.

73   Young (n. 15).

74   Hartsock (n. 9).

75   Catharine A. MacKinnon, 'Feminism, Marxism, Method, and the State: Toward Feminist Jurisprudence' (1983) 8 *Signs: Journal of Women, Culture, and Society* 635, 643, doi.org/10.1515/9780691186429-022.

76   Andrew Fraser, 'Feminism and Marital Rape' (1977) 46 *Arena* 14.

the intelligentsia of the Left, by defending the interests of the class of men, produces a counter ideology, which is in fact a "new look" ideology against women.'[77]

The ambivalence of feminists towards the state has influenced the development of a feminist theory of the state.[78] As Branson and Miller have pointed out in their trenchant critique of Fraser, the peculiar privatised and molecular nature of domestic labour within capitalist society has militated against any sort of unified activity for most women, and the only common ground has necessarily been in public institutions.[79] The task of producing a critical theory has therefore been effectively scuttled by the marshmallow nature of liberalism with its valiant attempts to be all things to all people. Indeed, the seductive appeal of recent liberal state reforms has succeeded in both modifying and mollifying the critical impulse.

Although an acceptable 'grand theory' has not yet eventuated, the feminist movement is believed to be producing a scholarship that is at the cutting edge of positive social change: 'The redressers of sexual oppression are currently producing a critical and analytic literature of an intellectual liveliness and practical relevance unmatched in any other field of social science.'[80] Despite such an optimistic acknowledgement from a male social scientist, feminism has generally had little impact on legal education or legal discourse to date, such as a general requirement that all law courses include a feminist component.[81]

Conclusion: The elusiveness of feminist jurisprudence

The androcentric standard constitutes a concealed trap for women. A feminist approach would have to eschew positivism—the essence of traditional jurisprudence—because it does not operate in a gender-neutral way any more than does gender-specific language, despite

---

77   Monique Plaza, 'Ideology against Women' (1984) 4 *Feminist Issues* 73.

78   MacKinnon (n. 75, 635) notes that feminism has a theory of power instead.

79   Jan Branson & Don Miller, 'Feminism and Class Struggle' (1977) 47–48 *Arena* 80, 90–91.

80   Raewyn Connell, 'Theorizing Gender' in Norma Grieve & Alisa Burns (eds), *Australian Women: New Feminist Perspectives* (Oxford University Press, 1986) 83.

81   Tove Stang Dahl, 'Taking Women as a Starting Point: Building Women's Law' (1986) 14 *International Journal of the Sociology of Law* 239.

endless disclaimers to the contrary.[82] But how far can a radical feminist perspective of law be developed given the constraints delineated in this chapter? Indeed, in one sense, 'radicalism and the law' is a contradiction in terms, no less than is 'women and the law'. Hence, is our vision of law so constrained that a feminist jurisprudence is no more than a phantasmagorical glimmer on the horizon when we desire it to be the reality to inform the way forward?

So entrenched is the notion of maleness as universal throughout all branches of knowledge that special efforts by feminists would seem to be necessary to overcome its distorting effects. So pervasive are the effects of the public/private split, the notion of the preeminence of the public sphere and the myth of neutrality cloaking legal reasoning and jurisprudence, the reform of a substantive area of law alone is going to have little impact. Furthermore, increasing the number of women in law will also make little difference if all students continue to be acculturated into the dominant tradition of legal positivism in our law schools and in practice. Thus, as observed by a feminist social scientist: '[I]t is not the malevolence of men but the malevolence of method which constitutes the true obstacles of their efforts.'[83] Indeed, method has become the central question for feminist scholars and it is one that must be addressed to effect any semblance of equality.[84] As Cole puts it, the question of method has always preoccupied the Left in its desire to achieve a praxis:

> Method is the bridge between theory and practice, between the theorist and the everyday world, and between substantive ends and procedural means. A successful critical social method collapses the opposition of theory and practice, substance and procedure, and reform and revolution.[85]

Cole believes, building on Habermas, that feminism has developed a method that is socially transformative in that its critique is informed by self-reflection and the search for intersubjectivity. This self-reflective method 'validates norms through consensus and discussion rather than by engaging in a search for objective truths'.[86]

---

82   Janice Moulton, 'The Myth of the Neutral Man' in Mary Vetterling-Braggin, Frederick Elliston & Jane English (eds), *Feminism and Philosophy* (Littlefield, Adams, 1977).
83   McCormack (n. 65) 10.
84   Phyllis L. Crocker, 'The Meaning of Equality for Battered Women who Kill Men in Self-Defense' (1985) 8 *Harvard Women's Law Journal* 121, 153.
85   Cole (n. 61) 59.
86   ibid., 67.

A feminist perspective corrodes the very essence of liberal legalism with its assumptions of universalism, formal equality and neutrality. Not only does it highlight the falsity of these assumptions, but also a feminist analysis brings out the inner core of meaning of an act for women; it rejects the high level of abstraction. Indeed, the experiential dimension may be all-important.[87] A feminist approach to law must also challenge the hegemonic, sex-based structures of capitalist formation. The fragility of recent feminist gains must alert the proponents to be ever watchful, for it is a function of legalism to constrain and hedge in radical political change to protect and maintain the status quo.

The iconoclasm of feminist critiques of the substance and form of law is a necessary step towards comprehending the role of the law in effecting the perversion of the feminine in its portrayal as a homogeneous and inferior standard. Feminist scholarship, then, aims to be 'perspective transforming'.[88] However, is this new feminist perspective, acquired because of the unmasking of the mystique of law, sufficient to constitute a feminist jurisprudence? Jurisprudence is defined as 'the science or philosophy of law' and, as Judith Shklar has pointed out, analytical jurisprudence is 'solely a science of definitions': 'The major part of any work entitled "jurisprudence" consists of demonstrations of the "real meaning of such terms as right, duty, tort, crime, and contract".'[89] The focus of jurisprudence, as it is presently understood, tends to be directed towards the exposition of the law as it is within narrow, positivistic parameters. There is little understanding of the study of law as an interdisciplinary, contextual and critical exercise, for it is accepted that the law is a complete entity that can produce 'right' answers.

The language of liberal jurisprudence reflects a society of free and equal individuals who act as independent, self-defining agents.[90] As has been pointed out, the seeds of invidiousness that attach to women as inhabitants of the private sphere have been used to deny them access to this society of equals. Law has underpinned and legitimised this exclusion and liberal jurisprudence ignores the way law is isolated from the social context in which it operates.[91] This ideology serves a functional purpose and

---

87   Kathleen Lahey, '… Until women themselves have told all they have to tell' (Conference Paper, European Conference on Critical Legal Studies, April 1986).
88   Strathern (n. 56).
89   Shklar (n. 57) 32.
90   Husson (n. 12).
91   Shklar (n. 57) 2.

jurisprudence is likely to be just as unresponsive to feminism as it has been to challenge by other social and intellectual movements such as Marxism, legal realism and critical legal studies—all of which have been assiduous in seeking to deconstruct the doctrines of liberal legalism. So elusive is the theoretical task of inquiry, let alone the task of transformation, that Stewart depicts the efforts of (non-feminist) sociologists of law as producing no more than a looking-glass effect: 'But through the looking-glass the sociologist can glimpse the carcasses of the attempts that since the Renaissance have repeatedly been made, then one after another abandoned, to enrich jurisprudence itself with a specific study of society.'[92]

While a feminist jurisprudential telos may be elusive, there is a danger that, if feminists are too assiduous in compressing feminist scholarship into an analytical jurisprudential framework in the short term, it may lose its critical edge. Scales' article 'Towards a Feminist Jurisprudence' would seem to be an example of this somewhat overly cautious approach.[93] Scales does not set out to postulate a theory of law, as she herself acknowledges, but to demonstrate 'the necessity of making a feminist evaluation of our jurisprudence and of taking a jurisprudential view of feminism'. While she recognises the fallacy inherent in the liberal vision—that is, the maleness of the norm of equality—her analysis focuses on the sex-unique problems arising from pregnancy and breastfeeding, as revealed in several US Supreme Court cases. Dismissing both the liberal and the assimilationist views that seek to minimise sexual difference, Scales proposes her own 'incorporationist' approach, which would recognise women's uniqueness in respect of female sex specificity.

However, a focus on reproductive differences alone is too limited to constitute a 'feminist jurisprudence' because it does no more than reaffirm women's association with nature and nurture, although it is recognised that it could have the potential to expose the law to the politics of reproduction—a fundamental area of human endeavour formerly invisible. The conflation of women and reproduction is also restrictive because it suggests a non-existent homogeneity among women. Indeed, the Scales model does not appear to be visibly different from conventional

---

92   Iain Stewart, 'Sociology in Jurisprudence: The Problem of "Law" as Object of Knowledge' in Bob Fryer, Alan Hunt, Doreen McBarnet & Bert Moorhouse (eds), *Law, State and Society* (Croom Helm, 1981).
93   Ann C. Scales, 'Towards a Feminist Jurisprudence' (1981) 56(3) *Indiana Law Journal* 375.

liberal jurisprudence that is able to accommodate sex-based differential treatment in cases where to do otherwise might be irrational—an asseveration that is ultimately damaging to the rule of law.[94]

A transformative vision requires not just that women be 'let in' to mainstream society with a perspective on 'women's issues',[95] but also that the entire gamut of jurisprudence be reappraised to take cognisance of the feminine. The focus on reproductive differences alone has the effect of perennially confining women to the margins and otherwise accepting the continued irrelevance of women to public-sphere concerns. It would allow the meretricious claim made by androcentrism that it represents the universal standard to remain unchallenged.

Feminist legal scholarship, in common with the feminist project generally, has the twin aims of challenging the existing norms and of devising a new agenda for theory: 'In other words, feminist theory is involved in both an anti-sexist project, which involves challenging and deconstructing phallocentric discourses; and in a positive project of constructing and developing alternative models, methods, procedures, discourses, etc.'[96] Given the fact, however, that women have been entirely excluded from a legal tradition that spans several millennia, it is ingenuous to imagine that a fully fledged feminist jurisprudence is likely to spring forth from the feminist movement instantaneously. Such naivety also fails to acknowledge that the impenetrability of the carapace of autonomy that envelops the law and immunises it against challenge is such that a transformed gynocentric jurisprudence must necessarily remain elusive— at least for the time being.

---

94   Scales' approach is also a reminder that there is unlikely to be one vision of feminist jurisprudence because of the multifarious strands of feminism. Jaggar (n. 8) identifies three main categories of feminism: liberal feminism, classical Marxist feminism and radical feminism. However, as Stanley and Wise point out, such typologies inevitably caricature. Liz Stanley & Sue Wise, *Breaking Out: Feminist Consciousness and Feminist Research* (Routledge & Kegan Paul, 1983) 38.

95   Angela R. Miles, 'Feminism, Equality, and Liberation' (1985) 1(1) *Canadian Journal of Women and the Law* 42.

96   Gross (n. 67) 195.

3

The Contradictions of Law Reform

Legality within the masculinist state

Within some sections of the feminist community, it is fashionable to denigrate attempts at law reform as misguided considering the current scepticism towards liberal legalism.[1] The fact that law is a central legitimating mechanism of the contemporary capitalist state, carrying with it baggage that is necessarily antipathetic to feminist ideals, has rendered suspect advocacy for a reformist path. The problem is nicely encapsulated in the well-known words of Audre Lorde: 'For the master's tools will never dismantle the master's house. They may allow us temporarily to beat him at his own game, but they will never enable us to bring about genuine change.'[2]

Despite the purist stance espoused by those eschewing the path of law reform, there is necessarily a reformist, as well as a transformative, dimension within the essence of feminism. That is, there is a desire to make society as we know it more tolerable for women, as well as a desire to transform that society. I wish to turn to the former: the reformist project.

---

1   Archana Parashar, 'The Anti-Discrimination Laws and the Illusory Promise of Sex Equality' (1994) 13(1) *University of Tasmania Law Review* 83, 84.
2   Audre Lord, 'The Master's Tools Will Never Dismantle the House', in Audre Lord, *Sister Outsider: Essays and Speeches* (The Crossing Press, 1984) 112.

A consciousness of the fact that many feminist political struggles have emanated from a liberal position means the assault on liberalism by critical feminism is likely to have been somewhat more ambivalent than that waged by critical male scholars.[3] The importance of law is summed up by Nicola Lacey:

> All feminist scholars with an interest in law start out from the assumption that law has an important, albeit not decisive, influence in constructing and maintaining social relations. Thus most feminist legal scholars believe, though to very different degrees, that law plays some part in consolidating, expressing, underpinning and supporting existing power relations in societies, including those between women and men.[4]

Considering the privileged status of law within our society, it cannot be neglected, or social relations will continue to be reproduced within legal discourse as they always have been—that is, from a mainstream masculinist point of view. I would nevertheless like to explore the reasons the lawful path is such an equivocal one for feminists.

Law is not univocal, for it operates from several different formal sites, in addition to exercising a pervasive normative presence. In Australia, law reform invariably means legislative reform.[5] A marked scepticism towards the courts as the locus of social change was long evinced by Australian feminist reformers, in contrast with their US sisters. This was partly because of the conservativism of the judiciary, but the absence of a bill of rights containing an equality guarantee has denied feminist reformers a mechanism utilised extensively by US feminists. The colonial heritage— long manifest in the excessive deference accorded decisions of English superior courts—together with a positivistic, acontextual and conservative style of adjudication, has deterred feminist reformers from turning to the courts for the running of test cases. Most Australian judges have been so conservative until relatively recently that they have been too timid to alter even the judicially created common law, despite startling instances of overt sex-based discrimination offensive to liberalism's commitment to formal equality before the law. Instead, a symbiotic relationship has developed between feminist law reformers and the legislature, albeit that

---

3   Deborah L. Rhode, 'Feminist Critical Theories' (1990) 42(3) *Stanford Law Review* 617, 627, doi.org/10.2307/1228887.
4   Nikola Lacey, 'Feminist Legal Theory' (1989) 9 *Oxford Journal of Legal* Studies 383, 385.
5   Jude Wallace & John Fiocco, 'Recent Criticisms of Formalism in Legal Theory and Legal Education' (1980–81) 7 *Adelaide Law Review* 309.

the swing to the right of the late 1980s led to a decline in interest in gender issues, aided by the rhetoric of 'post-feminism'. Nevertheless, 'women's issues' featured prominently on the political agenda of social liberalism for more than a decade and the masculinist corpus of statutory law impacting women and others was markedly altered by the inclusion of different voices, albeit sometimes only faintly discernible.

At one level of analysis, the state's attempts at beneficence may be seen as insidious attempts at cooption. Not only are subversive elements rendered quiescent by feminist-oriented reforms but also the bonds of dependency between women as a political constituency and the state are strengthened. Feminist law reform can therefore be understood as a means of expanding state power through political patronage. As the etymology of the word 'patronage' suggests, this realisation of state power is masculinised. The tripartite components of government, the legislature, the judiciary and the executive, are invariably dominated by benchmark men—that is, those who are Anglo-Celtic, heterosexual, able-bodied and middle class— as are the professions, business and the academy. In addition, the more covert manifestations of masculinist power in both the public and the private spheres, physical as well as metaphysical, should not be gainsaid. The power benchmark men exercise and the ideology of male superiority infuse and colour the concept of the state.

One of the most pervasive myths of liberal democracy, however, is that the state is neutral and autonomous, thereby denying its patriarchal character. The phrase 'feminist engagement with the state' underscores the marginal status of women, for to speak of 'masculinist engagement with the state' would be tautologous. Thus, although women, including racialised women, are incorporated into the state through reformist and welfare measures, they are not regarded as citizens in the same way as benchmark men. Women remain, as Carole Pateman has observed, in social exile simultaneously from both the state and civil society.[6] Since women are not accepted as members of the public sphere's 'society of equals', they must always approach the state in its lawmaking sense as supplicants. In addition, feminist reformers usually do not seek law reform directly on their own behalf, but on behalf of a particular constituency of women, such as those who have been subjected to domestic violence or sexual assault. The mediation of feminist reformers between female 'clients' and the state

---

6   Carole Pateman, 'The Patriarchal Welfare State' in Amy Gutmann (ed.), *Democracy and the Welfare State* (Princeton University Press, 1988) 236.

forms a triangular relationship that constitutes a further distinguishing feature regarding women's intersection with the state, underscoring the inadequacy of the normative binary model of citizen and state.

The partisanship of the liberal state towards masculinist norms is underpinned by the public/private dualism, which, in turn, continues to be a metaphor for male and female within the Western intellectual tradition. Men's association with governance of the state and the formal positions of power within civil society is claimed to signify their superior reason and association with culture.[7] Legality has therefore become a cherished example of Anglocentric masculinist culture—epitomised by abstract reasoning and rationality—while the private sphere continues to carry elements of the feminised association with nature, nurture and the nonrational. Assumptions pertaining to the nonrational arise from closeness to nature and have also been invoked to deny Indigenous people access to the public sphere, as epitomised by excessive paternalism and denial of citizenship until relatively recently. The meanings of maleness and femaleness are in fact multiplicitous when considered in conjunction with the characteristics of race, class, age, sexuality and disability—factors with which the one-dimensionality of liberal legalism is loath to grapple.

However, the binary oppositions of liberal legalism cannot be ignored, as a fundamental threshold dilemma for feminist law reform is posed by the asymmetry of the public/private dichotomy. The public world of men has been regarded as qualitatively superior to that of the private world of women throughout the Western intellectual tradition; culture always trumps nature. As the law is a notable artefact of male culture, women therefore must enter the masculinist realm, replete with its ambiguities, to access legal mechanisms. That is, they must lobby for and negotiate with the state to effect statutory law reform, embark on legal relations and institute litigation within civil society or they must deal with state agencies straddling the state/civil society divide. Regardless of which site is selected, it is apparent that interaction with law is not easily effected from within the private sphere qua family, despite the grossness and immediacy of the harms women suffer in the home. The corporeal and sexual strands of the private within liberal legalism add an additional layer of meaning for women.

7   Stanley I. Benn & Gerald F. Gaus, 'The Liberal Conception of the Public and the Private' in Stanley I. Benn & Gerald F. Gaus (eds), *Public and Private in Social Life* (Croom Helm, 1983) 40; Margaret Thornton (ed.), *Public and Private: Feminist Legal Debates* (Oxford University Press, 1995); Jeff Weintraub & Krishan Kumar (eds), *Public and Private in Thought and Practice: Perspectives on a Grand Dichotomy* (University of Chicago Press, 1997).

'The personal is political' is the familiar catchcry associated with Second-Wave Feminism. It rejects the centrality of the public/private dichotomy of liberalism and seeks to expose the reality of the harms suffered within the private sphere qua family. That is, far from the family being 'a haven in a heartless world', it is all too often a site of oppression, exploitation and violence for women from which egress is difficult. Thus, even those disparaged as 'liberal feminists' challenge the integrity of the public/private dichotomy, the pièce de résistance of liberal theory, when they focus on the inequitable position of women within the family. It is nevertheless undeniable that those issues involving corporeality, affectivity and desire highlight women's presumed association with nature and nurture that is assigned to one side of the dichotomised spheres approach—that is, the private sphere, which is historically regarded as a sphere of non-law.

In this chapter, I propose to focus briefly on domestic violence, rape and sexual harassment, although I could include abortion, pornography, in vitro fertilisation (IVF), surrogacy and a whole range of harms emanating from contemporary medical practice, all of which bring the body to the fore. I am adopting what appears to be an essentialist position in focusing on the paradigmatic sex/violence harms that are overwhelmingly perpetrated by men against women because they are women, regardless of race, ethnicity, sexuality or class, although these factors may affect the nature and extent of the harm. I nevertheless acknowledge the criticism of black women such as bell hooks that white, middle-class feminists tend to extrapolate from their own race/class experience to generalise about all women.[8]

Harms to women arising from sex and violence have been well-traversed by feminist scholars, but these injuries continue to remain elusive in respect of substantive reform. Harms suffered by women that do not have a corporeal dimension may be cognisable to law if they fit into existing paradigms. Equal employment opportunity (EEO), for example, has constituted a major site of feminist struggle, although legislation is not concerned with 'the complex causes of women's subordination, which transcend the public/private divide'.[9] Furthermore, women must show

---

8   bell hooks, *Ain't I a Woman: Black Women and Feminism* (Pluto Press, 1981). Available data reveal a disproportionality higher rate for Indigenous women as victims of crime, including domestic violence and sexual assault. See, for example, Australian Bureau of Statistics, *Recorded Crime: Victims, Australia, 2017* (ABS, 2018).
9   Susan Atkins, 'Equal Treatment for Men and Women: The Case for Legislative Reform' (1988) *Public Law* 320.

that they are like men to succeed. That is, they must demonstrate that they are just as rational as men. In practice, the private sphere exercises a centripetal pull on women's paid work participation, as women must cope with the double burden of paid and unpaid work. In addition, assumptions are made concerning women's preeminent role as sexual beings and as bearers and nurturers of children—that is, assumptions are made about women's essential irrationality that distort their status as paid workers and limit the usefulness of reforms that continue to accept the male model as the universal. Sexuality and affectivity continue to be largely discounted in respect of masculinity so far as citizenship is concerned.

To maintain its legitimacy, the state must *appear* to be fair in the invidious task of mediating dichotomous interests.[10] Thus, the state must simultaneously assuage both the male pressure to retain the status quo and the feminist pressure for reform. Liberalism's obsession with formal equality and formal justice operates to occlude the masculinist bias in the substantive operation of a law. Thus, feminist-inspired legislation may be undermined by the absence of effective sanctions so that its effect is little more than symbolic. Alternatively, the legislature might abdicate responsibility in politically sensitive areas by conferring a discretion on an administrative or judicial decision-maker. Despite the political attempts to contract the substance of any reform, there is nevertheless a small space in which to manoeuvre. Legal activism is an important public site of political activity. Battered women are compelled to look to the state for protection because they have no alternative. While I do not want to present women as universally powerless, the social reality is that the physical integrity and self-realisation of many women are frequently contingent on an individual man, the institutional power of men or the state itself.

Feminist reforms that have been generated over the past 100 years have caused what Sylvia Walby terms a transition from private to public patriarchy. The freedom women have acquired to leave unsatisfactory relationships has created new forms of oppression and control of women in female-headed households:

> The absence of a husband does not mean that women are freed from the work, responsibilities, and cost of child care. They still produce the next generation. While they lose their own individual patriarch, they do not lose their subordination to other patriarchal structures and practices. Indeed, they become even more exposed

10   E.P. Thompson, *Whigs and Hunters: The Origin of the Black Acts* (Allen Lane, 1975) 184.

to certain of the diffused public sets of patriarchal practices. Their income level and standard of living are no longer determined primarily by that of their husband, but instead either by the patriarchal state, if they are dependent upon welfare benefits, or [by] the patriarchally structured labour market.[11]

Many women therefore need the power and authority of the state, even though the relationship is a parlous one that is complicated by the fickleness of party politics. Women are better off having left violent relationships and what they receive from the state comes by way of entitlement rather than by way of the benevolence of an individual man, as Carole Pateman points out:

> In the welfare state, each woman receives what is hers by right, and she can, potentially, combine with other citizens to enforce her rightful claim. The state has enormous powers of intimidation, but political action takes place collectively in the public terrain and not behind the closed door of the home, where each woman has to rely on her own strength and resources.[12]

This empowering dimension of collective political action should nevertheless not be gainsaid, for it challenges private dominance that formerly went unchecked.

The loving web of interconnectedness that characterises many women's lives has led Carol Gilligan to posit the theory that women speak in a different moral voice to men, based on an ethic of care rather than a hierarchy of rights.[13] Although Gilligan uses the metaphor of the web to convey a sense of this interconnectedness in women's lives in a positive way, it becomes for many women a spider's trap from which there seems to be no escape. Interconnectedness constitutes a further impediment for law reform as the abstract legal subject of liberal theory is autonomous and unencumbered. The paradigmatic legal subject is male, although men in fact are not without ties to family and community. Legal subjects are assumed to be free to engage in legal relations—that is, within the realm of civil society, they are assumed to be free from interference by the state as well as from the burdens of affective family relations. Freedom

---

11   Sylvia Walby, 'From Private to Public Patriarchy: The Periodisation of British History' (1990) 13 *Women's Studies International Forum* 91, 102.

12   Pateman (n. 6) 256.

13   Carol Gilligan, *In a Different Voice: Psychological Theory and Women's Development* (Harvard University Press, 1982).

to enter a contract on whatever terms the parties' desire typifies the concept. The individualised approach is similarly apparent in tort law, where, provided an unbroken causal thread connects the plaintiff and the tortfeasor, the social context of an injury is irrelevant. In criminal law, there is a consistent endeavour to divorce the wrong from its social setting. The focus on what appears to be an aberrant or deviant individual is effectively secured by the metaphysical concept of *mens rea*, which entails an unbroken connection between the mind of the perpetrator and the *actus reus*, the criminal wrong.

The individualisation that is central to both civil and criminal law effectively deflects attention from the class-wide nature of gendered harms. Thus, each instance of a wrong—for example, an act of rape—is treated as the aberrant act of an individual. Generally speaking, there has been significant resistance to accepting gender-based harms, such as rape, as social phenomena.[14] Domestic violence is more widely understood as a social phenomenon although, again, the Anglo-Australian legal culture's fidelity to the individualised approach has been resistant to the 'battered woman syndrome', which is accepted within some US jurisdictions.[15] Even then, the focus has tended to be on the class of victims, not the class of perpetrators, which 'contributes to the myth that the victim is in some way responsible for the violence'.[16] The individualised model of harm that is central to the criminal law therefore represents a political impediment in attaining public acceptance of the gender-based extent of the harm and in devising prophylactic measures. It also constitutes a juridical impediment to developing class-wide remedies.

Domestic violence

Domestic violence has featured prominently on the feminist law reform agenda as sex-neutral assault laws were formerly not generally enforced against male perpetrators in the home.[17] The criminal law model has

---

14   For example, Susan Brownmiller, *Against Our Will: Men, Women and Rape* (Penguin, 1976); Adrian Howe, 'Social Injury Revisited: Towards a Feminist Theory of Social Justice' (1987) 15 *International Journal of the Sociology of Law* 423.

15   Lenore E. Walker, *The Battered Woman Syndrome* (Springer Publishing, 4th edn, 2016).

16   Rosemary A. Knight & Suzanne E. Hatty, 'Theoretical and Methodological Perspectives on Domestic Violence: Implications for Social Action' (1987) 22(2) *Australian Journal of Social Issues* 452, doi.org/10.1002/j.1839-4655.1987.tb00837.x.

17   Carol O'Donnell (ed.), *Family Violence in Australia* (Longman Cheshire, 1982); Jocelynne Scutt, *Even in the Best of Homes: Violence in the Family* (Penguin, 1983).

been utilised, based on common assault in a public place, although some special features have been included, such as express powers of entry for law enforcement personnel, which specifically challenge the notion that 'a man's home is his castle'. Other developments include the issue of telephone warrants and orders restraining future acts of violence. At the same time, the perpetration of violence has itself become more innovative, because of technology.[18]

As a result of the exposure of the underside of family life, the official stance of the police force has been turned around, but there appears to have been no discernible decline in the incidence of family violence.[19] Increased reportage may suggest an increase in assaults, but this may reflect an increase in public awareness of the phenomenon (the perception paradox). We know the question concerning the degree to which punishment acts as a deterrent within the criminal law generally is a vexed one.[20] The issue is compounded when dealing with so-called crimes of passion. That is, within the family, the sphere of affectivity and irrationality, it was long recognised by the criminal law that men might express anger and jealousy, and even hatred and revenge—emotions that could result in an act of physical violence against their female partners.[21] The law was prepared to partially excuse, if not tolerate, what were regarded as acts of masculine frailty although the batterer was conditioned to act differently within the rational constraints of the public sphere where respect for the physical integrity of others was the norm.

Domestic violence legislation goes to the heart of the public/private dichotomy, which may be why the measures devised have not been as successful as hoped. The police force has historically been imbued with the idea that 'real' crime occurs between strangers in a public place, despite the development of extensive education initiatives,[22] which highlights the ambivalence regarding the criminalisation of domestic violence. Although

---

18   Delanie Woodlock, Mandy McKenzie, Deborah Western & Bridget Harris, 'Technology as a Weapon in Domestic Violence: Responding to Digital Coercive Control' (2020) 73(3) *Australian Social Work* 368, doi.org/10.1080/0312407x.2019.1607510.

19   House of Representatives Standing Committee on Social Policy and Legal Affairs, *Inquiry into Family, Domestic and Sexual Violence* (Parliament of the Commonwealth of Australia, 2021) 17.

20   Barbara Hudson, *Justice through Punishment: A Critique of the 'Justice' Mode of Convictions* (Macmillan, 1987) 28.

21   For a thoroughgoing analysis of the role of masculinity in the criminal law, see Ngaire Naffine, *Criminal Law and the Man Problem* (Hart, 2019).

22   For example, Suzanne E. Hatty, *Male Violence and the Police: An Australian Experience* (School of Social Work, University of New South Wales, 1988) 107.

gender equality is a norm of liberalism, it is a norm that attaches only to the public sphere—the domain of the 'society of equals'. The very idea of a male head of a household precluded the realisation of equality within the family in the Aristotelian polis because a master exercised dominium over subordinates. The voices of the slave, the child or the woman could not be raised against the master—a vestigial reminder of subordination that is difficult to shake off. Even today, the very idea of equality between all members of the family, including children, strikes us as odd.[23]

In addition to the ontological perplexities that pervade equality discourse, the very language of 'domestic violence' is problematic because it borders on the oxymoronic. The home and hearth connotations of 'domestic' colour and soften society's repugnance towards the concept of violence, thereby reifying the popular stereotype epitomised by the stock police dismissal of a violent assault in the home as 'just another domestic'. The choice of language has the effect of undermining the very thing the legislation purports to do—that is, to have assaults in the home taken seriously. However, the vagaries of language are not easily overcome. On the one hand, 'wife abuse' or 'wife beating' may be more accurate but such terms are not empowering for women as they underscore the idea of women as eternal victims. On the other hand, 'spousal abuse' suggests a non-existent neutrality, although the term 'domestic violence' itself disguises which gender is responsible for the preponderance of the abuse. It is also notable that more attention is presently being given to nonphysical forms of violence. The favoured phrase is 'coercive control', which is defined as 'a pattern of controlling and manipulating behaviour designed to intimidate, isolate, and control a person', and is now expressly outlawed in several jurisdictions.[24]

The most problematic question for feminist law reformers is: does passing a law have a prophylactic or a preventative effect? A law constitutes a symbol of society's disapprobation of the impugned conduct and it may prescribe a remedy or course of conduct once the harm has occurred. As with medicine, legal prophylaxis has received considerably less attention than remediation. Of course, the fact that law is seeking to regulate the vagaries of human behaviour renders the predictive enterprise difficult

---

23   Deborah Kearns, 'A Theory of Justice—and Love: Rawls on the Family' in Marian Simms (ed.), *Australian Women and the Political System* (Longman Cheshire, 1984).

24   For example, *Family Violence Act 2004* (Tas.), ss 8, 9; *Serious Crimes Act 2015* (UK), s. 76; *Domestic Abuse (Scotland) Act 2018*.

and there is a lack of consensus as to how domestic violence might best be prevented. However, the problem is vast, with an estimated one in six women and one in 16 men experiencing family violence in Australia[25]— figures that are estimated to be even higher in the United States, where one in four women and one in 10 men are affected, with a noted increase in intimate partner violence victimisations between 2016 and 2018.[26]

Nevertheless, the realisation of a feminist vision of society surely involves more than simply creating a mechanism for dealing with an individual injury in an ad hoc way. Fundamental to any feminist vision of society is the non-subordination of women. Conventional legal remedies do little to bring about this end, although they undoubtedly have a symbolic effect. A civil remedy is designed to place a person in the position that she or he would have been in but for the injury. The most familiar way in which a court effects the make-whole principle is by means of an award of damages. When we endeavour to apply this principle to a domestic violence scenario, however, we immediately realise its inappropriateness in the context of an ongoing familial relationship. Money for the plaintiff is a clumsy tool of remediation at the best of times, despite our inurement to commodification. It is not only a poor salve for bruises and broken bones, but also affords little consolation for the psychological harm emanating from years of battering. The loss of the relationship itself, which is not a necessary concomitant of legal action, may be a relief but this is not necessarily so. We know many women desire a relationship to continue, for it has positive sexual and affective dimensions, particularly if there are dependent children, despite its darker side.

An order restraining the perpetrator from engaging in further violent acts or encountering the victim may be more practical as an immediate remedy. There is nevertheless a preventative dimension inherent in such orders that transcends traditional remedies. It is only if an order is breached that the imposition of criminal sanctions may occur. The focus, however, is limited as it is directed to the individual wrongdoer, not violent men as a class.

25 'Health Impacts of Family, Domestic and Sexual Violence', in Australian Institute of Health and Welfare, *Australia's Health 2020* (AIHW, 23 July 2020), available from: www.aihw.gov.au/reports/ australias-health/health-impacts-family-domestic-and-sexual-violence.

26 National Coalition Against Domestic Violence, *Domestic Violence* (NCADV, 2020), available from: assets.speakcdn.com/assets/2497/domestic_violence-2020080709350855.pdf?1596828650457.

Domestic violence initiatives show how the substance of feminist law reform challenges the status quo and stretches the parameters of legal knowledge. Nevertheless, the reality is that reforms cannot transcend mainstream legal forms to any marked degree. The essential harm of the systematic indignity, humiliation and subordination of women as a class is consequently not addressed. While the state must accommodate pressures for reform, it cannot lose sight of law's essential conserving role within society, which includes retention of the public/private dichotomy. Without this division, the liberal state would be deemed to be under threat. Much more is at stake, therefore, than the inactivity of the police. The inactivity by one state agency provides a convenient scapegoat that deflects attention away from the more fundamental problem.

The shocking and widespread incidence of femicide, particularly when women attempt to leave abusive relationships,[27] have compelled governments to transcend approaches that have been in use for the past 40 years and to develop proactive strategies to protect women and to provide safe refuges for them and their children. Following an inquiry and detailed report produced by a House of Representatives Standing Committee in 2021,[28] the Australian Government committed more than $1 billion for this purpose.[29] However, as the parliamentary report recognised, governments alone are unable to eliminate domestic violence;[30] deep-seated cultural change is also required.

Rape

The state avers that it is not interested in (hetero)sexual activity that takes place in private between consenting adults. It also acknowledges that rape is the quintessential harm against women—evidenced by its long history as a serious crime formerly punishable by death.[31] Feminist struggles to effect rape law reform have absorbed an inordinate degree of time and

---

27 Adrian Howe, '"Endlessly Valuable" Discursive Work: Intimate Partner Femicide, an English Case Study' (2019) 8(4) *Laws*, doi.org/10.3390/laws8040033.

28 House of Representatives Standing Committee on Social Policy and Legal Affairs (n. 19).

29 Benjamin Graham, 'Federal Budget 2021: Domestic Violence Prevention Receives $1.1 Billion Funding Boost', *news.com.au*, 11 May 2021, available from: www.news.com.au/finance/economy/federal-budget/federal-budget-2021-domestic-violence-prevention-receives-11-billion-funding-boost/news-story/7b307fd4f9118bc8124d921e67c3f32b.

30 House of Representatives Standing Committee on Social Policy and Legal Affairs (n. 19) x.

31 William Blackstone, *Commentaries on the Laws of England* (University of Chicago Press, 1979) IV.15, 215.

energy over the past 40 years, yet the essential harm has not been tractable to law reform efforts. The lack of unanimity as to the meaning of consent that lies at the heart of the problem of rape is highlighted by the polarised views of men and women and is affected by lingering misconceptions: when a woman says 'no', she means 'no', which may be reinterpreted by authoritative benchmark men to be when she says 'no', she means 'yes':

> Women who say no do not always mean no. It is not just a question of saying no, it is a question of how she says it, how she shows and makes it clear. If she doesn't want it she only has to keep her legs shut and she would not get it without force and there will be marks of force being used.[32]

Married women were long denied the exercise of free will in sexual relations, which is, paradoxically, the very essence of rape. Under the anachronistic doctrine of coverture, discussed in the Introduction, the wife's legal entity was absorbed into that of her husband on marriage and the consent of the wife to intercourse was legally irrelevant. The vestigial remains of this doctrine lingered until the end of the twentieth century, when the marital rape immunity was abolished.[33] The history of the derogation of autonomy contributed to the construction of women as incapable of willed action in contrast to the paradigmatic man of reason. However, an act of rape has little to do with rationality, which brings us back to the law's discomfort with the body and the liberal presumptive privacy of sexuality. If a man is satisfying his sexual desires, a complainant (or the prosecution on that person's behalf) encounters a considerable onus in rebutting a presumption that the act was consensual. Rape law is saturated with the idea of woman as a preeminently sexual and irrational being.[34] This irrationality is illustrated by the fact that her uncorroborated account of rape has had scant credibility within the courtroom, which partly accounts for the continuing low conviction rate. Despite decades of law reform, 'sexual offences remain under-reported, under-prosecuted and under-convicted'.[35]

---

32 Part of the summation to the jury by an English Crown Court judge in 1982. Cited in Fenton Bresler, *Sex and the Law* (Muller, 1988) 181.

33 *R v L* (1991) 174 CLR (Aust.) 379; *R v R* (1992) 1 AC 599 (UK).

34 Most victims of sexual assault in Australia in 2019 were female (83 per cent). See Australian Bureau of Statistics, *Recorded Crime: Victims, Australia, 2019* (Catalogue No. 4510.0, ABS, 2020).

35 New South Wales Law Reform Commission, *Consent in Relation to Sexual Offences (Report 148)* (NSW Law Reform Commission, 2020) 14.

The legal focus on the consent of the victim operates to set the crime of rape conceptually apart from other crimes. In murder, there must be a link between the *actus reus* (the homicidal act) and the *mens rea* (the guilty mind of the perpetrator). In rape, this relationship is required but it is obscure because the constituent elements are invariably contested. The *mens rea* may involve actual knowledge of lack of consent or a reckless disregard as to whether the victim was consenting or not. Whether a purely subjective test should be utilised in respect of recklessness or whether an objective test is preferable has been hotly debated since the House of Lords decision in *DPP v Morgan* (1975) 2 WLR 923. The subjective test has meant that it has traditionally been the alleged rapist's perception of the act that determines whether a crime has been committed, regardless of the reasonableness of the perpetrator's belief. What is more, the alleged rapist may understand that there is no difference between coercive intercourse and 'normal' intercourse.[36] This highlights the problem of what Susan Estrich calls 'real rape'—that is, rape without violence or threats.[37] The normalisation of a rape culture among young people that does not necessarily involve violence or threats was highlighted in Sydney in 2021 when 6,000 testimonies were gathered from school students who had been allegedly raped by their peers.[38]

Over time, a whole arsenal of tactics has been developed to resist rape charges supported by misogynistic myths. This folklore acquired the status of legal truths until major campaigns were conducted by feminist reformers in the 1970s and 1980s to make the complainant's role in rape trials less traumatic. The process had become so gruelling that complainants were persuaded to drop charges rather than be subjected to an ordeal that was certainly as injurious, or even more so, than the original attack, particularly when the chances of a conviction were low. The instrumental focus of reform has been designed to ensure that the conviction rate increases as well as to render the process less traumatic for victims. A notable reform has included broadening the definition of the crime to make it gender neutral, although the paradigm is heterosexed.

---

36 Andrea Dworkin believed all heterosexual intercourse involved a coercive dimension. See Andrea Dworkin, *Intercourse* (Martin Secker & Warburg, 1987).

37 Susan Estrich, *Real Rape* (Harvard University Press, 1987).

38 Bri Lee, 'Gauge of Consent', *The Saturday Paper* [Melbourne], 29 May–4 June 2021, 12. The official data reveal the highest rates of sexual assault reported are experienced by young people. See Australian Bureau of Statistics (n. 34) Table.

A central difficulty of the crime, regardless of the gender of the perpetrator, is that the substantive harm to the victim has not been tractable to reform. The masculinist bias in rape law has meant the psychological harm of forced penetration has barely been understood as a harm at all. Indeed, the greater emphasis placed on discernible evidence of the use of violent acts and objective criteria has underscored the way that harms cognisable in male terms are privileged. The influence of the *Criminal Sexual Conduct Statute 1974* (Michigan), which sought to downplay the question of consent altogether by focusing on the coercive behaviour of the assailant, has been significant as a model. This is not to say that having forced sex with a knife held at one's throat may not be worse than the same act of violation without the knife, but that the coercion involved in sexual assault without such threats is less likely to be comprehended by men as a harm. Robin West has brilliantly shown that what constitutes pleasure for men may be pain for women.[39]

The phenomenon of 'date rape' in which intercourse invariably involves a coercive dimension illustrates the point. While the Michigan model may not be able to obviate the consent question altogether, it does have the advantage of transferring the onus to the accused to prove it in defence rather than rely on the prosecution to prove that the perpetrator either knew or was reckless as to whether the woman was consenting or not, however perverse the circumstances. The appropriate concept, Carol Smart argues, is really submission, not consent,[40] which conveys no suggestion of free will. Again, it is a question of the bipolar perceptions of men and women as to the nature of sexual assault.

Reformist moves towards gender-neutral sexual assault laws were thought to be a positive step in jettisoning the entrenched medicolegal–popular mythology that stigmatised women as sex-crazed, venal and untrustworthy. However, insufficient cognisance was taken of the fact that the neutrality prescript within law operates to occlude the dominant values, not to guarantee substantive fairness. The inclusion of a definition of consent, such as one requiring 'positive co-operation in act or attitude pursuant to an exercise of free will' (*Penal Code* [1982] 261.6., California), suggests the influence of a more assertive feminist voice. Nevertheless, it still does not overcome the problem arising from the social construction of consent, which is a problem that would also apply to submission—

39   Robin L. West, 'The Difference in Women's Hedonic Lives: A Phenomenological Critique of Feminist Legal Theory' (1987) 3 *Wisconsin Women's Law Journal* 81.
40   Carol Smart, *Feminism and the Power of Law* (Routledge, 1989) 33–34.

that is, from whose perspective consent or submission is likely to be constructed. As Catharine MacKinnon observes, the prevailing definition of sexual intercourse within hegemonic masculinity is sadomasochistic since coercion is often redefined as consensual.[41]

As consent remains central to the crime of rape, a more pronounced focus on 'affirmative consent' has been developed, requiring the accused person to demonstrate that actual consent was given because of that person having said or done something rather than relying on the more familiar defence that there were reasonable grounds to believe the victim had consented. New South Wales reformed its criminal law in 2021 to incorporate this new standard.[42] The definition in the *Criminal Code Act 1924* (Tas.), s. 2A, was amended in 2019 to accord with a similar notion of affirmative consent, although it has been observed that it has not substantially changed the nature of criminal trials.[43]

Given the fact that the sphere of legality has traditionally been a masculinist preserve, feminists cannot expect to move into it and instantaneously effect radical reform. Rape laws, after all, were designed to protect men's honour and property; any benefit accruing to women, other than the purely symbolic disapprobation of rape, has been incidental. But how could it be otherwise when, as Carol Smart argues, law has been traditionally used as a mechanism for disqualifying and disempowering women?[44] While it is now theoretically easier for the victim to testify, the overall effect of the changes may be conducive to making rape laws more punitive, which renders a conviction difficult to secure. Satisfying the punitive ends of the law-and-order lobby, and making the criminal law equally repressive for all, hardly constitutes a feminist victory if it also means that securing a conviction is less likely. We see again the way in which the state must mediate dichotomous interests in effecting law reform so that feminist interests invariably face the possibility of being deployed to serve more powerful interests. Rape law reform involves not just using the master's tools, but also trying to work out how to use an activated crosscut saw without exacerbating harm to rape survivors and without entrenching their victimhood.

---

41   Catherine A. McKinnon, *Toward a Feminist Theory of the State* (Harvard University Press, 1989) 172.

42   *Crimes Act 1900* (NSW), s. 61HA. See also Department of Attorney-General and Justice, *Review of the Consent Provisions for Sexual Assault Offences in the Crimes Act 1900* (NSW Government, 2013), available from: www.justice.nsw.gov.au/justicepolicy/Documents/consent_review.pdf.

43   Greg Barnes, national criminal justice spokesperson for the Australian Lawyers Alliance.

44   Smart (n. 40) 26.

Carol Smart argues that women have colluded with the law in the projection of women as victims through rape narratives.[45] She suggests that feminist accounts of rape 'could become forms of resistance rather than victimization'.[46] I acknowledge the disabling victimhood status accorded rape survivors as quasi-juridical subjects. Resistance may mean not being raped but, for many, rape has resulted in disablement or death—the ultimate victim status. The adage 'innocent until proven guilty' places the perpetrator at the centre of any sexual assault trial, while the survivor is reduced to a bit player as the witness for the prosecution. It is apparent that the masculinist bias within sexual assault law inheres within the form of law itself.

Sexual harassment

Sexual harassment is a clear example of a feminist-inspired law reform over an action recognised as unlawful in Australia only as recently as 1984,[47] although the phenomenon has long been known to working women. Sexual harassment involves a range of conduct of both a specifically sexual and a sex-based nature.[48] The proscription operates within antidiscrimination legislation,[49] which means that sexual harassment is a civil wrong for which a remedy may be sought; it is not dealt with through the criminal law, as is the case with domestic violence and rape.[50] However, unlike rape law, which is not restricted as to place or circumstance, sexual harassment is proscribed only in certain aspects of the public sphere—primarily employment, although it may also be outlawed in education, the provision of accommodation and in access to goods and services; it does not extend to all facets of the public sphere to include the phenomenon of street-hassling, for example. Similarly, sexual harassment involving a range of relationships, such as that of co-student, co-purchaser and client, may also lack the necessary actual or putative characteristic that attracts liability. Such acts, unless constituting an assault, are more likely to fall under the

---

45   Carol Smart, 'Law's Power, the Sexed Body, and Feminist Discourse' (1990) 17 *Journal of Law & Society* 194, 208.
46   ibid.
47   *O'Callaghan v Loder* (1984) EOC ¶92-023 (NSW EOT).
48   Catharine MacKinnon, *Sexual Harassment of Working Women* (Yale University Press, 1979).
49   For example, *Sex Discrimination Act 1984* (Cth), ss 28.
50   Sexual harassment is nevertheless a generic term that is broad enough to encompass sexual assault. See, for example, *Aldridge v Booth* (1988) EOC ¶92-222 (HREOC).

rubric of 'private' and allow no course of action. Typically, an employer is vicariously liable for the sexually harassing acts of an employee committed during employment.

The point I want to stress is that it is only when sexuality—conduct that is preeminently private within the liberal paradigm—manifests itself within the market that it may constitute the subject of complaint under antidiscrimination legislation. Thus, sexual harassment is the attempt by men (and we are again talking about what is overwhelmingly a gender-specific phenomenon) to bring irrational activity into the sphere of rationality that is proscribed. Irrationality is not only tolerated within the private sphere; it is also normative, as we see with rape and domestic violence, but it is intolerable within those facets of civil society that are central to capitalism. Such acts not only disturb the harmony of the workplace, they also contribute to inefficiency and thereby detract from productivity. I suggest this helps to explain why the proscription of sexual harassment was accepted with alacrity by legislatures, by the judiciary and by management once feminists had persuasively established the extent of the phenomenon, in contradistinction to the tardiness and ineffectiveness associated with rape and domestic violence reforms. However, the fact that the proscription of sexual harassment in employment is deployed by the state to serve non-feminist ends is not a reason to jettison it, providing it is vigilantly monitored. The essentially mediative role of law means that feminist reform alone can never be the sole determinant of the state agenda.

However, there are problems with sexual harassment that might cause one to be less sanguine about the ostensible 'success' of this area of law reform. The variety and extent of conduct that can fall within the rubric of sexual harassment almost defy the imagination. It can include virtually any physical contact in addition to verbal, nonverbal and onanistic acts, such as the harasser exposing himself and masturbating in the presence of the complainant. There is no problem in finding that overtly sexual acts constitute sexual harassment as long as they can be proven, although the fact that such acts normally do not take place in the presence of third parties may constitute a probative burden for complainants, just as it does for those complaining about rape or domestic violence—a factor that can be exacerbated by an unequal power relationship in the workplace.[51]

---

51   In *O'Callaghan v Loder*, the disparity was marked: the complainant was a lift driver in the organisation, while the respondent was its most senior officer, the Commissioner of Main Roads, appointed by parliament.

Second, even if the harassment were to be proven to the satisfaction of a court, there could still be doubt in the mind of a male judge as to whether the complainant had suffered compensable harm. In *Hall v Sheiban*, Einfeld J found the complainants had been sexually harassed contrary to Section 28 of the *Sex Discrimination Act 1984* (Cth). Even though the impugned conduct included acts of both sexual and sex-based harassment, Einfeld J disparaged the harms perpetrated by a doctor against several female employees as being so trivial as to not warrant an award of damages. He initially found the harassment was explicable in terms of the 'tactile and amorous impulses' of the respondent,[52] but was compelled to repudiate this stance soon afterwards because of public criticism.[53]

The juridical doubt surrounding the harm in sexual harassment continues to beset complaints, as with rape allegations, resulting in successful complainants being awarded parsimonious damages compared with other areas of the civil law, such as defamation. The anomaly was rectified only in 2014, when Kenny J expressly drew attention to it—a decision that proved to be a watershed in taking sexual harassment more seriously.[54]

When a complainant is the sole woman in a traditionally male workplace, the collective harassment by her colleagues may be so gross that a quasi-judicial finding of sex-based harassment is relatively unproblematic.[55] Less overt acts are resistant to compression within legal form. Indeed, all working women are subjected to some degree of harassment in male-dominated workplaces, regardless of how 'successful' they are in conventional terms. This harassment may be so subtle and insidious that it is accepted as part of the organisational culture but is not tractable to amelioration within sex discrimination law. I am talking about the snubs women receive every day by virtue of gender, not being consulted on issues of which they have carriage, being put down or talked over at meetings, having their ideas rephrased by men who are then commended by other men for their originality, having their contributions ignored unless they are of use to men and so on. The daily replication of these

---

52   *Hall v Sheiban* (1988) EOC ¶96-269. For critique, see Jenny Morgan, 'Sexual Harassment: One Man's View' (1988) 13 *Legal Service Bulletin* 157. The decision to not award damages was challenged successfully before the Federal Court. See *Hall v A & A Sheiban Pty Ltd* (1989) EOC ¶92-250.

53   *Bennett v Everitt* (1989) EOC ¶92-244 (HREOC); *Kiel v Weeks* (1989) EOC ¶92-245 (HREOC).

54   *Richardson v Oracle Corporation Australia Pty Limited (No. 2)* [2013] FCA 359. For a thoroughgoing analysis of damages awards in sexual harassment complaints, see Madeleine Castles, Tom Hvala & Kieran Pender, 'Rethinking *Richardson*: Sexual Harassment Damages in the #MeToo Era' (2021) 49(2) *Federal Law Review*, doi.org/10.1177/0067205X21993146.

55   For example, *Hill v Water Resources Commission* (1985) EOC ¶92-127 (NSW EOT).

incidents constitutes a psychic harm that demeans all women, effectively reifying the belief that they do not quite belong in the professional world of paid work, other than to serve men in subordinate roles.

Conclusion

From my brief overview of the sex/violence problematic, it may be seen that there are significant conceptual constraints that operate to hedge in and delimit feminist attempts at law reform. The central legitimating, ideological role played by law within the liberal state has long ensured it maintains the hegemony of benchmark masculinity through the seeming naturalness of the public/private, male/female, mind/body dichotomies. The harms women suffer by virtue of sex/sexuality are deeply embedded within the private sphere qua family qua corporeality so they have not been tractable to effective reform. The legislature has not been altogether opposed to a reformist agenda, but law reform efforts have been impeded by the form of law and by a desire to maintain the dominance of benchmark masculinity buried deep within the social psyche.

Legal reform therefore carries with it all the ambiguous hallmarks of liberalism. Law is not apolitical and autonomous but profoundly political. Therefore, committed lawyers 'must attempt to integrate their work in insurgent cultures, and energize those cultures'.[56] Clumsy though the criminal law is, with virtually no remedial, rehabilitative or preventative value, its public role can effectively expose harms endured by individuals in private that would otherwise remain hidden. Police training courses and public awareness programs have been important corollaries of legislative reform. In Melbourne in 1990, several hundred men marched in support of women who had been raped—an extraordinary phenomenon.[57] While such an act may not have significantly reduced the number of rape victims, and this figure always remains elusive because of the low level of complaint and successful prosecution, the unprecedented demonstration of support for women provoked lively public debate and demonstrated solidarity with survivors. It showed that cultural change was definitely on the agenda.

---

56   Steve Bachmann, 'Lawyers, Law and Social Change' (1984) *New York University Review of Law & Social Change* l, 44.
57   *The Age*, [Melbourne], 29 August 1990.

Such actions also highlight the fact that law reform cannot be effected within the sphere of legality alone. To say that a woman has a right to not be subjected to domestic violence, to not be raped and to not be sexually harassed is true only in a very abstract sense. The law does not and cannot confer such rights in practice. The right to complain once a violation has occurred is the only genuine 'right' and that is likely to be cold comfort for survivors who may then feel they have been placed on trial, disbelieved and even ridiculed. The personal cost of pursuing a rights claim is high, although the assertion of a right is an important political act within an authoritative public forum.

A rights-based approach has been critiqued by some feminist legal scholars because it pays inadequate attention to the form of political discourse generated by the rights context. Thus, as Judy Fudge shows, an abstract equality right in the Canadian *Charter of Rights and Freedoms* was disproportionately resorted to in its early days of operation by men to resolve their 'equality' claims to a far greater extent than was the case for women,[58] even though the inclusion of the equality guarantee had been championed as a major feminist initiative. Fudge shows clearly that rights are not necessarily progressive, for they are always contingent on the political and linguistic contexts that inform them. The dilemma facing feminist reformers is whether to persevere with the realm of legality, which is embedded within an obtuse masculinist culture, as illustrated by the examples of domestic violence, rape and sexual harassment.

The seeds of invidiousness springing from women's assumed irrationality and unrestrained sexuality were sown so long ago within the ideologically fertile ground of subordinated femininity that pruning a few twigs fails to attack the roots. The straitjacket of legal form allows little scope for imaginative and creative solutions. The individualised focus encourages the view that the perpetrator is aberrant or deviant rather than being merely one manifestation of misogyny, with scant regard for race or age.[59]

---

58   For example, Judy Fudge, 'The Effect of Entrenching a Bill of Rights upon Political Discourse: Feminist Demands in Sexual Violence in Canada' (1989) 17 *International Journal of the Sociology of Law* 445. Cf. *Proudfoot, A v Human Rights and Equal Opportunity Commission* (1991) FCA 112; see also Parashar (n. 1).

59   Kyllie Cripps, 'Media Constructions of Indigenous Women in Sexual Assault Cases: Reflections from Australia and Canada' (2021) 33(3) *Current Issues in Criminal Justice* 1, doi.org/10.1080/10345329.2020.1867039.

There have also been scant attempts to develop communitarian forms within legal discourse that focus on the relational and the associative, as such approaches are antipathetic to the individualism of liberal legalism. Despite the general currency of feminist discourse, comparatively little political, educational or juridical attention has been paid to men as a class in respect of domestic violence, rape or sexual harassment.[60] By ignoring the collective responsibility of men and by focusing disproportionately on individual perpetrators, the law privileges masculinist perspectives and upholds the collective right of men to occupy dominant roles in both public and private life.[61]

Since law is enmeshed within a carapace of neutrality, while continuing to reproduce hegemonic masculinity, it is more likely to be lagging in the rear than leading social change. Nevertheless, law's central legitimating and ideological role does require space to be accorded a feminist voice, albeit a small one, to satisfy the rhetoric of inclusion. As benchmark men will not surrender their social power voluntarily, legislation designed to effect social justice is invariably a compromise solution.[62]

Although feminist reformers are properly resistant to the depiction of women as eternal victims, it is nevertheless clear that many men want women to remain quiescent and docile. If law can be used duplicitously to persuade women that they are full legal subjects within the society of equals, law can also be used to maintain their subordination while simultaneously tantalising them with promises of a new dawn. However, we know that the power of non-law will be used simultaneously. That is, women are going to continue to be beaten, raped and harassed regardless of what legal reforms are effected. Men have power in our society and it is this reality that constitutes an intractable obstacle to substantive law reform. I take Naffine's point that benchmark man or the 'man of law' is a middle-class man, not every man.[63] However, there is a homologous relationship between him and the 'man of non-law' that is reflected in domestic violence and rape law for, when the 'man of law' withdraws from

60 For example, Wendy Pollack, 'Sexual Harassment: Women's Experience vs Legal Definitions' (1990) 13 *Harvard Women's Law Journal* 35, 84.
61 Margaret Thornton, 'The Political Contingency of Sex Discrimination Legislation: The Case of Australia' (2015) 4(3) *Laws*, 314, 325–26, doi.org/10.3390/laws4030314.
62 Cf. Suzanne Franzway, Dianne Court & R.W. Connell, *Staking a Claim: Feminism, Bureaucracy and the State* (Allen & Unwin, 1989) 129.
63 Ngaire Naffine, *Law and the Sexes: Explorations in Feminist Jurisprudence* (Allen & Unwin, 1990) 119.

the public realm, he, too, becomes the 'man of non-law' who may use force to exert control over others with scant regard for his class position. The 'men of law' who dominate the public realm ensure that legislative reforms do not challenge unduly their status as superordinates in the private realm. Law reform focusing on the collective wrongdoings of men will therefore be resisted in favour of traditional forms of scapegoating aberrant individuals. Despite knowledge of the pervasiveness of male power, the imperative to enter the liberal world of legality with its authoritative and privileged discourses is a seductive one. The challenge for feminist reformers is how to manage the contradictions to secure liberatory outcomes for women and disfavoured groups without being caught by one of legality's many concealed traps. With this caveat, law reform can facilitate the structural change necessary to point the way towards a transformative vision of society, provided progressive invigilators are prepared to remain constantly alert.

Part III: Legislating for Equality

4

Feminism and the Changing State

The state of things

'The state' is an ambiguous and vexed concept for feminist scholars. Bringing women into the state was the primary focus of First and Second-Wave Feminism, which meant feminist campaigns for justice had to be directed to the instrumentalities of the same masculinist state that legitimated the injustices in the first place. That a demonstrably hostile entity was expected to transmute itself miraculously into a beneficent one has been a central paradox perennially besetting feminist reformism. Indeed, Wendy Brown suggests the notion of women seeking protection *from* masculinist institutions *against* men is more in keeping with a politics of feudalism than freedom.[1] The state must nevertheless *appear* to be fair to maintain its legitimacy, as E.P. Thompson reminds us,[2] and, despite misgivings, this veneer of fairness initially acted as a spur to feminist campaigners. The need for the liberal state to accommodate divergent interests also attests to the fact that it is not a unitary entity and the conventional lines of demarcation between state/civil society, state/market and state/family are unduly rigid.

---

1   Wendy Brown, *States of Injury: Power and Freedom in Late Modernity* (Princeton University Press, 1995) 170.
2   E.P. Thompson, *Whigs and Hunters: The Origin of the Black Acts* (Pantheon, 1975) 184.

The preponderance of political theory since the time of Aristotle has nevertheless sought to restrict the state to the sphere of government. The state that Marx critiqued was a centralised state 'with its ubiquitous organs of standing army, police, bureaucracy, clergy, and judicature', which served middle-class society in its struggles against feudalism.[3] Typically, Marx paid no attention to the gendered or racialised character of the state.

The Marxist critique fell out of favour with the collapse of communist regimes in Europe and the anti-essentialist swing induced by postmodernism. 'The state', with its politico-economic and centralist focus, came to be viewed as old-fashioned and one-dimensional. Foucault's concept of governmentality[4] shaped a more comprehensive and fluid understanding that comported with new ways of seeing. Reclaiming a broad meaning of government from the sixteenth century, Foucault focused on the way that fields of action were structured through discourse.[5] Rather than being understood as a discrete sphere, 'the state' includes the multifarious technologies and relationships through which subjects are constituted. Rather than being restricted to the public sphere, as in conventional political theory, every nook and cranny of society, including the family and the self, is a productive site of meaning. Governmentality also stresses the importance of power, which struck a chord with feminist poststructuralist accounts of the state.[6]

Nevertheless, an understanding of the dispersal of power does not mean we should go to the other extreme and regard the state as having 'withered away'. Neo-Marxist scholars believe postmodernists have gone too far in disaggregating the state:

> The postmodernist call to reject unitary or 'grand' theoretical perspectives (metanarratives) has inspired 'governmentality' theorists to move closer to an understanding of power as an

---

3   Karl Marx, 'The Civil War in France' in David McLellan (ed.), *Karl Marx: Selected Writings* (Oxford University Press, 1977) 539.

4   Michel Foucault, 'Governmentality' in Graham Burchell, Colin Gordon & Peter Miller (eds), *The Foucault Effect: Studies in Governmentality* (University of Chicago Press, 1991).

5   Hubert L. Dreyfus & Paul Rainbow, *Michel Foucault: Beyond Structuralism and Hermeneutics* (University of Chicago Press, 1982) 221.

6   For example, Clare Burton, *Subordination: Feminism and Social Theory* (Allen & Unwin, 1985); Suzanne Franzway, Dianne Court & R.W. Connell, *Staking a Claim: Feminism, Bureaucracy and the State* (Allen & Unwin, 1989); Rosemary Pringle & Sophie Watson, '"Women's Interests" and the Post-Structuralist State' in Michelle Barrett & Anne Phillips (eds), *Destabilizing Theory: Contemporary Feminist Debates* (Polity Press, 1992).

almost ethereal force, so dispersed throughout the body of society that it has little relation to the traditional centers of political and economic decision making in capitalist social orders.[7]

While I accept that the state is not a static entity, it is not ethereal either, for it remains a powerful masculinist force that is also racialised, heterosexed, able-bodied and classed. However, the deployment of a range of discourses about individual freedom, choice and success under the rubric of 'the market' effectively conveys the impression that the state may be ethereal.[8] The constitutional power of the state to determine the status of persons within its purview is undeniable—a power that is not diminished by the suprastate currents of globalisation.[9]

It is notable that the time 'the state' fell out of favour coincided with the collapse of the category 'woman'. This centrepiece of Second-Wave Feminism began to be attacked, like the state, as cumbrous, old-fashioned and essentialist. Disillusionment or disengagement was the result of reformist endeavours as the outcomes have not necessarily been empowering for women.[10] 'Engagement with the state' also lost its intellectual appeal for feminist scholars lured by the micropolitical and the seductiveness of bodies, sexualities and popular culture.

Women's studies centres in universities also came under attack and were either closed or replaced with configurations such as gender, sexuality and diversity studies. Despite the importance of acknowledging the variegated and heteroglossic nature of women, the disintegration of a unifying subject weakened the political commitment to feminism.[11] Once women had been 'let in' to public life, it became fashionable within popular and political discourses to aver that feminism was passé. Even former conservative Australian prime minister John Howard entered the fray by referring to the belief that we inhabit a 'post-feminist age'.[12]

7   Steve Tombs & Dave Whyte, 'Unmasking the Crimes of the Powerful: Establishing Some Rules of Engagement' in Steve Tombs and Dave Whyte (eds), *Unmasking the Crimes of the Powerful: Scrutinizing States and Corporations* (Peter Lang, 2003) 264, doi.org/10.3726/978-1-4331-3820-1.
8   For example, Alistair Davidson, *The Invisible State: The Formation of the Australian State 1788–1901* (Cambridge University Press, 1991); cf. Franzway et al. (n. 6).
9   Anna Yeatman, 'The Idea of the Constitutional State and Global Society' (2004) 8 *Law/Text/Culture* 83, 99.
10   Rachel Simon-Kumar, 'Negotiating Emancipation: The Public Sphere and Gender Critiques of Neo-liberal Development' (2004) 6(3) *International Feminist Journal of Politics* 485, 486.
11   Mary G. Dietz, 'Current Controversies in Feminist Theory' (2003) 6 *Annual Review of Political Science* 399.
12   Anne Summers, *The End of Equality: Work, Babies and Women's Choices in 21st Century Australia* (Random House Australia, 2003) 21.

The project of First and Second-Wave Feminism to place women in the state qua public life could be said to be reflective of an epistemic moment when a particular construction of 'woman' was politically and strategically necessary. This unidimensional woman also provided a point of contestation for those who felt excluded by virtue of their race, class or disability. While feminist theorists such as Gayatri Spivak,[13] Judith Butler[14] and Maria Drakopoulou[15] have alluded to the way the category 'woman' has been invoked epistemically to challenge its surface essentialism, a focus on the capillaries has served to deflect attention from the insidious power of the state. It is arguable that the fragmentation of the state in feminist theory, while itself a by-product of the postmodern movement, has also contributed to the marginalisation of a politics of economic justice for women.[16]

With remarkable rapidity, virtually all trace of feminist influence was erased from official discourses during the Howard regime (1996–2007), including government policies, other than in so far as subordinate, dependent, entrepreneurial or commodified subject positions were concerned. The 'femocrat', for example—a distinctive Australian neologism—virtually disappeared from feminist discourse, apart from the occasional allusion by an overseas scholar.[17]

Feminists were taken unawares by the speed of these changes while preoccupied with 'the capillaries'. Like other progressive scholars, they discovered they lacked either a politics or a theory to deal with the neoliberal swing that pulled the rug from beneath their feet. Indeed, some years earlier, Catharine MacKinnon had famously postulated that 'feminism has no theory of the state'[18]—a proposition that seems to have been illustrated more sharply with the neoliberal turn. Governmentality theory, with its multiple discourses and sensitivity to the play of power, does provide a way of understanding the dynamic constitution of the

---

13   Gayatri Chakravorty Spivak, *In Other Worlds: Essays in Cultural Politics* (Methuen, 1987).

14   Judith Butler, *Bodies that Matter: On the Discursive Limits of 'Sex'* (Routledge, 1993).

15   Maria Drakopoulou, 'Women's Resolutions of Lawes Reconsidered: Epistemic Shifts and the Emergence of the Feminist Legal Discourse' (2000) 11(1) *Law and Critique* 47, doi.org/10.1023/A:1008920005319.

16   Jane S. Jaquette, 'Feminism and the Challenges of the "Post–Cold War" World' (2003) 5(3) *International Feminist Journal of Politics* 331, 336, doi.org/10.1080/1461674032000122704.

17   For example, ibid., 339.

18   Catharine MacKinnon, *Towards a Feminist Theory of the State* (Harvard University Press, 1989) 157.

state regarding gender, but it may not go far enough in capturing the facilitative role of the neoliberal state in relation to the market within a global economy.

Franzway, Court and Connell asked with considerable prescience in the late 1980s: 'Will the state be captured by the New Right and transformed into a monetarists' heaven with devastating consequences for feminism including the femocrats?'[19] Several decades later, the answer must be an unequivocal 'yes'. The issue has acquired a singular urgency as feminist scholarship in the academy is being eviscerated because of ever-increasing state intervention in universities, which includes pressure to cheaply produce substantial numbers of job-ready graduates. Feminist scholars are expected to reinvent themselves or leave the academy altogether.[20] In a neoliberal environment that has fostered a resurgence of benchmark masculinity and the privileging of applied knowledge, critical theory has become something of a luxury.

In this chapter, I consider the shift from social liberalism to neoliberalism and show how this has impacted on sex discrimination legislation regarding paid work. I have selected sex discrimination legislation as an example of a feminist-inspired reform that is not only illustrative of the way the social liberal state was deployed by feminists, but also embodies a utopian promise of the way things might be. As Anna Yeatman points out, drawing on Durkheim, the state's role is to *think*—that is, to think through social problems and translate them into policy.[21] Slackening vigilance necessarily imperils feminist futures. I argue that a neoconservative morality has also become enmeshed with neoliberalism in such a way as to undergird the logic of the market. While I am not advocating a return to the values of the past—a futile aspiration—I would like to exhort at least some consideration of the neoliberal state by feminist scholars considering the dramatic trajectory of change that has occurred, including the unravelling of the feminist agenda.

---

19   Franzway et al. (n. 6) 161.
20   Margaret Thornton, 'Neoliberal Melancholia: The Case of Feminist Legal Scholarship' (2004) 20(1) *Australian Feminist Law Journal* 7, 20–22, doi.org/10.1080/13200968.2004.10854321.
21   Yeatman (n. 9) 100.

From social liberalism to neoliberalism

While freedom and equality are the key features of liberalism, they are counterpoised with one another. Freedom is maximised when conservativism is in the ascendancy, equality when progressivism triumphs. As a result of the tension between them, Wendy Brown suggests that liberalism perennially produces a Nietzschean notion of *ressentiment*[22] within one side or the other because of its paradoxical promise of both freedom *and* equality.[23] Thus, when the political pendulum swings to the left, prioritising collective good and equality, it arouses *ressentiment* on the part of conservatives, who believe their freedom is being constrained. Once the pendulum swings to the right, the *ressentiment* of the Left is roused, for the untrammelled freedom to satisfy individual desire prevents the realisation of equality. I do not wish to overstate the pendulum metaphor by suggesting the responses are automatic as, like all discourses, they are necessarily marked by discontinuities, breaks, thresholds and limits.[24] Nevertheless, it does capture something of the political tension within liberalism.

Feminist critiques have long unmasked the universal citizen of the liberal state as male.[25] He is the autonomous inhabitant of the public sphere who has been able to slough off the domestic sphere and its responsibilities that are compatible with neither freedom nor equality. Despite the best endeavours of feminist scholars to stress the importance of the symbiotic relationship between public and private life, relationality and care continue to remain marginal to liberal state theory. The social liberalism that is associated with the inchoate welfare state of the twentieth century took halting steps to respond to feminist claims that freedom and equality be reconceptualised, but the modest gains achieved have now been largely erased.

Under social liberalism, the untrammelled play of individual freedom was tempered by a notion of collective good. State regulation and progressive taxation were employed to effect a modicum of distributive

---

22   Friedrich Nietzsche, *On the Genealogy of Morals*, translated by W. Kaufmann & R.J. Hollingdale (Vintage Books, 1969) 127.

23   Brown (n. 1) 67.

24   Michel Foucault, *The Archaeology of Knowledge*, translated by A.M. Sheridan Smith (Tavistock, 1972) 31.

25   For example, Genevieve Lloyd, *The Man of Reason: 'Male' and 'Female' in Western Philosophy* (Methuen, 1984).

justice, bolstered by a vibrant civil society. In contrast, the cluster of values associated with neoliberalism maximises the individual freedom associated with the masculine and minimises the feminised values of collective good and distributive justice, thereby signalling what Marian Sawer refers to as a 'sex change' in the state.[26] Under neoliberalism, we find that deregulation is the order of the day as the state purports to have devolved the management of the economy to the market. The public sphere qua government has contracted and public goods such as utilities, transport, health and education have been privatised and commodified. Nothing is of significance unless it has use value in the market. It might be noted that neoliberalism is by no means peculiar to the Australian nation-state but has become the dominant political ideology of the Western world.[27] It is a corollary of globalisation and, as such, has become the metanarrative of our times.[28]

It was under the social liberalism of the late twentieth century that women were grudgingly accepted by the state as legal subjects after decades of struggle. In terms of liberal theory, exclusion and the most blatant inequalities could then be treated as aberrations that needed to be corrected because they did not comport with the liberal commitment to (formal) equality between citizens. Measures such as equal pay, no-fault divorce, the proscription of family violence, changes to sexual assault laws, the setting up of women's advisory units within state and federal governments and the passage of sex discrimination legislation were all notable examples of reformist initiatives designed to remedy the anomalies of the past.[29] The recognition of the category 'woman' coincided with the high point of social liberalism under Prime Minister Gough Whitlam in the early 1970s, but at that very moment the first seeds of neoliberalism were sown when Whitlam cut tariffs on imports by 25 per cent.[30] I suggest

---

26   Marian Sawer, *The Ethical State? Social Liberalism in Australia* (Melbourne University Press, 2003) 87.

27   Colin Crouch, 'Putting Neoliberalism in its Place' (2014) 85(2) *Political Quarterly* 114, doi.org/ 10.1111/1467-923x.12077; Loïc Wacquant, *Punishing the Poor: The Neoliberal Government of Social Security* (Duke University Press, 2009), doi.org/10.1215/9780822392255; David Harvey, *A Brief History of Neoliberalism* (Oxford University Press, 2005).

28   Peter Roberts, 'Rereading Lyotard: Knowledge, Commodification and Higher Education' (1998) 3(3) *Electronic Journal of Sociology*, available from: sociology.lightningpath.org/ejs-archives/vol003.003/ roberts.html.

29   Regina Graycar & Jenny Morgan, *The Hidden Gender of Law* (The Federation Press, 2nd edn, 2002).

30   Damien Cahill, 'New-Class Discourse and the Construction of Left-Wing Elites' in Marian Sawer & Barry Hindess (eds), *Us and Them: Anti-Elitism in Australia* (API Network, 2004) 89.

this privileging of market freedom over collective good, which was to gather momentum in subsequent decades, signalled the change of course. Since then, neoliberals have set out with a vengeance to reassert their freedom and neutralise the gains of social liberalism.

The neoliberal state began to slough off responsibility for what happens to its vulnerable and low-paid citizens. Instead of the social state, an ethic of individualism prevailed, in which citizens were expected to take responsibility for the course of their own lives. If they failed, they had only themselves to blame. The concept of individual responsibility had been popularised and made palatable by stressing the liberal rhetoric of individual freedom, autonomy and choice. In contrast, the ethic of care associated with social liberalism was dismissed pejoratively by neoliberals as a manifestation of the 'nanny state'.[31] The feminised language alerts us to the reassertion of the masculinity of the state and its latent hostility to the feminine. The state assistance previously available for social justice initiatives was curtailed within the new social Darwinist milieu and the 'crisis' of the welfare state was identified as a phenomenon of the 1980s.[32] Rather than equality and distributive justice as the fundamental underpinnings of the state, there was a discernible shift in favour of *in*equality—exemplified by the emphasis on competition policy, entrepreneurialism and the market. While inequality has always been an undeniable dimension of a free-enterprise society, its potential for excess was formally reined in by state regulation under social liberalism.

It should not be thought, however, that the state has altogether opted out under neoliberalism. While market freedom, deregulation and privatisation are the hallmarks of the neoliberal political economy, the state remains the driver of policy. While the state may have ostensibly devolved responsibility to the market for the good of the economy, it retained power for itself by operating insidiously through the market; there was no descent into anarchy. The appearance of self-regulation through the market was one of the most successful ploys of neoliberalism. It highlights the cogency of Foucault's governmentality thesis, for the discourse of the free market does not emanate from a discrete sphere but represents the voices of the powerful operating through multiple sites.

---

31 Sawer (n. 26) 91–94.
32 Anna Yeatman, *Bureaucrats, Technocrats, Femocrats: Essays on the Contemporary Australian State* (Allen & Unwin, 1990) 119–48.

Thus, the neoliberal state did not self-destruct, but remained firmly in control, albeit behind the scenes, single-mindedly pump-priming the economy and winding down social justice policies that are frequently dismissed as an 'impost on business'. The state qua government works to boost the market by restricting social welfare policies for individuals and sponsoring 'corporate welfare' to tempt profitable ventures away from global competitors. It is within this marketised and privatised incarnation of the state that social justice and gender equality are regarded as passé. The market has transformed citizens into consumers obsessed with lifestyle and the visible markers of success.[33] What sense do vestigial egalitarian measures make in a state committed to competition policy or inequality? The transformation leads Marian Sawer to ask why the defence of the welfare state is not 'the number one item on the agenda of politically mobilized women'.[34]

Sex discrimination legislation

Sex discrimination legislation is a casualty of the changing state. It has been unable to fulfil its promise of equality for women because of the force of the competing social norm of *in*equality—a corollary of freedom and the free market, which has been strengthened incrementally by the neoliberal turn.[35] The *ressentiment* of the Right represents a strand of the neoconservative swing that is not only antifeminist, but also anti-Aboriginal, anti–gay and lesbian and xenophobic, representing a moral conservatism that has become entwined with the economic conservatism associated with neoliberalism. I will briefly show how these twin ideologies have combined to extract the teeth from sex discrimination legislation, although some might think it was edentulous to start with! I will pay regard to the sphere of employment, which represents a crucial dimension of social life. It is also the site where the contradictions arising from the intersections of public and private life are acute for feminist and state interests alike.

33   Clive Hamilton & Richard Denniss, *Affluenza: When Too Much is Never Enough* (Allen & Unwin, 2005).
34   Marian Sawer, 'Constructing Democracy' (2003) 5(3) *International Feminist Journal of Politics* 361, doi.org/10.1080/1461674032000122722.
35   Susan Magarey, 'The Sex Discrimination Act 1984' (2004) 20(1) *Australian Feminist Law Journal* 127, doi.org/10.1080/13200968.2004.10854327.

The federal *Sex Discrimination Act 1984* (hereinafter *SDA*) was enacted by the Hawke Labor government just when the Australian economy had been officially opened to world markets.[36] Prime Minister Paul Keating further boosted the trend in favour of the market, although it was Prime Minister Howard who, in the 1990s and 2000s, more fervently embraced the free market than any other leader (with the possible exception of his northern hemisphere role models, Margaret Thatcher and George H.W. Bush). The change in state policy from protection to free trade affected all workers profoundly, but I suggest it exercised a disproportionate impact on women.

In the preferred model of antidiscrimination legislation, an individual complainant pursues a specified avenue of complaint in the hope of securing a remedy, usually in the form of damages. Sex discrimination was never treated as a criminal offence, despite the feminist hope that it would be.[37] On the contrary, the favoured approach has been a softly-softly one, in which there is an attempt to conciliate a complaint behind closed doors; a mere 2 per cent of complaints proceed to a formal public hearing.[38] Thus, far from perpetrators being hauled off to jail, even the most egregious discriminators have generally been able to avoid public scrutiny. We see here how the state has established discrimination procedures that operate to protect the interests of benchmark men by erecting a carapace of privacy around the conciliation process.

The express aim of the legislation is to 'eliminate discrimination' and effect equality between men and women, primarily in the areas of employment, education, accommodation and access to goods and services and clubs. As I have shown in detailed critiques of the legislation elsewhere,[39] the commitment to equality is lukewarm; the ambit of operation is narrow, its procedures tortuous and its exceptions legion, as well as being very expensive for a complainant to pursue to a formal hearing. What is more, it is impossible to 'eliminate' something that is constantly being produced

---

36 Hester Eisenstein, *Inside Agitators: Australian Femocrats and the State* (Temple University Press, 1996) 47.

37 The first Australian antidiscrimination legislation, the *Prohibition of Discrimination Act 1966* (SA), which proscribed discrimination on the ground of race, utilised the criminal standard of proof 'beyond all reasonable doubt', but the Act was a dismal failure because the standard was virtually impossible to meet.

38 Australian Human Rights Commission, *2019–20 Complaint Statistics* (AHRC, 2020) 3, available from: humanrights.gov.au/sites/default/files/2020-10/AHRC_AR_2019-20_Complaint_Stats_FINAL.pdf.

39 For example, Margaret Thornton, *The Liberal Promise: Anti-Discrimination Legislation in Australia* (Oxford University Press, 1990); Margaret Thornton, 'Equality and Anti-Discrimination Legislation: An Uneasy Relationship' (2021) 37(2) *Law in Context* 12, doi.org/10.26826/law-in-context.v37i2.149.

and reinscribed in the social script.[40] The language of 'elimination', which is taken directly from the UN Convention on the Elimination of All Forms of Discrimination against Women (CEDAW),[41] would seem to proceed from the fallacious assumption that inequality is a finite variable that each complaint of discrimination is progressively able to reduce. Furthermore, a free-enterprise society based on competition necessarily produces inequality, which antidiscrimination legislation does little to inhibit. Class is notably absent from antidiscrimination legislation as a proscribed ground[42]—a variable that has particular significance when intersecting with sex, race and disability.[43] Its exclusion is another manifestation of the liberal state's denial of the existence of power. There are also multiple conceptual problems arising from the liberal legal mode of adjudication that operate to delimit the aim of effecting equality, to which I briefly advert.

First, there is the individualised nature of complaint handling. This means a complainant at a formal hearing must carry the burden of proving that an identifiable respondent *caused* the discriminatory harm. Since sexism and sex discrimination are strands of our normative universe that have been socially and historically created, as well as legitimated by the state, how can an individual complainant sever her complaint from its political context to prove (on the balance of probabilities) that an individual respondent be held liable for the harm suffered? If responsibility cannot be sheeted home to an identifiable respondent, no discrimination will be found to have occurred—a finding that serves to normalise the discrimination. Indirect discrimination makes a half-hearted attempt to address systemic discrimination by purporting to consider practices that are neutral on their face but exercise a discriminatory effect. However, a complex legal test that includes the slippery subjectivity of reasonableness permits only the most overt instances to be captured.[44] Needless to say, such a test does

---

40   Margaret Thornton, 'Auditing the Sex Discrimination Act' in Marius Smith (ed.), *Human Rights 2004: The Year in Review* (Monash University, 2005).

41   *Convention on the Elimination of All Forms of Discrimination against Women*, opened for signature 18 December 1979, 1249 UNTS 513 (entered into force 3 September 1981); ratified by Australia in 1983.

42   Margaret Thornton, 'Social Status: The Last Bastion of Discrimination' (2018) 1 *Anti-Discrimination Law Review* 5.

43   Beth Goldblatt, 'Intersectionality in International Anti-Discrimination Law: Addressing Poverty in its Complexity' (2015) 21(1) *Australian Journal of Human Rights* 47, doi.org/10.1080/1323238x.2015.11910931.

44   For example, *State of New South Wales v Amery* (2006) ALR 196, which is one of the few sex discrimination cases to reach the High Court. See Beth Gaze, 'Judgment' in Heather Douglas, Francesca Bartlett, Trish Luker & Rosemary Hunter, *Australian Feminist Judgments: Righting and Rewriting Law* (Hart, 2014). See also Chapter 9, this volume.

not overcome the causation issue, which still requires that an identifiable respondent be held liable in accordance with the typical model of civil liability within the Anglo-Australian legal system. While it may be unreasonable to hold an employer responsible for a gendered harm that is buried deep within the social psyche and legitimised by the state, this is cold comfort for a complainant who is left high and dry with no prospect of a remedy. The individualistic approach not only serves to depoliticise complaints by sloughing off all reference to the context in which they occur, it also downplays the substantive harm, which is underscored by a judicial preference for the technocratic and the procedural.

Second, our intrepid complainant normally needs to prove that she was treated less favourably than a real or hypothetical male in the same or similar circumstances. Given the extent of sex segregation that persists within the Australian workforce, the comparability requirement constitutes a significant obstacle for those engaged in women's work or for those with caring responsibilities. A hypothetical comparator may be postulated but this may be difficult for a decision-maker to imagine.[45] The feminist campaigns for reform sought to address discrimination against *women*, not men, and even though sex specificity is supported by the CEDAW, Australian antidiscrimination legislation is couched in gender-neutral terms to conform to the liberal state's ideal of impartiality. That is, to not be seen to be conferring a benefit on women, men can also lodge complaints alleging sex discrimination, as though the masculinist state had historically excluded and marginalised men in the same way it had women.[46] In an endeavour to locate a gendered harm on a gender-neutral playing field, the essence of the harm as gendered must be muted or sloughed off altogether.

Comparability also favours a reductive and biological approach to sex. The legislation does not deny the social constructionist element of sex/gender but, unsurprisingly, it is not well understood in sex discrimination jurisprudence. Similarly, the way sex intersects with other variables of identity—especially race, sexuality and disability—remains elusive within the essentialised understanding of the phrase 'on the ground of

---

45 For example, *Curtis v T & G Mutual Life Society Ltd* (Victorian Equal Opportunity Board) 3 July 1981 (unreported). The complainant, who was secretary to the general manager of the respondent company, was expected to make the coffee and clean the silver, but she was unable to prove that this was sex discrimination as there was no comparable male secretary.

46 A notorious example involved a challenge to women's health centres: *Proudfoot v ACT Board of Health* (1992) EOC ¶92–417 (HREOC).

sex'. Sex discrimination legislation requires a relentless focus on this one characteristic of identity. Not only does this have the effect of heightening the burden of proof for Indigenous women, lesbians, older women or those with a disability,[47] it also requires one facet of identity to be privileged over all others, even though identities necessarily represent a complex amalgam of traits.

Third, sex discrimination legislation operates in conformity with the classic public/private dichotomy of liberal legalism that cordons off the family and treats it as though it were 'naturally' a regulation-free domain, although it is accepted that the state should make formal incursions into the family through law from time to time. Once again, we are reminded of the masculinist character of the state and the caveats it imposes when grudgingly 'letting in' the Other.

Even though the family represents a major source of inequality for many women, it remains largely out of bounds in the case of sex discrimination legislation. While the public/private dichotomy remains intractable, the ground of workers with family responsibilities was included, following Australia's ratification of the International Labour Organization (ILO) Workers with Family Responsibilities Convention, 1981 (ILO C156).[48] This ground is potentially transgressive in the way it purports to reach across the public/private divide but is limited in its operation. In the case of the *SDA*, for example, an individual may rely on this ground to complain of discrimination only in the case of dismissal from employment.[49] The ground falls far short of opening the private sphere to enable scrutiny of just who is doing the caring and under what circumstances. Under the guise of sex neutrality, it ensures that worker/carers are engaged in productive work. Hence, sex and parental status are a problematic intersection in the case of working mothers whose careers deviate from those of ideal unencumbered workers.[50] We see, therefore, that the state is prepared to make no more than a tiny aperture in the barrier between public and private; it is certainly not prepared to dismantle the dichotomy altogether.

---

47   For example, Karen O'Connell, 'Can Law Address Intersectional Sexual Harassment? The Case of Claimants with Personality Disorders' (2019) 4(4) *Laws* 34, doi.org/10.3390/laws8040034.

48   ILO Convention 156, *Workers with Family Responsibilities*, opened for signature 3 June 1981, ratified by Australia 1990, and accorded a legislative base in the *SDA* in 1992.

49   *SDA*, s. 14(3A). For example, *Transport Workers' Union of Australia v Atkins* [2014] FCCA 1553; *Wilkie v National Storage Operations Pty Ltd* [2013] FCCA 1056.

50   Beth Gaze, 'Quality Part-Time Work: Can Law Provide a Framework?' (2005) 15(3) *Labour & Industry* 89, 94, doi.org/10.1080/10301763.2005.10669319.

While all states and territories, except South Australia, contain a somewhat broader conceptualisation of the ground of family responsibilities than found in the federal Act, I reiterate that the legislation can be accessed only from the public qua employment side of the divide. Even then, a judge may delimit its ambit further, for the statutory language of sex discrimination is deliberately left opaque in an endeavour to appeal to dichotomous interests. The hermeneutic role of judges also represents an important site of masculinist state power, despite the belief that judging represents an independent and neutral site of decision-making.

The *Schou* case,[51] discussed in detail in Chapter 9, is illustrative. Deborah Schou, who had worked as a Hansard reporter in the Victorian Parliament for 17 years, had two children, one of whom was asthmatic. If parliament was sitting, she was expected to work until parliament finished, even if it was as late as 2 am. When she sought to do her transcription work at home for two days a week, permission was refused, and she resigned. Her complaint of discrimination was not conciliated and she lost her appeal before the Victorian Supreme Court. The freedom of the employer trumped a claim by a worker with caring responsibilities to work flexibly in the interests of equality. The majority judges evinced disbelief that an employee would challenge managerial prerogative regarding the site where the work would be conducted (even though the complainant had entered into a workplace agreement guaranteeing her 'flexible and progressive work practices'). It is notable that the idea of the masculinist state carried with it a particular cogency in this case because the respondent was the State of Victoria, which fought the case tenaciously, even being prepared to undermine the proscription of discrimination on the ground of status as a carer within its own legislation.[52]

Cases such as *Schou* rattle the barricades surrounding the private sphere, possibly even creating a few dents. Retaining the immunity of the private sphere from regulation, however, is a central project of the masculinist state. It remains a site where benchmark men are largely free from the constraints of inequality and unequal treatment meted out to women and 'Others'. Equality is a concept realisable only within the public sphere in liberal theory. In contrast, the private sphere has always been a site of

---

51   *State of Victoria v Schou* (2004) EOC ¶93–328 (VCA). See also Beth Gaze, 'Context and Interpretation in Anti-Discrimination Law' (2002) 26(2) *Melbourne University Law Review* 325.

52   Law firm Holding Redlich represented the complainant on a pro bono basis through the various hearings and was prepared to appeal to the High Court provided the State of Victoria did not sue for costs if Ms Schou were to lose, but no such undertaking was forthcoming.

inequality. A wife, children, extended family members and servants could never historically be the equal of the master, the *pater familias*. While the rhetoric of equality between adults may have been extended tentatively to the private sphere in popular discourse, it is far from the reality, as illustrated by the way it is cordoned off from sex discrimination and other regulatory regimes. If inequality in the private sphere qua family had been outlawed, we would be encountering a truly radical reform. However, far from even thinking about the pros and cons of extending the ambit of the legislation into the family, my immediate concern is with the evisceration of the legislation in respect of employment.

The impact of neoliberalism on sex discrimination legislation

The workplace is changing dramatically because of the depredations of neoliberalism. Rather than focus on the rights of employees and the conditions under which they work, which were a major concern of social liberalism, the state is now concerned primarily with the freedom of employers to maximise corporate profits within a global economy.[53] The preference is for flexible workplaces, which means that wages are static, conditions are poor and tenure is parlous. Everyone is expected to do more with less. If it is no longer profitable to keep workers on, they may be dispensed with; tenure cannot be justified. As a result, restructuring and redundancy now typify what has become a workplace culture of insecurity. The state, in facilitating the market, is prepared to sacrifice the interests of its citizens, particularly its most vulnerable workers. If workers cannot survive through their own endeavours, that is their responsibility.

The shift away from a social liberal regime in which the rights of (benchmark male) workers commanded respect to one obsessed with the maximisation of profits poses a conundrum for sex discrimination legislation, for discrimination is endemic in the new environment. What is more, the pervasiveness of a culture of insecurity neutralises the discriminatory impact. The new employment discourse averring that flexible work is 'good for the economy' has been accepted as orthodoxy within a remarkably short time. Accordingly, the state has resiled from

---

53   Harry Glasbeek, *Class Privilege: How Law Shelters Shareholders and Coddles Capitalism* (Between the Lines, 2017).

a regulated system of industrial relations and devolved responsibility to individual employers within the market. The turnaround has dramatically transformed the culture of work. Centralised wage-fixing and regulation of the conditions of work through state and federal awards reveal how social liberalism operated as a beneficent force. Women benefited from a state-regulated system, which sought to effect pay equity and superior workplace conditions for all workers.[54] The tripartite compact formerly effected between government, unions and employers minimised the exploitation of the most vulnerable. The move to a deregulated system in which workers, either individually or through an enterprise collective, bargain for the terms of their employment contract generally leaves them worse off.[55]

In the desperate scramble to be competitive within a global economy, which includes entering into free-trade agreements with countries that have inferior working conditions and lower wages, such as the United States and China, Australian workers' rights are rapidly being whittled away. Nation-states generally are engaged in a 'race to the bottom' by reducing workers' conditions to maximise profits. As a result, significant worker protections have been eroded, as illustrated by the neoliberal workplace reforms that began with the Howard government.[56] Deregulation means there are dramatic variations in pay between those doing the same job. Furthermore, workers are being engaged as independent contractors to bypass antidiscrimination laws and they have lost rights to permanency, occupying their positions at will, which means potential dismissal without cause at any time.

Also dramatic is the shift to part-time, casual and contract work in the interests of 'flexibility'. Contingent or precarious workers are expected to be available at any time at the behest of the employer to suit the needs of global capital.[57] Thus, flexible workers are expected to work harder and longer when demand is high but less when it is slack, regardless of the financial ramifications on them personally. Workers may enter alternative

---

54   Margaret Thornton, 'Equal Pay in Australia' in Francois Eyraud et al., *Equal Pay Protection in Industrialised Market Economies: In Search of Greater Effectiveness* (International Labour Office, 1992).
55   David Peetz, *The Realities and Future of Work* (ANU Press, 2019).
56   *Workplace Relations Amendment (Work Choices) Act 2005* (Cth); Anthony Forsyth & Andrew Stewart, *Fair Work: The New Workplace Laws and the Work Choices Legacy* (The Federation Press, 2009).
57   Iain Campbell & Robin Price, 'Precarious Work and Precarious Workers: Towards an Improved Conceptualisation' (2016) 27(3) *Economic & Labour Relations Review* 314, doi.org/10.1177/1035304616652074.

employment relationships with employers, such as that of independent contractor, in the belief they will have control over their working lives, but it is the employer's freedom—not theirs—that is being expanded, despite the rhetoric of family friendliness. Labour-law experts have pointed to the poverty of contract law in a changing employment context.[58] The increasing uncertainty of the employment relationship, as illustrated by casual or 'as required' workers, magnifies the difficulties.

Women, young people and migrant workers are overrepresented among precarious workers, but gender has once again become invisible as a category of analysis.[59] One must ask: What does the non-discrimination principle mean in a context where discriminatory treatment and the sacrifice of rights are the modus operandi of the contemporary reserve army thesis? Even if conditions of employment were less favourable than those of a similarly situated benchmark male worker, how could a precarious worker lodge a discrimination complaint? Complaining about conditions of work can be disastrous at the best of times. It can mean marginalisation or victimisation—if the complainant still has a job—or being blackballed by an entire industry.[60] Any course of action involving the lodgement of a complaint to an outside agency is imbued with risk as it will be regarded as damaging the 'brand' of the corporation. The worker is expected to put up with adverse conditions, however discriminatory, or leave and go elsewhere, for her job is held subject to the good graces of the employer. Like workers of the nineteenth century, contemporary neoliberal workers are expected to bear responsibility for their workplace experience, including less favourable treatment.

The insecurity of the contemporary workplace is by no means limited to the growing category of precarious workers within the gig economy, for the phenomenon now affects all workers. How can a worker prove that the loss of her job or a demotion on return from maternity leave was caused by discrimination rather than the employer's need to 'downsize' or restructure?[61] A neoliberal presumption in favour of the employer

---

58 For example, Mark R. Freedland, *The Personal Employment Contract* (Oxford University Press, 2003) 521; Jill Murray, 'Work and Care: New Legal Mechanisms for Adaptation' (2005) 15(3) *Labour & Industry* 67, 69–71.

59 For example, Caroline Criado-Perez, *Invisible Women: Exposing Data Bias in a World Designed for Men* (Vintage Publishing, 2019).

60 For example, *Hickie v Hunt & Hunt* (1998) EOC ¶92–910 (HREOC); *Dunn-Dyer v ANZ Banking Group* (1997) 92–897 (HREOC).

61 *Commonwealth Bank of Australia v Human Rights and Equal Opportunity Commission* (1997) 80 FCR 78, discussed in Chapter 9, this volume.

renders it virtually impossible to prove sex discrimination in restructured workplaces.[62] Globalisation may mean there is no longer an identifiable employer against whom a complaint can be lodged and a real or hypothetical comparator may prove to be even more elusive. The model of employment underpinning sex discrimination legislation—that of constant, full-time employment—is fast disappearing as the norm, although it is not possible to determine the extent to which this influences the lodgement of discrimination complaints reported at the federal level.[63] It is notable, however, that the preponderance of sex discrimination complaints relate to employment, most of which relate to sexual harassment, pregnancy or family responsibilities, which suggest that sex discrimination, far from being 'eliminated', has been absorbed into the culture of work.

As feminists believed that institutional initiatives were a more efficacious means of securing social change than the lodgement of myriad individual complaints, provision for affirmative action (AA) was originally included in Susan Ryan's sex discrimination bill, which did not survive. A separate Act was subsequently passed in 1986.[64] This was a very weak piece of legislation, which created no rights. It required that organisations with more than 100 employees lodge an annual report regarding their progress in the development of an AA program. The short history of this Act illustrates well the Nietzschean *ressentiment* thesis, as an ongoing attack on AA was maintained by conservative interests, including the Business Council of Australia. AA allegedly impeded the freedom of employers to be competitive, although no evidence was adduced in support. The 1986 Act was repealed in 1999. It was replaced with a weaker Act, which made no reference to AA whatsoever.[65] This Act carefully excised all reference to 'forward estimates' or 'objectives', because of the fear that quotas—regarded as code for appointing 'unqualified' women—would operate without regard to the merit principle. The continued opposition from the business lobby led to the third and current Act, the *Workplace Gender Equality Act 2012* (Cth) (hereinafter *WGEA*), which removed reference to 'women' and became gender neutral. Reflecting the neoliberal turn, it also expressly adverted to productivity and competitiveness as legislative objects (*WGEA*, s. 2A[e]).

---

62   Rosemary Hunter, 'The Mirage of Justice: Women and the Shrinking State' (2002) 16 *Australian Feminist Law Journal* 53, 63–65.
63   Australian Human Rights Commission (n. 38).
64   *Affirmative Action (Equal Opportunity for Women in the Workplace) Act 1986* (Cth).
65   The replacement legislation was the *Equal Opportunity for Women in the Workplace Act 1999* (Cth).

The anodyne concept of diversity, particularly 'managing diversity', has tended to replace the more threatening discourses of equal opportunity and AA within contemporary workplace practice.[66] While a diversity ideal is difficult to dispute, it is apparent that the language has been deployed to enhance the freedom of employers, particularly when examined in the light of patterns of restructuring, redundancy and precarious work. This new discourse, I suggest, contributes to the stifling of agonistic concepts such as 'discrimination' and 'inequality' in the context of antidiscrimination legislation. The transition from EEO to diversity has been carefully orchestrated by the state in the interests of the market.

Neoconservatism

Hand-in-glove with neoliberalism is 'neoconservatism'. The state's adoption of an ideologically conservative stance has resulted in the unravelling of the feminist agenda in conjunction with an antifeminist discourse, rendering 'women' passé as a category of analysis. The *ressentiment* of the Right is complete.

Reflecting the antifeminist agenda, the political focus is now more likely to be on 'the family' than 'women', 'feminism' or 'gender'. This transition occurred because of the intersection of economic neoliberalism and social conservatism borrowed from the US religious Right—a conjunction that was exposed brilliantly by Marion Maddox in respect of the Howard regime.[67] The revived discourse of 'the family' refers to the traditional two-parent heterosexual family, which may no longer be the norm in contemporary Australia. Moral conservatives have had to recognise that it is no longer feasible to corral women with young children behind the white picket fence, 1950s style, as women are now a legitimate part of the paid workforce. Neoliberalism has deployed this reality to its own ends. Full-time work is still frowned on for women with very young children, but women with school-age children have been seized on by the economy as the ideal flexible workers, echoing the reserve army theory of women's labour long identified by feminist scholars.[68] Women can be brought out

---

66 Margaret Thornton, 'The Political Contingency of Sex Discrimination Legislation: The Case of Australia' (2015) 4(3) *Laws* 314, doi.org/10.3390/laws4030314.

67 Marion Maddox, *God under Howard: The Rise of the Religious Right in Australian Politics* (Allen & Unwin, 2005). For a critique of religious discrimination laws, see Margaret Thornton & Trish Luker, 'The Spectral Ground: Religious Belief Discrimination' (2009) 9 *Macquarie Law Journal* 71.

68 For example, Brown (n. 1) 185.

of the home at times of high demand, such as the need to work in retail for two or three hours in the middle of the day, and be home again in time to collect the children from school.

Women are still primarily responsible for caring not just for children, the aged and sick family members, but also for their male partners and adult sons who are perfectly able to look after themselves.[69] The preference theory of labour market theorists such as Catherine Hakim[70] has struck a chord with neoliberals and neoconservatives alike,[71] for it naturalises the assignation of both paid precarious work and unpaid caring work to women in ways that crucially serve the state, thereby underscoring the symbiosis between public and private life in liberal theory. In brief, Hakim's thesis is that the differences between men's and women's labour market experiences and pay are explicable in terms of the lifestyle choices women make, including electing to work part-time or fewer hours. Hakim argues that 'work-centred women' can be equal at work because of initiatives such as antidiscrimination legislation but, by the same token, 'home-centred women' should not be denied equality because of the choices they have made. The third group, to which most women now belong according to Hakim's thesis, comprises the 'adaptive women' who fit in paid work around the needs of the family.

While many women may opt for flexibility at work, particularly when they have family responsibilities, as illustrated by the *Schou* case, this does not mean they favour precarious jobs that are exploitative. They may be compelled to consent to poor working conditions because there is no alternative or they lack bargaining power. Rational-choice theory underpins the neoliberal notion of individual responsibility, which conveniently glides over structural discrimination. This theory disguises the way in which increasing numbers of unskilled women workers, including those from non–English-speaking backgrounds, are subordinated through precarious work—a phenomenon that has been exacerbated by the Global Financial Crisis (GFC), the rise of the gig economy and the Covid-19 pandemic. By a certain sleight of hand, however, freedom and equality appear to be reconciled.

---

69   Nancy Fraser, *Unruly Practices: Power, Discourse and Gender in Contemporary Social Theory* (Polity, 1989) 148.
70   Catherine Hakim, *Key Issues in Women's Work: Female Diversity and the Polarisation of Women's Employment* (Routledge Contemporary Issues in Public Policy, 2nd edn, 2016).
71   Maddox (n. 67) 87–92.

While a great deal of attention has been paid to work–life balance (WLB) in recent years, the assumption is that women—the 'marginalised caregivers'—are the ones expected to do the balancing. Precarious work, as the descriptor graphically implies, denotes insecurity, inadequate pay, dependency and/or poverty, possibly at the time of working, as well as in old age. The rhetoric of WLB confirms that substantive equality remains a chimera for women. The low status accorded to the bearing of and caring for life, compared with the endangering and destruction of life, as in war, again signifies the way in which a gendered dichotomy is mapped on to the priorities of the neoliberal state. Childcare workers are so low-paid that agencies encounter difficulty recruiting and retaining qualified staff. In contrast, war service is extolled as heroic and still carries connotations of good citizenship as it did in antiquity.[72]

An environment has been created that insidiously unpicks policy and institutes new directions to circumscribe the freedom of women. Exemptions are a way of undermining the public nature of antidiscrimination legislative texts. Applications have been made from time to time for an exemption from marital status provisions to prevent single women and lesbians from having access to assisted reproductive technology,[73] and another on the grounds of sex to allow male-only scholarships to encourage young men to become primary schoolteachers.[74] Race exemptions have also been sought and granted to effect lucrative contracts,[75] which reveals how the market may be blatantly privileged over human rights.

Neoliberalism and neoconservatism have colluded in the development of an antifeminist agenda that has seen a sharp turn away from the concerns of social liberalism. Although neoconservatives have systematically attacked

---

72 This connection between combat and citizenship, or what Iris Marion Young terms the 'militaristic norms of honour and homoerotic camaraderie', has been a leitmotif of the Western intellectual tradition since antiquity—a congruence that has also been accepted as a desirable, if not essential, prerequisite for leadership. Iris Marion Young, 'Polity and Group Difference: A Critique of the Ideal of Universal Citizenship' (Symposium on Feminism and Political Theory, 1989) 99(2) *Ethics* 250, 253, doi.org/10.1086/293065.

73 Sex Discrimination Bill (No. 1) 2000 (Cth) (lapsed).

74 Sex Discrimination Amendment (Teaching Profession) Bill 2004 (Cth) (lapsed). The Australian Catholic University was granted an exemption on 31 March 2004, allowing it to offer 12 scholarships to men and 12 to women. Australian Human Rights Commission, 'Temporary Exemption Application—Catholic Education Office' (AHRC, 2002), available from: humanrights.gov.au/our-work/legal/temporary-exemption-application-catholic-education-office.

75 These exemptions relate to access to specialised aerospace technology. Margaret Thornton & Trish Luker, 'The New Racism in Employment Discrimination: Tales from the Global Economy' (2010) 32(1) *Sydney Law Review* 1.

the *SDA* and the *Affirmative Action (Equal Employment Opportunity for Women) Act 1986* (Cth) (hereinafter *AA Act*) from the outset,[76] it is only as neoliberalism and neoconservatism have coalesced that the masculinist character of the state has been able to expose itself with confidence once again. Anne Summers' book *The End of Equality*[77] shows graphically how social liberal policies designed to benefit women rapidly unravelled.[78] One could note the strength of the opposition to the paid maternity leave campaign,[79] the severe budget cuts to and downgrading of the Office of the Status of Women,[80] the privatisation of childcare[81] and the watering down of the *AA Act* to which I have referred. A particularly bizarre illustration of the discounting of women's interests at the millennial turn was the dispatch of an official 12-person delegation to an ILO conference on pregnancy and the workplace in Geneva in 2001 that did not include a single woman.[82] Indeed, one could go so far as to say that gender justice has been rendered both unseeable and unsayable by neoliberal discourse.

The discourse of freedom as rational choice has complemented the more overtly masculinist discourses to deflect attention from the struggles of Second-Wave Feminism. The new incarnation of the feminine that is acceptable is a commodified form that serves the market. 'Girl power' has been deployed to sell style in designer clothing, makeup and household goods. Packaged as 'Third-Wave Feminism', it is sexy, trendy and superficial. Second-Wave Feminism, with its trenchant exposé of the gendered partiality of the liberal state, can now be dismissed as so cumbrous and old-fashioned that it is best consigned to mothballs.

---

76   For discussion of the role of conservative groups such as Women Who Want to be Women, see Robin Rowland (ed.), *Women Who Do and Women Who Don't Join the Women's Movement* (Routledge & Kegan Paul, 1984).

77   Summers (n. 12).

78   Barbara Pocock, *The Work/Life Collision: What Work is Doing to Australians and What to Do About It* (The Federation Press, 2003). For an insightful analysis of the way in which Coalition policies construct heteronormativity to the detriment of gays and lesbians, see Carol Johnson, 'Heteronormative Citizenship: The Howard Government's Views on Gay and Lesbian Issues' (2003) 38(1) *Australian Journal of Political Science* 45, doi.org/10.1080/1036114032000056242.

79   Human Rights and Equal Opportunity Commission, *A Time to Value: Proposal for a Paid Maternity Leave Scheme* (Report, HREOC, 2002). Universal paid parental leave was introduced by the *Paid Parental Leave Act 2010* (Cth).

80   Rosemary Whip, 'The 1996 Australian Federal Election and its Aftermath: A Case for Equal Gender Representation' (2003) 18(40) *Australian Feminist Studies* 73, doi.org/10.1080/0816464022000056385.

81   Pocock (n. 78).

82   Whip (n. 80).

Conclusion

Understandably, complaint-based antidiscrimination legislation has been unable to realise its stated objective of 'eliminating' sex discrimination in our society. It was naive to imagine it could since it is perennially being reinscribed in the social script. The social liberal state managed to maintain no more than an uneasy truce between dichotomously opposing interests. The neoliberal swing means that not only has inequality become more pronounced as a norm within our society, but also social justice is treated as expendable so far as the market is concerned, unless use value can be attached to it. At the same time, sex discrimination legislation is an official text of the state and remains an important, if somewhat tarnished, symbol of equity and plurality.

The proscription of sexual harassment, a subset of sex discrimination, is touted as a feminist victory and—in a limited way—it is, although I argue in Chapter 5 that the focus on corporeality deflects attention from systemic discrimination. According to liberal theory, sexuality does not belong in the workplace; it is paradigmatically private activity that is viewed as likely to impede worker productivity. For this reason, complaints of sexual harassment that mirror heterosex have a reasonable chance of success.[83] In contrast, sex discrimination in the workplace, where it is necessarily entwined with managerialism, employer prerogative and the construction of merit, is resistant to challenge. A rational explanation can invariably be adduced to explain why a particular woman was not appointed that has nothing to do with gender. As I suggest, the diffusion of authority and power, together with the insecurity of the contemporary workplace, renders the possibility of success of complaints of sex discrimination even more elusive. The individualised approach to the handling of complaints has always been problematic because it cannot grapple with structural discrimination, but the neoliberal labour market stresses the notion that lodgement of complaints is outmoded because discrimination and inequality are pivotal to corporate success.

Sexual harassment clearly reveals that only those aspects of the feminist reform agenda that are compatible with the interests of the state are likely to be supported. While sex discrimination legislation was an initiative of

---

83 Gail Mason argues that same-sex harassment should not be equated with sexual harassment as presently conceptualised. Gail Mason, 'Harm, Harassment and Sexuality' (2002) 26(3) *Melbourne University Law Review* 596.

social liberalism, its passage also coincided with a period of unparalleled economic growth. Hence, it was desirable to encourage women into the workplace with the promise of a non-discriminatory environment, as they were viewed as a source of relatively cheap and expendable labour. The neoliberal promise is now one of 'work–life balance' and 'flexible work'—a promise that possesses a similarly superficial allure. Women are encouraged to engage in precarious and exploitative work because it allows them to demonstrate in a material way that they place their families first.

Far from there being a contraction of the state—as ostensibly appears to be the case with devolution, deregulation and privatisation—we are seeing a boosting of the power of the state through neoliberalism that includes a renewed emphasis on the construction of gendered subjects. We are once again being spun a story, clothed in the language of flexibility and choice, of a neutral and progressivist liberal state in which things are always getting better. The ostensible devolution to the market of responsibility for the economy tricks us into believing the state has disappeared. Just because it is less visible does not mean it is now ethereal. It is not the invisible hand of the market that is at work here, attenuating the inchoate commitment to equality, but the invisible hand of the state working through the market. By effecting an intimate liaison with the market, the state has played a key role in 'sustaining and intensifying the neoliberal project'.[84]

There is little space for social justice and the constellation of feminist values in the neoliberal state's single-minded pursuit of the interests of capital. As Sawer points out, markets are incapable of delivering equal opportunity, 'which is why welfare states were introduced in the first place'.[85] Competition and the bottom line, however, are all that matter to the players on the global economic stage. Equity for those who continue to undertake the preponderance of care is of little consequence. The success of a neoconservative ideology means the neoliberal state has been saved from having to expend energy in accommodating divergent interests, leaving it free to proceed with its agenda largely unimpeded. Redistributive justice can be effected only by the state qua government; it is not going to occur of its own volition. The swing from social liberalism to neoliberalism occurred because of pressure from the business sector and exponents of the free market. A swing in the other direction is unlikely to

---

84 Tombs & Whyte (n. 7) 264.
85 Sawer (n. 34) 365.

occur without significant energy being expended by feminist and social justice activists. Engagement with the state is fraught in that it always carries with it the danger of cooption, to say nothing of the ubiquitous conundrum of 'who speaks for whom?'. It can nevertheless serve 'both as a brake on the negative externalities of capitalism and as a positive force for material redistribution'.[86]

The fickle and treacherous character of the neoliberal state poses an ongoing challenge, but there is too much at stake to ignore it. The absorption of feminist energies by the capillaries has deflected attention from the market metanarrative. The change in the relationship between feminism and the state is so dramatic that it calls for a new episteme. I am exhorting not gender mainstreaming or a revival of femocracy in the vain hope of securing an instantaneous panacea, but critical engagement with the insidious workings of the antifeminist neoliberal state. It may be the only hope for developing the necessary groundswell to push the political pendulum back towards social justice again. This is the real challenge for Third-Wave Feminism.

---

86   Jane Mansbridge, 'Anti-Statism and Difference Feminism in International Social Movements' (2003) 5(3) *International Feminist Journal of Politics* 355, 356, doi.org/10.1080/1461674032000122 713.

5

Sexual Harassment Losing Sight of Sex Discrimination

Introduction: Embodiment at work

Legal proscriptions against sexual harassment in the workplace, accompanied by avenues of redress, have existed in Australia for almost four decades. The legal and popular discourses about sexual harassment have caused women to think about the way the phenomenon detracts from their personhood. They have the right not only to say 'no' to a boss or a colleague, but also to complain formally, either inhouse or to a human rights agency, if they are sexually harassed. The evidence suggests corporations are paying much more attention to internal grievance mechanisms than was once the case, although the incidence of sexual harassment continues to be high.[1]

While the recognition of sexual harassment as a legal wrong is an important step in securing human rights for women and non-dominant men, my support for the action is by no means unequivocal. I suggest that, while important, the disproportionate attention paid to the sexual

---

1   A large national survey conducted in Australia in 2018 established that 33 per cent of those surveyed (39 per cent women and 26 per cent men) had experienced workplace harassment in the previous five years. See, Australian Human Rights Commission, *Respect@Work: National Inquiry into Sexual Harassment in Australian Workplaces* (AHRC, 2020) 17.

in sexual harassment, as illustrated by recurring high-profile media cases,[2] has deflected attention from the sex-based discrimination that informs it.[3] The erection of a line of demarcation between sexual harassment and sex discrimination has been legitimated in Australia through legislation, despite the fact that the proscriptions against harassing and discriminatory conduct are contained in the same legislative instruments.[4] The construction of women workers as sexualised can have the effect of affirming the misogynistic subtext of the social script that the feminine is a dangerous and disorderly force within a sphere of rationality. It allows women to continue to be constituted as 'Others' to 'benchmark men'— that is, those who are Anglo-Celtic, heterosexual, able-bodied and middle-class and who are the normative inhabitants of the world of paid work. The corporealisation of women in positions where they are expected to display deference to senior men is a very effective mechanism for impugning the authority of the feminine.

Typically, men are the respondents in sexual harassment complaints and women are the targets.[5] This accentuates a heterosexed paradigm with its connotations of sexual desire that lies at the base of popular understandings of sexual harassment. However, in accordance with the glass ceiling theory, harassment is frequently perpetrated against women, irrespective of their sexual orientation, because they are not wanted in certain sectors of the

---

2   Many cases have involved prominent public figures, such as judges, including Justice Clarence Thomas of the District of Columbia Circuit Court of Appeals, now on the US Supreme Court. See Anita Hill and Emma Jordan (eds), *Race, Gender and Power in America: The Legacy of the Hill–Thomas Hearings* (Oxford University Press, 1995). Former justice Dyson Heydon was found in 2020 to have harassed six women who worked as associates when he was on the Australian High Court. See Naomi Neilson, '"We Must Do More": Legal Profession Responds to Dyson Heydon Findings', *Lawyers Weekly*, 24 June 2020, available from: www.lawyersweekly.com.au/biglaw/28674-we-must-do-more-legal-profession-responds-to-dyson-heydon-findings. One of the most notorious cases in recent years involved movie mogul Harvey Weinstein, who was found to have sexually harassed dozens of women, including prominent movie stars. The publicity resulted in the '#MeToo' movement, the global ramifications of which were profound, leading to a plethora of studies exposing the extent of sexual harassment in multiple workplaces—for example, AHRC (n. 1); Kieran Pender, *Us Too? Bullying and Sexual Harassment in the Legal Profession* (International Bar Association, 2019).
3   Cf. Vicki Schultz, 'Reconceptualizing Sexual Harassment' (1998) 107(6) *Yale Law Journal* 1683, 1687, doi.org/10.2307/797337.
4   See, for example, *Sex Discrimination Act 1984* (Cth).
5   AHRC (n. 1); Australian Human Rights Commission, *Set the Standard: Report on the Independent Review into Commonwealth Parliamentary Workplaces* (AHRC, 2021); Paula McDonald, 'Workplace Sexual Harassment 30 Years On: A Review of the Literature' (2012) 14(1) *International Journal of Management Reviews* 1, doi.org/10.1111/j.1468-2370.2011.00300.x.

workplace.[6] This harassment may be more appropriately characterised as discrimination at work; it is unlikely to have anything to do with desire. Similarly, non-dominant men may be the targets of harassment at work because they do not fit into prevailing masculinist cultures.[7]

The dominant heterosexed understanding of sexual harassment also needs to be placed in its broader sociopolitical context. Workplaces have generally become much less secure as conditions of work have been eroded at the expense of profitmaking. Short-term contracts, casualisation and precarious work underscore the culture of uncertainty that characterises the contemporary workplace.[8] Within this environment, workers learn to be docile, since those who complain about workplace conditions may soon find themselves dispensable. Those subjected to discrimination face a dilemma: complain and risk losing your job or keep quiet and retain it. However, by keeping quiet one may become complicit in the maintenance of a sexual regime in the workplace.

The privileging of the sexual in sexual harassment means the focus is on the aberrant behaviour of individuals rather than the structural and systemic manifestations of discrimination. It must be acknowledged, however, that the latter remains perennially elusive. How do we tell the difference between 'managing' and 'harassing' when workers have to be constantly cajoled into working harder and being more productive to increase profit margins? The emphasis on employer prerogative and the correlative de-emphasis on employee rights in an insecure environment mean it has become increasingly difficult for the targets of harassment to make out complaints. I suggest that the corporatised workplace operates to legitimise sex-based harassment of women and non-dominant workers, many incarnations of which are not tractable to remediation under antidiscrimination law.

---

6   Harassment has been a major concern for lesbians, at work and elsewhere. Chapman and Mason found in their study of discrimination and vilification complaints lodged on sexuality grounds that 46 per cent related to the area of employment. Anna Chapman & Gail Mason, 'Women, Sexual Preference and Discrimination Law: A Case Study of the NSW Jurisdiction' (1999) 21(4) *Sydney Law Review* 525, 531.

7   See, for example, *Daniels v Hunter Water Board* [1994] EOC ¶92–626 (NSW EOT). In this case, the complainant was able to rely on the ground of perceived homosexuality in s. 49ZG of the *Anti-Discrimination Act 1977* (NSW). Even more provocatively, in a claim of same-sex 'hostile environment' sexual harassment, the US Supreme Court found that actions by the heterosexual male harassers constituted sex discrimination: *Oncale v Sundowner Offshore Services*, 523 US 75 (1998).

8   Richard Sennett, *The Corrosion of Character: The Personal Consequences of Work in the New Capitalism* (W.W. Norton, 1998) 22–7.

Sexual harassment was not initially included in antidiscrimination legislation in Australia, but when it was, the proscription was accepted more readily than in the United States,[9] where sexual harassment was a judicial rather than a legislative creation.[10] The Australian legislatures adopted a more pragmatic approach because it was accepted at the outset that sexual harassment impacted adversely on productivity in the workplace, as I suggested in Chapter 3. Despite the proscription, articulating a complaint and obtaining a remedy are always fraught, particularly in a context where employer prerogative endows managers with considerable discretion. Furthermore, it is a flaw of the prevailing individual complaint-based model of antidiscrimination legislation that the individual act of sex discrimination is separated from sexism, just as racial discrimination is separated from racism, same-sex discrimination from homophobia, and so on.[11] While the class-wide factor is recognised in the lodgement of complaints, the probative burden, which includes connecting the impugned conduct with an identifiable respondent, is the responsibility of the individual complainant. The burden is one confronting all discrimination complainants. The sexual activity within sexual harassment complaints is often so overt that it takes centre-stage and overwhelms the discriminatory impact on the complainant class. I suggest, therefore, that the favoured reading of sexual harassment serves a significant ideological and political role in safeguarding the conventional gendering of workplaces.

I turn to a consideration of what might be imagined as a continuum of sexual harassment that bedevils mainly women workers, particularly within masculinist enclaves. I do not wish to suggest that the continuum is rigid or unchanging but that there is a discernible pattern, underpinned by the essentialised understanding of sexual harassment that prevails in legal and popular culture. I start with overtly sexual conduct at one end of the spectrum and argue that the more the harassing conduct is like heterosexed activity (conceptualised in terms of an active male harasser and a passive female 'victim'), the more likely it is to be accepted as sexual

---

9   USC§2000-e (1994) based on Title VII of the *Civil Rights Act of 1964*, Pub L No 88-352, 78 Stat 241.

10   The Supreme Court first determined that sexual harassment was a form of illegal discrimination in *Meritor Savings Bank v Vinson* 477 US 57 (1986).

11   Margaret Thornton, *The Liberal Promise: Anti-Discrimination Legislation in Australia* (Oxford University Press, 1990) 8.

harassment. The less sexualised, albeit sexed, the harassing conduct is, the more likely it is to be normalised within the workplace and the more difficult it is for a complainant to obtain a remedy.

I acknowledge that the language I am working with—especially 'sex' and 'sexuality'—is slippery, as these terms merge with one another and take their colouration from the context in which they operate.[12] After all, we are all sexed, as well as sexual, beings. While 'sex' may refer to a biological category, it is also a socially constructed term that incorporates gendered understandings of masculinity and femininity. This broad view of sex has selectively been incorporated into sex discrimination jurisprudence, although the linguistic leeway accommodates a biological reductionism when it suits. The legislation itself does not define 'sex', thereby investing tribunals and courts with considerable power to tell us what it means. The *Sex Discrimination Act 1984* (Cth) (*SDA*) (s. 5[1]) does no more than refer to the 'opposite sex', which suggests a clear binarism.[13] 'Sexual', like sex, however, can refer to both biological and political classifications of identity, as well as to the desires, appetites and practices associated with sexual expression. 'Sexual' is also undefined in the sexual harassment provisions of the *SDA* (s. 28[1]), although the references to 'an unwelcome sexual advance', a 'request for sexual favours' and 'conduct of a sexual nature' clearly signify sexualised conduct. Given the political and ideological quicksand surrounding the semiotics of sex, I recognise that my task is a daunting one.

Sexual harassment as heterosex

The sociolegal recognition of sexual harassment is of very recent origin, although the phenomenon itself has an ancient lineage. The term 'sexual harassment' emerged in the mid 1970s in the United States[14] and quickly

---

12   For a critique of the sex/gender distinction, see Moira Gatens, 'A Critique of the Sex/Gender Distinction' in Sneja Gunew (ed.), *A Reader in Feminist Knowledge* (Routledge, 1991) 139; Michelle Boivin, 'The Category of "Woman/Women" in Discrimination Based on Sex' (1999) 14(2) *Canadian Journal of Law and Society* 203, doi.org/10.1017/s0829320100006116.

13   More recent legislation tends to favour the term 'gender'—for example, the *Gender Equality Act 2020* (Vic.).

14   The term 'sexual harassment' is associated preeminently with the work of Catherine MacKinnon in the United States. Catherine MacKinnon, *The Sexual Harassment of Working Women* (Yale University Press, 1979), xi, 25–55. Schultz points out that several US authors used the term before MacKinnon from the mid 1970s. In particular, she notes that Carroll Brodsky used the term in a broader, less specifically sexualised manner than MacKinnon. Schultz (n. 3) 1696–705.

entered feminist and EEO discourses throughout the Western world.[15] The understanding of sexual harassment as conduct that is overwhelmingly perpetrated by men against women is reflective of the heterosexed nature of the typical workplace. That is, managerial positions are more likely to be masculinised, while those that are managed are feminised. Nevertheless, the principle of sex neutrality is favoured by federal and state legislation, which permit the lodgement of a complaint by a person regardless of gender or sexual orientation against another without regard to that person's gender or sexual orientation, but the same sexualised understanding of sexual harassment tends to colour the conduct.

The interpretative gloss on the legislative proscription of sexual harassment encompasses a broad range of conduct, including acts of masturbation and exposure,[16] the recounting of sexual exploits,[17] the interrogation of the complainants concerning their sexual practices[18] and remarks of a sexual nature.[19] As these sexualised instances of harassment invariably involve male actors and female targets—mirroring heterosex—it is perhaps not surprising that the paradigm of sexually harassing conduct involves importuning another for sexual favours.[20] At its most extreme, this may include criminally actionable sexual assault, although most workplace harassment falls short of criminality.[21] However, there are manifold heterosexed variations apart from soliciting favours, such as the case of the employer who stole sexually explicit photographs of the complainant from her home, enlarged them and carried them around in his briefcase[22] or the case involving a middle-aged man who stood in front of the desk of a young woman in her first job and stared at her all day.[23] While sexual obsession may underpin harassment of this kind, harassment may also be animated by a desire to intimidate. The general concern of the Australian

---

15   Rosemary Pringle, *Secretaries Talk: Sexuality, Power and Work* (Allen & Unwin, 1988) 93.

16   For example, *Greenhalgh v National Australia Bank Ltd* [1997] EOC ¶92–884 (HREOC).

17   This was one of the allegations from the Anita Hill–Clarence Thomas case (n. 2).

18   For example, *Hall v A & A Sheiban Pty Ltd* (1989) 20 FCR 217.

19   For example, *Fornaro v Strachan* [1998] EOC ¶92–955 (NTADC).

20   For example, *Hughes trading as Beesley and Hughes Lawyers v Hill* [2020] FCAFC 126 (24 July 2020).

21   A major scandal erupted in Australia in 2021 when it was revealed that political staffer Brittany Higgins had been allegedly raped in Parliament House two years earlier by another staffer. See, for example, James Massola, 'Brittany Higgins on How the Last Three Months Have Transformed Her Life', *Sydney Morning Herald*, 2 May 2021, available from: www.smh.com.au/politics/federal/ brittany-higgins-on-how-the-last-three-months-have-transformed-her-life-20210429-p57nkc.html.

22   *Lallard v Tweed Art Framing Co.* [1999] EOC ¶93–036 (NSWADT).

23   Inhouse inquiry conducted by the author.

legislation is that the actions of the respondent have created a hostile environment for the complainant.[24] Hence, the focus is directed towards the effect on the complainant; intent is of no legal relevance.

Sexual harassment as heterosex is rife against women in subordinate positions where a male boss exercises 'power over' them. A common scenario is that of a small business, such as a shop or restaurant, in which a young woman, often in her first job, is employed as a shop assistant, waiter, secretary or cleaner. The manager or sole proprietor is typically a middle-aged man who assumes that an unsophisticated young woman is fair game. He regards her personhood and autonomy as inferior and, in paying for her labour, he seems to assume that he can assert a right over her body. When she exercises her free will and rejects him, she may be victimised, downgraded or dismissed.[25] Of course, respondents in such cases know they do not have possessory rights in the person of the employee and, if challenged, will endeavour to rationalise their treatment in terms of incompetence.[26] Nevertheless, respondents in such cases are frequently serial harassers.[27]

With *O'Callaghan v Loder*,[28] New South Wales became the first Australian jurisdiction to accept that sexual harassment was a form of sex discrimination.[29] The NSW Equal Opportunity Tribunal (EOT) held that a person is sexually harassed if he or she is subjected to unsolicited and unwelcome conduct by a person who stands in a position of power over him or her.[30] In this case, the heterosexed nature of organisational power, or what Catharine MacKinnon has referred to aphoristically as 'dominance eroticised',[31] was clearly in evidence. The male respondent, the Commissioner of Main Roads (appointed by parliament), was the

---

24 *Whitlock v Bunnings, DP and DF* (2009) QADT 14; *Rail Corporation New South Wales v Hunt* [2009] NSWWCCPD 114.

25 See, for example, *Kalich v Es* [1999] EOC ¶92–961 (NTADC); *Q v John Defelice* [1999] EOC ¶93–051 (HREOC); *D v Berkeley Challenge Pty Ltd* [2001] EOC ¶93–150 (NSWADT).

26 A study of the US cases suggests that, in such instances, the burden on the employee is such that she must show she was virtually a perfect employee to succeed. However, such perfection can also work against the complainant, supporting an implication that the harassment was inconsequential. Susan Estrich, 'Sex at Work' (1991) 43 *Stanford Law Review* 813, 834–39, 846.

27 See, for example, *Hall v A & A Sheiban Pty Ltd* (1989) 20 FCR 217.

28 [1984] EOC ¶92–024 (NSWEOT) [hereinafter *O'Callaghan*].

29 In the United States, lower federal courts had recognised a cause of action since 1976. MacKinnon (n. 14) 59–77. The Supreme Court recognised the cause of action in 1986 in the case of *Meritor Savings Bank v Vinson* 477 US 57 (1986).

30 *O'Callaghan* [1984] EOC ¶92–024, 75516.

31 MacKinnon (n. 14) 162.

most senior person in the organisation, while the female complainant, a lift driver, was one of the lowliest. The commissioner was in the habit of inviting the complainant into his office with the explicit intention of soliciting sexual favours. Despite Mathews J's initial courage in acknowledging the discriminatory harm of sexual harassment, she faltered in applying the test to the crucial element of power. The harassing conduct was found not to amount to unlawful sex discrimination because the complainant had failed to make known to the respondent that his attentions were unwelcome. The implications of 'power over' were thereby undermined. Was the complainant to slap the commissioner's face and tell him to 'get lost'? She knew perfectly well that any intimation of rejection could have adverse repercussions, as she indicated at the hearing. Despite the unsuccessful outcome for the complainant, this was a trailblazing decision that laid the groundwork for new ways of thinking about gendered harms in the workplace.[32] Indeed, it led to the express proscription of sexual harassment within antidiscrimination legislation.[33]

Antidiscrimination legislation does not proscribe all sexual behaviour in the workplace, much of which may be pleasurable.[34] It is the unwanted character of the behaviour that transmutes ostensibly neutral behaviour into unlawful behaviour in the eyes of the law. The impact on the targeted person must be evaluated in the light of community norms, which is then filtered through the fictional standard of the reasonable person. This well-known albeit contested standard purports to bring a quasi-objective test to bear on the subjective reception of the conduct by the complainant—supposedly to foreclose the concern that employers might be held responsible for injury to hypersensitive employees.[35]

---

32 For example, Jenny Morgan, 'Sexual Harassment and the Public/Private Dichotomy: Equality, Morality and Manners' in Margaret Thornton (ed.), *Public and Private: Feminist Legal Debates* (Oxford University Press, 1995) 89–92.

33 As a matter of constitutional law, sexual harassment was found to constitute sex discrimination for the purposes of the *Convention on the Elimination of All Forms of Discrimination against Women*, opened for signature 18 December 1979, 1249 UNTS 13 (entered into force 3 September 1981). *Aldridge v Booth* (1988) 80 ALR 1, 14–16.

34 For example, Pringle (n. 15) 90–92.

35 In *Hall v Sheiban* [1988] EOC ¶92–227 (HREOC), Einfeld J referred to a 'reasonable woman' who was seemingly expected to tolerate unwanted sexual overtures and touching (at 77144)—a standard that was rejected by the Federal Court on appeal as an error of law, in *Hall v A & A Sheiban Pty Ltd* (1989) 20 FCR 217.

All Australian antidiscrimination legislation now includes a provision requiring the behaviour to be such that 'a reasonable person … would have anticipated that the person harassed would be offended, humiliated or intimidated'. As Jenny Morgan points out, however, the moralistic overtones of this formulation, particularly the word 'offended', detract from the inequality that sexual harassment creates in the workplace.[36] I concur with this assertion but, as foreshadowed, I wish to go further. I suggest that it is not only the moralistic and trivialising formulation that is the problem, but the emphasis on sexual in sexual harassment. This emphasis essentially camouflages the systemic discrimination that fosters the harassment. Hence, only the most overtly heterosexed and individualised examples of sexual harassment tend to be comprehensible within the terms of the legislation:

> This sexual desire–dominance paradigm governs our understanding of harassment. Its influence is reflected in the very fact that the category is referred to as 'sexual' harassment rather than, for example, 'gender-based' or 'sex-based' harassment. The most publicized harassment cases have accentuated this understanding.[37]

Harassment that is sexed, rather than sexualised, is theoretically covered by the general proscription against sex discrimination—less favourable treatment on the ground of sex—but the *expressio unius* principle of legal interpretation[38] renders this more difficult to bring within the ambit of the legislation, as I will demonstrate.

Thus, while feminists and progressive lawyers thought the inclusion of a proscription of sexual harassment was a significant development,[39] as indeed it was in many ways, insufficient cognisance has been accorded to the 'offended, humiliated or intimidated' formulation. In fact, the original wording of the *SDA*, which focused on unwelcome conduct that would disadvantage the complainant, took greater account of the discriminatory effect. The parliamentary debates relating to the amendment stress the move away from the need to prove disadvantage

---

36 Morgan (n. 32) 92–93.
37 Schultz (n. 3) 1692.
38 The Latin phrase in full is *expressio unius personae vel rei, est exclusio alterius* ('the express mention of one person or thing is the exclusion of another'). R.S. Vasan (ed.), *Latin Words & Phrases for Lawyers* (Godwin, 1980) 85. Applying the maxim here, the express proscription of sexual harassment in one part of the legislation implies those other unspecified forms of harassment may not be covered.
39 For example, Morgan (n. 32) 91.

as a positive step, as disadvantage is not always relevant, but the substitution of the new wording was not given further explication.[40] I am not suggesting that the previous wording was unproblematic as it also focused on sexual conduct, as distinct from sex discrimination, but the 'offended, humiliated or intimidated' requirement undermines the significance of the discriminatory effect of that conduct. Cordoning off sexual harassment and treating it as the aberrant conduct of individuals also encourage superficial and trivialising views, such as those equating sexual harassment with a breach of manners or sexual etiquette.[41]

Sexually permeated workplaces

When women endeavour to move into what is predominantly thought of as 'men's work' for the first time, the character of the harassment frequently shifts from the actions of a single harasser to the conduct of several co-workers or the members of an entire work unit. Their aim seems to be to create a hostile work environment in the hope that the interloper will leave. Harassment of this nature seems to be motivated by a fear that men's masculinity will be impugned if women are able to do the same job as well as them.

As we move away from individualised sexual overtures and sexual desire, the conduct tends to be less direct, albeit sexualised, as it consists of imagery that mimics heterosex with masculine actors and objectified women. Such conduct commonly includes pornographic displays, obscene language and crude, sexist jokes.[42] The display of pornographic images has served to mark certain workplaces as masculinised spaces—a practice that has been conventionally tolerated by management. Blue-collar workplaces, such as building sites and mines, are paradigmatic examples of workplaces where the entry of women has generated a high degree of resentment.[43]

---

40   See, for example, the discussion of the Sex Discrimination and Other Legislation Amendment Bill 1992 (Cth) in Commonwealth, *Parliamentary Debates*, House of Representatives, 3 November 1992, 2396 (Paul Keating, Prime Minister); Commonwealth, *Parliamentary Debates*, Senate, 8 December 1992, 4366 (Michael Tate, Minister for Justice).

41   For example, Jeffrey Minson, 'Second Principles of Social Justice' (1992) 10 *Law in Context* 1, 12–17. For a critique, see Morgan (n. 32) 108–9.

42   See, for example, *Horne v Press Clough Joint Venture* [1994] EOC ¶92–591 (WAEOT); *Carroll v Zielke* [2002] EOC ¶93–177 (NSWADT).

43   For example, Cynthia Cockburn & Susan Ormrod, *Gender and Technology in the Making* (Sage, 1993); Cynthia Cockburn, *Machinery of Dominance: Women, Men and Technical Know-How* (Pluto, 1986); Ann Game & Rosemary Pringle, *Gender at Work* (Allen & Unwin, 1983) 16.

The often-gross nature of the harassment enables the complainant to succeed in making out a complaint successfully, albeit that her career may be ruined by the time she lodges a complaint.

In *Hopper v Mt Isa Mines Ltd*,[44] the complainant was one of the first women to be selected as an apprentice diesel fitter. However, during her employment, she was subjected to persistent sexual harassment, including having gross comments made about her body and being surrounded by pornographic material. The sexualisation of the complainant was effective in constructing her as a figure of abjection,[45] rather than a competent worker. Her apprenticeship was also deleteriously affected, as she was assigned inappropriate and menial tasks, such as washing bolts. She broke out in a rash, suffered depression and had to abandon her apprenticeship after two years.

Harassment that involves inappropriate assignments is not sexual according to the legislative formulation, but sexed, because it constitutes less favourable treatment than would have been accorded a comparable male apprentice. In *Hopper*, the discriminatory activity was not disaggregated from the more overtly sexualised activity, so it did not prove to be a problem. It is when the harassment occurs in the absence of sexualised conduct that it is more difficult for the complainant to prove that it was sex-based. In any case, the sexualised conduct itself may be probatively problematic because a woman in a non-traditional workplace may not necessarily be 'offended, humiliated or intimidated' by the harassing acts—a point made by Quinn in discussing an interview in a North American study: 'In her job in construction, Judy was not offended per se by the male employees' crude remarks or the pornography in the construction trailer; in contrast, she found it childish and unprofessional.'[46] Because she was not 'offended, humiliated or intimidated', Judy would also encounter difficulty in making out her complaint successfully under the Australian sexual harassment provisions. This category of complaints underscores Morgan's point about the inappropriateness of the moralistic formulation at the expense of a focus on inequality.

---

44   [1997] EOC ¶92–879 (QADT).

45   Julia Kristeva, *Powers of Horror: An Essay on Abjection*, translated by Leon Roudiez (Columbia University Press, 1982). Kristeva posits the 'abject' as an otherness that cannot be assimilated, 'the jettisoned object' that is 'radically excluded' (at 1–2).

46   Beth A. Quinn, 'The Paradox of Complaining: Law, Humor, and Harassment in the Everyday Work World' (2000) 25(4) *Law and Social Inquiry* 1151, 1177, doi.org/10.1111/j.1747-4469.2000.tb00319.x.

The sexual harassment of women who encroach on and disturb masculinist workplaces is by no means confined to blue-collar work. The police force and the armed services are also well-known examples, despite conscious efforts at official levels to change the forces' image and clamp down on 'bastardisation' practices.[47] However, the existence of a non-discrimination policy does not automatically translate into civility and acceptance throughout the organisation. In *McKenna v Victoria*,[48] the complainant was a police officer who was subjected to unwelcome sexual advances, excessive criticism and derogatory remarks about her private life. After two years of abuse, she complained, at first within the force and then externally, but was victimised as a result, which culminated in successive breakdowns. In the eyes of the old-guard police officers, reporting the harassment to an outside body was a wrong that far outweighed the wrongful conduct itself, for it violated the cherished code that one should never 'dob'.

Williams v Robinson,[49] in which the complainant was a member of the Royal Australian Air Force (RAAF), evinces similar facts. Williams had been subjected to several instances of sexual harassment. The failure of superior officers to deal appropriately with the behaviour influenced the complainant's decision to leave when life in the RAAF became intolerable and she had to have psychotherapy. As with the closed culture of the police force, complaining about one's treatment to an outside body carried the risk of being branded a 'dobber'.

This 'whistleblower' mentality provides a powerful disincentive for a targeted person to complain because they know they are unlikely ever to win more than a Pyrrhic victory against a powerful institution. That is, complainants might have the satisfaction of eventually being told they are in the right, but their careers will have been reduced to tatters in the process. While 'dobbing' may be the language of both the police force and the RAAF, the same sentiment often prevails in private corporate cultures, as my research on the legal profession has shown.[50]

---

47   See Submission to Senate Standing Committee on Foreign Affairs, Defence and Trade, Parliament of Australia, *Inquiry into Sexual Harassment in the Australian Defence Force*, November 1993, 54 (Sue Walpole, Sex Discrimination Commissioner).
48   [1998] EOC ¶92–927 (VADT). The respondent's appeal to the Supreme Court of Victoria was denied. [2000] EOC ¶93–080.
49   [2000] EOC ¶93–112 (HREOC).
50   Margaret Thornton, *Dissonance and Distrust: Women in the Legal Profession* (Oxford University Press, 1996) 259–60.

Men who resist the dominant norms of the workplace may also be the targets of sexualised harassment by other men, even when non-dominant men are not gay. In *Daniels v Hunter Water Board*,[51] the complainant, an electrician, was subjected to a campaign of harassment because his co-workers thought he was gay. In addition to taking up jazz ballet, drama classes and modelling, he adopted a 'trendy' haircut and wore an earring. He was ridiculed and taunted with epithets such as 'weirdo', 'poofter' and 'gay boy'. He was also spat on and physically assaulted. Within the masculinist culture of the workplace, the co-workers made it known that the complainant was 'not one of the boys'.

In pursuing a remedy, the complainant was able to rely successfully on a provision in the NSW Act proscribing discrimination on the ground of 'perceived homosexuality'.[52] In US jurisdictions where proscriptions on the grounds of sexual preference are not available, male complainants have sought to rely on sex discrimination provisions. The Supreme Court has upheld a same-sex complaint by a heterosexual complainant whose harassers were also heterosexual men.[53] Extrapolating from this case to *Daniels*, the argument would be that but for his sex, the complainant would not have been harassed. In other words, had Daniels been a woman who took up jazz ballet, drama and modelling, his conduct would not have given rise to hostile environment sexual harassment in the workplace. The argument is a provocative one, as it confounds the biological binarism of sex that underpins antidiscrimination law, as discussed earlier.

Cases such as *Daniels* underscore the animosity towards the feminine as well as LGBTIQ+ in masculinist workplace cultures, no less than in *Hopper*, *McKenna* and *Williams*. The aggressive conduct often found in such cases clearly has more to do with resentment than desire. These cases illustrate how masculinist cultures of homosociality and heterosexism are effectively sustained.[54]

---

51 [1994] EOC ¶92–626 (NSW EOT).
52 *Anti-Discrimination Act 1977* (NSW) s. 49ZG.
53 *Oncale v Sundowner Offshore Services* 523 US 75 (1998). Cf. *Quick v Donaldson Co Inc.* 90 F 3d 1372 (8th Cir, 1996). See also Marianne C. DelPo, 'The Thin Line between Love and Hate: Same Sex Hostile Environment Sexual Harassment' (2000) 51(1) *Labor Law Journal* 15.
54 Richard Collier, *Masculinities, Crime and Criminology* (Sage, 1998); R.W. Connell, *Masculinities* (Allen & Unwin, 1995); Cynthia Cockburn, *In the Way of Women: Men's Resistance to Sex Equality in Organizations* (Macmillan, 1991).

The gender of authority

In the face of the ostensible imperative to modernise corporate workplaces by appointing women to authoritative positions, there has been a strong rearguard action to maintain the hierarchical status quo. The metaphor of the glass ceiling captures the way that well-qualified and competent women often reach a point in organisations beyond which they are not promoted. Whether one looks at private corporations, the professions, universities or public entities, the same gendered pyramidal structure is clearly discernible. Masculinist cultures of authority may implicitly condone the scapegoating and harassment of individual women who have been promoted to the higher echelons as a strategy for impugning their ability.[55] The vestiges of fraternity—still prominent in blue-collar employment, the police force and the armed services—are also discernible in professional and authoritative enclaves. The difference is that the harassing conduct is usually more insidious, in both its character and its effects, so it is difficult to make out a complaint. In other words, it may be less overtly heterosexed.

This category of behaviour includes a panoply of harassing acts, often of a petty and repetitive kind. It includes verbal putdowns, patronising or abusive remarks and excessive criticism of work performed.[56] It may also include marginalising conduct, such as failing to consult the complainant on matters over which she has responsibility,[57] or making it difficult for her to access resources and obtain the necessary approvals to carry out her job properly.[58] Any failures then appear to be her fault. As Schultz points out, 'characterizing women as incompetent … is a central component of the harassment'.[59] I suggest this behaviour is pervasive within the pyramidal apex of many organisations, long preserved as a masculinist domain of power and authority, albeit increasingly under challenge.

---

55   Julie Hare, 'The Paradox of Power: Why Men Target Women Leaders', *BroadAgenda*, 3 August 2020, available from: www.broadagenda.com.au/2020/the-paradox-of-power-why-women-in-leadership-are-targets-for-harassers/.
56   Judith Wyatt & Chauncey Hare, *Work Abuse: How to Recognize and Survive It* (Schenkman, 1997) 4–10.
57   Valerie Sutherland & Cary Cooper, *Strategic Stress Management: An Organizational Approach* (Palgrave Macmillan, 2000) 171.
58   Emily Bassman, *Abuse in the Workplace: Management Remedies and Bottom Line Impact* (Praeger, 1992) 43–50.
59   Schultz (n. 3) 1754.

The problem is that while harassing conduct is undoubtedly unwelcome, it may not constitute 'conduct of a sexual nature' for the purposes of a sexual harassment proscription, such as that of the *SDA* (s. 28A[2]). In the absence of a specifically sexual dimension, a complainant would have to rely on general sex discrimination provisions, such as denial of access to a benefit in employment (*SDA* s. 14[2][b]) or subjection 'to any other detriment' (s. 14[2][d]). The complainant then has the burden of proving that the discrimination occurred by virtue of sex (or marital status, pregnancy, sexual orientation or other ground under the *SDA*). While the burden of proof is onerous at any formal antidiscrimination hearing, harassment of this kind is even less tractable to remediation because it represents a manifestation of systemic discrimination that is ever-present at a subliminal level, constituting and reconstituting authority at work in masculinist terms. The complainant has the burden of proving that the unwelcome conduct was directed at her by virtue of her sex, rather than, say, because the harasser just happened to be an inept manager or an unpleasant person. Repeated micro-inequities also lack the dramatic impact of salacious heterosexed behaviour of the Harvey Weinstein kind that attracted worldwide attention and resulted in the #MeToo movement. The tendency of tribunals and courts to disaggregate and dissect a string of incidents separately can have the effect of detracting from the overall discriminatory effect of a complaint. A single heterosexualised act, marked by lasciviousness and lust, invariably trumps a succession of seemingly trivial putdowns, even though the latter may reveal more about structural discrimination on the ground of sex than the former.

This more insidious manifestation of harassment was recognised in New South Wales within a general proscription against sex discrimination, where the term 'sex-based harassment' was first used to distinguish it from the sexual variety. In *Hill v Water Resources Commission*,[60] the complainant had been appointed as the first clerical graded officer in her department where most of her co-workers were men. They said she would not fit in and ensured that she did not. There were no sexual overtures as such, although some sexually explicit material was displayed on noticeboards. For the most part, the harassment comprised an endless succession of petty acts, including nuisance telephone calls, threatening letters and heavy-handed 'jokes', such as pretending to have killed the complainant's goldfish. The NSW EOT held that the cumulative effect of the harassment contributed

---

60 [1985] EOC ¶92–127 (NSWEOT). The US Supreme Court recognised hostile workplace harassment as sex discrimination in *Meritor Savings Bank v Vinson* 477 US 57 (1986).

to the creation of a hostile working environment. The recognition that the petty vindictiveness and harassment, to which women pioneers in male-dominated workplaces are all too often subjected, constituted sex discrimination was an important step forward.

The second significant development in *Hill* related to the fact that the perpetrators of the harassment were not men in structural positions of 'power over' the complainant, as per the test articulated in *O'Callaghan*, but they were Ms Hill's co-workers. The senior men to whom she complained nevertheless condoned the harassment by failing to take action to stop it, thereby underscoring the fraternal bonds between the men in the organisation, regardless of their position in the hierarchy. Their inaction sufficed to make the statutory employer vicariously liable for the conduct of its employees. However, when the supervisors finally did act, their response was to transfer and demote the complainant, rather than the perpetrators— a resolution that would no longer be automatically accepted.[61]

Now that sexual harassment has been generally separated from sex discrimination in most legislation, it is doubtful whether Ms Hill would succeed if she were to lodge a complaint of sexual harassment under the current provisions. The decision established that a pattern of harassment arising from the sex of the complainant violates the proscription against sex discrimination; the conduct does not have to be sexual. In the case of women entering male-dominated areas of employment, the language of being 'offended, humiliated or intimidated' falls short of accurately capturing the discriminatory effect of the conduct to which Ms Hill was subjected. Under the NSW legislation, she would have to rely on the general prohibition of sex discrimination as 'less favourable treatment'. This is not only more difficult from a probative perspective, as the harassing conduct becomes entwined with the historical exclusion of women from positions of authority generally (which cannot be sheeted home to a particular respondent); it also becomes enmeshed with bona fide acts of management. It is notable, however, that the *SDA* was amended in 2021 to proscribe sex-based harassment (s. 28AA).

The masculinist nature of authority at the senior level of organisations, together with the countervailing antipathy towards the feminine, is clearly illustrated by *Dunn-Dyer v ANZ Banking Group Ltd*.[62] The complainant

---

61   For example, *Sharma v Bibby Financial Services Australia Pty Ltd* [2012] NSWSC 1157 (appeal dismissed: *Bibby Financial Services Australia Pty Ltd v Sharma* [2014] NSWCA 37).
62   [1997] EOC ¶92–897 (HREOC).

was appointed to a senior position in the banking industry—a domain where there are still comparatively few senior women.[63] Ms Dunn-Dyer complained of both sexual harassment and sex discrimination. The sexual harassment claim failed, although the dealing-room atmosphere was a masculinist and bawdy one that included posters of nude women and soft-porn magazines. At a 'Kris Kringle' Christmas Eve function, Ms Dunn-Dyer received a plastic jumping penis, although she had herself once donated a gift representing male genitalia. The inquiry commissioner was of the view that the onus of proof had not been satisfied to distinguish between 'consensual and harmless bawdiness' and a hostile workplace. The subtext here would seem to be that to succeed on the sexual harassment count, Ms Dunn-Dyer was expected to step into the subject position of woman as 'fragile flower' and demonstrate how she was personally offended, rather than demonstrate how such conduct created an environment that discriminated against women.

In the separate sex discrimination claim, the evidence revealed the complainant had been subjected to a constant barrage of disparaging remarks, including being referred to as 'mother hen' and her department as 'the kindergarten nursery' and the 'mothers' club'. The evidence of one senior manager denied that the term 'mother hen' was derogatory: 'I didn't introduce you as the mother hen. I introduced you, then described your role as a mother hen.' The commission disagreed with the witness, finding that the remarks were not only derogatory but also had influenced the assessment of the managerial qualities of the complainant, including the amalgamation of her department with that of another.[64] The decision to restructure and dispense with her position was found to be a calculated decision to get rid of her.

Nevertheless, the disparagement and construction of the complainant as someone unfit to hold a managerial position were held to be inadequate to establish why she was not appointed to the position of state treasurer with the bank. The long experience and seniority of the successful male appointee were accepted as foreclosing a finding of sex discrimination on this point. This aspect of the complaint underscores the difficulty of meeting the burden of proof in a context where the bona fide but elusive

---

63   Sara Charlesworth, 'Working Mums: The Construction of Women Workers in the Banking Industry' (1999) 4(2) *Journal of Interdisciplinary Gender Studies* 12, 14, 18–19.
64   Charlesworth has argued that even though Susan Dunn-Dyer did not have children, the disparaging references to motherhood were designed to suggest that she belonged to a category of workers who were not serious about their careers (ibid., 20).

concept of merit (discussed in Chapters 11 and 15) is all-important. The reasons for the restructuring and the redundancy were more obviously pretextual; they were extreme acts for which no credible rationale could be adduced.

The disaggregation of the sexual harassment and the sex discrimination in this case reveals the artificiality of the approach. Clearly, the dealing-room atmosphere and the disparagement of Ms Dunn-Dyer were related. A more holistic approach would have shown how the complainant's competence was systematically undermined by the various kinds of harassment—including sexualised displays and gender disparagement—all of which contributed to the creation of a hostile workplace environment, which would have been damaging for any woman in an authoritative position. *Dunn-Dyer* illustrates my point that disaggregation has the effect of trivialising sexual harassment claims by disconnecting them from the discriminatory factors that animate them.

Work rage

My next stop on the harassment continuum is bullying, which is reported to have increased as a corollary of increased managerialism.[65] Harassment is bullying by another name, which, in the case of repeated and unreasonable behaviour, is now proscribed in Australia under the *Fair Work Act 2009* (Cth), Part 6, although some workers who have experienced bullying and suffered significant psychiatric effects have secured substantial damages by recourse to tort law.[66] However, if the complainant can establish that the bullying behaviour occurred on the ground of sex (or other proscribed ground), they may have recourse to a remedy under antidiscrimination legislation. Petty acts of harassment may be successfully subsumed within the rubric of sex discrimination in the context of an attempt to expel the complainant from a masculinist workplace, as in *Hill*, but harassment and management are not otherwise easily disentangled. As Finn J points out, 'it is not workplace harassment for managers to manage'.[67] But where does management end and harassment begin? The neoliberal presumption in favour of employer prerogative has served to heighten the burden of

---

65   Lesley Wright & Marti Smye, *Corporate Abuse: How 'Lean and Mean' Robs People and Profits* (Macmillan, 1996) 50–54.
66   For example, *Swan v Monash Law Book Co-Operative* [2013] VSC 326; *Keegan v Sussan Corporation (Aust) Pty Ltd* [2014] QSC 64.
67   *Kelson v Forward* (1995) 60 FCR 39, 56.

proof for complainants. Unless a complainant can support an allegation of sex discrimination with persuasive evidence, such as being the first and only woman in a particular position (as with *Hill* or *Dunn-Dyer*), a presumption in favour of management prevails. Even if the harassment is conceptualised as the aberrant act of an inept manager, it is nonetheless deemed to be 'managing'.

In *Malone v Pike*,[68] the main allegation of sexual harassment was that the respondent poked the complainant in the chest and told her to do what she was told. The Human Rights and Equal Opportunity Commission (HREOC), while conceding that such behaviour was 'unwelcome, and reasonably likely to offend', held that it was not conduct of a sexual nature for the purposes of the *SDA*. In *Hosemans v Crea's Glenara Motel Pty Ltd*,[69] the HREOC held that calling the complainant a 'stupid bitch' and telling her that she had a 'fat arse' were personal abuse rather than sexual harassment. In contrast, the conduct in *Gray v Victoria*,[70] where the school principal shook a packet of Ratsak in the complainant's face and said that 'he would "get a rat"', was accepted as an element of victimisation waged against the complainant because she lodged a complaint alleging both sexual harassment and sex discrimination. The tribunal was of the view that a male teacher would not have been intimidated in the same manner.

One could come to a similar conclusion about being poked in the chest, especially as a woman's chest may be indistinguishable from her breasts— an undeniably erogenous zone. Furthermore, the 'stupid bitch' and 'fat arse' remarks also carry with them sexual overtones. Their rejection as sexual harassment by the inquiry commissioner reveals how sexual abuse has come to be normalised within everyday speech. It also underscores my point that sexual harassment is more likely to be legally cognisable if it involves heterosexed conduct. Verbal abuse may be found to constitute sexual harassment, provided it can be shown to have given rise to the requisite humiliation, loss of dignity or injury to feelings. However, it is not sexed or sex-based abuse, but sexual abuse that is necessary. Thus, it is the element of 'recurrent sexual innuendo' associated with the abuse that locates it within the terms of the legislative proscription.[71] Generally speaking, to succeed, the abuse needs to be combined with other instances of discrimination arising from specified grounds, as in *Hopper*.

---

68 [1996] EOC ¶92–868.
69 [2000] EOC ¶93–062.
70 [1999] EOC ¶92–996 (VCAT).
71 *Hall v Naismith* [1994] EOC ¶92–587(1) (HREOC).

The point is illustrated by *Djokic v Sinclair*,[72] in which the complainant's superior and co-workers at a meatworks regularly referred to her as a 'stupid wog bitch' and a 'fucking wog bitch'. In this case, the racist element was intermingled with incidents of sexual harassment and sex discrimination. The complainant succeeded in respect of all grounds, but there was some question about her ability to satisfy the burden of proof had the various incidents been disaggregated. The HREOC acknowledged that the threatening words constituted a serious abuse of power, which could be characterised as sexual harassment, but it questioned whether flicking the complainant's bra strap and touching the top of her trousers constituted deliberate touching of a sexual nature. While the HREOC accepted that the sustained hostility towards Ms Djokic amounted to sexual harassment in its broad sense, establishing the sexual in sexual harassment is not straightforward, even when it involves touching, unless it is unequivocally (hetero)sexualised.

In the absence of other manifestations of discrimination, sexualised verbal harassment—a common form of bullying—seems to fall into the space that has been created by the artificial line of demarcation between sexual harassment and sex discrimination. Abusive, infantilising and demeaning language directed towards women is woven into the social script. A study of women lawyers in the United States revealed that almost all women aged under 35 working in the private sector were vulnerable to gender disparagement, although being an older woman in a private law firm also afforded little protection.[73] Such conduct does not clearly meet the legislative test for sexual harassment and it is unlikely to satisfy the test for sex discrimination either. It is all too easy to aver that verbal taunts, physical assaults and other manifestations of hatred and dislike are perpetrated by rude, insensitive and mean-spirited bullies, rather than sex discriminators. However, the application of a simple 'but for' test rebuts a finding of sex neutrality: but for the fact the target was a woman, one might postulate she would not have been subjected to the demeaning conduct. Not only is it unlikely that benchmark man would be called 'a stupid bitch'; there is also no comparable phrase in common usage that encapsulates quite the same degree of sexualised contempt for men.

---

72   [1994] EOC ¶92–643.
73   Janet Rosenberg, Harry Perlstadt & William R.F. Phillips, 'Now That We Are Here: Discrimination, Disparagement, and Harassment at Work and the Experience of Women Lawyers' (1993) 7(3) *Gender and Society* 415, 429, doi.org/10.1177/089124393007003006.

Probative and psychic burdens

Conciliation remains the primary mode of dispute resolution in antidiscrimination legislation.[74] The confidentiality associated with the process, which normally extends to nondisclosure agreements, means few details are made public.[75] While 48 per cent of finalised sex discrimination complaints were conciliated successfully in 2019–20, a high proportion are withdrawn, lapse or are terminated.[76] A minuscule percentage of complaints lodged proceed to hearing, representing only the most dedicated of complainants and the most obdurate of respondents. The corporate respondents who hold out are determined to win at all costs, as discussed in Chapter 9, because a complaint to an outside body represents a threat to both managerial authority and fraternal integrity— hence, the strong disapprobation of 'dobbing'.

As a public lesson to any other employee thinking of complaining, respondents often set out to destroy a complainant's credibility by arguing that (she) improperly eroticised the workplace, displayed incompetence or otherwise transgressed professional norms. They are prepared to devote substantial resources to defending the action, which few complainants can match—particularly if they are unemployed at the time of a hearing, as is frequently the case. The case of *Dunn-Dyer*, discussed above, is exemplary. Ms Dunn-Dyer lodged her complaint in 1992, but a decision was not handed down until five years later. The case involved weeks of hearing, spanning 14 months. The transcript amounted to more than 4,000 pages. Although the complainant 'won' at the inquiry level, and the respondent bank chose not to appeal, few women have the fortitude, tenacity or resources to withstand such a gruelling experience if conciliation fails. There is not only a gross financial inequality between a large corporation and an unemployed individual (often lacking union support),[77] but also the corporate employer has a monopoly over the evidence and access to employee witnesses who may be fearful of being scapegoated and placing

---

74 Thornton (n. 11) Ch. 5.
75 Dominique Allen & Alysia Blackham, 'Under Wraps: Secrecy, Confidentiality and the Enforcement of Equality Law in Australia and the United Kingdom' (2019) 43(2) *Melbourne University Law Review* 384.
76 AHRC, *2019–20 Complaint Statistics* (AHRC, 2021), available from: humanrights.gov.au/sites/default/files/2020-10/AHRC_AR_2019-20_Complaint_Stats_FINAL.pdf.
77 A union cannot always be relied on. In *Horne v Press Clough Joint Venture* [1994] EOC ¶92–591, the union was held jointly liable for participating in the campaign of harassment and intimidation of the complainants.

their jobs in jeopardy if they decline to testify. There is no recompense for the additional trauma incurred by a complainant who withstands the years it may take to reach a settlement. Susan Dunn-Dyer received a mere A\$10,000 for emotional harm calculated to the time of lodgement of her complaint. Although she received A\$125,000 for economic loss,[78] no allowance was made for her legal costs—a sum that may have exceeded the damages award. In no way did the damages compensate her for the loss of her career. She had lost her job five years previously and the public nature of the hearing ensured she was unlikely ever to be employed by a bank again. Misogynistic images of 'the troublemaking and complaining woman' are difficult to dislodge for professional and high-status women who pursue justice through formal avenues.

In addition, there is always a psychic difficulty faced by the survivor who complains about having been harassed by either a boss or co-workers. To complain formally means one has to step into the shoes of 'the victim', which can be just as humiliating and disempowering as enduring the harassment itself—sometimes more so, particularly for senior women: 'To conform to the image of the proper victim, women must comport themselves as sexually pure, even passive, beings who have been violated by their co-workers' sexual predation.'[79] As with any civil action, harm must be proven by survivors. If they have survived seemingly intact due to self-help measures, which may include resigning and securing another position, they can expect minimal damages—a problem that inheres within the compensatory model of civil remediation. The fact that costs are not awarded in all antidiscrimination jurisdictions may induce rational targets to cut their losses and not pursue a legal remedy at all, unless they are altruistically committed to calling the respondent to account publicly. Having to assume the trappings of the 'victim' is one of the paradoxes of a statutory scheme geared towards compensation.[80] It may be easier for

---

78 Kenny J sought to remedy the undervaluation of damages in sexual harassment cases in *Richardson v Oracle Corporation Australia Pty Limited (No. 2)* [2013] FCA 359. See Madeleine Castles, Tom Hvala & Kieran Pender, 'Rethinking *Richardson*: Sexual Harassment Damages in the #MeToo Era' (2021) 49(2) *Federal Law Review*, doi.org/10.1177/0067205X21993146.

79 Schultz (n. 3) 1732.

80 The 'make whole' principle or restoring the injured person to the position he or she would have been in but for the wrongful act is the underlying principle of tort law—the closest analogy to antidiscrimination law. *Hall v A & A Sheiban* (1989) 20 FCR 217, 239 (Lockhart J). For a detailed discussion of remedies, see W. Covell, K. Lupton & L. Parsons, *Covell & Lupton Principles of Remedies* (LexisNexis, 7th edn, 2018).

the targets of heterosexed conduct to satisfy the probative burden than for those subjected to sex-based harassment. Indeed, the latter may agonise over whether to complain formally or not.

The experience of a woman lawyer whom I interviewed illustrates the point very well.[81] She was at lunch with a client and the senior (male) partner of her law firm when she said something that the partner did not like. He pretended to drop his napkin, bent down to pick it up and, in the process, slapped the woman on the thigh. She was outraged but felt that she could not do or say anything even though, technically, an assault had occurred. To whom could she speak? What words could she use? The indignity would have only been magnified were she to have recounted her experience to a person in authority. The effect of giving voice to the unwelcome behaviour would probably serve only to strengthen male solidarity, thereby confirming the outsider status of women in the legal workplace. The corporeal act remained ineffable because it demeaned the woman as an authoritative knower whether she complained or not. In formal terms, the conduct was also problematic. It was clearly sexed and discriminatory, in that it is doubtful whether the hypothetical benchmark man would ever be subjected to such treatment, but it was not clearly sexualised in terms of the legislative prescript. Thus, as I have argued, it is easier to pursue a complaint of sexual harassment than of sex-based harassment, but there are powerful psychic factors that inhibit the lodging of workplace discrimination complaints of any kind, either inhouse or externally. Complainants may then choose to ignore the harassment or deal with it in some other way—most commonly by leaving the workplace. Nevertheless, their silence may be interpreted as a form of complicity, for it lacks broader social impact. This is the paradox of sexual harassment.

Conclusion

The separation of sexual harassment from sex discrimination and sex-based discrimination reinforces the view that what is defined as 'sexual' is, like rape, based on a male perspective. That is, the paradigm involves a male subject who is the actor and an objectified woman or feminised man who is acted on. Thus, the conduct of a man importuning sexual favours or exposing himself is characterised as unproblematically

---

81 Thornton (n. 50) 248.

sexual. However, as soon as we move away from the paradigm, we begin to encounter problems. Abuse, taunts, insults and other everyday micro-inequities that are sexed are trivialised and dismissed because they are deemed to be insufficiently sexual. Over time, daily putdowns may exercise a more corrosive effect on the authority and sense of self of a targeted employee than a single unwanted sexual overture. The 'stupid bitch' remark denigrates all women, but is the 'reasonable person' likely to be 'offended, humiliated or intimidated' by it when such remarks have become normalised within everyday speech? As suggested, abusive epithets in common parlance are generally not regarded as sexual harassment, although words that suggest sexual intercourse and intimate body parts probably carry the requisite degree of sexualisation. The misogyny encapsulated by such language is a facet of systemic or society-wide discrimination that is not comprehensible within an individualised complaint-based regime. The propensity to adopt a 'biological' approach to sexual harassment and sex discrimination facilitates sloughing off the social to appear normal and even natural.

While it is a positive development that sexual harassment is now widely recognised as a compensable harm, it is a blunt instrument of remediation. The hegemony of the heterosexed paradigm has caused feminist, as well as legal and popular, discourses to lose sight of the ways that harassment at work is sexed, not just sexualised. Sexual harassment claims reify the liberal binarism that 'the mind', which biologically 'has no sex',[82] is masculine, while corporeality is marked as female or Other. While this gendered mind/sex binarism is under challenge every day, emphasising the sexual in sexual harassment simultaneously reproduces it. The normativity of the masculine body, especially when clothed in a dark suit, enables it to assume an aura of depersonalised authority within the workplace. A woman complaining about (heterosexed) sexual harassment to a male boss, male tribunal member or male judge in a hearing or courtroom invariably overflowing with male lawyers reifies that binarism. This is always the dilemma for complainants because there is a discursive power associated with naming that which was formerly suppressed.

---

82   Londa Schiebinger, *The Mind Has No Sex? Women in the Origins of Modern Science* (Harvard University Press, 1989) 1. The original quote, '*L'esprit n'a point de sexe*', is attributed to Francois Poullain de la Barre. See also Genevieve Lloyd, *The Man of Reason: 'Male' and 'Female' in Western Philosophy* (Macmillan, 1984).

Sexual harassment has entered public discourse only because individual women and non-dominant others have courageously spoken out. In the absence of challenge, all the hard work of the women's movement is quickly papered over. We see how dramatically this has occurred since the proscription was introduced—how a neoliberal social script rarely mentions women in public life, other than in subordinate positions or in sexualised subject positions.[83] The stressful bullying cultures legitimated by neoliberalism, in which workers are expected to work ever harder to increase profit margins, are not readily tractable to remediation through antidiscrimination avenues in which the complainant bears the burden of proof.

As systemic sex discrimination is entrenched within the culture of the workplace, more than a little tweaking of the present legislative model would be required to address widespread sexual harassment and effect substantive equality for women at work. The imposition of a positive duty on employers, as recommended by the AHRC in *Respect@Work*, would not necessarily eliminate sexual harassment as a manifestation of violence against women, but it could substantially minimise it. Lawyers' most powerful clients are corporations, as discussed in Chapter 9, and they will seek to define whatever words appear in legislation to their clients' advantage, which means there is comparatively little interest in the broader ramifications of social change.[84]

Perhaps the environment of neoliberalism has caused us all to be less vigilant in permitting a linguistic shift from discrimination to managerialism to occur, cloaking sex-based harassment in the workplace. Harassment not only demeans all women and non-dominant workers in respect of their professionalism and authority, but it also detracts from the idea that they are full citizens.

---

83   The scandal involving political staffer Brittany Higgins in Parliament House, Canberra, in 2021 is illustrative. See Massola (n. 21).

84   Cf. Beth Gaze, 'The *Sex Discrimination Act* at 25: Reflections on the Past, Present and Future' in Margaret Thornton (ed.), *Sex Discrimination in Uncertain Times* (ANU Press, 2010) 124, doi.org/10.22459/SDUT.09.2010.05.

Part IV: Engendering Legal Practice

6

Hypercompetitiveness or a Balanced Life?

Introduction

Reaching the tipping point

There is much talk of the feminisation of the legal profession in many parts of the world because of the rapidly changing gender demographic.[1] In a number of countries, including Australia, women now make up more than 60 per cent of law graduates[2] and more than 50 per cent of practising solicitors.[3] The apex of the pyramid, which is associated with autonomy, power and authority, long remained resolutely masculinised, but has changed in recent years in the large corporate firms,[4] although

---

1   Ulrike Schultz & Gisela Shaw (eds), *Women in the World's Legal Professions* (Hart, 2003).
2   Women make up approximately two-thirds of all law students in Australia and have represented a majority since 1993. See Andrew Norton & Ittima Cherastidtham, *Mapping Australian Higher Education 2018* (Grattan Institute, 2018), available from: apo.org.au/sites/default/files/resource-files/2018-09/apo-nid192826_0.pdf.
3   Law Society of New South Wales, *2020 National Profile of Solicitors: Final* (Urbis, 2021) 7–9, available from: www.lawsociety.com.au/sites/default/files/2021-07/2020%20National%20Profile%20of%20Solicitors%20-%20Final%20-%201%20July%202021.pdf.
4   This is now as high as 31 per cent for partnerships, but somewhat less for equity partners. See Hannah Wootton & Edmund Tadros, 'Women Grab Record Half of New Law Partner Promotions', *Australian Financial Review*, 9 December 2021, available from: www.afr.com/companies/professional-services/women-grab-record-half-of-new-law-partner-promotions-20211130-p59dda#:~:text=Women%20now%20comprise%201184%20of,the%20January%202022%20promotion%20period. In the 47 top-level UK firms that provided data, 23 per cent of equity partners were women in 2021. See Meganne Tillay, 'Which Law Firms Have the Most Female Equity Partners?', *Law.Com International*, 13 July 2021, available from: www.law.com/international-edition/2021/07/13/which-law-firms-have-the-most-female-equity-partners/?slreturn=20220229205631#:~:text=While%20all%2068

the pace of change has encouraged some women to establish their own firms.[5] Throughout the Western intellectual tradition, the feminine has been constructed as an unruly force that is corrosive of rationality,[6] which has cemented the conjunction between masculinity, law and authority.

The historical animus towards women in the legal profession began to recede only at the turn of the millennium. As women were often the top students at law school, they could not be ignored indefinitely,[7] not only because of acceptance of the principle of equal opportunity, but also because of the growth in the economy, which substantially increased the demand for legal services. However, the residual distrust of the feminine in positions of authority lingered and women often found they were confined to managed or 'manned' positions;[8] the principle of meritocracy did not extend to promotional positions or partnerships, other than in 'exceptional' cases.

Nevertheless, any expression of concern about the ethics of a skewed gender demographic has invariably been fobbed off with the familiar refrain 'It's just a matter of time'[9]—a refrain that has become less compelling three decades after the gender tipping point was reached in law schools. A Law Society of New South Wales report of 2011 revealed that approximately 50 per cent of women who entered private practice over the previous 20 years had left within five years.[10] While a significant proportion of men also left, the proportion of women, particularly young women, was greater.[11] The high attrition rate resulted in pressure being

---

%20firms%20provided,23%25%20of%20the%20equity%20partnership. Women are similarly underrepresented in major leadership roles in US law firms where they make up 23 per cent of equity partners. See Debra Cassens Weiss, 'Female Lawyers Still Underrepresented, Especially in Partnership Ranks; Which Law Firms Do Best?', *ABA Journal*, 16 September 2021, available from: www.abajournal.com/news/article/female-lawyers-still-underrepresented-especially-in-partnership-ranks-which-law-firms-do-best.

5   Housnia Shams, 'Female Lawyers Outnumber Males, But Advocates Say More Women Are Needed in Senior Roles', *ABC Radio Sydney*, 21 July 2021, available from: www.abc.net.au/news/2021-07-21/women-lawyers-australia-gender-equality-newlaw-law-society-/100309294.

6   Genevieve Lloyd, *The Man of Reason: 'Male' and 'Female' in Western Philosophy* (Methuen, 1984).

7   Margaret Thornton, *Dissonance and Distrust: Women in the Legal Profession* (Oxford University Press, 1990). Cf. Eli Wald, 'Glass Ceilings and Dead Ends: Professional Ideologies, Gender Stereotypes, and the Future of Women Lawyers at Large Law Firms' (2010) 78 *Fordham Law Review* 101, 137.

8   Thornton (n. 7) 177–80. Cf. Deborah L. Rhode, 'The "No-Problem" Problem: Feminist Challenges and Cultural Change' (1991) 100(6) *Yale Law Journal* 1731, doi.org/10.2307/796785.

9   Margaret Thornton & Joanne Bagust, 'The Gender Trap: Flexible Work in Contemporary Legal Practice' (2007) 45(4) *Osgoode Hall Law Journal* 773–811, 775; Wald (n. 7) 108.

10   Law Society of New South Wales, *Thought Leadership 2011: Advancement of Women in the Profession* (Law Society of New South Wales, 2011) 14.

11   ibid., 7, 14. Cf. Wald (n. 7) 119.

placed on firms by women lawyers' associations to develop flexible work policies and rethink the construction of merit predicated on the norm of full-time work.[12]

However, at the very moment the profession acknowledged the high cost of attrition and the desirability of developing flexible work policies, hypercompetitiveness insidiously became the dominant ideology of large firms—in Australia, as elsewhere.[13] A rapacious form of capitalism came to be associated with the super-elite law firms as they scanned the globe seeking new sites for expansion—a phenomenon comparable to that animating their clients, the multinational corporations.[14] Like them, the super-elites evince a strikingly masculinist character as they aggressively seek new markets. Hypercompetitiveness, as Wald argues, requires the 'ideal lawyer' to sacrifice any suggestion of a personal life. The discourse of hypercompetitiveness is compounding the residual bias towards women in authoritative positions despite the embrace of flexible work. Indeed, the incommensurability of the discourses of flexible work and hypercompetitiveness operates to sustain the masculinity of legal practice, even though partnerships are contracting in favour of organisational bureaucracy. John Flood describes this as a shift away from 'patriarchal domination',[15] but the rise of global firms is instantiating a new form of patriarchal domination.

In this chapter, I contrast the reporting of flexible work initiatives with that of the amalgamations effected between Australian corporate law firms and United Kingdom–based super-elite firms. The language used in respect of the latter is far stronger and more compelling than in the comparatively lukewarm reporting of the former, which leads me to suggest that the ethic of implementing a work–life balance is effectively trumped by hypercompetition.

---

12   Wilkins, while focusing primarily on Black American lawyers, makes a compelling business case for diversity. See David B. Wilkins, 'From "Separate is Inherently Unequal" to "Diversity is Good for Business": The Rise of Market-Based Diversity Arguments and the Fate of the Black Corporate Bar' (2004) 117(5) *Harvard Law Review* 1584, doi.org/10.2307/4093260.

13   Wald (n. 7) 126. Cf. Richard Collier, *Men, Law and Gender: Essays on the 'Man' of Law* (Routledge, 2010) 170.

14   Jean Comaroff & John L. Comaroff, 'Millennial Capitalism: First Thoughts on a Second Coming' in Jean Comaroff & John L. Comaroff (eds), *Millennial Capitalism and the Culture of Neoliberalism* (Duke University Press, 2001), doi.org/10.2307/j.ctv11cw8vz.

15   John Flood, 'From Ethics to Regulation: The Re-Organization and Re-Professionalization of Large Law Firms in the 21st Century', 20 September 2011, available from: papers.ssrn.com/sol3/papers.cfm?abstract_id=1592324.

Two discourses and their ramifications

It is only recently that flexible work became a topic of national interest in Australia, prompted by the introduction of a paid parental leave scheme.[16] This is despite the fact that women lawyers had been advocating flexible work for years as a way of enhancing the participation of women and staunching the haemorrhage from private practice.[17] With the neoliberal turn, workers everywhere have been expected to work harder and longer, causing the demands for a balance between work and life to become correspondingly more vociferous. Indeed, work–life balance has been described as '*the* topic of the 21st Century for families, employers and government'.[18] Nevertheless, there are far fewer stories about flexible work in corporate law firms compared with those dealing with striking transnational mergers, expansion into new areas of the globe and the making of huge profits. The publication of league tables of annual profits generated[19] attests to the way the 'market metanarrative'[20] has entered the soul of the legal profession.

Ashis Nandy coined the word 'hypermasculinity' to describe the dominant culture in India under the British Raj.[21] The characteristics of manliness identified by Nandy—namely, aggression, achievement, control, competition and power[22]—correlate to a remarkable degree with the values currently extolled by global legal practice. This is not the fragile and nuanced notion of masculinity associated with lawyer-fathers about which Richard Collier writes insightfully,[23] but a more aggressive form that might be thought of as occupying one end of the masculinity continuum. Just as the hypermasculinist aspects of European personality were glorified under the Raj to supplant the once-valued feminine traits

---

16 *Paid Parental Leave Act 2010* (Cth).

17 For example, Victorian Women Lawyers, *A 360 Review: Flexible Work Practices—Confronting Myths and Realities in the Legal Profession Firms* (Victorian Women Lawyers, 2002).

18 Sarah Squire & Jo Tilley, *It's About Time: Women, Men, Work and Family* (Human Rights and Equal Opportunity Commission, 2007) xi.

19 The International Financial Law Firm Rankings (IFLR1000) is available across jurisdictions from: www.iflr1000.com/.

20 Peter Roberts, 'Rereading Lyotard: Knowledge, Commodification and Higher Education' (1998) 3 *Electronic Journal of Sociology*, available from: sociology.lightningpath.org/ejs-archives/vol003.003/roberts.html.

21 Ashis Nandy, *The Intimate Enemy: Loss and Recovery of Self under Colonialism* (Oxford University Press, 1983).

22 ibid., 9.

23 Collier (n. 13).

associated with Indian men, I suggest the dominant values associated with globalisation have been able to suppress competing discourses in the context of contemporary corporate legal practice in a comparable way.

Indeed, Nandy believed that for hypermasculinity to survive, it needed to be sustained through a colonisation of the mind, or ideological colonisation.[24] Raewyn Connell's cognate concept of 'hegemonic masculinity'[25] carries with it a similar ideological message. Connell notes that the success of such a concept does not depend on being totalising or one-dimensional, as '"hegemony" does not mean total cultural dominance, the obliteration of alternatives. It means ascendancy achieved within a balance of forces, that is, a state of play.'[26] Thus, economic globalisation with its carapace of rationality can occlude its hypermasculinist underside. Just as hypermasculinity was ideologically functional to the British Raj, I suggest it also carries with it an ideological functionality because the feminisation of the legal profession looms as a reality. While aggression and competition have long been claimed as key characteristics of legal practice that have had a marginalising effect on women,[27] the hypercompetitiveness associated with globalisation has become a new site for the production of gender identity.[28] Thus, while the discourse of flexible work has come to the fore as the proportion of women in the legal profession has increased, it struggles to be heard in a global neoliberal climate in which the market has become the measure of all things.

In the news

To illustrate the intractability of the gender dynamic within the law firm culture, I examine the way corporate law firms and their activities were represented in the print media in the period 2011–12 in both the

24 Anshuman Prasad, 'The Gaze of the Other: Postcolonial Theory and Organizational Analysis' in Anshuman Prasad (ed.), *Postcolonial Theory and Organizational Analysis: A Critical Engagement* (Palgrave Macmillan, 2003) 3–43, doi.org/10.1057/9781403982292.

25 R.W. Connell, *Gender and Power: Society, the Person and Sexual Politics* (Allen & Unwin, 1987) 183–88, *et passim*.

26 ibid., 184. The concept of hegemony is derived from Antonio Gramsci, *Selections from the Prison Notebooks of Antonio Gramsci*, edited & translated by Quintin Hoare & Geoffrey Nowell Smith (International Publishers, 1971) 12–13, *et passim*.

27 Anne Spencer & David Podmore, 'Women Lawyers: Marginal Members of a Male-Dominated Profession' in Anne Spencer & David Podmore (eds), *In a Man's World: Essays on Women in Male-Dominated Professions* (Tavistock, 1987) 128.

28 Cf. Juanita Elias, 'Hegemonic Masculinities, the Multinational Corporation, and the Developmental State: Constructing Gender in "Progressive" Firms' (2008) 10(4) *Men and Masculinities* 405, 409, doi.org/10.1177/1097184x07306747.

United Kingdom and Australia. Not only had the *Australian Paid Parental Leave Act 2010* (Cth) just come into operation, but also the period coincided with a short burst of unprecedented activity involving mergers between London-based super-elite law firms and Australian national firms. Although it is recognised that newspaper readership is declining[29] as technological developments in e-space and social media take over,[30] reports of the global manoeuvring of corporate law firms are regularly included in the business and financial pages of certain broadsheets. Both *The Times* of London and *The Australian* devote a section each week to 'Legal Affairs'.

Newspapers as everyday sources of knowledge shape patterns of understanding about social phenomena. Conboy and Steel argue that the primary aim of newspapers is to create 'a selection of news tailored for a particular readership to create profit and/or exert influence on that readership'.[31] Hence, the 'quality' morning newspapers are able to 'dictate the dominant interpretation' of the important issues,[32] which aligns the 'news media coverage of the economy with the overall business interests of the corporate community'.[33] The globalisation of corporate law firms and their single-minded focus on profit maximisation comport with this coverage. The favoured standpoint endorses and legitimises the status quo and provides little critique. The conjunction of the values of aggression, competition, power and corporate legal practice become intimately imbricated with masculinity and success in the reporting of global deals. Through the exclusive focus on competition and capital accumulation, we see how 'linguistic representations have the power to simultaneously describe and produce phenomena'.[34]

---

29   For example, RonNell Anderson Jones, 'Litigation, Legislation and Democracy in a Post-Newspaper America' (2011) 68 *Washington and Lee Law Review* 557.

30   Professional electronic services such as *Lawyers Weekly* may be supplanting newspapers, with Twitter and social media serving a somewhat different purpose. See, for example, Patrick M. Ellis, '140 Characters or Less: An Experiment in Legal Research' (2014) 42(2) *International Journal of Legal Information* 303, doi.org/10.1017/s0731126500012075.

31   Martin Conboy & John Steel, 'The Future of Newspapers' (2008) 9(5) *Journalism Studies* 650, 651.

32   Geoffrey Craig, *The Media, Politics and Public Life* (Allen & Unwin, 2004) 8.

33   Christopher J. Kollmeyer, 'Corporate Interests: How the New Media Portray the Economy' (2004) 51(3) *Social Problems* 432, 435, doi.org/10.1525/sp.2004.51.3.432.

34   Marcel Broersma, 'The Unbearable Limitations of Journalism: On Press Critique and Journalism's Claim to Truth' (2010) 72(1) *International Communication Gazette* 21, 26, doi.org/10.1177/174804 8509350336.

In the process of conveying information, the media contributes to an understanding of 'the way things are', not through coercion but by what is essentially a form of 'soft power'.[35] In writing from the dominant perspective, the media can be seen as 'an agency supportive of élite interests and élite frameworks of interpretation'.[36] The positive representation of aggressive conduct insidiously normalises the hypermasculinist subtext and undermines the efforts of those seeking to improve the status of women in the profession. Indeed, media studies more generally have shown that women's voices, experiences and expertise continue to be regarded as less important than those of men.[37] The Global Media Monitoring Project, for example, which involves more than 100 countries, reveals that there has been a shift in the 15 years since the project began, but change is slow and equivocal as new forms of sexism have a habit of appearing. Global hypercompetition between super-elite law firms is one such new form as law firms have traditionally been almost entirely domestic in orientation. In the face of profit maximisation on the global stage, the progressive and ostensibly gender-neutral discourse of flexible work has retained the seeds of invidiousness associated with the feminine.

Although films, television sitcoms and novels are significant manifestations of popular culture that portray lawyers and law firm ideology insightfully,[38] the characters and settings are fictional—albeit sometimes thinly disguised—whereas newspaper accounts purport to report the doings of real people. This projection of 'the real' thereby enables newspapers to play a crucial role in the construction and production of the dominant form of masculinity together with the marginalisation of the feminine in the context of reporting the activities of super-elite corporate law firms. Another reason for looking at newspapers rather than more enduring scholarly texts is that comparatively little research has been conducted

---

35   John Corner, *Theorising Media: Power, Form and Subjectivity* (Manchester University Press, 2011) 14.

36   ibid., 40.

37   Karen Ross & Cynthia Carter, 'Women and News: A Long and Winding Road' (2011) 33(8) *Media, Culture & Society* 1148, doi.org/10.1177/0163443711418272. The visibility of men through the privileged status of sport is notorious. See, for example, Louise North, 'The Gendered World of Sports Reporting in the Australian Print Media' *Journalism, Media and Cultural Studies (JOMEC) Journal*, 2 November 2012, 1.

38   See, for example, Michael Asimow (ed.), *Lawyers in Your Living Room: Law on Television* (ABA Press, 2009); Michael D. Freeman (ed.), *Law and Popular Culture* (Oxford University Press, 2005); Richard Sherwin, *When the Law Goes Pop: The Vanishing Line between Law and Popular Culture* (University of Chicago Press, 2002); Margaret Thornton (ed.), *Romancing the Tomes: Popular Culture, Law and Feminism* (Cavendish Publishing, 2002).

on global mergers.[39] The print media is a valuable primary source that provides a snapshot of contemporary thinking at a given moment and inevitably influences the views of law firm elites and society more generally. It is suggested that the hypercompetitive ideology represented in the print media operates to sustain the conventional distinction between the masculinist movers and shakers at the apex of the super-elite law firms and the feminised underclass at the pyramidal base who are more likely to be associated with flexible work.

Searches were conducted through the electronic database Factiva, as well as hardcopies of newspapers where practicable. While leading newspapers in both the United Kingdom and Australia—broadsheets and tabloids— were searched, most accounts appeared in two leading broadsheets, *The Times* (London) and *The Australian* (Sydney).[40] The *Financial Times* (London) and the *Australian Financial Review* (Sydney) also contained many references to law firm amalgamations, but there were otherwise relatively few stories on the global growth of law firms or their flexible work policies. The tabloids were more interested in the transgressions of individual lawyers than the financial activities of law firms, unless the latter were also scandalous, but such representations were outside my study, as were the stereotypical representations of women in law.[41]

Work–life balance

I begin with the representation of flexible work practices, which are regarded as the key to a successful integration of work and life, including caring responsibilities.[42] The essence of flexible work is that workers themselves exercise a modicum of autonomy over when and where the

---

39   But see Kath Hall, *The expansion of global law firms in Australia and Asia* (ANU College of Law Research Paper No. 13-12, The Australian National University, 7 August 2013), available from: papers.ssrn.com/sol3/papers.cfm?abstract_id=2307333; Bruce E. Aronson, 'Elite Law Firm Mergers and Reputational Competition: Is Bigger Really Better? An International Comparison' (2007) 40 *Vanderbilt Journal of Transnational Law* 763, 777.

40   It is notable that both these papers are owned by News Corporation, which is controlled by media baron Rupert Murdoch. They both evince a conservative and pro-capitalist stance.

41   For an insightful study, see Hannah Brenner & Renee Newman Knake, 'Rethinking Gender Equality in the Legal Profession's Pipeline to Power: A Study on Media Coverage of Supreme Court Nominees (Phase 1, the Introduction Week)' (2012) 84(2) *Temple Law Review* 325, available from: www.templelawreview.org/article/84-2_knake-brenner/.

42   Barbara Pocock, Natalie Skinner & Philippa Williams, *Time Bomb: Work, Rest and Play in Australia Today* (NewSouth Publishing, 2012) 95.

work is carried out. As Reiter points out, work–life balance is primarily about maximising the satisfaction of workers.[43] As I will show in the next section, this individualised orientation contrasts with the hypercompetitive environment that characterises global legal practice.

Like hypercompetitiveness, flexible work is a concept that is neutral on its face but is undeniably gendered because it carries with it a cluster of values associated with caring that are marked as feminine in the social script. A linguistic study by Smithson and Stokoe confirmed the feminised connotations as participants regularly reproduced gender differences while maintaining the myth of working in a non-gendered organisation.[44] The characteristics associated with the feminine have conventionally led to women being expected to assume the preponderance of society's caring responsibilities—in the public as well as the private spheres. Hence, in law firms, women are more likely to play a role in so-called soft areas, such as human resources.[45] Alternatively, they find themselves confined to managed positions or are treated as invisible, as is the case with the large numbers of ancillary legal workers—paralegals and administrators—who work behind the scenes.[46] Despite the ethical ramifications for the careers of women lawyers, flexible work policies are functional for law firms as women have become an essential component of the legal workforce.[47]

Newspaper reports tell us we have moved beyond mere rhetoric and that a more progressive stance is now being adopted by corporate law firms towards men and women with family responsibilities, including those in senior positions. *The Australian*, which produces an annual flexible work survey of the top firms, revealed in its 2012 survey that formal 'working-from-home' arrangements rose by a 'staggering' 65 per cent in the top 13 Australian law firms in one year, of whom a small number proceeded to partner.[48] These data support my argument that there is a greater

---

43   Natalie Reiter, 'Work Life Balance: What DO You Mean? The Ethical Ideology Underpinning Appropriate Application' (2007) 43(2) *Journal of Applied Behavioral Science* 273, 289, doi.org/10.1177/0021886306295639.

44   Janet Smithson & Elizabeth H. Stokoe, 'Discourses of Work–Life Balance: Negotiating "Genderblind" Terms in Organizations' (2005) 12(2) *Gender, Work and Organization* 147, 159–60, doi.org/10.1111/j.1468-0432.2005.00267.x.

45   Lisa Pryor, *The Pinstriped Prison: How Over Achievers Get Trapped in Corporate Jobs They Hate* (Pan Macmillan, 2008) 78, 181.

46   Andrew Francis, *At the Edge of Law: Emergent and Divergent Models of Legal Professionalism* (Ashgate, 2011), 77 *et passim*.

47   For an international overview, see Schultz & Shaw (n. 1).

48   Ainslie van Onselen, 'Home is Where the Work is as Firms Get Flexible', *The Australian*, 18 January 2013, 25.

receptiveness on the part of corporate law firms towards flexible work for women lawyers in managed or 'manned' positions—a finding that is borne out by previous studies.[49]

References to flexible work policies often appear in media interviews with corporate law firms: 'We have flexible hours when needed and 22 per cent of our partners are female.'[50] This statement occurred in the context of a discussion of international travel but there was no advertence to the challenges that travel might pose for those with caring responsibilities.

There is nevertheless an apparent desire on the part of the print media to project law firms as progressive. Good news stories about flexible work practices abound and are clearly intended to encourage firms that are lagging in the development of policies. These stories are also intended to encourage women to enter or remain in private practice.[51] One account noted with approval that Freshfields in London permitted staff to 'pick up children from day-care, put them to bed and then work later in the evenings',[52] but there was no indication of just how far into the night they were expected to work. Typical of the good news stories was one that involved the appointment of a pregnant woman to a partnership at an Australian firm:

> Ms Walker worked three days a week and was about to head off on maternity leave to have her second child, but CBP's [Colin Biggers & Paisley] partners were undeterred. Ms Walker, whose son Andrew was born 11 weeks ago, said she was worried that her family commitments would make it too tough to be a partner but the law firm's management convinced her otherwise. 'I was a bit hesitant', she said. 'But they were really supportive. They said, "It doesn't make a scrap of difference whether you're pregnant or not; we want you as one of our partners".'[53]

---

49 Thornton & Bagust (n. 9).

50 Kate Weaver, Human Resources Director for DLA Piper, quoted in Louis White, 'Law Firm Puts its Breadth to Good Use', [Weekend Professional], *The Australian*, 23 July 2011, 3.

51 For example, Nicola Berkovic, 'Bid to Hang on to Women Sees Baby Leave Soar', *The Australian*, 22 July 2011, 29.

52 Jenny Knight, 'Flexibility Keeps the Talented on Track: Being Successful Need Not Mean Working from Nine to Five', *The Times*, [London], 13 April 2011, 11.

53 Nicola Berkovic, 'Top Firm Works Hard to Redress Balance', *The Australian*, 16 December 2011, 30.

This treatment is shown to be in sharp contrast to the woman's negative experience at her previous firm where she was forced to resign when she sought unsuccessfully to take six months off to have her first child, even though she was already a partner. As conceptualised, flexible work suits the exceptional woman. If she can manage a full-time job in four days, others can, too, particularly if they always remain connected to clients. We are told that Corrs Chambers Westgarth partner Kirsty Sutherland became one of the nation's leading litigators while working part-time.[54] She usually does not go into the office on Fridays, but 'still takes calls if necessary' and works shorter hours on other days.

There is nevertheless a disjuncture between the rhetoric and the reality of flexible work. The accounts of individual women being treated less favourably when pregnant are legion:

> As recently as this year … a young (recently engaged) woman making budget was being managed out of an underperforming practice group in a large firm. In terminating her employment, the male partner told her that losing her job would not be the end of the world because she would soon be married and at home having babies. No doubt her colleagues who survived the cut stayed silent, smugly congratulating themselves for being tougher, smarter and better employees, and thus perpetuating the means-of-survival myth.[55]

As more than 87 per cent of part-time lawyers in private practice in Australia are female,[56] the ambivalence about women in law, particularly in authoritative positions, continues to impact disproportionately on them, causing them to be viewed as an employment risk.[57] There is a discrepancy between the flexible work policies of law firms reported in the media and the attitudes displayed towards individual lawyers in practice. The firms are applauded in newspaper accounts for adopting flexible work policies but rarely display the same positive attitude towards those who avail themselves of such policies.[58] As one lawyer said: 'The firm's

---

54   Nicola Berkovic, 'Benefits in Culture Change', *The Australian*, 4 November 2011, 37.

55   Emma MacDonald, 'Life in the Firm Still No Picnic for Women', *Sydney Morning Herald*, 9 June 2011, 15.

56   Nicola Berkovic, 'Part-Time Lure's Full-Time Reward: Leading Firms Willingly Pay to Retain Talent', *The Australian*, 4 November 2011, 37.

57   Angela T. Ragusa & Philip Groves, 'Gendered Meritocracy? Women Senior Counsels in Australia's Legal Profession' (2012) 1 *Australian Journal of Gender and Law* 1, 3.

58   Thornton & Bagust (n. 9); Pryor (n. 45) 179.

policy is not worth the paper it is written on.'[59] Many respondents to an online survey conducted by the author between May 2012 and May 2013 endorsed this view, reporting that they had been treated less seriously or penalised in their career aspirations for working flexibly in a manner approved by their firm.[60]

A subtext of the flexible work stories is that it is a luxury associated with the good times but dispensable in the bad. When things deteriorate, retaining one's clients, whatever the cost, is paramount. In a UK piece reporting on a poll involving 24,000 inhouse lawyers, two-thirds of whom opted for a shorter working week, the author suggested that attention could once more be paid to work–life balance because 'the slash-and-burn days of redundancy' associated with the effects of the GFC were over.[61] In contrast, the research of Sommerlad et al. found that firms were more willing to adopt flexible work strategies during the recession to avoid redundancies,[62] with the situation being reversed following an upswing in the economy. There is clearly ambivalence about flexible work in a context favouring dynamic growth.

Once a global firm is set on moving into Asia, Africa or war-torn Libya, facilitating a work–life balance for its lawyers, particularly in accommodating caring responsibilities, is far from uppermost in its mind. Indeed, the emergence of the 'global client' has signalled a different type of lawyering from that of the past. It entails a fundamental shift from a focus on projects to a focus on the quality of the service delivery.[63] The competition between firms for global clients is intense and allows little scope for flexible work, even in the case of routine activities, for this is more likely to be managed through outsourcing and 'offshoring', where it is performed in different jurisdictions as part of a 24/7 operation.[64] The time-zone factor of globalisation appears to have resulted in an exponential increase in working hours for lawyers.[65]

---

59   Justin Whealing, 'Large Firms Lacking Balance', *Lawyers Weekly*, available from: www.lawyers weekly.com.au/sme-law/10120-large-firms-lacking-balance.

60   Margaret Thornton & Richard Collier, Balancing Law and Life, Australian Research Council, 2012-14 (DP120104785). Cf. Thornton & Bagust (n. 9).

61   Edward Fennell, 'Give Me a Break …', *The Times*, [London], 28 April 2011, 75.

62   Hilary Sommerlad, Lisa Webley, Liz Duff, Daniel Muzio & Jennifer Tomlinson, *Diversity in the Legal Profession in England and Wales: A Qualitative Study of Barriers and Individual Choices* (University of Westminster, 2012).

63   Susan Segal-Horn & Alison Dean, 'The Rise of Super-Elite Law Firms: Towards Global Strategies' (2011) 31(2) *Service Industries Journal* 195, 205, doi.org/10.1080/02642060802706956.

64   ibid., 207.

65   Hilary Sommerlad, 'Minorities, Merit, and Misrecognition in the Globalized Profession' (2012) 80(6) *Fordham Law Review* 2482, 2509.

Despite the phenomenon of 'job engorgement',[66] which now seems to typify corporate legal workplaces everywhere, the evidence suggests the younger generation of lawyers—men as well as women—places greater store on work–life balance than in the past. In a survey conducted by the London 'magic circle' firm Freshfields, and based on the views of 114 students and recent graduates aged 18–22, four in 10, or 42 per cent, ranked work–life balance as an important consideration and 29 per cent as more important than a competitive salary and bonus.[67] *The Australian* noted that 42 male staff took parental leave from top-tier national firm Clayton Utz in the period January–May 2012, following the introduction of paid parental leave,[68] which allowed lawyers to take three weeks' paid parental leave after three years' service. While primary carers were entitled to 18 weeks after five years' service, it is nevertheless notable that none of the male lawyers availed themselves of this extended leave. As Collier's interviewees recognised, for men to play the 'quality of life card' could amount to 'career suicide'.[69] Ironically, women who seek to work part-time in the interests of a better quality of life but do not have caring responsibilities are threatened with the same fate.[70]

Indeed, in contrast to the stories involving women lawyers, there was a dearth of flexible work stories in the press about men relating to family responsibilities,[71] especially in a global context. The nearest involved the Australian head of Baker and McKenzie, Chris Freeland, who attended the 2008 Beijing Olympics with his family while on a posting in China.[72] The implication was that fatherhood and international mobility are not necessarily incompatible, as is often assumed to be the case with lawyer-mothers. It reflects the stereotypical assumption that having a family is a mark of stability that assists male lawyers' careers but is harmful to women. Nevertheless, there is no evidence that the lawyer-father in this case was

66   Emily S. Bassman, *Abuse in the Workplace: Management Remedies and Bottom Line Impact* (Quorum Books, 1992) 77.

67   Features, 'New Generation Rates Life Quality Over Job', *The Times*, [London], 19 January 2012, 11.

68   Nicola Berkovic, 'Parental Leave a Big Hit with Men', *The Australian*, 21 September 2012, 30.

69   Collier (n. 13) 171–72.

70   Amelia J. Uelmen, 'The Evils of "Elasticity": Reflections on the Rhetoric of Professionalism and the Part-time Paradox in Large Firm Practice' (2005) 33(1) *Fordham Urban Law Journal* 81.

71   Cf. Collier (n. 13) 161.

72   Alex Boxsell, 'Freeland has Global Ambitions', *Australian Financial Review*, 13 August 2010, 39.

engaged in 'active fathering' in accordance with the 'new fatherhood framework'.[73] In other words, the lawyer-father relegates responsibility for primary caring to someone else, just as he has always done.

Work–life balance has a somewhat different meaning for young law graduates without family commitments as 'exciting challenges' are offered by global firms through postings to exotic places. Such opportunities, rather than the promise of flexible work as such, are already luring lawyers away from the top Australia-based firms.[74] DLA Piper, for example, another of the global super-elite firms, with multiple lawyers in 40 countries,[75] makes overseas secondments appear relatively easy with a range of short and long-term programs, as well as traineeships.

Images of a glamorous lifestyle overseas nevertheless contrast with the reality of legal life for many junior associates in their home city. Although a former chief justice of New South Wales was compelled to resile from a controversial reference to new recruits in corporate law firms as 'mindless drones' (which he subsequently replaced with 'mechanical drones'),[76] the imagery captures the relentlessness of corporate legal life dominated by routine work, billable hours and an inescapable sense of hierarchy and frustration arising from an absence of access to justice for ordinary people.[77] The culture of long hours and the relentless competition also suggest a balance between work and life is unattainable for either men or women.

Indeed, it is now acknowledged that the legal profession is plagued by depression, mental illness and suicide because of the relentless pressure on lawyers to maximise profits and chalk up ever more billable hours. The suicide of young Sydney lawyer Tristan Jepson focused attention on the mental health problems induced by hypercompetition. In conjunction with the Brain and Mind Institute at the University of Sydney, the Tristan Jepson Memorial Foundation sponsored research on the incidence of

---

73   Richard S. Collier, 'Fathers 4 Justice, Law and the New Politics of Fatherhood' (2005) 17(4) *Child and Family Law Quarterly* 511.
74   Georgina Dent, 'Locals Man the Barricades', *BRW*, [Melbourne], 15 September 2011, 38; Leanne Mezrani, 'Travel Bug Draws Lawyers to Merged Firms', *Lawyers Weekly*, 27 June 2012.
75   'The DLA Piper Story', available from: timeline.dlapiper.com/.
76   Chris Merritt, 'Bathurst Rethinks "Drone" Attack', *The Australian*, 11 May 2012, 33.
77   ibid. Cf. Alex Aldridge, 'Boozy Lunches Are Out but Long Hours and Flexible Working Are In', *The Times*, [London], 26 May 2011, 11.

depression among law students and lawyers.[78] The evidence revealed that legal professionals have a higher rate of depression than other professions and one that is considerably higher than the general population.[79]

The Tristan Jepson case nevertheless appears to have exerted little impact on the long-hours culture, although we are told the masculinist practices of the past, such as 'boozy lunches', are out and 'long hours and flexible work are in'.[80] Stuart Popham, a senior partner at Clifford Chance, London, reflected on the change in culture during his 35 years with the firm: 'Lawyers used to work from 9.30 am to 5.30 pm and switch on the answerphone. Suddenly it was a 24/7 environment.'[81] Clearly, the model of being permanently at the beck and call of corporate clients, particularly when they might inhabit a different time zone, frustrates any possibility of a balance between work and life and is unappealing to those with family obligations.[82]

What is significant about the flexible work discourse is that far from making inroads into hypermasculinity, it may strengthen it. The values of competition, aggression and acquisitiveness have become normalised in corporate legal practice, just like the long-hours culture. Individual lawyers—women as well as men—who espouse the normative professional values are likely to be handsomely rewarded, but it is hypermasculinity that sets the standard for successful global lawyering.[83] If a woman takes maternity or paid parental leave, which she is legally entitled to do, she is still considered to have disturbed the status quo and questions may be asked as to where her loyalty lies. Furthermore, if she voices a desire to work flexibly when she resumes full-time work, she is likely to find herself subjected to differential treatment.[84] While the technology simplifies the possibility of flexible schedules, such as working from home, physical presence is still taken to be a symbolic measure of loyalty.[85] The alternative

78   Norm Kelk, Georgina Luscombe, Sharon Medlow & Ian Hickie, *Courting the Blues: Attitudes towards Depression in Australian Law Students and Lawyers* (Brain and Mind Research Institute, University of Sydney, in conjunction with Tristan Jepson Memorial Foundation, 2009), available from: law.uq.edu.au/files/32510/Courting-the-Blues.pdf.
79   James Eyers, 'The Saddest Profession of All', *Australian Financial Review*, 21 August 2010, 30.
80   Aldridge (n. 77).
81   Edward Fennell & Frances Gibb, '"It's the Very Best Job in the Legal World": Stuart Popham on 35 Years at Clifford Chance', *The Times*, [London], 9 September 2010, 73.
82   Cf. Sommerlad (n. 65) 2507.
83   L.H.M. Ling, 'Sex Machine: Global Hypermasculinity and Images of the Asian Woman in Modernity' (1999) 7(2) *Positions* 277, 295, doi.org/10.1215/10679847-7-2-277.
84   Thornton and Bagust (n. 9).
85   Cf. Wald (n. 7) 139.

for many is to leave corporate practice and take up a position in a smaller firm, a government department or a private corporation as inhouse counsel where one is not subjected to the tyranny of time sheets or the expectation of 24/7 availability to clients,[86] although it has been suggested that inhouse legal practice has increasingly begun to resemble law firm practice.[87]

It is notable that a high attrition rate for women from corporate law firms is an international phenomenon.[88] Like their male colleagues, they know that 'taking advantage of family-friendly policies is not consistent with gaining high points toward partner profits'.[89] The exodus of lawyers from private law firms does little to challenge the long-hours culture and the competitive values associated with law-as-business, which continues to underscore the ambiguous status of women in law. Rather than the exodus being understood as a structural manifestation of inequality, it is conventionally conceptualised as a matter of fairness and choice.[90]

Towards hypermasculinity

Competition policy

While flexible work is undeniably a positive initiative for women lawyers that receives media approbation, I propose to show how it is marginalised by the dominant discourse associated with the pursuit of capital accumulation by large corporate law firms at the global level. I thereby seek to show how Nandy's notion of hypermasculinity— denoting aggression, achievement, control, competition and power[91]— conveys an ideological message through newspaper reporting that trumps that of flexible work.

---

86   Susannah Moran, 'In-House Lawyers Urged to Step Up', *The Australian*, 20 January 2012, 25.
87   Lisa H. Nicholson, 'Making In-Roads to Corporate General Counsel Positions: It's Only a Matter of Time?' (2006) 65 *Maryland Law Review* 625; Eli Wald, 'In-House Myths' (2012) 407 *Wisconsin Law Review* 407.
88   Reiter (n. 43) 289.
89   ibid., 290–91.
90   Cf. Smithson & Stokoe (n. 44) 147, 162.
91   Nandy (n. 21).

Competition, which could be said to be the leitmotif of the market generally, became a plank of Australian government policy in 1993.[92] By the millennial turn, it was officially adopted by the legal profession, generating a range of business initiatives, including multidisciplinary practices, the incorporation of law firms[93] and listing on the stock exchange[94]—all of which privilege the idea of law-as-business. These innovations were subsequently emulated in the United Kingdom.[95] The corporatisation and globalisation of law firms are key manifestations of the market embrace. After centuries of an almost exclusive focus on municipal law within nation-states, the super-elite firms in Australia and elsewhere have sought to transcend national borders by following their multinational clients to foreign sites in the hope of securing new clients.[96]

The primary media focus in reporting the newsworthy activities of the super-elites is on capital growth, with mergers and acquisitions represented as the modus operandi of corporate law firm life. The firms themselves justify the mergers as 'part of the inevitable globalisation and interconnectedness of the world of business'.[97] Several prominent UK firms have made alliances with Australian firms or established offices in Australia, not only to secure a share of the Australian legal market, but also to facilitate entry into Asia. Australian and UK corporate law firms are thereby simultaneously collaborating and competing, which heightens the hypercompetitive legal environment. A few mergers have been made with US firms, but the UK firms are described as generally being far more expansionist than US firms.[98]

---

92 Independent Committee of Inquiry into Competition Policy in Australia, *National Competition Policy* [Hilmer Report] (AGPS, 1993). The main recommendations of the report were incorporated into the *Competition Policy Reform Act 1995* (Cth).
93 Christine Parker, Tahlia Gordon & Steve Mark, 'Regulating Law Firm Ethics Management: An Empirical Assessment of an Innovation in Regulation of the Legal Profession in New South Wales' (2010) 37(3) *Journal of Law and Society* 466, doi.org/10.1111/j.1467-6478.2010.00515.x; Susan Fortney & Tahlia Gordon, 'Adopting Law Firm Management System to Survive and Thrive: A Study of the Australian Approach to Management-Based Regulation' (2012) 10(1) *St Thomas Law Review* 152.
94 For example, Andrew Grech & Kirsten Morrison, 'Slater & Gordon: The Listing Experience' (2009) 22 *Georgetown Journal of Legal Ethics* 535; Benjamin Esty & Scott E. Mayfield, *Creating the First Public Law Firm: The IPO of Slater and Gordon Limited* (Harvard Business Publishing, 2012).
95 *Legal Profession Act 2007* (UK).
96 Aronson (n. 39) 763.
97 Ashurst Australia Chairperson Mary Padbury, quoted in Leonie Wood, 'Law Firms Build Ties with Asia', *The Age*, [Melbourne], 1 March 2012, 6.
98 Flood (n. 15).

The language used by the media to describe the activities of the super-elites in a globalising context is increasingly aggressive and bellicose. The oft-repeated militaristic language glorifies competition, acquisitiveness and power—all concepts denoting masculinity. Law firms are reported to be engaging in 'a war',[99] 'a battle',[100] 'a conquest', 'a struggle for market share', 'cut-throat competition' or embarking on a common goal 'to conquer Asia',[101] where the intention is to 'crush the competition as they attack Asian markets'.[102] The law firms 'man the barricades',[103] 'blaze a trail',[104] go after a 'war chest',[105] engage in 'foreign invasions',[106] carry out 'daring raids' on rivals[107] or 'gobble them up',[108] 'throw down the challenge' and 'go head to head',[109] 'muscle in',[110] 'jostle for business'[111] in the 'cut and thrust of private practice',[112] engage in 'aggressive growth'[113] and embark on 'a fierce war for work',[114] 'a renewed war for partner-level talent'[115] or a 'war for talent [on an] expanded battlefield',[116] after which they tell 'war stories'.[117] The intention of the bigger firms is 'to crush the competition as they attack Asian markets'.[118] The top London firms are 'leading the charge into China, Australia and the Middle East',[119] but the invading forces are

99   George Beaton, 'Smart Firms Will Follow in Slater & Gordon's Footsteps', *The Australian*, 3 February 2012, 33.

100 Alex Boxsell, 'Cutthroat Asia Demands Deep Pockets', *Australian Financial Review*, 10 September 2010, 41.

101 ibid.

102 ibid.

103 Dent (n. 74).

104 Alex Spence, 'London Law Firm Follows Mining Trail to Africa', *The Times*, [London], 2 January 2012, 35.

105 Alex Spence, 'Law Firm Ready to Break New Ground with Listing on Stock Exchange', *The Times*, [London], 20 April 2011, 47.

106 James Eyers & Alex Boxsell, 'Foreign Invasion a Game-Changer for Law Firms', *Australian Financial Review*, 17 February 2011, 1.

107 Sarah Thompson & Paul Garvey (eds), 'Scale of Justice: Law Firm Giants Looking to Merge', *Australian Financial Review*, 19 January 2011, 16. Cf. Eyers & Boxsell (n. 106).

108 Michael Sainsbury, 'Navigating the Politics of Power', *The Australian*, 30 March 2012, 30.

109 Alex Boxsell, 'Freeland has Global Ambitions', *Australian Financial Review*, 13 August 2010, 39.

110 News, 'Merged Firm Hails Canada', *Lawyers Weekly*, 16 October 2012.

111 Annabel Hepworth, 'Taking Steppes to be Boom's Gobi-tween', *The Australian*, 3 August 2012, 20.

112 Alex Boxsell & James Eyers, 'In Good Company', *Australian Financial Review*, 10 December 2010, 53.

113 Eyers & Boxsell (n. 106).

114 ibid.

115 Alex Boxsell, 'Big Firms Compete for Top Talent', *Australian Financial Review*, 2 March 2012, 2.

116 Justin Whealing, 'Editor's Note', *Lawyers Weekly*, 4 May 2012, 13.

117 Aldridge (n. 77).

118 Boxsell (n. 100).

119 Alex Spence, 'Lawyers' Pay Marks Return of Boom Times', *The Times*, [London], 6 July 2011, 31.

not going in one direction. In the case of Herbert Smith Freehills, it was suggested 'the Freehills deal [would] almost certainly trigger paranoid talk in London of an Australian invasion'.[120]

If not fighting battles, corporate lawyers are likely to be engaged in other aggressive masculinist pastimes, such as annual hunting expeditions, including 'surviving the legal jungle'[121] or a 'flurry of poaching'[122] in the aggressive pursuit of top performers: 'Cutthroat competition for talent forced law firms to set their sights on rivals and large companies as partner poaching heated up.'[123] The takeover of the UK firm Russell Jones and Walker by the Australian-listed firm Slater and Gordon engendered 'the biggest beast in the new world of alternative business structures'.[124]

Perhaps the most aggressive hunting metaphor to have entered the lexicon is 'eat what you kill'—a far more graphic and hypercompetitive phrase than the neutral-sounding 'performance or merit-based remuneration system' that is replacing the familiar lockstep remuneration system of advancement based on seniority.[125] In this way, hypercompetitiveness animates relations within firms as well as between firms. Indeed, it is now much harder for associates to become partner.[126] While firms grow exponentially, the number of equity partnerships shrink and are replaced with non-equity or salaried partnerships.[127]

Competition is the modus operandi of global business, in respect of which lawyers play a vital role in effecting mergers and takeovers on behalf of their corporate clients. It is inevitable that the global firms themselves

120 Chris Merritt, 'Merger of Equals but Brits Develop an Aussie Accent', *The Australian*, 29 June 2012, 31.
121 Dent (n. 74).
122 Samantha Bowers, 'Law Firm Partners in Search of Greener Pastures', *Australian Financial Review*, 9 March 2012, 43.
123 Boxsell & Eyers (n. 112).
124 *UK Law Society Gazette* (n.d.), quoted in Beaton (n. 99).
125 Jonathan Ames, 'Will "Eat What You Kill" Replace Lockstep?', *The Times*, [London], 8 September 2011, 65; Alex Boxsell, 'Performance Coach On Board', *Australian Financial Review*, 20 April 2012, 42; Nicola Berkovic, 'Smaller Firms Need to Move Away from the "Lockstep" Model to Stay Competitive', *The Australian*, 11 May 2012, 33.
126 Once the major 'tournament' in which associates participated. See Marc Galanter & Thomas Palay, *Tournament of Lawyers: The Transformation of the Big Law Firm* (Chicago University Press, 1991). Galanter and Henderson have since revisited the issue given more recent developments. See Marc Galanter & William Henderson, 'The Elastic Tournament: A Second Transformation of the Big Law Firm' (2008) 60 *Stanford Law Review* 1867.
127 John Flood, 'Lawyers as Sanctifiers: The Role of Elite Law Firms in International Business Transactions' (2007) 14(1) *Indiana Journal of Global Legal Studies* 35, 44, doi.org/10.2979/gls.2007.14.1.35.

now mirror the competitive business ethos of their clients, evincing similar market-oriented values, although competition between firms is represented as an unequivocal good that will improve legal services and reduce fees.[128] Law firms may even be prepared to tolerate competitors if it means holding on to a valuable client—or a share of a client. One mining client with assets in China and operations staff in Australia and the United Kingdom, for example, was using four different law firms to secure a Hong Kong listing.[129] Scenarios such as this encourage increased deference towards corporate clients to retain them, with lawyers being expected to be at their beck and call 24/7 across jurisdictions in conjunction with a rapid professional response and turnaround of work.[130] There is little scope for flexible work that satisfies a notion of work–life balance for individual lawyers in this environment.[131] Flexibility has been redefined in terms of employer prerogative generally, which means evincing a willingness to work as required,[132] including all night if necessary. The ethic has become one of work–work, which impacts on all workers, particularly those with caring responsibilities.

Just as Kollmeyer's study of the economy found relatively few newspaper articles about economic problems affecting workers during a period when corporations and investors enjoyed robust growth,[133] comparatively little media attention is devoted to the conditions under which lawyers work, whether it be in terms of excessively long hours or being subjected to compulsory redundancy in straitened times. Corporate firms rarely display the same loyalty to staff that was once the case, although a semblance of loyalty may linger in small firms where clients are individuals seeking to resolve personal disputes.

The new competitive environment inhabited by national, transnational and global firms means the life of the typical associate is beset with insecurity, but the overwhelming focus of media reporting is on capital investment and profits, not the wellbeing of lawyer-workers. While the movement of a manufacturing plant offshore is familiar when a company

---

128 Dent (n. 74).
129 Boxsell & Eyers (n. 112).
130 Segal-Horn & Dean (n. 63) 195, 204.
131 As acknowledged by Galanter & Henderson (n. 126).
132 Labour relations in Australia were transformed by the Howard government through its WorkChoices policy in the 1990s. See Andrew Stewart & Anthony Forsyth, 'The Journey from Work Choices to Fair Work' in Anthony Forsyth & Andrew Stewart (eds), *Fair Work: The New Workplace Laws and the Work Choices Legacy* (The Federation Press, 2009).
133 Kollmeyer (n. 33) 449.

closes its doors and declares all workers redundant, a comparable phenomenon has only recently manifested itself in global law firms. Lawyers are being treated more and more like assembly-line workers so that the 'proletarianisation' of the legal profession, which Derber posited 30 years ago,[134] would seem to have become a reality for many associates, particularly women—a thesis developed by Joanne Bagust.[135]

The position of associates can be rendered even more parlous by decisions to shed staff and outsource work to a cheaper jurisdiction. This accords with the practices of multinational corporations as they flit from country to country in search of ever cheaper labour and reduced overheads. Outsourcing nevertheless remains contentious for law firms,[136] not only because of the liability issue but because of competition from other concerns. When Axiom Law, a US legal company, opened its first European outsourcing centre in Belfast, it was regarded as a 'threat' to the London law firms that dominated the market for commercial legal services.[137] The deleterious impact on staff was clearly of less concern.

The dispensability of legal professionals was starkly revealed in Europe and the United States during the GFC when massive cuts occurred following the decline in mergers and acquisitions,[138] but the broadsheets were almost entirely concerned with the economic performance of law firms, not the plight of individual lawyers. In 2009, Clifford Chance culled 15 per cent of its partners as well as 130 salaried lawyers and 115 business staff.[139] This action by one of the world's largest global firms with a 'massive footprint' (3,200 lawyers in 34 offices in 24 countries)[140]

---

134 Charles Derber, 'Managing Professionals: Ideological Proletarianization and Mental Labor' in Charles Derber (ed.), *Professionals as Workers: Mental Labor in Advanced Capitalism* (G.J. Hall & Co., 1982).

135 Joanne Bagust, 'Keeping Gender on the Agenda: Theorising the Systemic Barriers to Women Lawyers in Corporate Legal Practice' (2012) 21(1) *Griffith Law Review* 137, doi.org/10.1080/10383 441.2012.10854735.

136 Katharine Towers, 'Firms Split Over Offshore Services', *The Australian*, 20 January 2012, 25–26.

137 Alex Spence, 'Belfast's Young Lawyers Lead the Charge as Dominance of the Elite Starts to Crack', *The Times*, [London], 2 April 2012, 57.

138 In the United States, more than 12,100 employees, one-third of whom were lawyers, were laid off by major law firms in 2009. See Neil Joel Dilloff, 'The Changing Cultures and Economics of Large Law Firm Practice and Their Impact on Legal Education' (2011) 70(2) *Maryland Law Review* 341, doi.org/10.2139/ssrn.1819485.

139 Fennell & Gibb (n. 81). Allen & Overy cut about 450 jobs, including 47 partners. See Alex Spence, 'The Trick to Achieving Growth Now Lies Overseas', *The Times*, [London], 3 July 2012, 31.

140 While the size of such firms is unprecedented as far as law is concerned, it pales into insignificance compared with accounting firms, with PricewaterhouseCoopers boasting more than 140,000 professionals. See Flood (n. 127) 49.

reveals how hypercompetitiveness has become inextricably intertwined with profit maximisation and an obsession with being the biggest and the best—an idea that emerged only in the late twentieth century.[141] A firm's global footprint—measured by the number of lawyers and staff employed and the number of offices—may still popularly be taken as an indicator of success. National pride is evinced by a high ranking, which is regarded as akin to Olympic glory:

> The latest annual rankings of the legal industry's global heavyweights is draped in the Union Flag. Six of the ten biggest law firms in the world are now either fully or jointly run from London, with DLA Piper only narrowly off the top spot … The ranking underlines how the top British firms, despite coming from a far smaller domestic market than their American counterparts, have established themselves as powerful competitors as the legal market becomes increasingly international.[142]

This piece in *The Times* went on to rue the fact that '78 of the 100 biggest firms are American. And the elite New York firms are still much more profitable than their city counterparts.'[143] Nevertheless, a volatile economy means the global law firm, like any multinational corporation, is beset with risk that can lead to its demise.[144] Size and profitability can therefore affect hypercompetitiveness in different ways. It has been suggested that for London law firms to return to the same level of profitability to which they were accustomed before the downturn would entail them shedding about 5 per cent of all lawyers:

> The UK legal market is *over-lawyered* by about 3,000 fee-earners whom firms will have to fire as they cope with the twin demands of a gloomy macroeconomic environment and a profession undergoing its biggest structural changes in decades, according to new research undertaken by the Royal Bank of Scotland.[145]

---

141 Aronson (n. 39) 763, 765.

142 Alex Spence, 'Contenders Punching Way Above Their Weight', *The Times*, [London], 9 July 2012, 32, 33. The strategic growth model, however, challenges the idea that bigger is necessarily better. See Eli Wald, 'Smart Growth: The Large Law Firm in the Twenty-First Century' (2012) 80(6) *Fordham Law Review* 2867.

143 Spence (n. 142).

144 As occurred with the New York–based law firm of Dewey and LeBoeuf, which had 16 offices outside the United States, together with a London office comprising more than 100 lawyers. See Alistair Osborne, '200 London Jobs at Risk after Dewey Collapse', *The Telegraph*, [London], 7 May 2012, 3; Jonathan Ames, 'Will a UK Firm be the Next Dewey's?', *The Times*, [London], 10 May 2012, 50.

145 Caroline Binham, 'Law Firms "Need More Restructuring"', *Financial Times*, [London], 19 March 2012, 24. Emphasis added.

The tone of this piece, especially the depersonalised 'over-lawyered', points to the way firm profitability and efficiency are privileged over the interests of individual lawyers and conventional notions of the common good. The relentless focus on profitability does not portend well for work–life balance as a norm in corporate law firms, for it has transformed the governing professional ideology of large law firms.[146]

While global firms rapidly shed staff when the economy slows, such firms have no compunction about seducing talented lawyers from elsewhere when things improve—a practice that once was rare.[147] Lateral hiring has become the norm, paralleling the mergers and acquisitions of the law firms.[148] Corporate firms are prepared to pay substantial premiums, as well as high salaries, to lure resource specialists to sites of growth.[149] Firms will also 'cherry pick' partners but are wary about the amount of work they might bring with them in an environment of economic uncertainty. It is the calibre of the clients, not the lawyers, that is now the key: 'The best lawyers are people whose experience and skill is relied on to drive whole practice groups and secure close relationships with an enviable list of ASX 200 clients.'[150] The ability of lawyers to bring in business to make the firm more competitive is what is crucial, even if colleagues are losing their jobs.[151] The firm's power, after all, is not autonomously generated; it derives from its clients.[152] Hypercompetition, the key signifier of globalisation, has now become the modus operandi of relations between law firms as well as between lawyers themselves.

Legal imperialism

The hypermasculinist theme is thrown into high relief when we turn to the expansionist policies of the super-elite law firms as played out in the Asia-Pacific during 2011–12. The reporting of these activities would seem to slough off altogether any possibility of work–life balance.

---

146 Wald (n. 7) 119.
147 Cf. Dilloff (n. 138) 349.
148 Cf. Wald (n. 7) 116.
149 Debbie Guest, 'Rejuvenated Minters on a Growth Spurt', *The Australian*, 22 June 2012, 33–34.
150 Boxsell (n. 115). Cf. Bowers (n. 122).
151 Chris Merritt, 'Firms Freeze Hiring Amid Weak Outlook', *The Australian*, 7 June 2013, 25.
152 Flood (n. 15) 6.

It is difficult to keep up with the pace of change in corporate legal practice as new liaisons between firms are constantly being effected in the hypercompetitive environment of globalisation. Michael Rose predicted in early 2011 that international mergers and alliances were likely to become more common in Australia as consolidation overseas gathered pace[153]—a prediction that was soon borne out.[154] As Rose notes, internationalisation itself is not new, as Australian firms had begun to expand into the Asia-Pacific in the 1980s, but what is new are 'the scale and pace of change and the heightened importance of [the] region in the world economy'.[155] British firms were attracted to Australia as the key player in the Asia-Pacific and the 'biggest M&A [mergers and acquisitions] market in the Asia-Pacific'.[156] Thus, 'gaining a foothold in Australia' is regarded as the crucial first step in 'their wider ambition of developing in Asia', where 'legal business is booming'.[157] In addition, Australia's comparatively successful efforts to withstand the GFC coincided with a significant resources boom, the downturn in the European economy and a flat UK market—all factors that made Australia attractive.[158] The UK firms were also keen to 'break the stranglehold of the elite Wall Street practices—by far the world's largest market'.[159] The Australian firms have been described as having 'a huge lead on revenue growth' over the global firms seeking to effect alliances.[160] The Australian legal expertise in energy and natural resources was also appealing to the UK firms.[161] At the same time, the Australian law firms themselves were attracted by amalgamation as they recognised they needed to 'get global or face extinction'.[162]

---

153 Michael Rose, 'Rising to the Global Challenge', *The Australian*, 11 February 2011, 30.

154 Within seven months, four of Australia's top-tier firms moved to operate under new names because of mergers. See 'No Turning the Tide', *Lawyers Weekly*, 24 July 2012.

155 Rose (n. 153). Cf. Hall (n. 39).

156 Chris Merritt, 'Giants See Asia-Pacific Potential: Strong M&A Draws Global Players', *The Australian*, 6 May 2011, 29.

157 Alex Spence, 'Clifford Chance Plants Flag in Australia: Acquisitions Open Way for Growth in Asia', *The Times*, [London], 17 February 2011, 43.

158 ibid. Questions were nevertheless raised about the sustainability of the Australian 'boom' considering the volatility of the Chinese economy. See Chris Merritt, 'Ruling Is In: Minerals Boom Over', *The Australian*, 31 August 2012, 29.

159 Spence (n. 119).

160 Chris Merritt, 'Local Revenue Boost Key to Generating Global Alliances', *The Australian*, 27 July 2012, 30.

161 Caroline Binham, 'Ashurst to Merge for Asian Growth', *Financial Times*, [London], 27 September 2011, 18; Chris Merritt, 'Top Firm in Global Alliance: Allens Links Up with Linklaters', *The Australian*, 23 April 2012, 19–20. Canadian firm HopgoodGanim was reported to be keen to 'muscle in' on the lucrative Australian energy and resources market with Perth-based firm Q Legal. See 'Merged Firm Hails Canada', *Lawyers Weekly*, 17 October 2012.

162 Dent (n. 74).

Rose also drew attention to the way wealthy commercial clients drove the imperative in favour of globalisation. The former Australian firm of Allens Arthur Robinson (now Allens Linklaters) opened an office in Ulaanbaatar, the Mongolian capital, to assist Rio Tinto in a project described as 'the world's largest undeveloped copper and gold mine'.[163] A second Australian firm, Minter Ellison, followed its corporate clients 'in the stampede to Mongolia'[164] to exploit its mineral wealth. The opening of Myanmar's doors to foreign interests was also seen as a source of 'opportunity for Australian firms'.[165]

The most dramatic change in direction, however, has been from the United Kingdom to Australia. Allen & Overy, the United Kingdom's fourth-largest firm, arrived in Australia after a 'daring raid' on Clayton Utz.[166] Other leading United Kingdom–based firms, keen to develop global reach, followed: Norton Rose, Clifford Chance and DLA Piper, together with several US firms. As one Australian commentator drily observed: 'The managing partners of Australia's national law firms must feel like paperclips facing the magnetic might of legal globalisation.'[167] Their fears are not baseless, as a new tier of high-profile firms soon began to emerge headed by the 'glamour globals'.[168]

A notable shift in the balance of power in the world economy has occurred in favour of Asia as the United States begins to lose its economic dominance.[169] The global firms see the Asia-Pacific legal market as 'booming', with 'Asia the prize'.[170] They are described as 'international suitors' seeking to attract 'international dance partners'.[171] Imagery of this kind suggests the arrival of the super-elites on Australian shores is benign, but other imagery, such as 'locals man the barricades',[172] suggests a distinctly cooler welcome. In light of the history of British imperialism, a headline in *The Times* appears particularly provocative: 'Clifford Chance

---

163 Merritt (n. 161).
164 Hepworth (n. 111).
165 'Burma Opens to Foreign Investment', *Lawyers Weekly*, 14 September 2012.
166 Sarah Thompson & Paul Garvey, 'Scale of Justice: Law Firm Giants Looking to Merge', *Australian Financial Review*, 19 January 2011, 16.
167 Eyers & Boxsell (n. 106).
168 Merritt (n. 151).
169 Tony Boyd, 'Chinese Companies Lawyer Up', *Australian Financial Review*, 31 March 2012, 64.
170 Alex Spence, 'Asia the Prize as City Lawyer Seals Deal', *The Times*, [London], 29 June 2012, 39.
171 Shane Barber, 'Global Arrivals No Cause for Alarm', *The Australian*, 29 July 2011, 29.
172 Dent (n. 74).

plants flag in Australia.'[173] On the same day, the headline in the *Australian Financial Review* reporting Clifford Chance's merger with two Australian firms included the words 'foreign invasion'.[174] Even more explicit was the message in *Lawyers Weekly*: 'Global law firms have arrived on our shores all guns blazing.'[175] This language signals the ambivalent response to 'the men with suits and attaché cases [who still] see [Australia] as a land of opportunity' and 'the back door to Asia'.[176] However, they no longer come with weapons but cap in hand seeking alliances with local law firms that are keen to take advantage of the global brand names but harbour a residual suspicion towards them.

Asia has become a prime site where hypercompetition is being played out in the name of globalisation as China is regarded as 'relatively undeveloped' in terms of legal services.[177] With China's gross domestic product estimated to exceed US$18 trillion by 2050,[178] the potential for profits is huge. The Chinese Government's policy of encouraging foreign investment or effecting alliances with the best in the world—known as 'going out'—has been seized on with alacrity by Australian and UK law firms.[179] The 'race to grab hold of the opportunities on offer'[180] is illustrated by the formation of the first Sino-Western global firm, King & Wood Mallesons, resulting from a Chinese–Australian amalgamation in 2012. King & Wood's chief executive, Stuart Fuller, insisted that even 'a decision by China's Ministry of Justice to make all lawyers pledge allegiance to the Chinese Communist Party will have no affect [sic] on the firm's strategy, business or clients',[181] and was one for which 'many global firms would give their eye teeth'.[182] In this neocolonial moment, we are able to discern shades of Orientalism,[183] for China, like Mongolia, if not conceptualised exactly as passive and feminised, is certainly depicted

---

173 Spence (n. 157).
174 Eyers & Boxsell (n. 106).
175 Whealing (n. 116).
176 Spence (n. 137).
177 Briana Everett, 'Chasing China', *Lawyers Weekly*, 5 April 2012.
178 News, 'Merger Mixed Bag', *Lawyers Weekly*, [Sydney], 30 August 2012.
179 For an analysis of the role of the Chinese Government in constituting the corporate law market (before the formation of King & Wood Mallesons) and the boundary-blurring it induces, see Sida Liu, 'Globalization as Boundary-Blurring: International and Local Law Firms in China's Corporate Law Market' (2008) 42(4) *Law & Society Review* 771.
180 Everett (n. 177).
181 Michael Sainsbury, 'Navigating the Politics of Power', *The Australian*, 30 March 2012, 30.
182 Georgina Dent, 'Third Time Lucky', *BRW*, [Melbourne], 20 October 2011, 42.
183 Edward Said, *Orientalism: Western Concepts of the Orient* (Penguin Books, 1978).

as in need of modernisation through Western law. The move into China enables us to clearly see the conjunction of hypermasculinity, globalisation and development.[184]

Asia is not the only site of growth for global law firms, which have also been venturing into sub-Saharan Africa in the hope of capitalising on the 'boom' in energy and mining deals there.[185] Again, echoes of aggressive nineteenth-century imperialism and the competition between nation-states for land with little ethical concern for the colonised are discernible. Another of the top-10 UK firms, Eversheds, has also been reported as 'chasing capital' and setting up business with a consortium of local lawyers in Iraq as US troops withdraw.[186] The focus is on markets in postwar reconstruction projects, but the rising price of oil makes the Middle East particularly attractive. Multibillion-dollar contracts in Libya following the war there have similarly attracted some of Europe's biggest companies and at least one London-based law firm.[187]

Indeed, anywhere in the world that is resource-rich holds allure for global law firms. As Ashurst's former Australian managing partner John Carrington pointed out, 'in the long term a leading global firm would need coverage in South America, Canada, Africa and Eastern Europe "on a much vaster scale"'.[188] The acquisitiveness, the competitiveness and the desire for control are clearly in evidence. Elias has argued that 'the mainstream study of multinational corporations effects a set of gendered assumptions that construct the firm as a hegemonically masculine political actor'.[189] I suggest the same could now be said for the global corporate law firms that have made the transition from domestic partnerships by cross-jurisdictional amalgamations. The top UK and US firms wish to effect mergers with Australian firms to maximise their chances of success in areas where they formerly lacked a presence. At the same time, some of the large Australian firms have been deliberately safeguarding their independence, while building up a presence in Asia and effecting ties with a range of Asian, US and UK firms.[190]

---

184 Cf. Elias (n. 28) 408; Ling (n. 83).

185 Spence (n. 137).

186 Caroline Binham, 'Mideast Expansion Deal Takes Eversheds into Iraq', *Financial Times*, [London], 25 May 2011, 4.

187 Caroline Binham & Lina Saigol, 'Clyde & Co to Open Law Office in Libya Led by Gaddafi Defector', *Financial Times*, [London], 11 July 2012, 22.

188 Chris Merritt, 'Blakes, Ashurst Set Profit Pool Goal', *The Australian*, 2 March 2012, 33–34.

189 Elias (n. 28).

190 Alex Boswell, 'Unaligned Drawn to Slaughter', *Australian Financial Review*, 3 August 2012, 36; Chris Merritt, 'Independence Has its Benefits in Land of the Giants', *The Australian*, 3 August 2012, 19.

It may be seen from the invocation of hypermasculinist militaristic language how neo-imperialism is deeply imbricated with a desire for domination. The primary dealmakers are invariably senior and powerful men whose profiles are commonly linked with reports of mergers and takeovers to ensure the success of their firms at the expense of competitors. 'International best practice' refers to the application of English law.[191] This is interpreted in procedural and formalistic terms with little regard for the effect on humans, whether they are indigenous inhabitants of the subject country or the firm's own employees. It is at this ethical crossroads that hypermasculinity collides with the contemporary discourse of work–life balance.

Conclusion

I have sought to show through the contrasting gendered representations of flexible work and the merger of Australia and London-based law firms in the print media that super-elite global practice remains a masculinist domain that is resistant to the feminine.

In an earlier study, I argued that although women had been 'let in' to legal practice, they remained 'fringe-dwellers' of the jurisprudential community.[192] Having surpassed the tipping point 25 years later, the descriptor is not quite apt. Nevertheless, while the advent of the super-elite global law firm has changed the legal landscape, a palimpsest of the gendered social script can be discerned as the masculinity of the legal culture is subtly reasserted through the globalisation of law firms and media representations of international mergers. While it is acknowledged that the print media is only one manifestation of popular culture, I have sought to show how it conveys crucial insights into attempts to reassert the dominance of masculinity and the 'otherness' of the feminine in the face of the imminence of the gender tipping point.[193]

---

191 Susannah Moran, 'Riding the Global Boom Out of Sub-Saharan Africa', *The Australian*, 20 January 2012, 25.
192 Thornton (n. 7).
193 Margaret Thornton, 'Authority and Corporeality: The Conundrum for Women in Law' (1998) 6 *Feminist Legal Studies* 147, 168, doi.org/10.1007/BF03359628.

Collier argues that the masculinity of the legal profession is a contested terrain, as male lawyers also seek recognition of fatherhood through flexible work practices.[194] Nevertheless, within the super-elite sphere of corporate practice, aggression, competition, acquisitiveness and 24/7 service—not flexible work practices—are represented as the desirable characteristics for successful lawyering. The lawyers who display the qualities of relentless aggression and acquisitiveness on the world stage are most likely to succeed. The language of hypercompetitiveness has become normalised in global practice, whereas the softer language of flexible work and work–life balance remains undeniably feminised despite persistent attempts to neutralise it. The undervaluation of caring in a society seduced by a culture of rapacious capitalism is insidiously invoked to detract from the competence and authority of women as legal players on the global stage. With its undercurrent of biological determinism, flexible work entrenches that element of the social script averring that caring for children is primarily the concern of mothers, not a shared parental responsibility in a heterosexual relationship. While women are ostensibly welcome as legal practitioners, the flexible work discourse suggests that welcome is qualified, for it entails being channelled into subordinate positions. This leaves the power of the upper echelons of the super-elite firms, the global 'highfliers' and the dominant ideology of hypercompetitiveness untouched.

While law firms have sought to present a more diverse face to the world by increasing the proportion of female partners in recent years, it is startling to learn that the global firms are reported to be presently resiling from gender initiatives in favour of 'cultural change' as they move into Asia.[195] Although sensitivity to ethnic, cultural and religious diversity is highly desirable in plural societies and the characteristics of diversity inevitably intersect with gender,[196] it is notable that express advertence to gender is absent in the characteristics associated with 'cultural change'. A blatant instrumentalism would seem to underpin the express move away from 'gender' in favour of a degendered notion of 'culture' in the belief that the latter is more appealing to the Asian corporate client base.

194 Collier (n. 13) 152–94.
195 Nicola Berkovic, 'Asian Shift Broadens Diversity Focus', *The Australian*, 6 July 2012, 29.
196 Diversity issues are presently being addressed by the Legal Services Board (England and Wales). See Sommerlad et al. (n. 62).

What is of preeminent importance in global practice, as we are repeatedly reminded by the media accounts, is capital accumulation—how much each partner generates, how much the firm generates vis-a-vis their competitors and how more and more money can be made by engaging in spectacular mergers and acquisitions all over the world. The more money a firm generates and the more ruthless it is in dealing with competitors, the more it is likely to be lauded.[197] While power, aggression, achievement, acquisitiveness and competition are accepted as the modus operandi of global firms as they merge, effect takeovers and forge new identities, the ideological dimension insidiously operates to normalise these values not just within corporate legal practice but also within society more generally—a process that is powerfully performed through the media, as I have sought to show. The ethic of work–life balance purports to demonstrate that corporate legal practice is welcoming to workers with family responsibilities in accordance with the contemporary spirit of egalitarianism, but these workers, the overwhelming proportion of whom are women, are in fact largely confined to subordinate and dispensable positions. This reality contrasts with the dominant ideology of hypercompetitiveness associated with positions of power and wealth that remain undeniably masculinist.

---

197 For example, News, 'DLA Piper's Billion-Dollar Payday', *Lawyers Weekly*, 8 February 2013.

7

The Flexible Cyborg

Introduction: Perpetually connected

More than 20 years ago, Haraway described the cyborg as 'a hybrid of machine and organism, a creature of social reality as well as a creature of fiction'.[1] I am invoking the cyborg to signify the idea of a lawyer who is always 'connected'—to the internet or a mobile phone—although Turkle has suggested that '[w]e are all cyborgs now'.[2] The metaphor captures the fluidity, hybridity and permeability associated with the dramatic pace of technological change. Despite the eagerness with which the latest apparatus is greeted, its impact is not politically neutral, for as each iteration of the relationship between the human and the technological is normalised, a new field of power comes into play. The impact on law firms of the explosion in technological innovation has been profound.[3] As technology does not recognise borders, the 'law of any place' prevails. Technology is now of such importance to legal practice that it has even been suggested minimum competency might need to be demonstrated as a prerequisite for lawyers to hold a practising certificate,[4] thereby elevating knowledge of technology to the same level as the legal competencies presently required for admission, such as negotiation, advocacy or drafting.

---

1   Donna J. Haraway, *Simians, Cyborgs, and Women: The Reinvention of Nature* (Free Association Books, 1991) 149.
2   Sherry Turkle, *Alone Together: Why We Expect More from Technology and Less from Each Other* (Basic Books, 2011) 152. Cf. Haraway (n. 1) 150.
3   Richard Susskind, *The End of Lawyers? Rethinking the Nature of Legal Services* (Oxford University Press, 2008).
4   Leanne Mezrani, 'Opting Out of Technology No Longer an Option', *Lawyers Weekly*, 10 March 2015, available from: www.lawyersweekly.com.au/news/16247-opting-out-of-technology-no-longer-an-option.

Hardt and Negri describe legal practice as a form of immaterial labour, which they define as labour that produces a continual exchange of information, knowledge and affect in the form of services.[5] Nevertheless, as with material labour, the aim is one of capital accumulation. The global law firms located in strategic parts of the world emulate the modus operandi of their multinational clients in the way they flit from place to place in the pursuit of profits. The analytic and symbolic tasks associated with processing and transmitting vast quantities of knowledge and information are dependent on accessible technology. This has significant ramifications for the conditions of lawyers' work compared with fixed sites, such as the factories that are associated with material labour.

Globalisation has hastened the reliance on technology by law firms because of the need to be available to corporate clients anywhere in the world 24 hours a day, seven days a week. The series of amalgamations that took place between Australian national law firms and elite London-based firms in 2011–12 had the effect of heightening competition not only between the burgeoning number of global firms, but also between individual lawyers in the competition for partnership, as discussed in Chapter 6, which resulted in what Wald refers to as a 'hypercompetitive professional ideology'.[6] While promotion to partner was once the normal expectation of lawyers, the growth of global firms with several thousand employees means few associates now have any prospect of becoming partner, despite working harder and longer.

Hypercompetition means a small percentage of elite lawyers—the equity partners—dominate the apex of the organisational pyramid of law firms, while the productivity of associates is managed through techniques of surveillance such as billable hours.[7] The pyramidal structure of law firms remains gendered even though women now make up more than 50 per cent of practitioners,[8] although the tendency is to appoint more women

5   Michael Hardt & Antonio Negri, *Commonwealth* (Harvard University Press, 2009) 132.
6   Eli Wald, 'Glass Ceilings and Dead Ends: Professional Ideologies, Gender Stereotypes, and the Future of Women Lawyers at Large Law Firms' (2010) 78(5) *Fordham Law Review* 2245.
7   Iain Campbell & Sara Charlesworth, 'Salaried Lawyers and Billable Hours: A New Perspective from the Sociology of Work' (2012) 19(1) *International Journal of the Legal Profession* 89, doi.org/10.1080/09695958.2012.752151.
8   An Australian national demographic profile of the practising profession in 2020 revealed that 53 per cent of solicitors were women, with the proportion of women increasing more rapidly than that of men. Law Society of New South Wales, *2020 National Profile of Solicitors: Final* (Urbis, 2021) 7–9, available from: www.lawsociety.com.au/sites/default/files/2021-07/2020%20National%20Profile%20of%20Solicitors%20-%20Final%20-%201%20July%202021.pdf.

as salaried rather than equity partners,[9] particularly as women are now the majority of senior associates. The result, as Bolton and Muzio point out in the UK context, is that male elites can extract an increasing share of surplus labour from the expanding cohorts of female subordinates: '[W]omen solicitors are opportunistically deployed as a reserve of relatively cheap salaried labour, which is subjected to work intensification … and the presence and exploitation of female solicitors has become essential to the legal profession's profitable survival.'[10]

Two decades ago when society was on the cusp of the technological revolution, the new technology was viewed as the way of the future for women lawyers, for it was believed it would enable them to work flexibly to combine work and family.[11] Women lawyers have argued for some years that if they had the opportunity to work flexibly, they would have a modicum of control over their working hours, they would be more likely to be represented in the upper echelons of law firm hierarchies and the haemorrhage of women from legal practice would be staunched.[12]

The genesis of flexibility in the labour market is in fact less benign as the concept was introduced to enable employers to exert greater control over workers by avoiding the rigidities of Fordism.[13] The idea was that those who worked part-time or casually would be employed to supplement the primary labour market when required. More significantly, this peripheral labour force would make it easier to exploit the labour power of women.

9   The gendered organisational pyramid is a familiar phenomenon elsewhere. In the United States, for example, women constitute approximately 22 per cent of equity partners. American Bar Association, *Women in the Legal Profession: Demographics* (ABA, 2022), available from: www.abalegal profile.com/women.php#anchor2. In the United Kingdom in 2019, 22 per cent of equity partners and 36 per cent of non-equity partners were women: *Transforming Women's Leadership in the Law: Current Approaches to Improving Gender Diversity at Senior Levels in Law Firms and Correlated Success. Research Study 2019* (Thomson Reuters, 2019), available from: blogs.thomsonreuters.com/legal-uk/wp-content/uploads/sites/14/2019/06/Current-approaches-to-improving-gender-diversity-at-senior-levels-in-law-firms-and-correlated-success.pdf.
10   Sharon C. Bolton & Daniel Muzio, 'Can't Live with 'Em; Can't Live without 'Em: Gendered Segmentation in the Legal Profession' (2007) 41(1) *Sociology* 47, 60, doi.org/10.1177/00380385 07072283.
11   Mary Jane Mossman, 'Lawyers and Family Life: New Directions for the 1990s (Part Two)' (1994) 2(2) *Feminist Legal Studies* 159, 167, doi.org/10.1007/bf01105176.
12   Law Council of Australia, *National Attrition and Re-Engagement Study (NARS) Report* (Law Council of Australia, 2014).
13   David Harvey, *The Condition of Postmodernity: An Enquiry into the Origins of Cultural Change* (Oxford University Press, 1990) 147.

Just as the cyborg tends to be associated with the feminine in science fiction,[14] 'being connected' by 'working from home' during normal working hours is a manifestation of flexible work that is overwhelmingly feminised. While Haraway's fable draws strength from her vision of an alternative to a male-centred society, it is far from clear whether worker-cyborgs possess the ability to create an alternative society, although women lawyers are undoubtedly challenging orthodoxy through the establishment of new forms of legal practice, as I will suggest. At the same time, portable technology, or what Bauman refers to as 'light capitalism',[15] has niftily adapted to colonise the private sphere as a new site of productivity.

I am not suggesting that all women are necessarily exploited in the way Harvey identifies,[16] but the deleterious impact of 'working from home' has undoubtedly been accorded short shrift. In focusing on this issue, I also consider the significance of flexible work for full-time workers—male, as well as female—who remain 'connected' by continuing to work and respond to emails at night, at weekends and on vacation. As a result, I conclude that the economic sphere is in danger of colonising the sphere of intimacy by stealth.

To acquire a better understanding of the way legal work is encroaching on private life, I conducted an Australia-wide web-based survey completed by male (25 per cent) and female (75 per cent) lawyers in private firms (n = 424) in 2012–13. I also conducted 54 follow-up interviews, eight of which were with Australian lawyers working for global firms based in London. The focus was on work–life balance (WLB) in private law firms, particularly large corporate law firms.

I was interested in establishing lawyers' perceptions of the impact of WLB, individual wellbeing and family harmony considering the increased competition both within and between law firms following the acceptance of competition policy at the turn of the twenty-first century. Competition was ratcheted up as global law firms based in the northern hemisphere began to enter the legal services market and to amalgamate with prominent Australian national firms. I wished to explore the views of respondents as to whether they thought WLB was attainable or whether

---

14   J. Andrew Brown, *Cyborgs in Latin America* (Palgrave Macmillan, 2010).
15   Zygmunt Bauman, *Liquid Modernity* (Polity, 2000) 54, 57–59.
16   Harvey (n. 13).

work was leaching into the private sphere and the intimacy of the home. Respondents' experiences of WLB and the differential impact of the flexibility stigma on men and women were also considered.

The elusiveness of a balanced life

The feminisation of work refers to the rapid increase of women in wage labour that has occurred all over the world since the 1990s.[17] The feminisation of the legal profession is a notable manifestation of the phenomenon. It is remarkable that women now make up approximately two-thirds of Australian law students, given that only a century ago, women were struggling to be 'let in' to the profession.[18] The liberal view was that once women had been admitted to law school in equal numbers, the momentum would be maintained and equal numbers would automatically flow through into all areas of the practising profession, including the upper echelons. However, this ignores the entrenched masculinity of the profession and the residual antipathy towards women in authoritative positions, which is buried deep within the legal culture but continues to manifest itself in discrimination, harassment and bullying.

As paid work has become numerically feminised, a qualitative shift towards what Hardt and Negri refer to as 'temporal flexibility' has occurred regarding when and where work is performed.[19] While the eight-hour working day was regarded as a great achievement of the labour movement for the working man in the nineteenth century,[20] it was based on the normative male artisan with an 'economically inactive wife',[21] and this model has been resistant to conversion to the 'working woman' or the 'economically active wife'. Women have continued to assume and are expected to assume responsibility for the domestic sphere, or realm of necessity, without any real accommodation of this reality in the workplace.

---

17   Hardt & Negri (n. 5) 133–34.
18   Margaret Thornton, *Dissonance and Distrust: Women in the Legal Profession* (Oxford University Press, 1996).
19   Hardt & Negri (n. 5) 133.
20   Julie Kimber & Peter Love, 'The Time of Their Lives' in Julie Kimber and Peter Love (eds), *The Time of Their Lives: The Eight Hour Day and Working Life* (Australian Society for the Study of Labour History, 2007) 1, 4.
21   Guy Weir, 'The Economically Inactive Who Look After the Family or Home' (2002) 110(11) *Labour Market Trends* 577.

It is women themselves who have been expected to adapt to the prevailing norms of work, including the long-hours culture that typifies professional legal work.

Indeed, the hours women expend in paid work have increased greatly, which has led to intense friction. Hypercompetitiveness has exacerbated this problem for lawyers, who were never subject to the eight-hour day. Despite the rhetoric, the ideal legal worker is still expected to be unencumbered by private-sphere responsibilities to be able to devote (him)self unconditionally to work.[22] The hope of the women's movement that men would share in the demands of family life equally with women has not been realised.[23] While there is some evidence that fathers in general are taking a more active role in childcare responsibilities, as discussed in Chapter 8, the long-hours culture of corporate law firms militates against this trend.[24] Indeed, as far as the two-career heterosexual family is concerned, it was usually agreed by interviewees in my study that it was economically rational for the male partner to remain in full-time employment (because he was invariably paid more) and for the woman either to put her career on hold for a few years or to work flexibly; it was not feasible for them both to work 12-hour days. Whether opting out or working flexibly, the impact on a woman's career is marked—a factor that operates to entrench the gendered configuration of power in the organisational hierarchy.

The feminisation of labour brought part-time work and irregular hours in its wake so that women might continue performing traditional caring and household responsibilities, but law firms have been slow to accommodate the needs of women and law societies have been hesitant about mounting a wholesale critique of the long-hours culture.[25] The median weekly hours worked by survey respondents (calculated from the previous month) was 50, with hours worked ranging from four to more than 100 hours. The long-hours culture, in conjunction with systemic gender discrimination, has resulted in an exceptionally high rate of attrition of

---

22   Joan Williams, *Unbending Gender: Why Family and Work Conflict and What to Do about It* (Oxford University Press, 2000).

23   Judy Wajcman, *Pressed for Time: The Acceleration of Life in Digital Capitalism* (University of Chicago Press, 2015) 69, doi.org/10.7208/chicago/9780226196503.001.0001.

24   Richard Collier, 'Naming Men *as Men* in Corporate Legal Practice: Gender and the Idea of "Virtually 24/7 Commitment" in Law' (2015) 83(5) *Fordham Law Review* 2387, 2393.

25   Melissa Gregg, *Work's Intimacy* (Polity, 2011) 4.

women from private practice.[26] A study by the Law Society of New South Wales in 2011 revealed that 50 per cent of women left private practice within five years.[27] Another study, undertaken by Victorian Women Lawyers, found that 75 per cent of women leave the profession between the ages of 35 and 55 years.[28] In addition, some global firms have an 'up or out' policy, which means senior associates have to leave if they have not made partner by a certain time.

Support for WLB was nevertheless boosted by the inclusion of s. 65(5A) of the *Fair Work Act 2009* (Cth), which permitted a limited right by an employee with young children or children with a disability to request a change in working arrangements. The request can be declined by the employer on a range of reasonable business-related grounds, including cost, which would be difficult for a law firm to justify. While falling short of conferring a legal right to flexible work, this legislation, together with the *Paid Parental Leave Act 2010* (Cth), placed WLB firmly on the public agenda.

While it might be averred that the term 'work–life balance' suffers from a lack of conceptual clarity,[29] it is commonly understood in terms of the absence of work–life conflict—that is, work should not consume all of one's energies and there should be time for family life, socialising, rest and relaxation, as well as time to pursue interests in music, theatre, art or sport. However, Drew, Datta and Howieson suggest that inadequate attention is paid to positive aspects of WLB, such as enrichment, which refers to the benefits that both work and life bring to the other. Drawing on Carlson, Grzywacz and Zivnuska,[30] Drew et al. identify development, affect, capital and efficiency as examples of work-to-life enrichment and life-to-work enrichment,[31] although they do not address the way these

26   Law Council of Australia (n. 12) 57; Iain Campbell, Sara Charlesworth & Jenny Malone, 'Part-Time of What? Job Quality and Part-Time Employment in the Legal Profession in Australia' (2012) 48(2) *Journal of Sociology* 149, doi.org/10.1177/1440783311408970. Wald (n. 6, 2255) notes a similar phenomenon in the United States.
27   Law Society of New South Wales, *Thought Leadership 2011: Advancement of Women in the Profession. Report* (Law Society of New South Wales, 2011) 14.
28   Stefanie Garber, '"Outdated Attitudes" Holding Back Women', *Lawyers Weekly*, 17 April 2015, available from: www.lawyersweekly.com.au/news/16395-firms-outdated-attitudes-holding-back-women.
29   Natalie Mei-Chuen Drew, Doita Datta & Jill Howieson, 'The Holy Grail: Work–Life Balance in the Legal Profession' (2015) 38(1) *University of New South Wales Law Journal* 288, 294.
30   Dawn S. Carlson, Joseph G. Grzywacz & Suzanne Zivnuska, 'Is Work–Family Balance More than Conflict and Enrichment?' (2009) 62(10) *Human Relations* 1459, doi.org/10.1177/00187267 09336500.
31   Drew et al. (n. 29) 295.

characteristics, especially affect, are gendered. As caring for young children is intense and requires a disproportionate amount of 'life-time' for a few years, balancing work and caring responsibilities tends to be the primary understanding of WLB. This is even though lawyers juggling both work and care are sceptical that any sort of balance is achievable:

> Sometimes work demands more time, sometimes family. It is a seesaw or a rollercoaster, not a balance. (Survey respondent #262, female, managing solicitor, state/territory single office)

> WLB simply means more connectivity and so a greater ability to be contactable and working at all hours. There has been a shift from face time to virtual time. (Survey respondent #90, female, paralegal, national firm)

Temporal flexibility

The ease of managing large quantities of documents, including their storage and portability, is hastening the embrace by the legal profession of working remotely:

> There would be 50 archived boxes plus documents on a USB stick. So, a consultant working from home would have to be able to store all of those boxes safely, and that could be a real issue for people who live in apartments and units; it's a huge amount of documentation. So, a USB stick is so much easier for everybody ... There's been a big increase in clients providing jobs to us on a stick, so we're all getting better at working electronically. (Interviewee, female, managing solicitor, state/territory single office)

Lawyers also regard the technology as a source of liberation from the office:

> The Blackberry gives you the freedom not to be in the office ... There were many, many nights that I would've sat in the office 'til three o'clock, four o'clock because you had to be by the telephone or the fax machine. Now you don't. You can go out to dinner. You put the Blackberry on the table. You say to the person you're having dinner with, 'I'm sorry, I'm gonna have to look at this' ... You can go to the theatre and check your emails in the interval. I mean, it's given so much freedom. People forget that you [once] just sat in the office all night. (Interviewee, female, consultant, former partner, global firm)

As mentioned, 'flexible work' is an indeterminate term, encompassing both formal and informal dimensions. The formal understanding refers to alternative arrangements that workers might negotiate with their employers in lieu of regular hours spent at the office. The informal understanding of flexible work refers to the time (and place) that workers might spend working in addition to the formal hours of work. This usually means 'working from home' at night or on weekends. These two meanings of flexible work merge with one another as I shall show, but the language does not distinguish between them.

In the formal understanding, respondents used flexible work to refer to a variety of arrangements, such as an adjustment of hours (not necessarily fewer), including compressing the working week into several very long days, working remotely from a few hours to several days a week, time-in-lieu, working part-time on a regular basis, working casually, taking unpaid leave from time to time (such as during school holidays), purchasing additional leave and job-sharing, with many variations in between:

> We leave it to them [employees] because it's not one size fits all … She took nine months, I think, and then came back three days a week and then came back four days a week. Then, because her mother wasn't available, I think it's three days one week and then four days the next, but we can be flexible … The risk in part-time inevitably is that because they're not going to be there the whole time, they don't get the really significant work where the expectation of the client will need access to someone the whole time. (Interviewee, male, partner, global firm)

> I'm a single man with two young children, a 10-year-old and a six-year-old, whom I have only half the time, and the ability for me to work extremely long Mondays and Tuesdays, get out the door at five o'clock on a Wednesday to pick them up, leave at three o'clock on a Thursday to meet them when they arrive home from school … the ability to work with extended days and short days, and masses of time in the week when I don't have them in the school holidays, and then work shorter days and juggle things when the kids are around … has been absolutely fantastic. (Interviewee, male, partner, global firm)

In some cases, the 'flexibility' appeared to be minimal. One survey respondent who identified himself as a 'young, single male' said: 'I can leave work at 5pm on Tuesdays and Thursdays during the summer to attend cricket training' (Survey respondent #308, lawyer, national firm).

Flexible arrangements of the formal kind were not available to everyone. In some firms, those engaged in transactional work, junior lawyers, childless lawyers and male lawyers were ineligible: 'Categorically a man wouldn't have been allowed to have the flexible work arrangements that I've got' (Interviewee, female, litigator, national firm). The ability to work remotely—even if it is for only a few hours a week—represents the heart of the technological revolution that is threatening to collapse the walls of the office.

On its face, it would seem that (formal) flexible work has been widely accepted by the legal profession. A 2014 poll revealed that 89 per cent of Australian firms offered flexible work arrangements,[32] and in the survey I conducted, 40 per cent of respondents indicated they were theoretically able to undertake some form of flexible work, but only 6 per cent indicated they had a formal flexible arrangement at the time, while 16 per cent worked part-time. Numerous respondents alluded to the gap between the rhetoric and the reality in their firm. While lawyers who work full-time and who undertake additional work at home at night or on weekends (informal flexible work) attract approbation, suspicion frequently attached to those who work at home during business hours, despite having an approved arrangement:

> If you work from home, it is perceived by my partners as not actually working. (Survey respondent #42, male, lawyer, state/territory single office)

> I think most firms pay lip-service to flexible practices. It does not suit most men in firms who are generally the leaders, and they only say they provide flexible practices because they want to get government clients. (Survey respondent #365, female, associate, national firm)

There was a sense that when times were more difficult and competition increased, there was greater resistance to approving formal flexible work arrangements:

> Flexibility and WLB are a challenge for all firms, largely because of the demands of clients and the competitive pressure firms face. (Survey respondent #76, male, partner, global firm)

---

32   John MacLean, 'Closing the Gender Gap', *Lawyers Weekly*, 17 October 2014.

With the advent of the global firm, firms are more interested in profit than employee retention. (Survey respondent #108, female, partner, state/territory single office)

The deleterious impact of flexible work on a lawyer's career has been noted elsewhere.[33] Indeed, while approximately 25 per cent of the survey respondents in the current project took carer's leave at some stage of their career, which could have included a formal flexible work arrangement, 33 per cent of them recorded having suffered negative repercussions as a result, such as being placed on the 'mummy track' because they were 'no longer viewed as fully committed'.[34] This meant not just being offered inferior assignments, but also finding their career progression had stalled:

> I think people are reluctant … to be involved in a flexible work arrangement because that is seen in practice as somebody who's not willing to commit entirely to their career. So, if you want to progress in your career, you certainly wouldn't put your hand up for flexible work arrangement[s]. (Interviewee, female, special counsel, national firm)

Despite the rhetoric and the functionality of formal flexible work, the ongoing stigma was not easily sloughed off, even when a period of working flexibly ended. There was also guilt on the part of the flexible worker for being absent from the office—a factor that was likely to be exacerbated by the resentment of colleagues. Nevertheless, some respondents thought that leave had a positive effect on their career as it gave them the confidence to reassess their priorities: 'I reflected on what I was passionate about … and it gave me the opportunity to give up half of my practice and … focus on the area I was passionate about. I returned a much more efficient practitioner' (Survey respondent #145, female, partner, global firm).

Seeking to work flexibly to realise a balanced life unrelated to family responsibilities may also carry with it a heightened degree of stigma. Uelmen writes of the likelihood of 'professional suicide', about which she was warned, even though the 'part-time' schedule she sought amounted to a 40-hour week.[35] What is more, the stigma against women who work

---

33 For example, Margaret Thornton & Joanne Bagust, 'The Gender Trap: Flexible Work in Corporate Legal Practice' (2007) 45(4) *Osgoode Hall Law Journal* 773, 787–800.
34 ibid. Cf. Australian Human Rights Commission, *Supporting Working Parents: Pregnancy and Return to Work National Review. Report* (AHRC, 2014) 23; Campbell et al. (n. 26) 158.
35 Amelia J. Uelmen, 'The Evils of "Elasticity": Reflections on the Rhetoric of Professionalism and the Part-Time Paradox in Large Firm Practice' (2005) 33(1) *Fordham Urban Law Journal* 81.

flexibly—for whatever reason—would appear to not have a rational basis as the evidence reveals they are generally the most productive members of the workforce.[36] The flexibility stigma may therefore be a trope for the residual animus against women in law.

Despite the popular discourse of 'flexibility for dads',[37] the impact of the flexibility stigma for men may be even more severe than for women.[38] This is because men who assume the role of primary carer for young children are subjected to a 'femininity stigma' arising from the feminisation of caring in the social script.[39] As a result, if men had time off for family reasons, it was usually restricted to one or two weeks' paternity leave. This factor, together with the financial disincentive for men to become primary carers, sustains the masculinisation of equity partnerships and the control of capital within law firms.

It has been suggested that the flexibility stigma that affects both men and women can be explained partly in terms of a generational difference. Palfrey and Gasser single out the millennial generation, who, as 'digital natives', are at ease with technology.[40] The 'Millennials', or 'Generation Y', are those born between the early 1980s and the mid 2000s who have grown up with digital media. As Otey notes, there is something of a gap in the use of technology between the Millennials and the older generation.[41] While the older generation of lawyers uses computers and laptops, they are less likely to feel the need to be connected all the time. Millennials and Generation Xers (those born between the mid 1960s and early 1980s) may also place high importance on schedule flexibility as they are more likely to have a young family.

36   Amy Poynton & Louise Rolland, *Untapped Opportunity: The Role of Women in Unlocking Australia's Productivity Potential* (Ernst & Young Australia, 2013) 3.
37   Collier (n. 24) 2395.
38   For example, Scott Coltrane, Elizabeth C. Miller, Tracy DeHaan & Lauren Stewart, 'Fathers and the Flexibility Stigma' (2013) 69(2) *Journal of Social Issues* 279, doi.org/10.1111/josi.12015.
39   For example, Joan C. Williams, Mary Blair-Loy & Jennifer L. Berdahl, 'Cultural Schemas, Social Class, and the Flexibility Stigma' (2013) 69(2) *Journal of Social Issues* 209, 226, doi.org/10.1111/josi.12012.
40   John Palfrey & Urs Gasser, *Born Digital: Understanding the First Generation of Digital Natives* (Basic Books, 2008).
41   Brittany Stringfellow Otey, 'Buffering Burnout: Preparing the Online Generation for the Occupational Hazards of the Legal Profession' (2014) 24(1) *Southern California Interdisciplinary Law Journal* 147.

Nevertheless, given the rapidity with which technology has become central to legal practice, the generational distinction would no longer seem to be compelling as a basis for the flexibility stigma, although the older (male) lawyers are the ones who continue to dominate the ranks of equity partners. They are inevitably going to be ultrasensitive to the needs of corporate clients as a source of wealth for the firm—a factor that does not sit easily with (formal) flexible work:

> It's part of client service. The rhetoric … is that to stand out from the rest, your client should have access to you 24/7 and that's unfortunately the view perpetuated across the board. So, if your partners are available, that trickles down and you're then forced to become available … outside of work hours. I don't understand why. If you look at accounting firms by comparison, the number of hours they're required to write on their budget are significantly less than law firms. (Interviewee, female, litigator, national firm)

> The client is always king … Often the client will ring in at five o'clock on a Friday afternoon, expecting something first thing Monday morning and then sit on it for two weeks before responding. Clearly, it wasn't that urgent, but they feel they're entitled to expect things from a law firm straight away—because they're paying for the service—but it places unrealistic pressure on those who work part-time to meet those unrealistic demands … Part of the solution is trying to encourage more creative ways of working, whether you work from home or work remotely. Part of it is re-educating the client as to what is realistic to expect. But no law firm's going to do that because, if they do, they'd lose the client. I'd like to see a shift in time recording to just charging for a particular job and then working to get that job done within a reasonable amount of time and it doesn't matter if you're in the office or out of the office when you get it done. (Interviewee, female, community lawyer, formerly with global firm)

> I was in a position for about three years where I worked under two senior women who were job-sharing. And the only way it worked for them was because I was there all the time to fill in all the gaps. That wasn't their fault; the clients expected us to be a full service—24-hour, pretty much—resource for them that we'd turn everything around when they needed it and that's why they paid us a lot of money for our services. So, I think maybe in the mid-tiers or in certain niche areas where the work is less transactional and urgent, working part-time might be more viable, but in my area, I just don't feel that optimistic about how it will work. (Interviewee, female, senior associate, global firm)

Despite the pro-flexibility rhetoric espoused by law firms, the physical workplace, which necessitates 'face time', visibility or 'presenteeism', remains at the heart of private legal practice, even though it does not necessarily equate with optimal performance. While it was one thing for independent contractors to be working from home during normal working hours, employees were viewed differently, and respondents thought the lack of visibility exercised negative ramifications on their careers. The occasional woman who works flexibly may be promoted to partner, but this is still likely to be regarded as newsworthy;[42] no comparable examples involving male lawyers were encountered. A partnership is usually awarded only after several years of demonstrated loyalty, 'rainmaking' (generating new business for the firm) and exceptional productivity. Presence has for so long been associated with power and masculinity in law firms that the absence of male lawyers is regarded as more significant than the absence of women, who may still be regarded as dispensable. While the concerted pressure from women lawyers' associations in favour of formally approved flexible work, together with the increasing sophistication of the technology, may diminish the flexibility stigma over time, the issue of conservative law firms having to adapt to the new norms remains unresolved:

> The firm is full of women. They are now having babies and I think this is the real test for the firm. They need to figure out how they're going to deal with the situation and there have been incidents of people leaving because it just didn't work, or the partners that supervised them couldn't accept the arrangements—I'd like to say, 'needed a bit more training' … We've had to work it out … and the partner who was supervising me for most of these past years had to remember when I wasn't around and be aware of and sensitive to that. The hours are flexible and I'm flexible, too. So, if I knew there was a pressing matter that just takes me two minutes to fill in the gap, I would. That might be on a day that I'm at home and not, in a sense, contactable. I will say if I'm not and that's respected … What'll be interesting is those who are in real, fast-paced corporate work and the ones who are just on the cusp of getting partnership … It's hard when you're primarily responsible for a client … And clients—it's not their job to be reasonable—the demands are still there, and you can understand where they're coming from because they have to meet deadlines and nobody is going to say, 'But this poor person is only able to work these days'. They need the results. (Interviewee, female, consultant, global firm)

---

42   Campbell et al. (n. 26) 158–59.

Although Haraway believed women must use technology as a means of both power and pleasure,[43] competition policy and capitalism have been able to seize on the positive aspects of 'being connected' to turn flexible work to its advantage. Technology is proving to be a means of reaffirming the masculinity of the power and wealth of the legal profession just when it has been confronted by the prospect of feminisation. This is because presence and visibility in situ are still accepted as tacit criteria not only for promotion, but also for the allocation of work.

The theft of time

The internet has enabled the relentless financialisation and commodification of more and more regions of individual and social life. Technology was meant to facilitate flexibility and ease of working, but the tyranny of email requiring instant responses generates pressure. Thus, in hastening the pace of life, we have less time, not more.[44]

Crary suggests that work time, consumption time and marketing time have taken over so that no possible harmonisation between living things and 24/7 capitalism is possible,[45] despite the trend towards 'work/life integration'. This phenomenon is apparent as globalisation has caused the large corporate law firms to become multinational entities for which capital accumulation is the modus operandi. This has hastened the introduction of practices directed towards greater efficiency, such as offshoring and the use of new technologies. Marx is very relevant for this new phase of capitalism, as Wendling notes.[46] Just as the machinery of the Industrial Revolution was regarded as an affront to pastoral time and the rhythm of the natural world, technology has hastened the shift to abstract time. Marx recognised 'free time' as the product of the accumulation of wealth, but temporal flexibility means there is no end. If there were no need for sleep, capital would take the full 24 hours of the day.[47]

---

43 Haraway (n. 1) 180–81.
44 Wajcman (n. 23) 2.
45 Jonathan Crary, *24/7: Late Capitalism and the Ends of Sleep* (Verso, 2013) 100.
46 Amy E. Wendling, *Karl Marx on Technology and Alienation* (Palgrave Macmillan, 2009).
47 Karl Marx, *Capital*, translated by Eden and Cedar Paul (J.M. Dent & Sons, 1962) 268. Cf. Crary (n. 45).

Numerous writers, such as Arendt, have also expressed the view that a protected sphere away from the harsh glare of public activity is necessary so that regeneration can occur.[48] However, technology has assisted in penetrating the carapace around the private sphere. The incipient conflation of the economic and the domestic spheres has attracted little attention to date as it has occurred by stealth—beginning with the occasional email when the technology was a novelty and potentially expanding to full-time virtual work. Also, the opportunity to work flexibly was eagerly sought by women lawyers as a step towards effecting WLB, but without regard to the possible pitfalls.

Temporal flexibility has significant ramifications for the intimacy of home life. Although working from home is often restricted by law firms to one day a week, this arrangement can be augmented by the informal understanding of flexible work, or 'job creep'.[49] This means lawyers working from home are expected to be available, not just at the specified times, but also at other times of the day or night. This idea of having received a 'favour' from the firm may be internalised by employees who feel guilty for spending time away from the office. They are grateful for being able to work at home; they love their work and want to do the best job they can. In addition, meeting billable hours targets may be impossible in an official working week in the office, which necessitates that time be made up at home. Thus, in the battle between home and work, work all too often emerges as the winner. Gregg describes the 'partial presence' of the worker who is 'connected' at home and only partially present to his or her family.[50] This may arise not only from the pressure to meet targets, but also from a form of 'internet addiction', in which emails are frequently checked, including at mealtimes and late at night:

> For that precise reason, I do not have a Blackberry ('crackberry').
> I don't want to take work home. I'll take work home when I have
> to, if I have a hearing or something, but if I'm not at work, I'm not
> working. If I need to work, I go to the office to do it. (Interviewee,
> male, associate, national firm)

---

48   Hannah Arendt, *The Human Condition* (University of Chicago Press, 1958) 71.
49   Ellen Ernst Kossek, Rebecca J. Thompson & Brenda A. Lautsch, 'Balanced Workplace Flexibility: Avoiding the Traps' (2015) 57(4) *California Management Review* 5, 8, doi.org/10.1525/cmr.2015.57.4.5.
50   Gregg (n. 25) 126.

> If you get into the habit of checking emails and that kind of thing late at night, you are setting yourself up for being constantly available. Some people prefer to be very flexible, maybe not work so much during the day and be available at all hours … and I think your clients get used to that way of working as well. (Interviewee, female, senior associate, global firm)

Time poverty has been described as the 'modern malaise', arising from 'longer working hours and fewer boundaries between work and free time'.[51] 'The potential for work to invade every nanosecond is said by some to spell the end of pure, uninterrupted leisure time.'[52] Although the use of technology at home undermines domestic and family time, it is encouraged, for it extends working time:

> Firms … are freely providing laptops, Blackberries, that sort of thing … under the pretence of making it easier for you to work. Now, of course, the flipside is that you never leave the office because while you're not physically standing or sitting in it, you have your Blackberry and people can call you or email you at all times of the day—and I mean at all times of the day. You get emails at three o'clock in the morning. And if you've got a laptop and it has the Citrix system, you can log in remotely to their server and access all your documents … and it becomes infinitely easier to work at home … So, there is certainly intrusion on your out-of-work time in that respect, but it's got some benefits, like when I go to hearings … but for other people, it's, 'I can do more work; I can do it at home after I've spent my mandatory hour with my family'. (Interviewee, male, associate, state/territory single office, formerly with national firm)

> I have had different types of flexible working. I did purely working from home for six weeks after my son was born. And then flexible hours in the workday in the office and then also working from home both during business hours and working from home in the evenings … I don't like working at home … I'd rather be in the office doing my work. It just feels like a better environment to do it in. I don't like taking the stress of work home with me. (Interviewee, female, inhouse, formerly with national firm)

51   Josh Fear, Serena Rogers & Richard Denniss, *Long Time, No See: The Impact of Time Poverty on Australian Workers* (Policy Brief No. 20, The Australia Institute, November 2010) 5.
52   For example, Wajcman (n. 23) 137.

So seamlessly are the practices of message-monitoring and email-checking absorbed into home life that employees frequently discount these activities as work. Workloads are thereby insidiously increased, with employees reporting that they work not only at night and on weekends, but also on sick leave and holidays. Thus, while flexible work is ostensibly a source of liberation, it is also a new form of theft of workers' time, or what Cottle, Keys and Masterman-Smith refer to as 'time banditry'.[53] An Australia Institute study from 2019 computed that Australian workers who work from home donate on average six weeks a year of unpaid labour to their workplaces.[54] While figures are unavailable for the legal profession, and it would be impossible to disaggregate informal and formal flexible work, I suggest the windfall for law firms would be at least comparable as so many survey respondents and interviewees alluded to this factor:

> I'm working full-time. So, I do four days in the office and Friday is my work-from-home day, although … the actual work hours I perform on the weekends or in the evenings. On the Friday, I'm expected to be available on the phone to do business and checking my emails. (Interviewee, female, inhouse, formerly state/territory single office)

> Ultimately, I reverted to full-time because I was effectively performing a full-time workload but only being paid for four days per week. (Survey respondent #286, female, partner, national firm)

> Q: So, do you find that you must work during the night sometimes because of your clients being overseas?

> A: Yes. I have to catch them if, say, we've got a deadline coming up and I can't wait another day for them to get instructions to me. I do that when there are major filing projects on and instructions need to go overnight. Most of the time if I do work at night, it's more to catch up on time. So, I see it as a flexibility issue … I'm willing to spend some of my time at home to do the work after the children have been dealt with. I think that's fair enough, you know, because the firm is a business; they have to make money. (Interviewee, female, consultant, global firm)

---

53   Drew Cottle, Angela Keys & Helen Masterman-Smith, 'A Political Economy of Labour Time' in Julie Kimber and Peter Love (eds), *The Time of Their Lives: The Eight Hour Day and Working Life* (Australian Society for the Study of Labour History, 2007) 205.
54   Bill Browne, *Excessive House and Unpaid Overtime: 2019 Update* (Centre for Future Work at The Australia Institute, 2019), available from: australiainstitute.org.au/report/excessive-hours-and-unpaid-overtime-2019-update/.

While some donors of time are the guilt-ridden lawyers who feel they always must do more because their request to work flexibly has been accommodated, others felt the exploitation of staff was a conscious endeavour to maximise the extraction of surplus labour from them, regardless of their formal work arrangements:

> The more 'flogged' their staff are, the better the business. The partners I work for barely bother to disguise this hard truth. Despite the rhetoric of the top-tier firms, from my experience, they do not offer genuine working-from-home options, rather the ability to contact you at any time of the day when you are at home and for you to be equipped to work there and then. (Survey respondent #57, female, associate, national firm)

> There is no choice but to take work home in the evenings and weekends to meet a budget that acts both as a billing mechanism for clients and an (often false) representation of a lawyer's performance. (Survey respondent #118, female, lawyer, state/territory single office)

To justify the intrusiveness of the technology, an inhouse senior legal consultant at a legal recruitment and search consultancy firm in Sydney tells us the term 'work–life balance' is passé and should be replaced with 'work–life integration': 'Work/life integration means checking emails and doing work outside of business hours and taking time out of work to take care of personal affairs.'[55] Here, we have explicit managerial recognition of the fact that the line of demarcation between work and home has not just blurred but collapsed altogether. This reflects the findings of several studies regarding the intrusive effect of smart devices and social networking.[56] Work–life integration is undoubtedly the reality for many women, if not the ideal, in which juggling and multitasking are the norm—with corporate clients on the telephone while supervising their children on the beach, for example. Once seen as a blight, multitasking has been recast as a crucial skill that enables work to secure the upper hand by stealth.

Gregg, in her study *Work's Intimacy*, percipiently captures the way new technology is invading the home.[57] She shows how the effect of the dissolution of the boundary between work and home has expanded the

---

55   Felicity Nelson, 'Jury Still Out on In-House vs Law Firms', *Lawyers Weekly*, 12 March 2015, available from: www.lawyersweekly.com.au/news/16263-in-house-vs-law-firms-the-verdict.

56   Turkle (n. 2); Gregg (n. 25); Otey (n. 41).

57   Gregg (n. 25).

time allocated to work. In emphasising the blurred boundaries between labour and life, and between production and reproduction, Hardt and Negri draw attention to the distinctly feminised connotations of these relationships.[58] Thus, far from flexible work being able to produce equality for women in the legal profession, as was hoped, it may be producing a new iteration of subordination.

Not only does the zeal for 'being connected' mean that the firm receives a windfall, but also temporal flexibility has significant ramifications for the gendering of work in law firms. It is well established that male lawyers without domestic or familial responsibilities can satisfy the unstated promotion criteria of 'presenteeism' and are more likely to be rewarded in their careers.[59] These 'ideal workers', about whom Joan Williams has written persuasively,[60] not only dominate the upper echelons of the profession and control the accumulation of capital, but also assist in countering the fear of feminisation of corporate power.

As suggested, men are discouraged from working flexibly to care for children—even if they would like to do so—and may suffer a flexibility stigma because of the feminised connotations of caring. This entrenches the homologous relationship between masculinity and the long-hours culture so that male lawyers remain consistently visible to gatekeepers and clients, thereby strengthening their position as favoured candidates for promotion. 'Homosocial reproduction'[61] (replacing like with like) allows male lawyers to retain domination of the apex of the legal and professional hierarchy, where power, influence and the control of capital reside in conjunction with equity partnerships. The control of capital in corporate law firms therefore remains highly masculinised via either a traditional partnership formation, incorporating the firm, or floating it on the stock exchange, as with Slater & Gordon.[62] These initiatives reveal how the norms of legal practice are subtly moving away from professionalism and closer to those of business and capital accumulation, replicating the modus operandi of a corporate firm's multinational clients.

---

58   Hardt & Negri (n. 5) 134.
59   Mary Jane Mossman, 'Lawyers and Family Life: New Directions for the 1990s (Part One)' (1994) 2(1) *Feminist Legal Studies* 61, 70, doi.org/10.1007/bf01117250.
60   Williams (n. 22).
61   Jean Lipman-Blumen, 'Toward a Homosocial Theory of Sex Roles: An Explanation of the Sex Segregation of Social Institutions' in Martha Blaxall and Barbara Reagan (eds), *Women and the Workplace: The Implications of Occupational Segregation* (University of Chicago Press, 1976) 15.
62   For example, Steven Mark & Tahlia Gordon, 'Innovations in Regulation: Responding to a Changing Legal Services Market' (2009) 22(2) *Georgetown Journal of Legal Ethics* 501.

The shifting relationship between capitalism and the regulatory state is captured by Bauman's allusion to the 'melting of solids' that has become a feature of 'fluid modernity'.[63] This proposition is illustrated by the expansion of the market because of the neoliberal turn, leading to a rolling back of state regulation and a privatising of many of the functions of the state. So important has the economy become, Davies suggests, that neoliberalism has done away with the liberal conceit of 'separate economic, social and political spheres, evaluating all three according to a single economic logic'.[64]

As noted, being able to work anywhere at any time is an example of 'light capitalism' in contrast to the 'solid modernity or heavy capitalism' of the past.[65] Thus, the incidence of 'working from home' suggests that Davies' insight regarding the application of 'a single economic logic'[66] to the economic, social and political spheres might also fruitfully be extended to encompass the domestic sphere. In this way, the multiple incarnations of flexible work all contribute to the way capital is colonising private life.

Conclusion

The imbrication of flexible work with new technologies is beset with ambiguity. On the one hand, being able to work flexibly is appreciated, particularly by women lawyers with caring obligations. They can continue with meaningful work at their own pace while raising their children or caring for an elderly parent or sick partner. However, the numbers in large law firms who avail themselves of (formal) flexible work arrangements appear to be small at any one time. As studies have shown that workers are more productive when they are happy—producing as much as an additional 12 per cent of output[67]—there is a clear economic incentive for law firms to accede to formal requests to work flexibly. At the same time, there are negative connotations for workers as flexibility has meant that work has the potential to leach into and colonise their personal space. This is the case with lawyers who work long hours in the office but also

63   Bauman (n. 15) 6.
64   William Davies, *The Limits of Neoliberalism: Authority, Sovereignty and the Logic of Competition* (Sage, 2014) 20.
65   Bauman (n. 15) 139, 144.
66   Davies (n. 64) 20.
67   William Davies, *The Happiness Industry: How the Government and Big Business Sold Us Well-Being* (Verso, 2015) 108.

work at home after hours (informal flexibility). Some lawyers are obliged to work at night when their corporate clients operate in a different time zone, but work–work can quickly become a habit, or even an addiction.

For others, dissatisfaction with the model of the large law firm, with its rigid hierarchy, long-hours culture and relentless billable hours has resulted in the search for alternative models of practice. Williams, Platt and Lee have carried out a thorough study of 'NewLaw' developments in legal practice in the United States, which they describe as 'disruptive innovations'.[68] As a reaction against the marble, mahogany and Monets favoured by large law firms, for which clients must pay, NewLaw may do away with offices altogether to keep overheads low. Among the most significant factors regarding the new models are their exceptionally flexible work schedules, which allow lawyers to choose their hours of work. These models have frequently been initiated by women lawyers and make a point of hiring women, some of whom elect to work as few as 10 hours a week. By starting off with a clean slate rather than accepting the prevailing masculinist norms, NewLaw has largely eliminated the flexibility stigma.[69] There is still a risk that the need to 'be connected' sustains the applicability of the cyborg metaphor. However, a seemingly radical measure to avoid trespassing on intimate space may include informing clients that lawyers do not check emails after hours or at weekends.

While the virtual features of NewLaw are appealing to women lawyers when faced with the needs of small children, presenteeism and visibility in traditional law firms continue to ensure preservation of the masculinity of the apex of the organisational pyramid of the law firm hierarchy where wealth and power are concentrated. Wald suggests that hypercompetitive meritocracy 'forecloses, by its very nature, the possibility of reduced or flexible schedules and reliance on technology to allow for work-from-home alternatives'.[70] While the technology facilitates working remotely, the prevailing ideology in corporate legal practice requires 'physical attendance as a symbolic measure of loyalty, 24/7 commitment, and near-instant responsiveness'. The conservative ideology that positions motherhood, children and families in opposition to careers is endorsed by

---

68   Joan C. Williams, Aaron Platt & Jessica Lee, *Disruptive innovation: New models of legal practice* (Legal Studies Research Paper Series, University of California Hastings College of Law, 2015) 5–6. See also Margaret Thornton, 'Towards the Uberisation of Legal Practice' (2019) 1(1) *Law, Technology and Humans* 46, doi.org/10.5204/lthj.v1i1.1277.

69   Williams et al. (n. 68) 10.

70   Wald (n. 6) 2283.

many senior men in law firms. If they are married, their female partners are frequently not in the paid workforce, at least not full-time. Even if they are well-qualified lawyers, the women tend to abandon their careers in favour of their male partners when choices must be made as to who should be the primary carer in the relationship—not only because men's earning potential is greater, but also because a lingering suspicion remains that once a woman has had a child, she is not serious about her career.

Substantive feminisation of the legal profession is thereby counteracted by the entrenched masculinist norms of homosociality. If women are dissatisfied with the prevailing conditions, they are free to leave, and large numbers do, as illustrated by the high attrition rates. They frequently go inhouse: 'They still work reasonably hard there but there's no billing and it's not as crazy' (Interviewee, female, associate, state/territory single office). The sustained attempts by women lawyers to change the prevailing norms of private legal practice, including the long-hours culture, have had remarkably little impact. Indeed, it has been suggested that the proliferation of law graduates 'sustains poor working-time conditions and high turnover rates',[71] as those who exit can be quickly replaced. It may be that the issue of supply outweighs competing factors such as the retention of top talent, improved performance, commitment, morale and satisfaction.

Of course, the use of technology in the home was never going to remain a stable social form; as a new productive site, it was inevitably going to be deployed by capitalism, as Marx predicted.[72] The ramifications are so profound they are changing the traditional configuration of the public/private dichotomy as the division between the economic realm and the home dissolves.

While law firms have been able to maintain surveillance over employees working flexibly through conventional disciplinary mechanisms, such as billable hours, the technology also harbours new forms of surveillance that have the potential to be utilised in respect of those working at home. Televisions are now able to record conversations in our living rooms and transmit them to the manufacturer[73] and a similar technology is built into

---

71   Campbell et al. (n. 26) 162.
72   Crary (n. 45) 37.
73   Lance Whitney, 'Watch Out: How to Stop Your Smart TV From Spying on You', *PC Mag Australia*, 27 April 2020, available from: au.pcmag.com/dvd/66546/how-to-stop-smart-tvs-from-snooping-on-you.

mobile phones and other spy apps. The Highster Mobile, for example, is a device that enables employers to monitor their employees' use of devices and websites in the workplace.[74] This technology not only further blurs the distinction between the body of the worker and the technology, but also totally eradicates the idea of an intimate space where the lawyer-worker can be free of scrutiny and the pressures of work.

While Haraway argues that the cyborg possesses a subversive power to transgress boundaries,[75] I am less optimistic, as the contemporary cyborg must be alert to the deployment of power from unexpected sources. Hence, flexible work may not represent the great advance for women workers that it was initially believed to be. Not only does it enable work to leach into the private sphere and colonise it, but also it is being deployed to retain the subordination of women in the legal profession just when the tipping point has been reached.

---

74   'Free Highster Mobile Alternatives' (AlternativeTo: Crowdsourced Software Recommendations, 17 May 2021), available from: alternativeto.net/software/highster-mobile/?license=free.
75   Haraway (n. 1) 152.

8

Who Cares? The Conundrum for Gender Equality

Introduction: More than numbers

When women sought to be admitted to the practice of law in the late nineteenth century, they encountered sustained resistance.[1] In addition to specious arguments regarding their intellectual ability and the likely negative impact of higher education on their reproductive capacity,[2] courts even went so far as to hold that women were not persons for the purposes of admission.[3] The animus towards women persisted long after they were grudgingly admitted, and their numbers remained small until the 1970s when growth in the economy and the impact of the women's movement encouraged them to enrol in law schools in substantial numbers. In 2020, 53 per cent of lawyers in Australian private practice were women—a proportion that is increasing faster than the male rate.[4]

---

1 Mary Jane Mossman, *The First Women Lawyers: A Comparative Study of Gender, Law and the Legal Professions* (Hart Publishing, 2006); Margaret Thornton, 'Squeezing the Life Out of Lawyers: Legal Practice in the Market Embrace' (2016) 25(4) *Griffith Law Review* 471–91, doi.org/10.1080/10383441.2016.1262230; Margaret Thornton, *Dissonance and Distrust: Women in the Legal Profession* (Oxford University Press, 1996).

2 See, for example, Herbert Spencer, *The Principles of Biology. Volume 2* (Williams & Norgate, 1867) 512–13.

3 Albie Sachs & Joan Hoff Wilson, *Sexism and the Law: A Study of Male Beliefs and Legal Bias in Britain and the United States* (Free Press, 1978). For an Australian example of a Persons' Case, see *Re Edith Haynes* [1904] 6 WALR 209, which is discussed in Chapter 1.

4 Law Society of New South Wales, *2020 National Profile of Solicitors: Final* (Urbis, 2021) 7, available from: www.lawsociety.com.au/sites/default/files/2021-07/2020%20National%20Profile%20of%20Solicitors%20-%20Final%20-%201%20July%202021.pdf.

Despite the changing gender composition of the legal profession, the seeds of invidiousness continue to cling to the feminine, particularly in relation to authoritative positions. Hence, women tend to be clustered at the lower echelons of the typical law firm hierarchy and the percentage of women partners remains less than 25 per cent in both common law and civil law countries.[5] Even if women are promoted, they are more likely to be assigned to less prestigious salary or non-equity partnerships. The masculinised nature of senior leadership positions not only creates an environment in which it is difficult for women to progress,[6] but it also enables men to extract an increasing share of surplus labour from women.[7] The dichotomy is built on a deeply embedded substructure of gender difference that is by no means peculiar to law.[8]

Nevertheless, if feminisation is understood in terms of numerosity alone, it appears that gender equality has been achieved and the masculinist subtext is ignored; however, 'fixing the numbers' is only the first stage towards gender equality, as Londa Schiebinger points out.[9] The next stage she identifies is 'fixing the institutions' (effecting structural change), which is followed by 'fixing the knowledge' (integrating gender-based knowledge

---

5   Jane Ellis & Ashleigh Buckett, *Women in Commercial Legal Practice* (Report, International Bar Association, December 2017) 20. The US figure is 30 per cent (but only 20 per cent of AmLaw 200 firms). See Meghan Tribe, 'New Report Finds Female Path to Law Firm Partnership a Sluggish Crawl', *The American Lawyer*, 10 October 2018, available from: www.law.com/americanlawyer/2018/10/10/new-report-finds-female-path-to-law-firm-partnership-a-sluggish-crawl/?slreturn=20190211235254. The UK figure is 33 per cent (29 per cent in large firms). See Solicitors Regulation Authority, *How Diverse Are Law Firms?* (SRA, 2017), available from: www.sra.org.uk/sra/equality-diversity/archive/law-firms-2017/. The 2018 Australian figure is 27 per cent. See Michael Pelly & Edmund Tadros, 'Legal Partnership Survey 2018: Herbert Smith Freehills' Perfect Record on Women', *Australian Financial Review*, 5 July 2018, available from: www.afr.com/news/legal-partnership-survey-2018-herbert-smith-freehills-perfect-record-on-women-20180625-h11uif.

6   Law Council of Australia, *National Attrition and Re-Engagement Study (NARS) Report* (Urbis, 14 March 2014), available from: www.lawcouncil.asn.au/docs/a8bae9a1-9830-e711-80d2-005056be66b1/NARS%20Report.pdf. Cf. Roberta D. Liebenberg & Stephanie A. Scharf, *Walking Out the Door: The Facts, Figures, and Future of Experienced Women Lawyers in Private Practice* (Report, American Bar Association & ALM Intelligence, 2019), available from: www.americanbar.org/content/dam/aba/administrative/women/walking-out-the-door-4920053.pdf. This study documents the disproportionately high attrition rate for senior women lawyers in the United States.

7   Sharon C. Bolton & Daniel Muzio, 'Can't Live with 'Em; Can't Live without 'Em: Gendered Segmentation in the Legal Profession' (2007) 41(1) *Sociology* 47, 60, doi.org/10.1177/0038038507072283.

8   Joan Acker, 'Hierarchies, Jobs, Bodies: A Theory of Gendered Organizations' (1990) 4(2) *Gender and Society* 139, doi.org/10.1177/089124390004002002.

9   Elsevier, *Gender in the Global Research Landscape: Analysis of Research Performance through a Gender Lens across 20 Years, 12 Geographies, and 27 Subject Areas* (Report, 6 February 2017) 74–76, available from: www.elsevier.com/__data/assets/pdf_file/0003/1083945/Elsevier-gender-report-2017.pdf.

into research). Because of the durability of gendered institutions,[10] it is apparent that we are still wrestling with structural change. Formal equality has focused on 'letting women in' to workplaces as they are because of the dominant view that gender is irrelevant to the way they are constituted.[11] This has proven to be particularly problematic for those with caring responsibilities and it continues to be the case despite the extensive research on the 'work–family interface'.[12]

Women have conventionally been expected to take responsibility for the demands of the private sphere for love—as they have always done: caring for children, the aged, people with disabilities and the sick, as well as running households and looking after grown men 'perfectly capable of looking after themselves'.[13] At the same time, women are expected to compete with those same men in the workplace. In view of the unequal distribution of caring responsibilities, it is perhaps unsurprising that women report greater work effort than their male colleagues.[14] Indeed, I suggest that the question of 'who cares' represents the last bastion of the struggle for gender equality in the legal workplace.

Even though gender equality in the legal profession has been an issue of concern for decades, it is somewhat surprising that gender-neutral modes of caring have been accorded comparatively little attention. The focus of attention is invariably skewed towards what is viewed as a woman's problem, with motherhood positioned as the key factor.[15] A paradox therefore arises because the realisation of gender equality is predicated on gender specificity. It is only with the millennial turn that the emphasis began to shift and men's parenting practices began to be questioned,

---

10   Cf. Joyce S. Sterling & Nancy Reichman, 'Overlooked and Undervalued: Women in Private Law Practice' (2016) 12 *Annual Review of Law and Social Science* 373, doi.org/10.1146/annurev-lawsocsci-120814-121705.

11   Robin J. Ely & Debra E. Meyerson, 'Advancing Gender Equity in Organizations: The Challenge and Importance of Maintaining a Gender Narrative' (2000) 7(4) *Organization* 589, 604, doi.org/10.1177/135050840074005.

12   Joan C. Williams, Jennifer L. Berdahl & Joseph A. Vandello, 'Beyond Work–Life "Integration"' (2016) 67 *Annual Review of Psychology* 515, 516, doi.org/10.1146/annurev-psych-122414-033710.

13   Cf. Nancy Fraser, *Unruly Practices: Power, Discourse and Gender in Contemporary Social Theory* (University of Minnesota Press, 1989) 148.

14   Elizabeth H. Gorman & Julie A. Kmec, 'We (Have to) Try Harder: Gender and Required Work Effort in Britain and the United States' (2007) 21(6) *Gender & Society* 828, 844, doi.org/10.1177/0891243207309900.

15   Richard Collier, 'Rethinking Men and Masculinities in the Contemporary Legal Profession: The Example of Fatherhood, Transnational Business Masculinities, and Work–Life Balance in Large Law Firms' (2013) 13(2) *Nevada Law Journal* 410, 417.

which led to modest changes in public policy. Apart from the work of Richard Collier in the United Kingdom,[16] there is a dearth of scholarship on the role of fatherhood in the legal profession.

In this chapter, I address the question of 'who cares', considering its significance for women's equality in the legal workplace. Rather than continuing to devise more creative ways for women to accommodate caring responsibilities in their working lives, it is argued that gender equality in the legal profession is unattainable unless men share equally in caring responsibilities.

To give the reader a sense of why we seem to have reached an impasse in the struggle for gender equality, I first overview the main measures introduced by the state to accommodate caring responsibilities as women began to be recognised as economic actors. Second, drawing on interviews with lawyers in corporate firms, I analyse the efficacy of flexible work. While this was thought to be the way forward, it was found to incur a stigma when undertaken by men. Third, I draw on supplementary interviews with lawyers in 'NewLaw' firms, in which both technology and flexibility are central. Perhaps, unsurprisingly, these studies did not rebut the presumption in favour of women as primary carers. Fourth, I turn to a brief consideration of the experience of the Nordic countries to consider the pros and cons of a stronger interventionist stance on the part of the state to encourage fathers to take time off work to share in caring responsibilities, although studies of lawyer-fathers are sparse, as they are elsewhere. Fifth, as the success of such initiatives has been limited, I explore the reasons lawyer-fathers are resistant to spending time as full-time carers, despite the contemporary rhetoric that a 'good dad' should not be an absent father. I conclude that it is apparent that male lawyers, like professional men generally, remain committed to their careers and are prepared to make no more than a token contribution to caring, such as taking one or two weeks' paternity leave after the birth of a child.

As Acker has argued, those with the greatest commitment to the workplace are deemed more suited to responsibility and authority, whereas those with divided commitments are consigned to the lower ranks.[17] Hence,

---

16   ibid. See also Richard Collier, *Masculinity, Law and the Family* (Routledge, 1995); Richard Collier & Sally Sheldon, *Fragmenting Fatherhood: A Socio-Legal Study* (Hart Publishing, 2008); Richard Collier, *Men, Law and Gender: Essays on the 'Man' of Law* (Routledge, 2010).
17   Acker (n. 8) 149.

while models of fatherhood are slowly changing, they fall short of the shared parenting ideal, which I suggest is the essential prerequisite to gender equality in the legal workplace.

Towards fixing the institutions

Accommodating the feminisation of care

When women were first 'let in' to the legal profession, they were expected to choose between a career and motherhood. Marriage was customarily a signal for women to leave the workforce and assume unpaid responsibilities in the private sphere. This was legitimised by the Australian Public Service requirement until 1966 that a woman must resign on marriage.[18] Ingrained within the culture was the idea that a 'good mother stays home, and a good man goes to work and is a full-time breadwinner'.[19] It was assumed the lawyer-mother would be unable to show concern for her children and focus on work. This understanding was influenced by many prominent thinkers of the Western intellectual tradition, such as Rousseau[20] and Freud,[21] who propounded the view that there was a *natural* association between women and the private sphere. This contrasted the image of the paradigmatic male worker, the unencumbered monad of liberalism, who was deemed to be able to slough off responsibility for the private sphere once he left home. It was assumed he had an 'economically inactive wife'[22] who would take responsibility for caring and housework.

The feminisation of labour refers to the worldwide movement of women into full-time employment that occurred in the late twentieth century.[23] It directly challenged the liberal separation of the public and private spheres. As women became an indispensable source of labour

---

18   *Public Service Act (No. 2) 1966* (Cth). See also Marian Sawer (ed.), *Removal of the Commonwealth Marriage Bar: A Documentary History* (Centre for Research in Public Sector Management, University of Canberra, 1996).

19   Calla Wahlquist, 'Gender Bias Still Rife in Legal Profession Despite Rhetoric, Says Kate Jenkins', *The Guardian*, 2 June 2017, available from: www.theguardian.com/world/2017/jun/02/gender-bias-still-rife-in-legal-profession-despite-rhetoric-says-kate-jenkins.

20   Jean-Jacques Rousseau, *Émile*, translated by Barbara Foxley (Dent, 1974).

21   Sigmund Freud, 'Some Psychical Consequences of the Anatomical Distinction between the Sexes' in James Strachey (ed.), *The Standard Edition of the Complete Psychological Works of Sigmund Freud. Volume 19* (Hogarth Press, 1961) 248.

22   Guy Weir, 'The Economically Inactive Who Look After the Family or Home' (2002) 110(11) *Labour Market Trends* 577.

23   Michael Hardt & Antonio Negri, *Commonwealth* (Harvard University Press, 2009) 133.

during postwar economic growth, both governments and employers were compelled to adapt to the fact that society also expected women to continue to take primary responsibility for the care of families and the running of households.

To accommodate the increasingly significant role of women as economic actors, initiatives gradually emerged in the mid twentieth century at the international level and were implemented in domestic legislation. The most significant instrument was the CEDAW,[24] accompanied by a raft of other ILO conventions and recommendations.[25] All these instruments implicitly recognised that the public and private spheres could no longer be treated as discrete, as had been the case in the Western intellectual tradition. As a result, pregnancy, potential pregnancy, breastfeeding and family responsibilities were expressly included as subsets of sex discrimination legislation in employment.[26] From the 1970s, maternity leave was introduced, which allowed a woman to retain her job and return to work after pregnancy. Although this was initially unpaid, a period of paid leave subsequently became the norm. The gender-specific language of 'maternity leave' eventually morphed into 'parental leave', but it continued to be aimed principally at mothers,[27] although two weeks' paid paternity leave was made available to fathers.[28] The gender-neutral language of 'parental' leave also occludes the tension between employment and welfare that underpins the history of parental leave policies in Australia and the United Kingdom, with 'employment' having a masculinist bias and 'welfare' carrying feminised overtones.[29]

24 *Convention on the Elimination of All Forms of Discrimination against Women*, opened for signature 18 December 1979, 1249 UNTS 13 (entered into force 3 September 1981).
25 See, for example, *Convention Concerning Equal Opportunities and Equal Treatment for Men and Women Workers: Workers with Family Responsibilities, 1981 (No. 156)*, opened for signature 23 June 1981 (entered into force 11 August 1983); *Part-Time Work Convention, 1994 (No. 175)*, opened for signature 24 June 1994 (entered into force 28 February 1998); *Maternity Protection Convention (Revised), 1953 (No. 183)*, opened for signature 28 June 1952 (entered into force 7 February 2002).
26 See, for example, *SDA*.
27 For a detailed history and analysis of policies, see Marian Baird & Margaret O'Brien, 'Dynamics of Parental Leave in Anglophone Countries: The Paradox of State Expansion in Liberal Welfare Regimes' (2015) 18(2) *Community, Work & Family* 198, doi.org/10.1080/13668803.2015.1021755.
28 See, for example, *Paid Parental Leave Act 2010* (Cth). More than one-quarter (27 per cent) of fathers and partners (of a total of 1,001) surveyed for the National Prevalence Survey reported experiencing discrimination when requesting or taking parental leave or when they returned to work, despite the short period (less than four weeks) usually sought. Only 2 per cent of the men affected lodged a complaint with a government agency. See Australian Human Rights Commission, *Supporting Working Parents: Pregnancy and Return to Work National Review* (Report, AHRC, 2014) 48, 53, available from: www.humanrights.gov.au/sites/default/files/document/publication/SWP_Report_2014.pdf.
29 Baird & O'Brien (n. 27) 206.

Despite these public policy initiatives, pregnancy and childcare have continued to be persistent sources of less favourable treatment for women in the workplace,[30] signalling the difficulty of effecting a transition of the materiality of care from the home to the environment of paid work. In fact, 49 per cent of respondents reported in a 2014 national survey that they experienced discrimination in the workplace during pregnancy, parental leave or on return to work on at least one occasion.[31] Thirty-two per cent of 'professionals' surveyed (of a total of 595) reported experiencing discrimination either when requesting parental leave or during parental leave, and 35 per cent reported experiencing discrimination on return to work. This included being made redundant, having their position restructured, being dismissed or not having their contract renewed. As is the case with most national surveys, this one did not provide disaggregated figures for lawyers. However, a national survey by the Law Council of Australia, also conducted in 2014, found that 55 per cent of women lawyers who were primary carers were likely to experience discrimination.[32] These studies reveal a significant gap between the legal framework and the reality, which underscores the residual animus towards motherhood at work.

In contrast, fatherhood is construed positively in the legal workplace because of the higher status associated with being a good provider than with active caring. Kay, Alarie and Adjei found that the more children a male lawyer had, the more secure was his position in the firm, whereas the 'hazard ratio' for women associated with leaving private practice increased with each child.[33] Indeed, the 'absent father' is the paradigmatic unencumbered subject of liberalism. He is the 'ideal worker' who continues to work 'full time and overtime and takes little or no time off for childbearing or child rearing'.[34] In the process, the actual parenting practices of men tend to fade from view so they become de-gendered, embodying 'a form of "bleached out" legal professionalism'.[35] To spend time as a primary carer carries a stigma that may be even more marked

---

30   Law Council of Australia (n. 6) 23–24.

31   Australian Human Rights Commission (n. 28) 26.

32   Law Council of Australia (n. 6) 34.

33   Fiona M. Kay, Stacey Alarie & Jones Adjei, 'Leaving Private Practice: How Organizational Context, Time Pressures, and Structural Inflexibilities Shape Departures from Private Law Practice' (2013) 20(2) *Indiana Journal of Global Legal Studies* 1223, 1251, doi.org/10.2979/indjglolegstu. 20.2.1223.

34   Joan Williams, *Unbending Gender: Why Family and Work Conflict and What to Do About It* (Oxford University Press, 1999) 1.

35   Richard Collier, 'Fatherhood, Gender and the Making of Professional Identity in Large Law Firms: Bringing Men into the Frame' (2019) 15(1) *International Journal of Law in Context* 68, 71–72, doi.org/10.1017/s1744552318000162.

for men than for women. The failure to pay heed to this factor causes the gender inequality gap to widen.[36] However, employers prefer to champion the 'ideal worker' norm that is dependent on the full-time labour availability of men.[37]

Flexible work

While the feminisation of labour resulted in positive initiatives for women workers, they were still expected to assume responsibility for the primary care of children while conforming to the demands of the standard working day. The irreconcilable tension between these competing ends resulted in a high rate of attrition of women from full-time work, including legal practice.[38] In an endeavour to stop the haemorrhage, the Australian Government created a right for workers to request flexible working hours and modified arrangements rather than adhere to a rigid schedule, such as nine to five.[39] Flexible work can take a range of forms, such as part-time work, job-sharing, working from home and adjusting the hours of the working day, as discussed in Chapter 7. While flexible work policies are couched in gender-neutral terms, this has not altered the feminised identity of the primary carer.[40] Indeed, a statistical overview of family employment patterns in Australia over the past two decades reveals that while mothers' employment changed considerably after having a child, fathers' employment showed little change.[41] Indeed, only one in 20 fathers in the general population takes primary parental leave.[42]

The resistance by employers to their employees working flexibly was borne out by an online Australia-wide survey (n = 424) and follow-up interviews (n = 54) undertaken by the author that involved male and

36   Linda Haas & C. Philip Hwang, 'Workplace Support and European Fathers' Use of State Policies Promoting Shared Childcare' (2019) 22(1) *Community, Work & Family* 1, 2.
37   ibid., 7.
38   See, for example, Fiona M. Kay, Stacey L. Alarie & Jones K. Adjei, 'Undermining Gender Equality: Female Attrition from Private Law Practice' (2016) 50(3) *Law & Society Review* 766, doi.org/10.1111/lasr.12214. Cf. Liebenberg & Scharf (n. 6).
39   *Fair Work Act 2009* (Cth) ss 65–66.
40   A respondent to the National Prevalence Survey who was in a same-sex relationship objected to the term 'primary carer' on the basis that 'we are both primary, we are equally important parents'. See Australian Human Rights Commission (n. 28) 89.
41   Jennifer Baxter, *Fathers and Work: A Statistical Overview* (Research Snapshot, Australian Institute of Family Studies, May 2019), available from: aifs.gov.au/aifs-conference/fathers-and-work.
42   Parents at Work, *Advancing parental leave equality and introducing shared care in Australia: The business case for action* (White Paper, PAW, 2018) 4, available from: parentsandcarersatwork.com/wp-content/uploads/2018/08/PAW_White-Paper-Parental-Leave-Equality.pdf.

female lawyers in corporate law firms in 2012–14, 'Balancing Law and Life'.[43] The aim was to establish lawyers' perceptions and experiences of the impact of work–life balance, wellbeing and family harmony in light of competition policy that had been accepted in the legal profession as a result of the conjunction of the *Competition Policy Reform Act 1995* (Cth) and the liberalising measures effected in the Australian legal profession since the millennial turn.[44]

While a survey of Australian law firms conducted by *Lawyers Weekly* found a very significant 89 per cent supported flexible work,[45] numerous respondents in the Balancing Law and Life study noted there was a marked gap between the rhetoric and the reality.[46] A high level of productivity was not enough to dispel the flexibility stigma associated with a lawyer (invariably the mother) working part-time, leaving the office early to pick up children from school or working from home for, say, one day a week. Flexible work also exerted a negative effect on the quality of the lawyers' assignments and their future careers.[47] The masculinist norms of an unbroken career pattern and being seen (presenteeism) continued to be accepted as evidence of serious commitment to one's career and presumptive eligibility for partnership.[48] This pressure to be seen has been internalised by lawyers in accordance with the Foucauldian idea of governing the self.[49] Several male interviewees mentioned they barely saw their children during the week as they left home early in the morning and

---

43   Australian Research Council DP 1020104785 ('Balancing Law and Life'). Law societies and women lawyers' associations assisted with the distribution of the survey. The anonymity of subjects was guaranteed as a condition of ethics approval, which was obtained from the Human Research Ethics Committee of The Australian National University in 2012. The questionnaire was completed by lawyers in corporate law firms, with a gender breakdown of 25 per cent male and 75 per cent female, with roughly equal numbers of men and women in the follow-up interviews. For detailed analyses of this study, see Margaret Thornton, 'Work/Life or Work/Work? Corporate Legal Practice in the Twenty-First Century' (2016) 23(1) *International Journal of the Legal Profession* 13, doi.org/10.1080/09695958.2015.1093939; Thornton, 'Squeezing the Life Out of Lawyers' (n. 1).

44   Joanne Bagust, 'The Legal Profession and the Business of Law' (2013) 35(1) *Sydney Law Review* 27.

45   John MacLean, 'Closing the Gender Gap', *Lawyers Weekly*, 16 October 2014, available from: www.lawyersweekly.com.au/careers/15824-closing-the-gender-gap.

46   Thornton, 'Work/Life' (n. 43) 23–24.

47   Stephanie Bornstein, 'The Legal and Policy Implications of the "Flexibility Stigma"' (2013) 69(2) *Journal of Social Issues* 389, 392, doi.org/10.1111/josi.12020; Iain Campbell, Sara Charlesworth & Jenny Malone, 'Part-Time of What? Job Quality and Part-Time Employment in the Legal Profession in Australia' (2011) 48(2) *Journal of Sociology* 149, 158–59, doi.org/10.1177/1440783311408970.

48   Margaret Thornton & Joanne Bagust, 'The Gender Trap: Flexible Work in Corporate Legal Practice' (2007) 45(4) *Osgoode Hall Law Journal* 773.

49   Michel Foucault, 'Governmentality' in Graham Burchell, Colin Gordon & Peter Miller (eds), *The Foucault Effect: Studies in Governmentality* (Harvester Wheatsheaf, 1991) 87.

did not return until late at night. If a male lawyer wished to work flexibly, he tended to move from a corporate law firm to a workplace with regular hours or set up as an independent contractor.

It is apparent that few Australian fathers are as heavily involved in the care of their children as their mothers, despite the widespread view that they should be.[50] Indeed, in the case of a heteronormative lawyer couple with young children, it is deemed to be economically rational for the female partner to take time off to look after the children or to work part-time as she tends to be paid less than her spouse.[51] It could be some years before she returns to work full-time, in which case it is very difficult to make up for lost time. She may choose to pursue an alternative form of work that is less demanding or to work part-time or casually rather than struggle to rebuild her career. In the meantime, her partner's 'unbroken' career path may have flourished, resulting in a partnership, which is likely to elude her permanently, although she may have a chance in a small firm. The financial benefit associated with his success in the 'tournament' for partnership[52] may act as a further disincentive for her to persevere with a legal career, which confines her to a 'managed' position and endorses the gendered hierarchy within law firms.

Corroborated by studies in the United States,[53] Balancing Law and Life found the stigma associated with working flexibly was even more marked for men, although less so if they worked flexibly to accommodate a non-caring activity, such as sport.[54] However, men acting as primary carers are rated higher on feminised traits as being weak, naive, insecure and emotional in a way that is deemed to detract from their manhood.[55] This stigma contributes to the fact that flexibility programs are underutilised by men everywhere,[56]

---

50   C. Starla Hargita, 'Care-Based Temporalities and Parental Leave in Australia' (2017) 26(4) *Griffith Law Review* 511, 516, doi.org/10.1080/10383441.2017.1552554.

51   Linda Haas & C. Philip Hwang, 'The Impact of Taking Parental Leave on Fathers' Participation in Childcare and Relationships with Children: Lessons from Sweden' (2008) 11(1) *Community, Work & Family* 85, 91, doi.org/10.1080/13668800701785346.

52   Marc Galanter & Thomas M. Palay, *Tournament of Lawyers: The Transformation of the Big Law Firm* (University of Chicago Press, 1991).

53   For example, Laurie A. Rudman & Kris Mescher, 'Penalizing Men Who Request a Family Leave: Is Flexibility Stigma a Femininity Stigma?' (2013) 69(2) *Journal of Social Issues* 322, doi.org/10.1111/josi.12017; Joan C. Williams, Mary Blair-Loy & Jennifer L. Berdahl, 'Cultural Schemas, Social Class, and the Flexibility Stigma' (2013) 69(2) *Journal of Social Issues* 209.

54   Joseph A. Vandello, Vanessa E. Hettinger, Jennifer K. Bosson & Jasmine Siddiqi, 'When Equal Isn't Really Equal: The Masculine Dilemma of Seeking Work Flexibility' (2013) 69(2) *Journal of Social Issues* 303, 304, doi.org/10.1111/josi.12016.

55   Rudman & Mescher (n. 53) 329, 332.

56   Vandello et al. (n. 54) 304.

despite the desire expressed by individual lawyer-fathers that they want to be 'good dads', not just breadwinners.[57] While they might aspire to a more active role with their children than that of their own fathers,[58] the focus on work intensification and profit maximisation that was exacerbated by the GFC[59] accentuated the importance of career success for men.

One female interviewee surveyed the male lawyers in her former international firm to ascertain the extent of support for part-time work and parental leave. She found the men were unanimously opposed to working less than full-time because 'they didn't want to take a step down in their career'. Thus, despite the widespread advocacy of flexible work, the ideal worker continues to be constructed as the stereotypical unencumbered monad of liberalism. This means the worker who works flexibly, including part-time or casually, to manage family responsibilities is more likely to be female and is deemed to be a less-than-ideal worker. The intractability of the gendered dichotomy at work operates to preserve the gendered division of labour within the heteronormative two-parent family.[60] Women lawyers are expected to be grateful for being able to combine parenting with work they care about, albeit in a subordinate role. While they may be commended socially for placing their family first, they will not be rewarded in career terms.

Even as recently as 2019, a panel of senior legal practitioners at a Sydney roundtable were reported as unanimously expressing the opinion that 'for a female lawyer to achieve a senior role, she must either delay having a family, return to work very soon after giving birth to prove her commitment to the firm or find a new pathway to achieve her goals'.[61] The four lawyers on the panel were of the view that Small Law, particularly starting one's own practice, was a more attractive option for many women in law than Big Law, despite the fact that Big Law firms were striving for, and sometimes reaching, gender parity targets.

---

57   Collier (n. 35) 74–77.
58   ibid.; Collier (n. 15) 424; Jamie Atkinson, 'Shared Parental Leave in the UK: Can It Advance Gender Equality by Changing Fathers into Co-Parents?' (2017) 13(3) *International Journal of Law in Context* 356, doi.org/10.1017/s1744552317000209.
59   Hilary Sommerlad, '"A Pit to Put Women In": Professionalism, Work Intensification, Sexualisation and Work–Life Balance in the Legal Profession in England and Wales' (2016) 23(1) *International Journal of the Legal Profession* 61, 65, doi.org/10.1080/09695958.2016.1140945.
60   Rosabeth Moss Kanter, *Work and Family Life in the United States: A Critical Review and Agenda for Research and Policy* (Russell Sage Foundation, 1977) 15.
61   Jerome Doraisamy, 'Women May Be Better Off in "Small Law"', *Lawyers Weekly*, 12 March 2019, available from: www.lawyersweekly.com.au/sme-law/25237-women-may-be-better-off-in-small-law.

Such statements make it clear that responsibility is still being placed on women to adapt to the prevailing masculinist norms of the workplace, with the result that the rhetoric of work–life balance sounds increasingly hollow. If they received a request from a client at five o'clock on Friday, they had to stay back and work, regardless of the inconvenience. Indeed, several respondents to the Balancing Law and Life study expressed the view that any reference in their firm to work–life balance amounted to no more than window dressing, as such a balance was impossible given the demands placed on them by the firm. The notion of part-time work in corporate firms tended to be just as hollow, as women lawyers who were paid for a four-day week were often expected to be available on the fifth day for telephone calls and emails.

Flexible law

'NewLaw' is the generic descriptor given to a cluster of innovative ways of practising law in which flexible work is central.[62] It is a business model where labour arbitrage (in which an advantage is taken of a price difference between two or more markets) is used in the delivery of legal services. It represents a radical change from a full-time office presence as it is dependent on technology, which may mean never coming to the office at all. This can include not meeting with clients face-to-face when email, video conferencing and automated platforms will suffice. As the literature on NewLaw is scant, and to ascertain the possibility that it might dispel the likelihood of overcoming the femininity stigma associated with flexible work in traditional legal practice, the author conducted a small follow-up study to Balancing Law and Life, involving 38 interviews (30 in Australia and eight in the United Kingdom) in 2018.[63] Potential interviewees were identified with the assistance of law societies and websites; anonymity was a condition of ethics approval (ANU Ethics Protocol 2017/597).

---

62 The term is believed to have been coined by Eric Chin in 2013. See Josef Legal, 'Interview with Eric Chin, the Man Who Coined the Phrase "NewLaw"', *Josef*, [Blog], 9 April 2019, available from: joseflegal.com/blog/interview-with-eric-chin-the-man-who-coined-the-phrase-newlaw. See also Joan C. Williams, Aaron Platt & Jessica Lee, 'Disruptive Innovation: New Models of Legal Practice' (2015) 67(1) *Hastings Law Journal* 1.

63 The lawyers in NewLaw firms accorded little significance to place, as reliance on the internet facilitated a global clientele. For a comprehensive analysis of NewLaw, see Margaret Thornton, 'Towards the Uberisation of Legal Practice' (2019) 1(1) *Law, Technology and Humans* 46, doi.org/10.5204/lthj. v1i1.1277.

As a small qualitative study, its findings do not purport to be representative of all lawyers engaged in NewLaw, particularly young lawyers, whose positions are less secure. Because minimal oversight is associated with working away from the office, NewLaw prefers lawyers with a minimum of two to four years' experience in elite private practice, whereas other firms, especially those with a corporate clientele, specify at least 10 years' post-qualification experience.

Few NewLaw lawyers worked full-time in a firm unless they worked on secondment for corporate clients. The majority of them were able to choose where they worked, when they worked and how much they worked so they could integrate the practice of law with other aspects of their lives. This integration contrasted significantly with the Balancing Law and Life study, where a strict boundary existed between work and family, as borne out by the antipathy towards lawyers working flexibly. If NewLaw lawyers were engaged in caring activities, they did not feel they had to disguise it: 'I can say to a client, "I pick up my children from school on Monday, but I can do the job for you on Tuesday", which I think people like. They want to know that you're human' (Principal, female, UK).

Another principal rejected the idea of a fixed routine altogether, fitting work around the needs of her family. She was not afraid to act unconventionally:

> Today, I'll go and pick up my daughter at three o'clock and then I'm having a meeting with one of my team members at the park from three till five so that my daughter can play in the park, my six-month-old can sit next to us, and we can discuss some of the projects that [my team member] is working on. (Principal, female, Australia)

Several lawyers interviewed—all women with young children—worked as independent contractors at beachside locations in Australia, hundreds of kilometres from the city and the principals to whom they reported. Contractualism maximised their autonomy, enabling them to work for as little as 10 hours a week if they wished. As 'working mums', some of these women nevertheless suspected they were vulnerable to exploitation in negotiating terms of employment because they were unable to work full-time in an office.

The flexibility of NewLaw enabled fathers to participate in active parenting without the stigma it attracted in corporate law firms. Fathers could easily spend a day or more a week engaged in childcare, if they wished, without drawing attention to it; or, if employed, they could negotiate longer periods off. Independent contractors were free to choose whatever suited them. Baxter's study of Australian fathers' work arrangements reveals an increase in flexible work by fathers with children aged under 12,[64] but few fathers in the NewLaw study reported working part-time to care for young children, even though it could be easily accommodated. Men appeared to be more interested in using their flexible schedules to advance their paid work interests, as Brandth and Kvande found in the case of Norwegian fathers, whereas mothers used their flexible schedules to achieve a work–family balance.[65]

All the lawyers—male and female—interviewed for the NewLaw project in both the United Kingdom and Australia were very satisfied with their experience. This was the case whether they were principals of firms, employees or independent contractors. This satisfaction contrasted markedly with the Balancing Law and Life study conducted in traditional law firms.[66] The NewLaw interviewees found working flexibly to be relatively stress-free, frequently describing themselves as 'happy'—a descriptor rarely invoked by the interviewees in corporate law firms who struggled to satisfy the competing demands in their lives. The NewLaw interviewees loved the autonomy NewLaw afforded them, as well as the freedom that allowed them to choose when, where and how much to work. They particularly appreciated the opportunity to set up their own firm free of the constraints associated with traditional law firms.

While NewLaw is in its early stages, it is growing rapidly as lawyers embrace opportunities for innovation, as well as being attracted by the allure of flexibility, autonomy and control. Total mobility has meant lawyers are able to dispense with hardcopy and filing cabinets as all documents can be stored in the Cloud and accessed anywhere at any time. 'Disruptive innovation'—the phrase coined by Clayton Christensen to capture radically new ways of working[67]—encapsulates not only

---

64   Baxter (n. 41).
65   Berit Brandth & Elin Kvande, 'Fathers and Flexible Parental Leave' (2016) 30(2) *Work, Employment and Society* 275, 278, doi.org/10.1177/0950017015590749.
66   Ellis & Buckett (n. 5) 24.
67   Clayton M. Christensen, *The Innovator's Dilemma: The Revolutionary Book that Will Change the Way You Do Business* (Collins Business Essentials, rev. edn, 2003).

the idea of the creation of new markets, such as working inhouse for corporate clients, but also the impact of NewLaw on existing markets. Hence, traditional firms are now more willing to accept flexible work, at least to a limited extent, particularly when their senior lawyers begin to leave, taking their clients with them. However, is NewLaw the answer to the caring conundrum that lies at the heart of gender inequality in the legal profession?

Flexible work enables work and family life to be managed, although it has been shown to have negative consequences for professional workers more generally because of the need to 'be seen'. The Australian Human Rights Commission's National Prevalence Survey on pregnancy and return to work found there was a common perception in the workplace that those who worked part-time or flexibly lost professional standing and experienced a reduced likelihood of attaining a senior management position.[68] The long experience of northern European countries attests to this problem that besets the caring conundrum, as I will show in the next section. While the Scandinavian initiatives are held up as a model throughout the world, a 'Nordic gender equality paradox' nevertheless exists because the very policies that encourage long breaks from work prevent women from reaching the most senior positions.[69] The result is a Nordic glass ceiling, with the proportion of women in senior positions disappointingly low.

The Nordic experience

Although the precise details may vary between the Nordic countries, they all have a common goal of ensuring that fathers share parental leave in the interests of realising a 'gender-egalitarian society based on the dual-earner/dual-career family model' that accords with a generous social welfare philosophy.[70] The most distinctive feature of the Nordic parental leave policies is the 'use it or lose it' principle, involving father and mother-specific non-transferable leave entitlements. The Scandinavian research shows that fathers are much more likely to take leave when it

---

68   Australian Human Rights Commission (n. 28) 91–92; cf. Brandth & Kvande (n. 65) 277.

69   Nima Sanadaji, *The Nordic Glass Ceiling* (Policy Analysis No. 835, CATO Institute, 8 March 2018) 12, available from: www.cato.org/policy-analysis/nordic-glass-ceiling.

70   Linda Haas & Tine Rostgaard, 'Fathers' Rights to Paid Parental Leave in the Nordic Countries: Consequences for the Gendered Division of Leave' (2011) 14(2) *Community, Work & Family* 177, 192, doi.org/10.1080/13668803.2011.571398.

is a right, rather than an entitlement shared with mothers.[71] The second significant aspect of the framework is the provision of an earnings-based wage replacement. It is apparent that a change in the gendered nature of parental leave may be affected only if there is well-compensated non-transferable fathers' leave, but this poses a difficulty for the public purse when incomes in private legal practice are likely to be high. Low replacement compensation makes it economically rational for the parent earning less—invariably the mother—to take any shared entitlement. A low take-up rate by fathers serves to entrench the masculinist non-caring norm. While free choice accords with liberal values, it invariably leads to women assuming the preponderance of responsibility for parental leave, which interrupts their career prospects and confirms their secondary role in the legal labour market.[72]

The Swedish Government is aware that couples are more likely to share parental leave when fathers' compensation levels are higher.[73] As well as promoting gender equality, it is recognised that parental leave for fathers has a positive effect on their relationships with their children. Sweden provides 480 days of subsidised parental leave per child, which either parent may take, but at least three months must be allocated to each parent on a 'use it or lose it' basis. After 40 years, this intervention appears to be making inroads into the stereotypical feminisation of care. Indeed, the Swedish Social Insurance Agency reported that in 2017 fathers claimed 27.9 per cent of parental leave.[74] Although well short of 50 per cent, it represents a step towards de-gendering parental leave and is far ahead of most other countries.

In a comparative study of 21 European countries, the examples of Norway, Sweden and Iceland show that quotas are the only effective way to mainstream men's acceptance of their entitlements,[75] and granting leave without pay is ineffective. This study revealed that the highest percentage of men's use of non-transferable parental leave occurred in the countries with the highest rates of pay: Spain (80 per cent of take-up, 100 per cent pay); Denmark

71   ibid., 186.
72   Carmen Castro-García & Maria Pazos-Moran, 'Parental Leave Policy and Gender Equality in Europe' (2016) 22(3) *Feminist Economics* 51, 55, doi.org/10.1080/13545701.2015.1082033.
73   Haas & Hwang (n. 51) 91.
74   'Dads in Sweden Took More Paternity Leave Than Ever in 2017', *The Local*, [Stockholm], 17 January 2018, available from: www.thelocal.se/20180117/dads-in-sweden-took-more-paternity-leave-in-2017.
75   Castro-García & Pazos-Moran (n. 72) 57.

(89 per cent take-up, 90 per cent pay); Sweden (90 per cent take-up, 80 per cent pay); and Iceland (91 per cent take-up, 80 per cent pay). The duration of leave was also not a token one or two weeks, as in Anglophone countries, but extended to more than eight weeks.

The contrast in European countries between non-transferable and transferable leave is striking, as women overwhelmingly take the latter. Castro-García and Pazos-Moran show that the proportion of women to men taking up transferable leave ranged from 96:0.6 per cent in the case of Austria to 90:18 per cent in Sweden. The authors devised a Parental Leave Equality Index based on the promotion of co-responsibility, in which the leading countries were Iceland, Norway, Portugal and Sweden. Countries in the second group—considered to be 'incidental collaborators in childcare'—included France and Germany, which offered a few weeks of non-transferable, highly paid parental leave. The third group—which included Austria, Italy, Ireland and the Czech Republic—did not consider men to be 'even marginally responsible for childcare'. These countries left the responsibility to the mother and were deemed to be the most likely to reinforce the gendered division of labour, even if they offered short periods (one or two weeks) of (unpaid) paternity leave following the birth of a child.

Although informative, these European studies of parental leave did not focus on male lawyers, in respect of which studies are scant. Choroszewicz and Tremblay, together with Choroszewicz and Kay, have compared male lawyers in Helsinki and Montreal.[76] Although the number of subjects is also small, such studies nevertheless establish a link between lawyers' professional ethos and male lawyers' attitudes to fatherhood that are supportive of the Balancing Law and Life findings. These authors found that only seven of the 38 lawyer interviewees in their common study used their statutory leave while working in private practice. This was even though both the Finnish and the Québécois fathers were eligible for a period of non-transferable paternity leave. Even then, the female spouse tended to assume primary responsibility for childcare, taking from a year to 18 months of maternity and parental leave.

76   Marta Choroszewicz & Diane-Gabrielle Tremblay, 'Parental-Leave Policy for Male Lawyers in Helsinki and Montreal: Cultural and Professional Barriers to Male Lawyers' Use of Paternity and Parental Leaves' (2018) 25(3) *International Journal of the Legal Profession* 303, doi.org/10.1080/0969 5958.2018.1456435; Marta Choroszewicz & Fiona Kay, 'The Use of Mobile Technologies for Work-to-Family Boundary Permeability: The Case of Finnish and Canadian Male Lawyers' (2019) 73(10) *Human Relations* 1388, doi.org/10.1177/0018726719865762.

It is also notable that despite access to paternity leave, the Québécois interviewees preferred to use holiday leave rather than paternity leave. Like the lawyers interviewed for Balancing Law and Life, Finnish and Québécois male lawyers were fearful that leave associated with caring for young children would stigmatise them and jeopardise their careers. The male lawyers tended to accept the conventional gendered organisation of family life, particularly as their spouses received more generous maternity leave. Paternity leave was generally less stigmatised in Finland due to its longer tradition and national outreach, but only one Finnish male lawyer in the study was fully compensated for part of his paternity leave.

Choroszewicz and Kay focused on the use of mobile technologies to assess the degree of permeability in the work-to-family boundary of Finnish and Canadian male lawyers. Although the Finnish lawyers more readily embraced family responsibilities, which they had done since the birth of their children, the male breadwinner model remained strong in both countries. Mobile technologies reinforced a gendered professional norm for lawyers to prioritise career over family life and allow work demands to cross over into family time. What is significant, despite the rhetoric, is that the pressure on male lawyers to be available to clients 24/7 signalled the social disregard for their caregiving responsibilities. Thus, even in jurisdictions that appear progressive, men's commitment to work and careers is prioritised over family. Fathers will not use shared leave entitlements when it is a matter of choice.[77] While the father's quota is the only way to ensure paternal participation, the leave will not be taken up if it is dependent on financial compensation from the state, as this is likely to be only a fraction of what the typical lawyer earns in private practice. The men who took short stints of parental leave struggled with the tension in their roles between the 'new involved father' and the 'ideal worker'.[78]

While Australia's 12 to 24 months' 'Dad and Partner Pay' leave undoubtedly represents an important symbolic step towards cultural change in the gender of caring, its unpaid character is likely to induce few well-remunerated male lawyers to avail themselves of it unless their law firms are prepared to step into the breach. However, it is a question not only of male lawyers wishing to be paid more, but also of the need for organisational and peer support.

---

77   Haas & Rostgaard (n. 70) 193.
78   Brandth & Kvande (n. 65) 286.

Towards refashioning fatherhood

Research on men and masculinity has expanded considerably since the 1970s, largely in response to feminist scholarship. However, as Hearn observes, it was not as though men were not studying men before then; it was just that they 'call[ed] it "History", "Sociology", or whatever'.[79] Similarly, the study of law and lawyers also had a masculinist focus that presented itself as the universal—a standard that has been extensively critiqued by feminist legal scholars.[80]

Raewyn Connell's theory of hegemonic masculinity, one of the most influential theories, throws light on the resistance to men as carers. Influenced by Marx[81] and Gramsci,[82] Connell defines hegemonic masculinity as 'a social ascendancy achieved in a play of social forces that extends beyond contests of brute power into the organisation of private life and cultural processes'[83]—that is, ideas emanating from the dominant social class come to be taken for granted by virtue of its status and similarly accepted by others without coercion. While the theory of hegemonic masculinity may perhaps be losing something of its popularity,[84] the seeds of invidiousness linger, which help to explain the deep-seated resistance on the part of law firms to male lawyers assuming caring roles. Caring, together with maternity leave, flexible work and WLB, has been conventionally marked as a 'women's issue', and is therefore regarded as marginal to legal practice. Hence, the formal changes to public policy in respect of parental leave that have been documented above will not suffice to effect an instantaneous change to values that are buried deep within the social psyche. In traditional law firms, a partnership is still regarded as the pinnacle of a successful legal career, although it has become more elusive because of globalisation and the emergence of mega-firms. Billable hours, the generation of profits, the long-hours culture and competition policy

---

79   Jeff Hearn, 'From Hegemonic Masculinity to the Hegemony of Men' (2004) 5(1) *Feminist Theory* 49, doi.org/10.1177/1464700104040813.

80   For example, Catharine A. MacKinnon, 'Feminism, Marxism, Method, and the State: Toward Feminist Jurisprudence' (1983) 8(4) *Signs* 635, 638–39, doi.org/10.1086/494000.

81   Karl Marx, *A Contribution to the Critique of Political Economy* (Progress Publishers, 1970) 19.

82   Antonio Gramsci, *Selections from the Prison Notebooks of Antonio Gramsci*, edited & translated by Quintin Hoare & Geoffrey Nowell-Smith (Lawrence & Wishart, 1971).

83   R.W. Connell, *Gender and Power: Society, the Person and Sexual Politics* (Allen & Unwin, 1987) 184.

84   Kalle Berggren, 'Is Everything Compatible? A Feminist Critique of Hearn's Composite Approach to Men and Masculinity' (2018) 33(97) *Australian Feminist Studies* 331, 340–41, doi.org/10.1080/08164649.2018.1542590.

lie at the heart of the modus operandi of these firms. Such characteristics are the indicia of success to which a lawyer who wishes to 'get on' must pay heed.[85]

When children are young, they need constant care, but this is usually the stage when ambitious (male) lawyers feel the greatest pressure to work the longest hours to succeed. As mentioned in the introduction to this chapter, Richard Collier is one of the few legal scholars to have addressed the often contradictory elements of identity besetting male lawyers— that is, the problem of simultaneously being a 'family man', a 'good dad' and a 'good lawyer'.[86] As Collier points out, it is often only when the children have grown up that there is an appreciation of what might have been 'lost'.[87] Although the multiple meanings that attach to masculinity are acknowledged,[88] the workaholism that is associated with 'success' is resistant to the idea of a flexible workplace that takes account of caring for children and family members. In the past, the workaholic father consoled himself with the belief that he was a good provider for his family—an assumption that is now passé, certainly as far as those committed to the pursuit of gender equality are concerned. Nevertheless, just what variables constitute a good lawyer-father remain uncertain.[89]

Today, there is a growing interest in 'New Fatherhood',[90] which focuses on the active involvement of men in the care of their children based on what it means to be a 'good dad' in a way that was not expected of professional men in the past. Despite this cultural shift, however, the vexed issue that remains at the heart of the caring conundrum is that men are fearful of the impact on their careers of taking caring leave. Men in the United States, where there is no national paternity leave policy, have reported that they do not take leave, even if eligible, for fear it may hurt their careers.[91] Caregiving is antipathetic to the hypermasculinist norms associated with a successful career in law: the long-hours culture, 24/7 availability, 'rainmaking' (bringing new business to the firm) and the generation of

85   Collier (n. 35) 70.
86   Collier, *Masculinity* (n. 16) 215–18 ff.; Collier (n. 35) 74 ff.
87   Collier (n. 35) 81.
88   Collier (n. 15) 437.
89   Collier (n. 35) 73–74.
90   Collier (n. 15) 423.
91   Joan C. Williams, Marina Multhaup, Su Li & Rachel Korn, *You Can't Change What You Can't See: Interrupting Racial & Gender Bias in the Legal Profession* (American Bar Association & Minority Corporate Counsel Association, 2018) 8.

significant income.[92] Whereas the idea of men as good providers for their families dovetails with the idea of profit maximisation that is valued highly by the firm, hands-on caregiving necessarily disrupts it. The potential collision of values between transnational hypermasculinity and New Fatherhood[93] is highly problematic. As Wald notes, the hypercompetitive culture requires a 24/7 commitment in which there is little room for flexibility to accommodate caring.[94]

Williams, Berdahl and Vandello identify the contemporary workplace as the cause of the problem. They acknowledge that a change has occurred on the part of fathers in how they relate to their children, but the workplace has not kept up with social trends.[95] As discussed above in the context of flexible work in corporate law firms, a stigma attaches to lawyers who work flexibly, which discourages them from doing so. The US studies that Williams, Berdahl and Vandello reviewed identify a range of material disincentives to which those working flexibly have been subjected. They include slower wage growth, fewer promotions and fewer performance reviews. Those who worked flexibly were generally perceived to be less dedicated than those who conformed to the unencumbered 'ideal-worker template'.

In a further US study coordinated by Williams, the authors argue that work is a 'masculinity contest' in which men set out to prove themselves.[96] They argue that this contest generates behaviour that includes toxic leadership, bullying and sexual harassment. Law, with its extreme work hours and cutthroat competition, was one of the workplace types giving rise to this type of unedifying behaviour. Far from masculinity being a biological given, they argue that gender 'represents a socially created, enforced, and reproduced axis of power and inequality'. They draw on the theory of hegemonic masculinity to argue that masculinity is not fixed but adapts according to context. However, by transgressing gender boundaries, masculinity moves to the status of devalued femininity, which signals the resistance experienced by male lawyers who take carers' leave.

---

92   Eli Wald, 'Glass Ceilings and Dead Ends: Professional Ideologies, Gender Stereotypes, and the Future of Women Lawyers at Large Law Firms' (2010) 78(5) *Fordham Law Review* 2245. See also Chapter 6, this volume.
93   Collier (n. 15) 423 ff.
94   Wald (n. 92) 2263.
95   Williams et al. (n. 12) 516.
96   Jennifer L. Berdahl, Marianne Cooper, Peter Glick, Robert W. Livingston & Joan C. Williams, 'Work as a Masculinity Contest' (2018) 74(3)[SI] *Journal of Social Issues* 422, doi.org/10.1111/josi.12289.

As Williams, Berdahl and Vandello note, it is easier to change workplace norms that do not threaten the identities of the 'mostly' men at the top of organisations. This tends to favour the status quo, with women continuing to be the primary carers. While this does not necessarily mean relegating women to full-time caring once more, it does mean any accommodation of caring in the workplace continues to be feminised and demeaned. It follows that caring leave of any kind, including flexible or part-time work, is going to be stigmatised when undertaken by men, thereby ensuring that the gendered organisational pyramid remains intact, with men dominating the apex, the site of power and prestige, and women the pyramidal base as secondary or even disposable workers, which replicates the well-established pattern.

Conclusion: Competing narratives

De-gendering the identity of the primary caregiver and moving to a shared parenting regime are essential prerequisites to gender equality, but, as Collier observes, such a change will not occur in the legal profession unless there are organisational solutions that make men feel more comfortable about taking parental leave.[97] They need significant incentives to enable them to do so, which cannot be said to be the case with Australian Government policy until recently. In addition to 18 weeks of paid maternity leave for the birth mother and two weeks of paid Dad and Partner Pay leave (at the minimum wage), the *Fair Work Act 2009* (Cth) (ss 70–76) enabled either parent to take 12 months' unpaid parental leave, which could be extended for another 12 months. In the 2022–23 federal Budget, it was announced that the Dad and Partner Pay scheme would be abandoned and 20 weeks of paid parental leave would be made available to either parent in a two-parent family, with single parents able to access the full 20 weeks.[98] While such reforms are ostensibly designed to alter the gendered division of labour in the public sphere, choice tends to preserve the gendered division of labour in the private sphere, as it is almost always mothers in a heteronormative family who undertake parental leave available to either parent.[99] While fathers are likely to be responsive to family emergencies or to be amenable to

---

97   Collier (n. 35); cf. Choroszewicz & Tremblay (n. 76).
98   The increased household income test of $350,000 means many lawyers would be eligible, whereas this was not formerly the case.
99   Castro-García & Pazos-Moran (n. 72) 55, 65.

a short period of paternity leave, they are unwilling to take up a caregiver role if it is financially detrimental for them. McCurdy's study reveals that 86 per cent of fathers indicated they would be likely to take paid parental leave if paid at a replacement rate, compared with only 10 per cent if paid at the Australian minimum wage.[100]

In discussing the Balancing Law and Life project, advertence was made to the feminised stigma associated with working flexibly that disproportionately impacted male lawyers. However, even men in NewLaw firms, where flexibility was the norm, tended to minimise their caring time to devote more time to work. 'Success' in the market has conventionally been associated with the unencumbered lawyer—a model that is counterpoised by a residual animus towards caring buried deep within the social psyche. As the burden of caring has historically fallen on women, this role has served to normalise their subordination in the legal workplace.

While the dominant ideas of masculinity have been challenged by numerical feminisation as suggested, this has not sufficed to effect substantive change. We must be wary of liberal progressivism—that is, the idea that things are inexorably moving forward. The rhetoric of the 'good dad' has undoubtedly begun to make inroads into conventional norms as to 'who cares', but it has made no more than a few dents in ancillary norms such as conventional indicia of success, including highly paid partnerships in global firms that appear in published league tables.

As the prevailing workplace culture constitutes a formidable barrier to fathers' leave, 'structural change', as Schiebinger advocates,[101] cannot be effected by means of a simple policy change. In the past, different theories about women and femininity have been in the ascendancy in an endeavour to address the underrepresentation of women in male-dominated occupations, such as law. These include 'fixing' the numbers, valuing the feminine and reducing bias, but they have failed to alter the norms and values of the workplace, such as the long-hours culture and the sometimes-fierce competition.[102] The narrative of the 'good dad' does not

---

100 Samone McCurdy, 'Fathers, Work and Care: Opt Out or Lock Out?' (Research Results, Monash University), available from: www.monash.edu/__data/assets/pdf_file/0020/1474220/resultsoverview brochure-2-3.pdf.
101 Elsevier (n. 9) 74–76.
102 Berdahl et al. (n. 96) 440–42.

mesh with these values. The 'good dad' is one who plays an active caring role with his children; the model eschews that of the absent father typical of the previous generation.

A more interventionist role on the part of the state in accordance with the Nordic model is superficially appealing, but the studies comparing Finnish and Québécois male lawyers suggest this is likely to be only partially successful, as few men take other than a brief period of paternity leave on the birth of a child. Furthermore, based on the two-week Dad and Partner Pay scheme, any compensation is likely to be at the rate of the basic wage in Australia, which would invariably fall far short of a typical lawyer's remuneration. Even then, the lack of visibility that would ensue from a protracted workplace absence would be a disincentive for men strongly invested in their careers.

While it may be more cost-effective for firms to pay lawyer-fathers to go on parental leave than to lose them, only a minuscule number of prominent law firms is believed to have introduced gender-neutral policies to date.[103] As Australia, like the United States, was resistant to the introduction of paid maternity leave, even greater resistance could be expected in the case of extended paid leave for fathers,[104] as intimated by the Nordic example.

Nevertheless, legal and policy discourses have tentatively begun to move away from an exclusive focus on mothers as primary carers to shared parenting. In 2006, for example, the *Family Law Act 1975* (Cth) (s. 61DA [1]) was altered to include a presumption in favour of 'equal shared parental responsibility'. Despite these incipient changes within legal discourse, which clearly show that shared parenting is not far-fetched, it is not carrying over into the legal workplace itself, other than rhetorically. In the popular imagination, the language of 'primary carer' continues to be construed as feminine.

The major obstacle to effecting social change is the devotion of male lawyers to work and their unwillingness to take other than a brief period of paternity leave. What lawyers (and other professional men) seem to fear is a variation of the Nordic gender equality paradox, in which extended

---

103 Jerome Doraisamy, 'Ashurst Launches 26-Week Parental Leave Policy', *Lawyers Weekly*, 28 July 2021.
104 For a detailed comparative analysis of paid parental leave in the United States and Australia, see Deborah A. Widiss, 'The Hidden Gender of Gender-Neutral Paid Parental Leave: Examining Recently-Enacted Laws in the United States and Australia' (2021) 41 *Comparative Labor Law & Policy Journal* 723, doi.org/10.2139/ssrn.3505553.

periods away from work have the potential to impact their careers deleteriously, despite the desire to be a good father. I am therefore not optimistic about the likelihood of change in the short term, although it is apparent that shared caring is the essential prerequisite for gender equality in the legal profession.

Until the idea of equal shared parental responsibility at work is accepted—substantively, not just rhetorically—gender equality in the legal profession will necessarily remain elusive. Hence, it is not the 'woman question' on which we should be focusing, but the 'man question'[105]—or really, the 'man at work question'.

---

105 Cf. Collier (n. 35).

Part V: Gender and Judging

9

Sex Discrimination, Courts and Corporate Power

Introduction: Creating new norms

The concept of equality has been a familiar tenet of democratic theory since antiquity, but it has always been a skewed notion. In Athens, the birthplace of democracy (*demokratia*: 'the power of the people'), women and slaves were excluded from 'the people' so far as life in the polis was concerned. Aristotle believed this exclusion was justified because women and slaves were inferior *in phusei* ('by their natures').[1] The idea that 'justifiable' discrimination could be invoked selectively to derogate from equality continues to be the case today. What is justifiable is determined by those with power, just as it always has been. Equality between humans, therefore, is a contingent and permeable notion; absolute equality belongs only in the world of the quantifiable and the mathematical. While women and Others have been 'let in' to public life, the past continues to lie like a dead weight on equal participation.[2]

To address the more egregious manifestations of sex discrimination in accordance with the prevailing liberal commitment to formal equality, legislation proscribing sex discrimination first appeared in Australia in the 1970s and 1980s.[3] This was ostensibly radical legislation as the

---

1   Aristotle, *Politics*, edited & translated by John Warrington (J.M. Dent, 1961) s. 1254.
2   Sandra Berns, *Women Going Backwards: Law and Change in a Family Unfriendly Society* (Routledge, 2002), doi.org/10.4324/9781315186948.
3   *Sex Discrimination Act 1975* (SA); *Equal Opportunity Act 1977* (Vic.); *Anti-Discrimination Act 1977* (NSW); *SDA*.

common law had never recognised the concept of discrimination. Indeed, the common law had been engaged in reifying regimes of discrimination against women and disfavoured Others for centuries.[4]

It is testament to society's faith in the beneficence and neutrality of the courts that we accept judges as the arbiters of the non-discrimination principle, just as we accepted them—a mere nanosecond ago—as the arbiters of discrimination. Herein lies the nub of the problem, even though it may appear somewhat paradoxical to argue that a legislative instrument that purports to be progressive and remedial can in fact exert a deeply conservative effect. In one sense, of course, this is unsurprising as the legislature may have to accommodate multiple divergent interests in the one instrument. In the case of the public debate before passage of the *SDA*, the scale and diversity of opinion were such that unanimity was impossible. Vying with one another were women's groups lobbying for equal rights, moral conservatives who argued that women's place was in the home and employer groups, such as the Business Council of Australia, anxious to preserve employer prerogative.[5]

A familiar technique adopted by the legislature in controversial areas is to minimise the detail in legislation so the interpretative role is expanded. The *SDA* is a prime example of such a text, for the legislature has left so much unsaid. Instead, it has charged decision-makers—primarily judges—with the crucial hermeneutic role of endowing the trailblazing text with meaning. Ambiguity could have been minimised by including a stronger statement of objects or by investing an agency such as the AHRC with enhanced powers of enforcement, but I suggest that such a course of action was deliberately eschewed because it was not politically palatable. Furthermore, the typical legislative instrument purporting to proscribe discrimination is riddled with exceptions that further amplify the uncertainty of meaning.

---

4   Coverture, in which a woman entered into a state of civil death on marriage, is a startling example, captured most famously by Blackstone: 'By marriage, the husband and wife are one person in law; that is, the very being or legal existence of the woman is suspended during the marriage, or at least is incorporated and consolidated into that of the husband, under whose wing, protection, and cover, she performs everything.' William Blackstone, *Commentaries on the Laws of England* (University of Chicago Press, 1979 [1765–69]) 442. See also Mary Lyndon Shanley, *Feminism, Marriage, and the Law in Victorian England, 1850–1895* (Princeton University Press, 1989).

5   Margaret Thornton & Trish Luker, 'The *Sex Discrimination Act* and its Rocky Rite of Passage' in Margaret Thornton (ed.), *Sex Discrimination in Uncertain Times* (ANU Press, 2010), doi.org/10.22459/SDUT.09.2010.01.

Stare decisis, the primary security blanket on which judges conventionally rely to support their reasoning, has been of remarkably little help, as there were initially no precedents—at least none with binding authority. Judges could look to overseas jurisdictions—the United States, Canada or the United Kingdom—for guidance, but a propulsion towards parochialism and self-referentialism has generally constrained them. Instead, they tend to fall back on their own subjective appreciation of what is right. This does not mean they necessarily act in a way that is arbitrary or capricious, for they must draw on the *nomos*, or normative universe, which they inhabit to engage in what Robert Cover refers to as 'jurisgenesis', or the creation of meaning.[6] The *nomos* includes judges' 'commonsense ideas about the world' based on their own experiences and observations.[7] This element of judicial subjectivity enables judges to select what to notice and what to disregard.

Cover identifies two jurisgenerative patterns: the 'paideic' and the 'imperial'. He defines the paideic (educational; from the same root as pedagogical) as 'world creating' and the imperial as 'world maintaining'.[8] This distinction is useful in the context of adjudication and discrimination jurisprudence where, Janus-like, judges simultaneously look both to the past and to the future. The paideic approach can be understood to refer to a situation where judges wrestle to produce a beneficent and creative interpretation of novel legislation in the absence of either judicial precedents or legislative guidance.

Sex discrimination legislation, by virtue of its very existence, exercises a paideic effect—a role some judges believe should be respected.[9] The paideic approach, however, is in constant tension with the imperial, or world-maintaining, approach that looks to the past. *Stare decisis* is necessarily backward-looking, which underscores the world-maintaining predilection of judging. This innate conservatism is strengthened by the classed, racialised, heterosexed and gendered milieus inhabited by judges. The paideic and imperial patterns nevertheless endlessly circulate and compete with one another within the *nomos*, which means there is rarely a clear line of demarcation between them. This gyration of values also puts paid to the liberal notion of the linearity of progress.

---

6   Robert Cover, '*Nomos* and Narrative' (1983) 97 *Harvard Law Review* 4, 11.
7   Regina Graycar, 'The Gender of Judgments: An Introduction' in Margaret Thornton (ed.), *Public and Private: Feminist Legal Debates* (Oxford, 1995) 275.
8   Cover (n. 6) 12–13.
9   For example, *New South Wales v Amery* (2006) 226 ALR 196 (Kirby J).

Sex discrimination is an inescapable dimension of the normative universe that we all inhabit. It is embedded within the history and culture of the Western intellectual tradition, where the seeds of invidiousness that attach to the feminine have been nurtured for centuries and used to justify the exclusion of women from the public sphere, including universities and the professions. The normativity of masculinity heightens the burden of proof for an individual woman alleging discrimination. It is not enough to claim that the harm is systemic—that is, buried deep within the *nomos*—as this immediately exculpates the individual respondent. Practices that are neutral on their face but exercise a discriminatory effect may constitute indirect discrimination. However, as I will suggest, such practices have usually acquired an aura of legitimacy by virtue of age and convention that renders the causative links required by indirect discrimination even harder to establish.

The conceptualisation of the private sphere as a realm beyond law is a key element of the liberal universe.[10] The contemporary reality is that women continue to perform the overwhelming preponderance of life-sustaining work in the private sphere, which informs contemporary constructions of the feminine and produces discrimination at work for women in the form of less favourable terms and conditions, including unequal pay and exclusion from the most authoritative positions. The problem of the so-called work–life balance has been described as 'the topic of the 21st Century for families, employers, and government'.[11] The residual animus towards the feminine in the public sphere is enmeshed within the *nomos* and forms the backdrop to individual complaints of discrimination from which it may be impossible to disaggregate the individual complaint.

Whereas conciliation is the primary mode of dispute resolution under all antidiscrimination legislation in Australia,[12] a complainant may initiate a formal hearing before a tribunal or court if conciliation is unsuccessful.

---

10   For example, Jeff Weintraub and Krishan Kumar (eds), *Public and Private in Thought and Practice: Perspectives on a Grand Dichotomy* (University of Chicago Press, 1997).

11   Human Rights and Equal Opportunity Commission, *It's about time: Women, men, work and family* (Final Paper, HREOC, 2007) xi. Work–life balance has attracted extensive commentary in recent years. See, for example, Berns (n. 2); Barbara Pocock, *The Work/Life Collision: What Work is Doing to Australians and What to Do About It* (The Federation Press, 2003); Belinda Smith & Joellen Riley, 'Family-Friendly Work Practices and the Law' (2004) 26(3) *Sydney Law Review* 395; Jill Murray (ed.), *Work, Family and the Law* (2005) 23(1)[SI] *Law in Context*.

12   Margaret Thornton, *The Liberal Promise: Anti-Discrimination Legislation in Australia* (Oxford University Press, 1990) Ch. 5; Dominique Allen & Alysia Blackham, 'Under Wraps: Secrecy, Confidentiality and the Enforcement of Equality Law in Australia and the United Kingdom' (2019) 43(2) *Melbourne University Law Review* 384.

Depending on the jurisdiction, less than 2 per cent of complaints proceed to a formal hearing.[13] It follows that the proportion likely to be appealed from that decision through the court hierarchy will necessarily be minuscule. Indeed, in 40 years, the High Court has heard only three cases arising from sex discrimination complaints, even though thousands of complaints are lodged every year with federal, state and territory agencies.[14]

The cost of legal representation tends to place appeals beyond the reach of most individual litigants, whereas the possibility of litigation is built into the risk management plan of corporations, as the cost can be passed on to consumers or is borne by the public purse. Nevertheless, the comparatively few appellate decisions, particularly those that emanate from the most authoritative court, carry a great deal of weight; they are heard in public and are reported in full by both general and specialist court reporters. Not only do High Court decisions have binding authority on lower courts and tribunals, but also their effect may percolate down to the conciliation level, which operates within the shadow of the law. Accordingly, it is worth taking a closer look at sex discrimination jurisprudence at the appellate level.

The courts, of course, do not operate in isolation and I stress the homologous connections between them, the legislature, the executive and corporate power in shaping sex discrimination jurisprudence. Despite the artifice of the separation of powers doctrine, the respective arms of government form part of the same state. What is notable about the litigation emerging from sex discrimination and antidiscrimination legislation generally is the disproportionate number of powerful corporations—public as well as private—that appear as parties. In the cases considered in this article, these corporations include Ansett Airlines (one element of an airline duopoly at the time), the Commonwealth Bank, Australian Iron & Steel (a subsidiary of what was then Australia's largest and most powerful corporation, Broken Hill Proprietary Limited), as well as the states of New South Wales and Victoria—the two wealthiest and most populous Australian states.

---

13 Australian Human Rights Commission, *2019–20 Complaint Statistics* (AHRC, 2020) 3, available from: humanrights.gov.au/sites/default/files/2020-10/AHRC_AR_2019-20_Complaint_ Stats_FINAL.pdf.
14 For example, in 2019–20 at the federal level, 2,307 complaints were received by the AHRC. However, if counted by grounds and areas of complaint, the numbers would increase to 4,941 and 3,030, respectively (ibid., 2).

In one sense, the prominence of corporate elites is unsurprising as they not only have the resources to embark on protracted and sometimes extravagant litigation, but also may be habitual respondents who are bound to be concerned about the prospective operation of the instant case, for there are always going to be similar cases waiting in the wings. Marc Galanter's classic work on the role of the 'repeat player' (the corporate respondent), as opposed to the 'one-shotter' (the individual litigant), highlights the disparity between the typical complainant and corporate respondent in litigation.[15] These corporate players may have working for them a veritable army of top-tier lawyers whose responsibility it is to resist the substantive allegations made against their clients by recourse to whatever procedural means they can devise. I have argued elsewhere that 'constitutionalisation' is one such technique that confounds the complainant and renders irrelevant the substance of a dispute.[16] The adversarial system of justice assumes equality of bargaining power between the parties, regardless of their respective resources and tactics utilised. This procedural neutrality conveniently obscures the way the scales are tilted in favour of corporate respondents and 'world maintaining' decisions.[17]

The cartography of antidiscrimination legislation

In this chapter, I do not propose to embark on an analysis of antidiscrimination legislation generally, which I have done elsewhere,[18] as I wish to focus on the adjudicative role. However, I would initially like to draw attention to some of the key structural characteristics of the legislation that limit its impact from the outset, despite the radical rhetoric. These limitations subtly operate to support an imperial interpretation of the text.

---

15   Marc Galanter, 'Why the "Haves" Come Out Ahead: Speculations on the Limits of Legal Change' (1974–75) 9(1) *Law & Society Review* 95, doi.org/10.2307/3053023.
16   Margaret Thornton, 'Towards Embodied Justice: Wrestling with Legal Ethics in the Age of the New Corporatism' (1999) 23(3) *Melbourne University Law Review* 749.
17   Gaze suggests the neutrality in drafting was deliberately designed to 'avoid acknowledging the asymmetrical reality of social disadvantage'. See Beth Gaze, 'Context and Interpretation in Anti-Discrimination Law' (2002) 26(2) *Melbourne University Law Review* 325, 329.
18   For example, Thornton (n. 12). See also Chapter 4, this volume.

First, there is a presumption of sex neutrality. While the *SDA* is based on the sex-specific CEDAW,[19] the legislation is couched in sex-neutral terms.[20] That is, the legislation applies to both men and women, despite the sex-specific focus of the CEDAW, which authorises the enactment of remedial legislation to assist women, not men, in light of the centuries of less favourable treatment. The underlying presupposition of liberal democratic theory is that men and women are formally equal in fact, and individual instances of discrimination are mere aberrations that need to be corrected. However, as recognised by Aristotle, to treat as equal those who are unequally situated is to perpetuate injustice.[21] It is sex consciousness rather than sex neutrality that is required to address sex discrimination. A veneer of sex neutrality, or formal equality, conveniently occludes the normativity of systemic sex inequality. The presumption of sex neutrality conforms with the notion of formal equality that is central to the Anglo-Australian mode of adjudication. The presumption discourages a standard of strict scrutiny that discriminatory conduct demands from courts.

Second, the legislation has the effect of individualising complaints of discrimination. A focus on the individual harm must be clearly linked by a linear thread to both the complainant and the respondent, which also has the effect of formally deflecting attention away from the systemic nature of the discrimination. The paradigmatic case of direct discrimination is based on comparability. The complainant must establish that he or she was treated less favourably than another in the same or similar circumstances, by virtue of sex or race or disability or other proscribed ground. The effort in detaching the individual instance from system-wide discrimination heightens the burden of proof for the complainant. Courts are also loath to make a finding of discrimination because of the moral odium associated with labelling someone 'a discriminator'.[22] With specific reference to race discrimination, Jonathon Hunyor has discussed the high standard of evidence courts seem to require in the discrimination jurisdiction.[23] If a complainant cannot prove that the respondent caused the harm, the

---

19   *Convention on the Elimination of All Forms of Discrimination against Women*, opened for signature 18 December 1979, 1249 UNTS 513 (entered into force 3 September 1981).

20   The principle of neutrality was upheld following a constitutional challenge in *Aldridge v Booth* (1988) 80 ALR 1.

21   Aristotle (n. 1) s. 1282b.

22   Gaze (n. 17) 335.

23   Jonathon Hunyor, 'Skin-Deep: Proof and Inferences of Racial Discrimination in Employment' (2003) 25(4) *Sydney Law Review* 535. The evidentiary standard of 'reasonable satisfaction' was established by Dixon J in *Briginshaw v Briginshaw* (1938) 60 CLR 336.

complaint will founder at the threshold and no discrimination will be found to have occurred. When the complainant 'fails' to make out his or her case, the act of discrimination is legitimated and the respondent vindicated. Such failures assist in normalising discrimination. The persistent failure of discrimination complaints before the High Court underscores this phenomenon.

Third, the ambit of operation is restricted to specified areas of public and quasi-public life—namely, employment, education and access to goods and services, with the preponderance of complaints arising in the context of employment.[24] Given the centrality of employment to an individual's identity and wellbeing, this is unsurprising. The significance of the public ambit is that the focus is on those areas that affect individual citizens in the polity, civil society and the market. In contrast, private life qua family is quarantined from scrutiny, about which there is nothing unusual. Liberal legalism has traditionally drawn a line between public and private life, with law's empire being confined to the public side of the divide and the private side historically falling under the law of the father, the *pater familias*. This line became much more permeable in the twentieth century with the development and strengthening of general laws regulating conduct formerly characterised as private, such as sexual assault and violence in the home, as discussed in Chapter 3. Nevertheless, sex discrimination legislation upholds the traditional public–private dichotomy of liberalism, even though the wellspring of socioeconomic inequality for women is typically associated with the private sphere qua family: sexuality, reproduction and care; sex discrimination is not something that emanates from the market disconnected from private life. Discrimination on the newer grounds of potential pregnancy, parental responsibilities, breastfeeding, sexual orientation, gender identity and intersex directly challenges the public–private dichotomy. I will endeavour to show, however, that the judiciary, with assistance from the legislature, prefers to restrict incursions into the private sphere qua family through its jurisgenerative role. The attempt to uphold the line of demarcation between the world of work and the private sphere qua family may prove fatal for those with parenting responsibilities (invariably women) who seek to make out complaints of discrimination arising from the interconnectedness of the two spheres, as I will demonstrate.

24   In 2019–20, 64 per cent of complaints lodged with the AHRC under the *SDA* were on the ground of employment (n. 13, 19).

It might be noted that ambiguity also surrounds the private sphere qua market with which private employment is associated, for it is characterised as public for the purposes of the legislation. While discrimination is legislatively proscribed, neoliberalism has seen a pronounced move away from workers' rights in favour of employer prerogative. This shift is discernible also in case law, suggesting that so-called private employment is being quarantined from public scrutiny and treated more like the private sphere qua family, which further underscores the permeability of the line between public and private. The renewed emphasis on employer prerogative is also affecting public employment, as revealed by two of the cases I consider—namely, *New South Wales v Amery* (*Amery*)[25] and *State of Victoria v Schou* (*Schou*).[26] The fact that public-sphere employment is becoming more like private-sphere employment is undoubtedly a corollary of the propensity of neoliberalism to privatise public goods—a further complicating factor for judges in untangling what is public and what is private.

The blindness of justice

In recent years, there has been a shift from specialist to generalist tribunals and courts, which may have contributed to the decline in discrimination complaints proceeding to the inquiry level. Not only does increased formalism favour corporate respondents,[27] but also a greater focus on procedure rather than substance means there is a greater chance of a complainant losing a legal claim and being faced with the respondent's costs as well as their own—most notably, at the Federal Court level. As appeals lie only on questions of law, the merits tend to be relegated to the background so the focus shifts to points of legal doctrine, procedure or constitutionality. The difference between a question of fact and a question of law poses an existential dilemma for judges—one that is accentuated in the case of antidiscrimination law where case law is scant. This branch of law is primarily concerned with substantive justice, and the propensity to treat it as though it were merely an offshoot of administrative law, as Stella Tarrant argues, has a distorting effect that further favours respondents.[28]

---

25   (2006) 226 ALR 196.
26   (No 2) (2004) 8 VR 120.
27   Galanter (n. 15) 123 ff.
28   Stella Tarrant, 'Reasonableness in the Sex Discrimination Act: No Package Deals' (2000) 19(1) *University of Tasmania Law Review* 38. Cf. Gaze (n. 17) esp. 331–33.

A formalistic approach may also cause the paideic purpose of the legislation to be lost altogether, but there is a predilection in favour of formalism and retention of the status quo that lies at the heart of legal positivism, which remains the dominant mode of adjudication in the common law world. Loughlin suggests that Bentham, Austin and Dicey were responsible for a positivistic approach to public law, to sever it from its political roots.[29] De-politicisation fosters the belief that the process of adjudication entails a scientific method, the foundational myth of which is that judges do not make law, but merely declare it. Not only is a positivistic approach assumed to be disconnected from the political,[30] but the scientific veneer gives the impression that the decision is untouched by the subjective values of the judge—that justice is in fact blind. However, the subjectivity of the judge can never be entirely sloughed off, but merely disguised by the familiar techniques of depersonalisation, such as the use of the third person, rules consciousness and recourse to precedent as a means of authorising a particular outcome. The self-referentialism of legal positivism ensures that decisions are in tune with the dominant strands of the *nomos*, which remain conservative and masculinist. The resistance to citing commentators unless they belong to the canon of dead, white, male legal philosophers and historians,[31] who favour the imperial over the paideic, is a variation on the positivist theme. What is more, one does not need to have conducted an ethnographic study to know that judges themselves are overwhelmingly white, middle-class, heterosexual men who are the products of private schools,[32] despite the significant increase in the number of women appointed since the millennial turn.[33] The benchmark men of law, as I term them, who are likely to have had little personal experience of discrimination, constitute the sentinels of the interpretative community. However, legal positivism effectively cloaks their masculinised identity, just as wigs and gowns traditionally masked their physical person. Judicial meaning and authority are thereby constituted by a complex and subtle intersection of the socio-cultural,

---

29   Martin Loughlin, *Public Law and Political Theory* (Oxford University Press, 1992) 20–21, 230.

30   Hart, one of the major exponents of legal positivism, seeks to draw a line between law and history, law and politics, and law and social values of all kinds, including law and morality. H.L.A. Hart, *The Concept of Law* (Clarendon, 1961) 253n.

31   Bentham, Austin and Dicey are exemplary. See Loughlin (n. 29).

32   Gaze (n. 17) 338–40; Robert Thomson, *The Judges* (Allen & Unwin, 1987) esp. 37–43.

33   In 2020, 38.8 per cent of all judges and magistrates in Australia were women. See Australian Institute of Judicial Administration, *AIJA Judicial Gender Statistics: Number and Percentage of Women Judges and Magistrates at 30 June 2020* (AIJA, 2020), available from: aija.org.au/wp-content/uploads/2020/07/2020-JUDICIAL-GENDER-STATISTICS-v3.pdf.

the political and the textual within the normative universe. The effect is to uphold the *is* of law—that is, the status quo—so there is a shying away from the *ought* of law, the path of justice and the paideic.[34] The neutral cloak of legal formalism occludes the ideological significance of what is occurring.

The gendering of the text

I am critical of the use of the word 'elimination' in the CEDAW, which is replicated in Australian legislation, as it conveys the impression that discrimination is finite and will eventually disappear as a result of the operation of antidiscrimination legislation.[35] This is a furphy, for the legislation glosses over the way that legislatures and courts, as well as social institutions more generally, are in fact perennially engaged in constituting and reconstituting discrimination against women and Others as a taken-for-granted dimension of the *nomos*. While the reference to 'activist judges' tends to be invoked by conservatives as a pejorative term for those judges who are politically progressive (as elaborated on in Chapter 10), the phrase masks the way that all adjudication, including that which is world maintaining, necessarily entails an active process of interpretation and jurisgenesis.

The requirements of legal form within legislative texts set the scene by establishing specific conceptual categories with which a complaint must conform. Two primary understandings of discrimination are established legislatively, both of which have a delimiting effect so that systemic discrimination is prevented from being tractable to remediation. Direct discrimination—the most familiar form of discrimination—necessitates a complainant establishing that he or she was treated less favourably than another in the same or similar circumstances on the ground of sex or other specified ground. While ostensibly straightforward, the absence of a comparator, real or hypothetical, may still render this form of discrimination difficult to prove.[36]

---

34   Cf. Sandra Berns, *To Speak as a Judge: Difference, Voice and Power* (Ashgate, 1999) 159.
35   Margaret Thornton, 'Auditing the Sex Discrimination Act' in Marius Smith (ed.), *Human Rights 2004: The Year in Review* (Castan Centre for Human Rights Law, Monash University, 2005) 21.
36   For example, *Purvis v New South Wales (Department of Education and Training)* (2003) 217 CLR 92, which is discussed in Chapter 10, this volume.

Indirect discrimination goes somewhat further than direct discrimination in seeking to address practices that are neutral on their face but have a disproportionate effect by virtue of sex (or race or another characteristic). A simple illustration of indirect discrimination involves the historical requirement that police or prison officers be of a certain height and weight,[37] which disproportionately impacted on women and Asian people (men and women) by excluding them because the specified minima were based on Anglo-Celtic male norms. Indirect discrimination, nevertheless, cannot really capture the more subtle instances of systemic discrimination that are embedded in the social fabric because there is still the need to establish an identifiable discriminator that is clearly linked to the complainant through the impugned conduct. It is not possible to institute an action against 'society', although indirect discrimination does endeavour to transcend the simple model of comparability, the paradigm of direct discrimination, which can capture only the most overt instances.

Despite its promise, the legislative test for indirect discrimination has become increasingly complex as new meanings are invariably contested by corporate respondents.[38] While there are variations between jurisdictions as to the components of the test, its most common manifestation involves: 1) a requirement or condition with which the complainant is expected to comply; 2) a substantially higher proportion of members of the comparator class being able to comply than the class to which the complainant belongs; 3) the unreasonableness of the requirement in the circumstances; and 4) the aggrieved person being unable to comply with the requirement or condition. (The proportionality test was removed from the *SDA* in 1995 in favour of a simpler test, but the two High Court cases involving indirect discrimination that I address arose under the NSW *Anti-Discrimination Act 1977*, which retains proportionality.)

Complaints may involve elements of both direct and indirect discrimination as the line between them can be permeable. A complaint may also involve forays into other jurisdictions, which may raise quite different issues. For example, the first of the three sex discrimination cases that went to the High Court, *Ansett Transport Industries (Operations) Pty Ltd v Wardley* (*Wardley*),[39] began life as an instance of direct discrimination

---

37   For example, *Dothard v Rawlinson*, 433 US 321 (1977).
38   For a sustained analysis of the elements of indirect discrimination, see Rosemary Hunter, *Indirect Discrimination in the Workplace* (The Federation Press, 1992).
39   (1980) 142 CLR 237.

but reached the High Court as a constitutional dispute. In contrast, *Australian Iron & Steel Pty Ltd v Banovic* (*Banovic*)[40] and *Amery* were both instances of indirect discrimination that went to the High Court by way of appeal. I now turn to a brief consideration of these cases to illustrate the movement between the paideic and the imperial.

Wardley (1980) 142 CLR 237

This was the first discrimination case heard by the High Court and was made possible only by the fundraising efforts of women's groups to assist the complainant, as she lacked union support. Ms Wardley's application to be a trainee pilot had been rejected on the ground of her sex—because she was a woman of childbearing age. The case began as a relatively simple instance of direct discrimination under the former *Equal Opportunity Act 1977* (Vic.) (*EOA*) in which the complainant alleged she was treated less favourably than a man in the same or similar circumstances. The evidence was unequivocal as Ms Wardley scored demonstrably higher on the quantitative tests than several successful male applicants. The application of a simple 'but for' test clearly suggests more than a prima facie case: but for the fact that Ms Wardley was female, she would have been appointed.

Despite the strength of the complainant's case, Ansett sought to frustrate it from the outset by resorting to various legal tactics by virtue of its superior power and resources. First, it sought and obtained a writ of prohibition from the Victorian Supreme Court because of a comment made by a member of the Victorian Equal Opportunity Board during the initial hearing. This was alleged to constitute bias and resulted in the matter having to be heard *de novo*. Success before the reconstituted board led to Ms Wardley being appointed to a traineeship but her status remained parlous. Ansett appealed to the Supreme Court and, when the outcome was not looking propitious, the issue was transmuted into a constitutional dispute before the High Court. Such a strategy deflects attention from the substantive complaint altogether—a technique that also succeeds in rendering the complainant voiceless and irrelevant.[41]

Ansett argued an inconsistency between the federal Airline Pilots Agreement (1978) and the *EOA* (Vic.). Unsurprisingly, the agreement made no reference to pregnancy or sex as it was not envisaged that

40   (1989) 168 CLR 165.
41   Thornton (n. 16).

women would apply to become pilots. Relying on s. 109 of the Australian Constitution, which specifies that in the case of inconsistency between a federal and a state law, the federal law prevails, Ansett argued that no discrimination had occurred because the operation of the *EOA* (Vic.) was vitiated by the agreement. The majority, Justices Stephen, Mason, Murphy and Wilson, rejected this argument. They held in separate judgements that the agreement was not to be read in isolation from the general law. As elaborated by Stephen J, the majority view was that there could be no inconsistency because the agreement and the Act dealt with different subject matter, the former dealing with industrial disputes and the latter with discrimination on the ground of sex and marital status in a variety of areas.[42] In an endeavour to create innovative legal norms in accordance with the aims of the novel legislation, we see the embrace of a paideic approach by the majority.

However, an expansive view of the federal law could lead one to an altogether different conclusion—a position espoused by the minority. Aickin J, with whom Barwick CJ agreed, accorded precedence to the federal *Conciliation and Arbitration Act 1904* (Cth) under which the pilots' agreement was made. This Act enabled the relevant body 'to prescribe the industrial relations between employer and employee in relation to every matter the subject of a dispute'.[43] Such an approach comported with the imperial, or world-maintaining, view, which would have eviscerated the sex discrimination provisions of the *EOA* pertaining to employment altogether had it prevailed.

Although the High Court was divided, *Wardley* coincided with the high point of social liberalism in the late 1970s when the old gender norms were being renegotiated. Sex discrimination legislation was one strategy designed to remedy past wrongs perpetrated against women. The absolute exclusion of women from employment as airline pilots was such an egregious manifestation of sex discrimination that it encouraged a paideic interpretation, even though the focus was no longer on the merits because of constitutionalisation.

---

42   *Wardley*, 250–53.
43   ibid., 280 (Aickin J).

Banovic (1989) 168 CLR 165

The second sex discrimination case heard by the High Court occurred a decade after *Wardley*. The power disparity between the unemployed complainants and the corporate respondent was again palpable. The case involved a group of women, predominantly from non–English-speaking backgrounds, who had been employed in non-traditional work at Port Kembla, NSW, with Australian Iron & Steel (AIS). Soon after being employed, the women lost their jobs because of the application of the 'last on–first off' rule when there was a downturn in the economy. The complainants were successful before both the NSW Equal Opportunity Tribunal[44] and the NSW Court of Appeal,[45] but this did not deter their powerful adversary from appealing to the High Court. To assist them with legal representation, the 34 women applied on four occasions for legal aid before they were successful with the help of the Public Interest Advocacy Centre and the NSW Women's Advisory Council, which lobbied the state premier for a one-off grant of $10,000. In contrast, an entire floor of an elite corporate law firm was reputed to have been devoted to supporting the appeal on behalf of AIS.

Whereas *Wardley* was a clear instance of direct discrimination based on comparability, *Banovic* was an instance of indirect discrimination, as it involved a practice that was facially neutral but disproportionately impacted women. The 'last on–first off' rule is an example of such a practice, because the women had only recently been employed by AIS. As they had waited a long time before being employed, proportionately more women than men were retrenched. The requirement with which an ironworker needed to comply to avoid dismissal was to have commenced employment before a specified date. The wrong cut-off date could be misleading and produce a skewed result. A great deal of effort then went into establishing the mathematical niceties of proportionality before both the NSW Court of Appeal and the High Court. What was the numerator and what was the denominator? How were the respective pools to be constituted? Was the focus to be confined to the AIS workforce or calculated more broadly—within the region, the state or the country?

44   *Najdovska v Australian Iron & Steel Pty Ltd* (1985) 12 IR 250.
45   *Australian Iron & Steel Pty Ltd v Najdovska* (1988) 12 NSWLR 587.

By means of what Julius Stone terms the 'leeways of choice',[46] judges are invested with significant discretion to determine the outcome of a decision, despite the constraining factors besetting them within their hermeneutic universe. Although the last on–first off policy could not in itself be impugned as discriminatory, its impact had been exacerbated by the adverse effects of the respondent's resistance towards women ironworkers in the past. However, the history of exclusion by AIS had been resolved only shortly before the lodgement of the complaint because of extensive negotiations with the NSW Anti-Discrimination Board. The very long waiting time for women to be employed, compared with men, obscured the disproportionate impact on women of the last on–first off policy.

The majority judges, Justices Deane, Dawson and Gaudron, were sensitive to the history of women and work, holding that past discrimination could not be used to justify the existence of conduct that disproportionately impacted on women in the present. As with *Wardley*, we see how a paideic approach within the jurisgenesis of indirect discrimination in the context of 'letting in', which recognises the significance of historical exclusion, made all the difference to the outcome. In contrast, the minority judges adopted a strict construction of the legislative provision in comparing compliance on the ground of sex: '[I]t is beside the point that the respective sex groups are the product of discrimination.'[47] A narrow legalistic approach that sloughs off historical context can be very effectively invoked to sustain the imperial world.

The majority did not focus on the question of the history of discrimination against women in non-traditional work generally, but rather the discriminatory effect of the recruitment practices of AIS.[48] If the causative nexus between these practices and the complainants could not be established, the respondent would have been exonerated. Thus, we see a delicate balance between systemic discrimination and the instant case. If systemic discrimination is sloughed off, the complainant is in jeopardy because the focus will be on a workplace practice that is disconnected from the discrimination, while an exclusive focus on the systemic issue may lose sight of the essential causative nexus implicating the respondent. It is this inextricable linkage of the practice and the systemic discrimination that is so difficult to capture in indirect discrimination.

---

46 Julius Stone, *Legal System and Lawyers' Reasonings* (Maitland, 1968) 325–30, *et passim*.
47 *Banovic*, 206 (McHugh J; Brennan J agreeing).
48 ibid., 180 (Deane & Gaudron JJ), 191 (Dawson J).

Amery (2006) 226 ALR 196

Two decades after *Banovic*, and three after *Wardley*, sex discrimination had culturally moved beyond the threshold 'letting in' questions to the more complex systemic questions embedded within the normative universe. The assumption by women of responsibility for the preponderance of society's caring work lies at the heart of much of the discrimination against women in paid work—a factor with which policymakers continue to wrestle. The remaining cases I consider involve indirect discrimination arising from issues of care and its nexus with the workplace. They all directly challenge the public–private dichotomy of liberal legalism that goes to the core of the *nomos*. The majority judges, however, unlike those in *Wardley* and *Banovic*, now tended to favour a literal approach to the text, with scant regard for systemic discrimination. This comports with an imperial approach to issues of sex discrimination. What is of interest is the resistance to the paideic approach that was adopted by many of the High Court judges in the 1970s, 1980s and 1990s.[49] The majority began to evince a preference for the world-maintaining approaches of the past through an exclusive focus on doctrinalism in preference to the creation of new meanings.

Amery—only the third High Court decision dealing with sex discrimination—illustrates a number of themes in contemporary discrimination jurisprudence: the way legal formalism is able to slough off the systemic background of a complaint to the disadvantage of complainants; the inequality of bargaining power between the parties; the role of state governments in supporting public sector respondents in a way that undermines their own legislation; and the swing from social liberalism to neoliberalism, with its correlative favouring of employer prerogative over worker rights. These sociopolitical factors create a hostile climate for women and Others, which fosters textual interpretations that are narrow and regressive.[50] The favouring of a universalistic mode of adjudication disavows the societal shift from a formal to a more substantive understanding of equality.[51]

---

49   Of note are the race and disability cases *Koowarta v Bjelke-Petersen* (1982) 153 CLR 168; *Mabo v Queensland (No 2)* (1992) 175 CLR 1; *Wik Peoples v Queensland* (1996) 187 CLR 1; and *Waters v Public Transport Corporation* (1991) 173 CLR 349.

50   The judgement in *Amery* has been rewritten as an imagined feminist judgement. See Beth Gaze, 'Judgment' in Heather Douglas, Francesca Bartlett, Trish Luker & Rosemary Hunter, *Australian Feminist Judgments: Righting and Rewriting Law* (Hart, 2014).

51   For example, Amelia Simpson, 'The High Court's Conception of Discrimination: Origins, Applications, and Implications' (2007) 29(2) *Sydney Law Review* 263, esp. 278.

In *Amery*, a group of 13 women teachers in New South Wales, who were employed on a casual basis, alleged they were subjected to sex discrimination, based on the principle of equal pay for work of equal value, because they were paid less than those on the permanent staff. The linchpin of the complaint was that all teachers performed essentially the same work, regardless of whether they were casual or permanent.[52] The pay differential between casual and permanent staff was clear from the two separate pay scales. There were five steps in the casual scale and 13 steps in the permanent scale, and the top of the casual scale, where all the complainants were located, was equivalent to Level 8 of the permanent scale. This amounted to a 20 per cent differential in terms of the real pay received. Each of the complainants had taught for at least eight consecutive weeks in the one school. The gravamen of the sex discrimination complaint was that to access the higher rate of pay, the women had to have satisfied the prerequisite of permanency, which was easier for men to do than women. The disproportionate impact on women of the permanency requirement is readily apparent from the statistics. While 80 per cent of teachers in the NSW Teaching Service were women, 20 per cent more men than women were permanent and women made up approximately 83 per cent of all casual staff.

The complaint was lodged under the *Anti-Discrimination Act 1977* (NSW) in 1995 and took 11 years before being heard by the High Court. Following an unsuccessful attempt at conciliation, the complaint proceeded to four hearings. First, the NSW Administrative Decisions Tribunal (ADT) found in favour of the complainants and awarded damages totalling $250,000;[53] second, the ADT Appeals Panel overturned the decision in favour of the respondent;[54] third, the NSW Court of Appeal (2:1) reinstated the decision of the ADT in favour of the complainants;[55] and fourth, the respondent appealed to the High Court (*Amery*), which found 6:1 in its favour. The long history of litigation and the oscillation between the paideic and imperial positions attest not only to the determination of the complainants, but also to the volatility of the jurisdiction.

---

52   The NSW Administrative Decisions Tribunal found there was little or no discernible difference in the tasks or responsibilities of teachers, whether permanent or supply casual. See *Amery v New South Wales* (2001) EOC ¶93–130 (NSW ADT) 75 289.

53   *Amery v New South Wales* (2001) EOC ¶93–130 (NSW ADT) (P. King [Judicial Member], K. Edwards and O. McDonald [Members]).

54   *New South Wales v Amery* (2003) 129 IR 300.

55   *Amery v New South Wales (Director-General NSW Department of Education and Training)* [2004] NSWCA 404.

The sticking point was the threshold issue in establishing indirect discrimination—namely, the identification of a requirement or condition. The Education Department's practice had been to not pay over-award payments, and the complainants argued that permanent status was a condition of securing access to the higher salary rates. The condition of permanency was accepted as unproblematic by all bodies until overturned by the High Court. The majority—Gummow, Hayne and Crennan JJ (Callinan J agreeing)—held that 'the terms or conditions of employment which the employer affords the employee' referred to the 'actual employment' engaged in by a complainant.[56] That is, employment as a casual teacher, not employment in general. The majority judges held that it was an error to conflate the casual and permanent categories because the bifurcated structure of the teaching service was not merely a bureaucratic practice of the department, but a legislative requirement imposed by the *Teaching Service Act 1980* (NSW):

> There is an element of incongruity in describing as a requirement or condition, compliance with which is required in the terms and conditions of employment as a casual teacher, a requirement that in order to access higher levels of salary, one must cease to be a casual teacher and obtain permanent appointment.[57]

In contrast to this restrictive approach, which regarded the two classifications as discrete, the minority felt it was necessary to go beyond the value of the work to consider the teachers' rights and obligations. It is impossible not to agree with Kirby J (dissenting) that the interpretation adopted by the majority is 'narrow and antagonistic' to the beneficial and purposive approach mandated by the legislation.[58] He held that the majority's deference to the employer's historical and gendered categorisation of casual and permanent staff, despite repeal of the statutory exception, had the effect of defining the discrimination complaint 'out of existence'.

Ironically, Gummow, Hayne and Crennan JJ, in the course of articulating a restricted meaning for the phrase 'requirement or condition', noted that the legislation was to be given a broad rather than a technical meaning.[59] They stated that it was wrong to ask 'what was the requirement or

---

56   *Amery*, 213–14; relying on the interpretation of Lee J in *Allders International Pty Ltd v Anstee* (1986) 5 NSWLR 47, 55.
57   *Amery*, 214.
58   ibid., 230 (Kirby J).
59   ibid., 213.

condition' rather than 'whether the perpetrator engaged in a proscribed form of discrimination'.[60] It seems the requirement or condition must be established before ascertaining whether it exerted a discriminatory effect or not. In this case, the permanency requirement disproportionately impacted on the complainants because they were women.

The restrictive interpretation adopted by the majority avoids consideration of the gendered nature of casual employment and why women 'choose' to do it or feel duty bound to accept it. The majority position is striking because all but two of the 13 complainants had formerly occupied permanent positions in the teaching service. In most cases, the explanation for the transfer to the casual category was simple: they had resigned to care for their families—a sacrifice not expected of their male partners.[61] When the women subsequently sought to return to the teaching service, permanency entailed them accepting a posting anywhere in the state, but they were not free to relocate because of family commitments. The social norm prevailed that they follow their partner's place of work and accommodate the needs of their families. Accordingly, they accepted casual positions that were accessible to their homes.

The powerful norms that govern gender and familial relations, to which I have adverted, have long shaped the employment conditions of women. A positivistic reading of the text of the *ADA* effectively sloughs off the historical discrimination inhering within the differential pay scales. The narrow stance adopted by the majority contrasts markedly with the earlier judgement of *Banovic*, in which Justices Deane, Dawson and Gaudron determined that past discrimination could not be used to justify conduct that continued to discriminate unfairly against women.[62]

While *Amery* adopts a technocratic approach in the interpretation of a requirement or condition that appears to be neutral and depoliticised, its meaning is shaped by the juridical hermeneutic world, which, in turn, is shaped by the shifts and turns within the broader sociopolitical *nomos*. This includes the neoliberal swing in favour of flexible work that is casual and precarious, but which suits employers because it cuts costs. Such work is overwhelmingly feminised.[63] Precarious work also suggests

---

60   ibid.

61   *Amery v NSW* (2001) EOC ¶93–130 (NSW ADT) 75290.

62   *Banovic*, 180 (Deane & Gaudron JJ), 191 (Dawson J).

63   Judy Fudge & Rosemary Owens (eds), *Precarious Work, Women, and the New Economy: The Challenge to Legal Norms* (Hart, 2006).

a greater deference to employer prerogative, as we see in *Amery*; workers' rights, including the principles of non-discrimination, are no longer in the ascendancy.[64]

Focusing on the value to the employer of contingent or precarious work at the expense of employees also reifies the conventional public–private dichotomy of liberalism, as it cloaks the reasons women predominate in this type of work and how it contributes to systemic discrimination in the workplace. While the normative universe comprises an unstable mixture of imperial and paideic elements, and various shades in between, neoliberalism, in conjunction with the prevailing neoconservatism, has legitimated the contemporary imperial turn in adjudication on issues of sex discrimination.

Courts of appeal and reasonableness

The concept of reasonableness—invariably the most vexed element of the indirect discrimination test—deserves comment as it represents a classic instance of the abdication of responsibility by the legislature, which I have identified as a marked characteristic of antidiscrimination legislation. This familiar standard is left to judges to interpret and invest with meaning within a particular context, or it is otherwise devoid of meaning. For this reason, Julius Stone described reasonableness as a concept that is 'slippery and even treacherous'.[65] Its open-ended character allows judges to determine whether to look to the future or the past and whether to favour the perspective of the complainant or the respondent. Some legislation now includes criteria to which the courts should pay heed when addressing the reasonableness test,[66] which gives the appearance of objectivity and certainty. While such mechanisms serve to obscure the subjectivity of the judge, the leeways of choice are inescapable. This is the case whether the onus of proving reasonableness is on the complainant or whether it has shifted to the respondent.

The test of reasonableness is frequently the sticking point in indirect discrimination complaints, although the case law is not necessarily illuminating. The longevity of a practice can endow it with a veneer

---

64 For example, Rosemary Owens & Joellen Riley, *The Law of Work* (Oxford University Press, 2007); David Peetz, *The Realities and Future of Work* (ANU Press, 2019), doi.org/10.22459/RFW.2019.
65 Julius Stone, *Human Law and Human Justice* (Maitland, 1965) 328.
66 See, for example, *SDA*, s. 7B(2); *Equal Opportunity Act 2010* (Vic.) s. 9(3).

of reasonableness, which may have been a factor in *Amery*, although reasonableness was discussed only by Gleeson CJ (Callinan and Heydon JJ agreeing). Gleeson CJ was of the view that while the nature and quality of a permanent officer and a casual teacher may be identical, the issue of deployability in a large geographical area could not be ignored.[67] He determined that it had not been shown to be unreasonable to pay the two categories differently. Thus, even if this case had not foundered on the identification of the requirement or condition with which the complainants were expected to comply, the application of the reasonableness standard could have proven fatal.

I propose to consider two appellate decisions that turned on the issue of reasonableness in the domain of sex discrimination to illustrate the extent and power of the hermeneutic role at the authoritative level: *Commonwealth Bank of Australia v Human Rights & Equal Opportunity Commission* (*Commonwealth Bank*),[68] a decision of the Full Bench of the Federal Court, and *Schou*,[69] a decision of the Victorian Court of Appeal. These decisions may be fruitfully considered alongside *Amery* because they involve indirect discrimination arising from maternity leave and caring responsibilities that disproportionately impacted women. In both cases, the complainants failed because of the favouring of a managerial perspective over the interests of the complainants, which had the effect of upholding the status quo.

It might be noted that both cases would probably have gone to the High Court had the complainants been able to afford it. Based on *Amery* and other recent discrimination cases, however, it would not necessarily have been advantageous for them. In these cases, the leaning towards retention of an imperial world would not only have implicitly privileged corporate power and benchmark men—the unencumbered subjects of liberal legalism—but also managerial prerogative would have been privileged over workers' rights. Recourse to the convenient catch-all concept of 'reasonableness' authorises the legitimation of this ordering by judges.

While reasonableness is normally an issue for an initial hearing, I have chosen to focus on appellate decisions, where the jurisgenerative role is respected and well established. Reasonableness confounds the fact/law

---

67 *Amery*, 203.
68 (1997) 80 FCR 78.
69 (2004) 8 VR 120.

distinction, since a matter of fact cannot be determined in the abstract, although, as a matter of law, reasonableness involves an objective test in weighing up the evidence. Although reasonableness may be a question of fact, appellate judges are the ones charged with its review. They say it is to be determined by 'weighing all the *relevant* factors'.[70] Relevance is a category of illusory reference, no less than reasonableness, which further underscores the undeniable play of judicial subjectivity, despite asseverations to the contrary.

'Reasonableness' is a trope that allows discrimination against women to be justified and legitimated by the powerful today, no less than in the past, albeit less overtly. As a bona fide instrument within the hermeneutic toolkit of discrimination law, reasonableness selectively instantiates an imperial approach to issues of gender in the workplace that sustains the separation of the public and private spheres of liberal legalism. The message is that caring for young children belongs in the private sphere and is a responsibility that should be disconnected from the world of work. This approach is immune to the contemporary rhetoric of flexible work and WLB. The imperial view is that the workplace is a domain where employer prerogative reigns supreme, free from the 'unreasonable' demands of maternity leave and sick children.

Commonwealth Bank of Australia v Human Rights & Equal Opportunity Commission (1997) 80 FCR 78

This complaint was instituted by the Finance Sector Union on behalf of more than 100 female employees of the Commonwealth Bank. The bank engaged in a major restructure that entailed the loss of about 7,500 staff, because of which employees had the option of either taking a redundancy package or applying for a new position. It was argued that the restructure disproportionately impacted women because those on extended family leave, including maternity leave, did not have access to redundancy packages. As far as the new positions were concerned, employees had to be available to take them up within four weeks of appointment. For women on maternity leave, including those who either had recently had a baby or were about to give birth, this was unlikely to be practicable.

---

70   For example, *Waters v Public Transport Corporation* (1991) 173 CLR 349, 395 (Dawson & Toohey JJ). Emphasis added.

The inability to apply for a superior position instantiated the idea of women as primary carers but secondary workers in accordance with the prevailing neoconservative ethos.

While the Human Rights and Equal Opportunity Commission (HREOC) found in favour of the union in the first instance,[71] the Federal Court held on appeal that the condition was not unreasonable and reversed in favour of the bank.[72] The reasoning of the court was that the HREOC had failed to take sufficient account of the fact that women on maternity leave were entitled to a comparable position when they returned from leave. The HREOC had acknowledged the commercial imperative but rejected the necessity of the four-week requirement. The effect was that the complainants missed out on the possibility of superior positions that they might have been prepared to take up after the elapse of more than four weeks. In this case, we see judicial deference to corporate power and convenience.

Tarrant is critical of the Federal Court for what she terms its adoption of the 'package-deal approach'.[73] That is, rather than focus solely on the effect of the detriment arising from the requirement or condition, the court takes into account any other benefit allegedly conferred, which, in this case, was the availability of comparable positions: '[T]he primary mischief in the package deal approach is that it puts it in the power of the respondent unilaterally to assess and determine the needs of a complainant.'[74] As Tarrant points out, there is no authority in *Waters v Public Transport Corporation*[75] for the package-deal approach, despite the Federal Court's purported reliance on its interpretation of reasonableness. However, I would take issue with Tarrant regarding the power of the bank as the primary mischief here, for this power would have been of little avail without the crucial legitimating role of the judges of the Federal Court. As with *Amery*, the judges were able to relegate the principle of equality for women at work and the values underpinning sex discrimination legislation to the background under the rubric of reasonableness.

The Finance Sector Union ran the case on behalf of the complainants, but it was not prepared or could not afford to pursue an appeal to the High Court. Because of the high cost of representation and the risk of losing

---

71   *Finance Sector Union v Commonwealth Bank of Australia* (1997) EOC ¶92–889 (HREOC).
72   *Commonwealth Bank*, 113 (Sackville J).
73   Tarrant (n. 28).
74   ibid., 47.
75   (1991) 173 CLR 349.

the case, which could entail paying the bank's costs as well as its own, the union's male members were reputed to be opposed to an appeal. This chance element in litigation points to the way that the victors—invariably corporate entities with power and resources—can write sex discrimination jurisprudence in their own image. The homologous relationship between these corporate players and the judiciary induces judges to privilege the arguments of respondents over those of complainants. It also means that any successful utilisation of antidiscrimination legislation in the wake of a restructure would be virtually impossible.[76]

State of Victoria v Schou (2004) 8 VR 120

Schou represents yet another variation on the theme of the woman worker as carer and highlights the difficulty of combining work and family considering the competing values within the normative universe, despite the prevalence of the rhetoric of WLB. Indeed, as a manifestation of the changing discourse from the rights of individual workers to what is best for families, the alleged discrimination is based not on sex per se, but on the more recent ground of status as a parent or carer.[77]

The complainant was a Hansard reporter who had worked for the Victorian Parliament for 17 years. Because she had a chronically ill child, she sought to do her transcription work at home for two days a week when parliament was sitting (sometimes until 2 am), which was possible with a computer and a modem, to which the employer had initially agreed. The requirement or condition with which the complainant was unable to comply was that she attend work full-time at Parliament House on sitting days. Neither the conceptualisation of the requirement nor the issue of proportionality was contentious, as it was accepted that a higher proportion of people without parental or caring status could comply with the requirement. As with *Commonwealth Bank*, the focus was on the reasonableness of the attendance requirement. The Victorian Civil and Administrative Tribunal found (twice)[78] that the requirement was not

---

76 Cf. Rosemary Hunter, 'The Mirage of Justice: Women and the Shrinking State' (2002) 16(1) *Australian Feminist Law Journal* 53, 63–65, doi.org/10.1080/13200968.2002.11106904.

77 Australia ratified *ILO Convention (No. 156) Concerning Equal Opportunities and Equal Treatment for Men and Women Workers: Workers with Family Responsibilities*, opened for signature 23 June 1981 (entered into force 11 August 1983), in 1990. In 1992, the ground of family responsibilities was included as a proscribed ground within the *SDA*.

78 *Schou v Victoria (Department of Parliamentary Debates)* (2000) EOC ¶93–101 (VCAT); *Schou v Victoria (Department of Parliamentary Debates)* (2002) EOC ¶93–217 (VCAT).

reasonable as there was a practical alternative to working in situ, which was working online at home, and awarded the complainant damages of more than A$160,000.

Once again, we find a restrictive approach being adopted by appellate courts before, first, a single judge[79] and, second, a majority of the Full Bench of the Victorian Supreme Court.[80] While Gaze presents a trenchant critique of the judgement of Harper J in the first appeal to the Supreme Court for his less-than-adequate grasp of the elements of indirect discrimination,[81] a similar charge could be levelled against the majority judges in the subsequent appeal to the Full Bench. Both Harper J, sitting as a single judge, and Phillips JA (Buchanan JA agreeing) of the Full Bench held that the focus of the reasonableness provision should have been directed to the attendance requirement without regard to the modem proposal. In the disaggregation of issues, we see the same narrow technocratic interpretation as in *Amery* although, in this case, particularly so far as Phillips JA (Buchanan JA agreeing) was concerned, there was little attempt to disguise the preference for managerial prerogative. Phillips JA found it 'almost inconceivable' that the attendance requirement could be regarded as not reasonable as a matter of law, since it was authorised by the employment contract.[82] Common law, however, was not the end of the matter as the complainant had entered into an individual workplace agreement that guaranteed to promote 'flexible and progressive work practices and reasonable changes in the way work is organised'.[83] This agreement was ignored by the Supreme Court judges, which would seem to discount the legislative requirement that 'all the relevant circumstances of the case be taken into consideration' in weighing up the meaning of reasonableness[84]—a position supported by the High Court judges in *Waters*.[85] Callaway JA, in a brief dissent, rejected the narrow view, holding that the question of reasonableness was a matter of fact for the tribunal.

---

79   *Victoria v Schou* (2001) 3 VR 655.
80   *Schou*.
81   Gaze (n. 17); cf. K. Lee Adams, 'A Step Backward in Job Protection for Carers' (2002) 15(1) *Australian Journal of Labour Law* 93; K. Lee Adams, 'Indirect Discrimination and the Worker-Carer: It's Just Not Working' in Jill Murray (ed.), *Work, Family and the Law* (2005) 23(1)[SI] *Law in Context* 18.
82   *Schou*, 128 (Phillips JA).
83   *Deborah Schou v Victoria* (2000) EOC ¶93–100 (VCAT), 74424; *Schou v Victoria Melb (Department of Parliamentary Debates)* (2002) EOC ¶93–217 (VCAT), 76507–9.
84   *EOA 1995* (Vic.) s. 9(2).
85   *Waters v Public Transport Corporation* (1991) 173 CLR 349, 393 (Dawson and Toohey JJ).

The semiotics of 'choice' and 'flexibility' have changed our understanding of work. This language has been deployed by neoliberals to place responsibility on individual employees for the course of their lives and to deflect attention away from prevailing social structures and the profitmaking imperative.[86] Choice was invoked in *Amery* to explain the unwillingness of the complainants to accept teaching positions outside nominated geographical areas. While the Anti-Discrimination Tribunal recognised the socially constructed nature of this choice, in that it was not merely a 'personal' or 'lifestyle' choice, the propensity of conservative judges to individualise it deflects attention from the structural factors that require women to place their families first in determining work location. Hence, Buchanan JA in *Schou* suggested that the modification of a general requirement to accommodate one person's special needs is not what the indirect provisions of the Act are about.[87] Equality as sameness was also stressed by Harper J: '[T]he Act forbids discrimination. It does not compel the bestowing of special advantage.'[88] This stance virtually guarantees the failure of any complainant's case that entails any accommodation of difference.[89]

Charlesworth has observed that there is a propensity to treat 'working mums' as transient workers with little commitment to the workplace.[90] The secondary-worker status for women with children is a prominent strand of the *nomos* and, through *Schou*, together with *Commonwealth Bank* and *Amery*, we can see the power of judges in keeping alive this imperial construction. When a choice must be made, there is an unwillingness to find that the interests of women workers with childcare responsibilities could possibly take precedence over powerful institutional and corporate interests. In this way, the hermeneutic role of judges may be invoked to retard the promise of sex discrimination legislation to promote women's equality.

---

86   See, for example, Peter Self, *Government by the Market? The Politics of Public Choice* (Macmillan, 1993).

87   *Schou* (2004) 8 VR 120, 137.

88   *Victoria v Schou* (2001) 3 VR 655, 661 (Harper J).

89   Cf. *Purvis v New South Wales (Department of Education and Training)* (2003) 217 CLR 92.

90   Sara Charlesworth, 'Working Mums: The Construction of Women Workers in the Banking Industry' (1999) 4(2) *Journal of Interdisciplinary Gender Studies* 12.

Conclusion

The trajectory of sex discrimination cases highlights the symbiotic relationship between the sociopolitical climate and the adjudicative norms of the day. There is never going to be a precise congruence because of the ad hoc nature of adjudication, such as the fortitude and resources of a complainant to persist with an appeal, as well as the knowledge and understanding of the judge assigned to the case. The movement away from an expansive and paideic view of the legislation to a more restrictive and imperialistic approach over three decades is discernible in appellate decisions.[91] This has crystallised into what former High Court judge Michael Kirby referred to as a 'hostile litigious environment in which claims of the present kind are typically litigated'.[92] To some extent, the change mirrors the shift from social liberalism to neoliberalism, which is antipathetic to social justice. A similar observation could be made about the US Supreme Court, which was regarded as the champion of civil rights under Chief Justice Earl Warren (1953–69),[93] but the appointment of conservative judges under presidents Ronald Reagan, George H.W. Bush and George W. Bush saw the gradual unpicking of significant civil liberties victories in respect of race and sex discrimination.[94]

State-funded legal aid for sex discrimination complaints and for civil litigation generally has been another casualty of neoliberalism, which favours a user-pays philosophy.[95] A law firm could agree to act pro bono, but it might hesitate when faced with a powerful corporate respondent with deep pockets. The NSW Women's Advisory Council, which advocated on behalf of the 34 women of non–English-speaking background in *Banovic*, has been abolished and there is no replacement body with access to government ministers. In *Amery* and *Schou*, the respondent state governments of New South Wales and Victoria supported the respondents' appeals to the High Court, thereby undermining their own antidiscrimination legislation.

---

91 For example, *Purvis v New South Wales (Department of Education and Training)* (2003) 217 CLR 92. At the appellate court level, compare *Schou* and *Commonwealth Bank*.

92 *Amery*, 219.

93 See, for example, Lucas A. Powe Jr, *The Warren Court and American Politics* (Belknap/Harvard University Press, 2000).

94 Including the cause célèbre, *Regents of the University of California v Bakke*, 438 US 265 (1978), in which the Supreme Court struck down quotas for racial minorities but upheld a commitment to diversity.

95 Mary Anne Noone & Stephen A. Tomsen, *Lawyers in Conflict: Australian Lawyers and Legal Aid* (The Federation Press, 2006), esp. Ch. 6.

Of course, access to the courts is by no means the end of the matter. Inevitably, the power and resources of corporate respondents determine the course of the litigation and shape the jurisprudence that emerges. Three sex discrimination cases before the High Court in 40 years is not many. In reflecting on why more race than sex cases have gone to the High Court,[96] Jocelynne Scutt speculates that it is because key race cases such as *Koowarta*[97] and *Mabo*[98] were framed in terms of property rights rather than human rights or discrimination.[99] While the discourse of human rights has become more prominent in recent years, the normalisation of sex discrimination has militated against it being perceived as a human rights violation. However, there has been a resiling from the recognition of rights of all kinds in favour of 'the good of the economy'. The diminution of workers' rights because of neoliberalism is salutary, for there has been a correlative enhancement of employer prerogative that has augmented the burden of proof confronting complainants in discrimination cases. In *Amery*, for example, we see deference towards the idea of respondents defining a requirement or condition in their own interests against which earlier courts warned.[100] One of the express aims of the *SDA* is to 'promote recognition and acceptance within the community of the principle of the equality of men and women'. A narrow positivistic reading of the indirect provisions effectively nullifies this principle of equality. Even in the case of direct discrimination, the tendency is to recognise only those instances that lie close to the surface.[101]

Judges always encounter leeways of choice between the imperial and the paideic approaches, but a neoliberal milieu with its promotion of market values and moral conservatism is unlikely to champion the rights of women workers and the ideals of gender equality. Judges, moreover, are invariably more comfortable with the world-maintaining norms of the past, despite their jurisgenerative role as they comport with the doctrine of precedent. Substantial lacunae within the legislative texts

---

96   It is notable that there was a cessation of successful race discrimination cases before the High Court after the controversial decision of *Wik Peoples v Queensland* (1996) 187 CLR 1.

97   *Koowarta v Bjelke-Petersen* (1982) 153 CLR 168.

98   *Mabo v Queensland (No 2)* (1992) 175 CLR 1.

99   Jocelynne A. Scutt, 'Without Precedent: Sex/Gender Discrimination in the High Court' (2003) 28(2) *Alternative Law Journal* 74, doi.org/10.1177/1037969x0302800205.

100 For example, *Waters v Public Transport Corporation* (1991) 173 CLR 349, 394 (Dawson & Toohey JJ).

101 Thornton (n. 12) 245.

endorse the predilection in favour of the imperial turn. The interpretative community is most comfortable with a positivistic paradigm in which justice is incidental.

One could go a step further and distinguish the earlier cases dealing with the 'letting in' of women to non-traditional areas of work, such as *Wardley* and *Banovic*, from the subsequent cases—namely, *Amery*, *Commonwealth Bank* and *Schou*. It might be averred that 'letting in' a few women to non-traditional workplaces, when their exclusion is egregious, is significantly less destabilising than radically challenging established work practices emanating from the old master–servant relationship, such as the employer's right to determine the structure of the workplace, the site of work and the terms and conditions of employment. Despite the legislative prescripts of antidiscrimination legislation, the conservative view is that conferring gender equality on women with caring responsibilities is corrosive of the core values at the heart of the normative universe. The malleable hermeneutics of adjudication allow judges to sustain benchmark masculinity by adopting an imperial approach that is legitimated by the rule of law. The imperial approach represents an unstable position, however; faith in the rule of law demands the adoption of a paideic approach towards antidiscrimination legislation—at least some of the time.

10

The High Court and Judicial Activism

Introduction

Former Australian High Court judge Dyson Heydon, in a provocative paper postulating the death of the rule of law, was anxious to restrain the subjectivity of judges, which he equated with arbitrariness.[1] He reserved the strongest disapprobation for the 'activist judge' who invoked judicial power 'for a purpose other than that for which it was granted, namely, doing justice according to law'.[2] However, the assertion is weakened by the ambiguity besetting the terms he uses and the way they are shaped by the epistemological standpoint of the speaker. Heydon would certainly not go as far as Iain Stewart in describing law as a 'dark performative' that has no meaning of itself other than that which is constituted through the act of speech,[3] but he does concede that the rule of law possesses a 'range of meanings'.[4] Heydon does not qualify judicial activism in the same way, although it has been described as lacking defined content.[5] What these observations underscore is that the search for clear meanings is likely to be fruitless because the term is always politically contestable.[6]

---

1   Dyson Heydon, 'Judicial Activism and the Death of the Rule of Law' (2003) 23 *Australian Bar Review* 110.
2   ibid., 113.
3   Iain Stewart, 'The Use of Law' in Michael Freeman (ed.), *Law and Sociology* (Current Legal Issues Vol. 8, Oxford University Press, 2006) 259.
4   Heydon (n. 1) 111.
5   Frank B. Cross & Stefanie A. Lindquist, 'The Scientific Study of Judicial Activism' (2007) 91(6) *Minnesota Law Review* 1752.
6   Tom Campbell, 'Judicial Activism: Justice or Treason?' (2003) 10(3) *Otago Law Review* 307.

Judicial activism is nevertheless a useful phrase, for it reminds us that judges are perennially engaged in what Robert Cover calls a 'jurisgenerative' process—that is, the creation of meaning;[7] activist judging is not an idiosyncratic act undertaken by a few radicals. Julius Stone draws attention to the fact that, within their hermeneutic universe, judges are compelled to exercise what he famously called the 'leeways of choice' at every step of the adjudicative process.[8] Furthermore, activism is central to the role of appellate courts:

> Courts of final appeal are properly activist. To suggest otherwise would require the suspension of reality in face of the facts—why else have a second layer of appeal if the role of such a court is not to make law?[9]

To deny the importance of the activist role comports with the well-known positivist myth that judges do not make law, although many judges adopt a more realistic stance.[10]

I do not propose to embark on a thoroughgoing critique of Heydon's position, which has been ably undertaken by others,[11] but to use it as a springboard for examining the Australian High Court's approach to disability discrimination legislation. Thus, rather than focus on either constitutional or common law adjudication—the more conventional sites of the critique of judicial activism—I turn the spotlight on statutory interpretation. I argue that an ostensibly formalistic approach, far from revealing deference to the rule of law, may actually frustrate legislative intent—although ascertaining the meaning of intent is always contestable.[12] Indeed, I turn Heydon's notion of activism on its head and suggest that the judges of the High Court post *Mabo*[13] and *Wik*,[14]—particularly

---

7   Robert Cover, '*Nomos* and Narrative' (1983) 97(4) *Harvard Law Review* 4, 11.

8   Julius Stone, *Legal System and Lawyers' Reasonings* (Maitland Publications, 1968) 325–30, *et passim*.

9   Fiona Wheeler & John Williams, '"Restrained Activism" in the High Court of Australia' in Brice Dickson (ed.), *Judicial Activism in Common Law Supreme Courts* (Oxford University Press, 2007) 65, doi.org/10.1093/acprof:oso/9780199213290.003.0002. Cf. Michael Kirby, 'Judicial Activism: Power without Responsibility? No, Appropriate Activism Conforming to Duty' (2006) 30 *Melbourne University Law Review* 576.

10   For example, Anthony Mason, 'Legislative and Judicial Law-Making: Can We Locate an Identifiable Boundary?' in Geoffrey Lindell (ed.), *The Mason Papers: Selected Articles and Speeches by Sir Anthony Mason AC, KBE* (The Federation Press, 2007).

11   Allan C. Hutchinson, 'Heydon Seek: Looking for Law in All the Wrong Places' (2003) 29 *Monash University Law Review* 85; John Gava, 'Unconvincing and Perplexing: Hutchinson and Stapleton on Judging' (2007) 26 *University of Queensland Law Journal* 67.

12   Natalie Stoljar, 'Postulated Authors and Hypothetical Intentions' in Ngaire Naffine, Rosemary Owens & John Williams, *Intention in Law and Philosophy* (Ashgate/Dartmouth, 2001) 271.

13   *Mabo v Queensland* (1992) 175 CLR 1 (*Mabo*).

14   *Wik Peoples and Thayorre People v Queensland* (1996) 141 ALR 129 (*Wik*).

the 'rampant conservatives'[15] of the Gleeson court (1998–2008)—were insidious activists in contrast to the moderate social liberals of the Mason court (1987–95),[16] who acknowledged their activism. Leslie Zines notes the more democratic approach of the High Court that emerged, at least as far as constitutional adjudication was concerned, following passage of the *Australia Act 1986* (Cth).[17]

Antidiscrimination law could be described as a paradigm of social liberalism because the legislation that first emerged in the 1970s and 1980s is designed to promote equality between all citizens regardless of sex, race, sexuality, disability, age or other characteristic of identity.[18] While the legislation is not entrenched and is riddled with exceptions, it is the nearest instrument to a bill of rights in most Australian jurisdictions, which heightens its sensitivity to changes in the political climate. The neoliberal turn that began in the 1980s became pronounced in the 1990s. The key characteristic of neoliberalism is the adulation of the free market, although it is accompanied by a constellation of politically and morally conservative values that are supportive of the market, including the privileging of employer prerogative over employee rights, administrative convenience, efficiency, the maximisation of profits and promotion of the self. Correspondingly, we see a resiling from broad human rights principles. These changes are reflected in the values of the court, although they are subtle and evocative, rather than overt, as the adjudicative process is cloaked in a carapace of technocratic rules.

The activism of interpretation

Kent Roach argues that activist judging is a 'loaded and slippery term'[19] that has emerged from a two-century debate about the role of the US Supreme Court and the US Constitution.[20] The debate focuses on whether judges should be free to interpret the constitution as they think fit or whether

---

15   Brice Dickson, 'Comparing Supreme Courts' in Brice Dickson (ed.), *Judicial Activism in Common Law Supreme Courts* (Oxford University Press, 2007), doi.org/10.1093/acprof:oso/9780199213290.003.0001.

16   Wheeler & Williams (n. 9) 65.

17   Leslie Zines, 'Judicial Activism and the Rule of Law in Australia' in Tom Campbell & Jeffrey Goldsworthy (eds), *Judicial Power, Democracy and Legal Positivism* (Ashgate/Dartmouth, 2000) 397.

18   Margaret Thornton, *The Liberal Promise: Anti-Discrimination Legislation in Australia* (Oxford University Press, 1990).

19   Kent Roach, *The Supreme Court on Trial: Judicial Activism or Democratic Dialogue* (Irwin Law, 2001).

20   Cross & Lindquist (n. 5).

they should exercise restraint and be more deferential to the legislature.[21] It is this American-centric critique, Roach argues, that has spread like an epidemic around the globe and extended from constitutionalism to statutory and common law adjudication.[22]

It would seem the neoliberal turn induced Australian conservatives to adopt the populist North American understanding of judicial activism, which avers that if judges are not elected, any 'lawmaking' in which they engage must necessarily be undemocratic.[23] This very point was made by conservative newspaper columnist Janet Albrechtsen shortly before the 2007 Australian federal election.[24] Fearing the prospect of a Rudd Labor government, she denigrated Rudd's team for what she claimed would be its likelihood of favouring the appointment of judges with little time for 'democratic traditions'.[25] That is, Labor-appointed judges would want to make law themselves rather than defer to the legislature.

When we turn to discrimination legislation, we see that the aims are clearly articulated in terms of effecting equality between all persons and eliminating discrimination. Of course, these aims are expressed at a high level of abstraction and require creativity on the part of judges to interpret them meaningfully considering the facts of the instant case, but the positive injunction is undeniable. When conservative judges focus on statutory construction and disregard the objects of the legislation, they are committing the very sins that critics such as Heydon and Albrechtsen deplore. The aims of antidiscrimination legislation are grounded in a democratic political system and, as Tom Campbell points out, if the objects are reasonably clear, citizens have a right to expect statutes to mean what they say.[26]

The attacks on so-called activist judges are most vociferous when there is a victory by litigants from outside the ranks of the socially powerful, as in the case of Indigenous communities (for example, *Mabo* and *Wik*). In other words, when the political pendulum swings away from formal justice, which favours the hegemony of the powerful, and moves towards substantive equality, in an endeavour to redress the inequitable position

21   Ronald Dworkin, *Law's Empire* (Belknap/Harvard University Press, 1986) 369 ff.
22   Roach (n. 19) 98.
23   ibid., 99.
24   Janet Albrechtsen, 'Activist Judiciary a Looming Menace', *The Australian*, 31 October 2007, 16.
25   ibid.
26   Tom Campbell, 'Legislative Intent and Democratic Decision Making' in Ngaire Naffine, Rosemary Owens & John Williams (eds), *Intention in Law and Philosophy* (Ashgate/Dartmouth, 2001) 291.

of the less powerful, the backlash is sharp and furious. As Wheeler and Williams show in their considered analysis of the attack by conservatives on the Mason court for its 'judicial activism', the attacks were motivated by the substantive outcomes in landmark cases rather than by the court's adjudicative style.[27]

Conservatives reserve a particular animus for the progressive judge who is concerned with substantive equality, as can be seen in the disparagement by Heydon of the judgements of the late Justice Lionel Murphy as a 'series of dogmatic, dirigiste and emotional slogans',[28] which lends support to the view that criticisms of judicial activism are ideologically based and analytically unhelpful.[29] The epistemology of standpoint is crucial here. While conservative commentators suggest that judicial activism is the improper usurpation of the role of the legislature by progressive judges, the conservative judges who subvert legislative intent are depicted as exercising restraint.[30] A value-free neutrality simply cannot be supported in adjudication.[31] It is a fiction designed to mask the political, which is yet another 'category of illusory reference'.[32] While 'the political' may broadly encompass all aspects of citizen–state relations, on the one hand, or be restricted to the party–political, on the other, I am more interested in the political philosophies that underpin adjudication.

I am not sure I would go as far as Hutchinson and assert that law *is* politics,[33] as there are always powerful steadying factors at work in appellate courts that arise from acculturation in law.[34] Nevertheless, the competing views of judicial activism are undoubtedly shaped by the prevailing political philosophy of the court, despite the rhetoric averring judicial autonomy. Wendy Brown, drawing on Nietzsche, suggests that a concept of *ressentiment*[35] inheres within liberalism—the dominant political philosophy of the Western world—because of the way liberalism simultaneously promises both freedom and equality:

---

27   Wheeler & Williams (n. 9) 29.
28   Heydon (n. 1) 122.
29   Michael Coper, 'Concern about Judicial Method' (2006) 30 *Melbourne University Law Review* 554, 562, 573; Cross & Lindquist (n. 5).
30   Herman Schwartz, *The Rehnquist Court: Judicial Activism on the Right* (Hill & Wang, 2002).
31   Anthony Mason, 'Rights, Values and Legal Institutions: Reshaping Australian Institutions' in Geoffrey Lindell (ed.), *The Mason Papers: Selected Articles and Speeches by Sir Anthony Mason AC, KBE* (The Federation Press, 2007).
32   Stone (n. 8).
33   Hutchinson (n. 11).
34   Stone (n. 8) 322.
35   Friedrich Nietzsche, *On the Genealogy of Morals*, translated by Walter Kaufman & R.J. Hollingdale (Vintage Books, 1969) 127.

> A strong commitment to freedom vitiates the fulfilment of the equality promise and breeds *ressentiment* as welfare state liberalism—attenuations of the unmitigated license of the rich and powerful on behalf of the 'disadvantaged'. Conversely, a strong commitment to equality, requiring heavy state interventionism and economic redistribution, attenuates the commitment to freedom and breeds *ressentiment* expressed as neo-conservative anti-statism, racism, charges of reverse racism, and so forth.[36]

I suggest these pendulum swings in the contemporary political realm are obliquely reflected within the process of adjudication, despite the formalistic facade and the myths of objectivity. The fluctuations on the political continuum and the subjectivity of the judge are further disguised by the powerful discourse of merit that surrounds judicial appointments, which avers that the best person for the job is appointed, as discussed in Chapter 11.

Swings and roundabouts

When decisions that upheld the human rights of Indigenous people[37] and women[38] began to be handed down for the first time, the *ressentiment* of the Right began to manifest itself through agitation against progressive decisions—most notably, those of *Mabo* and *Wik*. The court's upholding of native title against the property interests of powerful landholders was viewed by detractors as an arrant manifestation of judicial lawmaking.[39] The attack on the court in the wake of *Wik* paralleled the trenchant attack by conservatives on the US Supreme Court under Chief Justice Warren following *Brown v Board of Education*[40]—one of that court's most famous decisions.[41]

---

36 Wendy Brown, *States of Injury: Power and Freedom in Late Modernity* (Princeton University Press, 1995) 67.

37 For example, *Koowarta v Bjelke-Petersen* (1982) 153 CLR 168.

38 *Ansett Transport Industries (Operations) Pty Ltd v Wardley* (1980) 142 CLR 237.

39 Garfield Barwick, 'Chief Justice Comments on Fundamental Issues Facing the Judiciary' in Geoffrey Lindell (ed.), *The Mason Papers: Selected Articles and Speeches by Sir Anthony Mason AC, KBE* (The Federation Press, 2007) 398; Zines (n. 17) 406–8; David Marr, 'No More Than They Deserve' in David Marr, *The High Price of Heaven* (Allen & Unwin, 1999).

40 *Brown v Board of Education of Topeka* 347 US 483 (1954).

41 John D. Carter, *The Warren Court and the Constitution: A Critical View of Judicial Activism* (Pelican Publishing, 1973).

Wik coincided with the election of Prime Minister John Howard in 1996, signalling a sharp swing to the right and the embrace of a neoliberal political agenda. A dramatic manifestation of the Howard government's intention following *Wik* was the announcement by then acting prime minister Tim Fischer that the government would appoint 'Capital C Conservatives' to the High Court to replace retiring judges.[42] The six new appointments to the court (of seven), including Murray Gleeson as chief justice in 1998, were intended to reflect the neoconservative turn and, as in the United States, a major transformation was initiated through a 'right-wing phalanx'.[43] While not all the judges may have identified themselves as capital-C Conservatives, the High Court's style of adjudication changed markedly. Wheeler and Williams describe the return to legalism as 'a recalibration of doctrine in key areas suggestive of a desire to check the perceived activism of the Mason era'.[44] Most significantly, I suggest, it retreated from an inchoate rights-based jurisprudence that recognised the changing position of women and disfavoured Others, including people with disabilities.

In all the discrimination appeals decided by the High Court during the decade of Howard's tenure as Australian prime minister (1996–2007), the complainants lost, in sharp contrast with comparable cases in the preceding decade. It is noteworthy that, considering the conservative outcry against *Mabo* and *Wik*, none of these decisions dealt with race; instead, one dealt with sex (*Amery*),[45] one with age (*Christie*)[46] and three with disability (*IW v City of Perth*,[47] *X v Commonwealth*[48] and *Purvis*).[49] In each instance, the majority judges interpreted the legislative texts in ways that undermined the proscriptions against discrimination. Justice Kirby, consistently in dissent, reminds us that antidiscrimination legislation is beneficial legislation that requires regard for its aims that can only be frustrated by narrow technical readings.[50] I suggest, however, that far from being the rogue activist out on a limb, Justice Kirby was the only

---

42   Nikki Savva, 'Fischer Seeks a More Conservative Court', *The Age*, [Melbourne], 5 March 1997, 1–2.

43   Ronald Dworkin, 'The Supreme Court Phalanx' 54(14) *New York Review of Books*, 27 September 2007, 92.

44   Wheeler & Williams (n. 9) 58.

45   *New South Wales v Amery* (2006) 226 ALR 196, discussed in Chapter 9, this volume.

46   *Qantas Airways Ltd v Christie* (1998) 193 CLR 280.

47   *IW v City of Perth* (1997) 191 CLR 1.

48   *X v Commonwealth* (1999) 200 CLR 177.

49   *Purvis v New South Wales (Department of Education and Training)* (2003) 217 CLR 92.

50   For example, *Amery*, 213.

judge, except for Justice McHugh, who exercised restraint in the Howard years by deferring to legislative intent in the terms ostensibly favoured by Heydon.

Heydon is dismissive of 'talk of policy and interests and values'.[51] However, antidiscrimination law does not lend itself easily to a technocratic approach without distorting legislative intent, for it is an area of law necessarily shaped by 'policy and interests and values'. It is not enough simply to enjoin judges to 'apply the law', as recommended by conservative commentators.[52] Historically, the common law did not recognise the non-discrimination principle at all, and law itself was engaged in reifying the inequitable status of women and disfavoured Others vis-a-vis benchmark men who represented the white, Anglo-Celtic, heterosexual, able-bodied, middle-class, male standard that underpins discrimination complaints. An injunction in favour of 'strict and complete legalism'[53] makes little sense in novel areas of law where there may be no precedent or other signposts. In such cases, judges must draw on their own subjective values and those of the normative universe they inhabit.[54] Beneath the seemingly neutral guise of technocratic 'black letter' law, conservative judges may be engaged in a hermeneutic process that is deeply political. Hence, I suggest they may be the rogues, not those denigrated as activist or 'hero judges'.[55]

Litigation may arise from a failure to conciliate a complaint of discrimination, whereupon one of the parties initiates a formal hearing within a tribunal or court. The greater the degree of formalism, the more favourable is the process to the respondent. Formalism exercises an ideological role in three ways: first, by favouring points of procedure and sloughing off the merits; second, by deterring appeals by other complainants because of the prospect of paying a respondent's costs as well as their own; and third, by formally orienting the jurisprudence towards a respondent perspective. The result can be a somewhat skewed notion of justice.

---

51   Heydon (n. 1) 119.
52   For example, Gava (n. 11) 81.
53   Owen Dixon, 'Swearing In of Sir Owen Dixon as Chief Justice' (1952) 85 *Commonwealth Law Reports* xi, xiv; Owen Dixon, 'Concerning Judicial Method' in Owen Dixon, *Jesting Pilate and Other Papers and Addresses, Collected by Judge Woinarski* (Law Book, 1965).
54   Cover (n. 7). Cf. Regina Graycar, 'The Gender of Judgments: An Introduction' in Margaret Thornton (ed.), *Public and Private: Feminist Legal Debates* (Oxford University Press, 1995) 262.
55   John Gava, 'The Rise of the Hero Judge' (2001) 24 *University of New South Wales Law Journal* 747.

In the war of attrition waged by respondents to resist a finding of discrimination, there may be multiple hearings before a matter reaches the High Court, although most complainants fall by the wayside, abandoning their claims through either exhaustion or a lack of resources. Cost is relatively unproblematic for corporate respondents, whether they are government departments or private sector corporations, as they either have recourse to the public purse or can pass the costs on to consumers. The juridification of discrimination disputes augments the inequality of bargaining power between what is typically a powerless individual and a powerful corporate respondent. The latter, with the aid of a substantial legal team, usually must do little more than raise a procedural point to deflect attention from the merits of the case, which then assumes a life of its own with little chance of success for the complainant. Legal formalism not only occludes the merits, but also allows a discriminatory rationalisation to be adduced in respect of the impugned conduct, as will be seen. It is therefore in the interests of corporate respondents to remove a complaint from an administrative or quasi-judicial body to a formal court at an early stage.

The discrimination jurisdiction is a paradigm of Marc Galanter's analysis in his iconic 1970s essay, 'Why the "Haves" Come Out Ahead'.[56] Applying his typology, the complainant is the one-shotter who may be interacting with the legal system for the first time and is baffled by its disregard for justice—that is, justice in a substantive sense. In contrast, the repeat player is typically a corporate respondent whose knowledge, homologous relationship with lawyers and virtually unlimited resources enable it to wear down the complainant by focusing on procedural justice. A snapshot of recent age and disability discrimination jurisprudence in the High Court shows how an ostensibly formalistic adjudicative style invariably favours the repeat player, who is exonerated when the court finds that no discrimination has occurred or, if it did, it was justifiable.

The litmus test of discrimination

I consider the discourse of judicial activism by first comparing a pair of disability discrimination cases. I take the first from the period when social liberalism was in the ascendancy and the second from the period following

---

56   Marc Galanter, 'Why the "Haves" Come Out Ahead: Speculations on the Limits of Legal Change' (1974–75) 9 *Law & Society Review* 95, doi.org/10.2307/3053023.

the neoliberal turn post *Wik* to reveal contrasting views of activism considering the human rights aims of the legislation. I then consider another pair of cases from the latter period, arising from age and disability relating to the inherent requirements of a job, in which the High Court privileged employer prerogative over human rights. A final case dealing with HIV underscores the idea that a neoconservative morality invariably accompanies the neoliberal turn.

Two facets of activism: For and against disability

Waters v Public Transport Corporation (1991) 173 CLR 349

Waters represents the high point of social liberalism and may be contrasted with the harsher direction in disability discrimination cases evinced at the turn of the millennium. The case was brought under the former *Equal Opportunity Act 1984* (Vic.) (*EOA*) by and on behalf of people with various physical and intellectual disabilities who alleged that the removal of conductors from trams and the introduction of scratch tickets constituted indirect discrimination against them. While there were differences of opinion between the judges regarding the elements of indirect discrimination that included the imposition of a requirement or condition with which a disproportionate percentage of the complainant class was unable to comply, and the vexed standard of reasonableness, the seven judges—Mason CJ and Brennan, Deane, Dawson, Toohey, Gaudron and McHugh JJ—were, in a rare feat, unanimous in finding for the complainants.[57]

Of course, the judges of the High Court were making law because they were confronting and having to determine the ambit of the legislative proscription against disability discrimination in the provision of services for the first time, but they deferred to the intention of the legislature, not corporate power or bureaucratic convenience. The inference is that the court regards legislation proscribing discrimination on the ground of disability as a positive initiative: 'A measure of the civilisation of a society is the extent to which it provides for the needs of the disabled.'[58] A narrow technocratic view of the rule of law may have paid more attention to the

57 For analysis, see Glenn Patmore, 'Moving Towards a Substantive Conception of the Anti-Discrimination Principle: *Waters v Public Transport Corporation of Victoria* Reconsidered' (1999) 23 *Melbourne University Law Review* 121.
58 *Waters*, 372 (Brennan J).

exception under *EOA* s. 39(e)(ii) regarding compliance with another Act. In this case, the respondent had endeavoured to argue that it was not bound by the *EOA* because it was acting under the *Transport Act 1983* (Vic.) s. 31(1). However, the court read down the provision and held that the respondent could not rely on it if there were no specific duty to remove conductors from trams or do away with scratch tickets.[59]

The familiar legal standard of 'reasonableness', as discussed in Chapter 9, may also prove to be a sticking point,[60] as its open-endedness provides a fertile field for jurists. Julius Stone describes reasonableness as a concept that is 'slippery and even treacherous',[61] but the reasonableness criterion was not interpreted in a way that favoured the corporate respondent. Brennan, Deane, Dawson and Toohey, together with McHugh JJ, construed the term to encompass all the circumstances of the case, including the financial situation of the respondent,[62] whereas a more restrictive view was articulated by Mason CJ and Gaudron J, who determined that it be ascertained by reference to 'the scope and purpose of the Act'.[63] In other words, legislative intent was privileged over financial exigencies. As the issue of reasonableness is treated as a matter of fact, it was remitted to the Victorian Equal Opportunity Board for determination.

There is a significant disjuncture between the high level of generality contained in the wording of the legislative proscription of discrimination in access to goods and services and the specific example in *Waters*—namely, the removal of conductors from trams and the introduction of scratch tickets, signifying the jurisgenerative scope for interpretation. In *Waters*, the court reconciled the law and the facts by deferring to legislative intention, which would seem to accord with Heydon's viewpoint. Mason and Gaudron JJ (Deane J agreeing) go further, however, and stress the increased importance of legislative intention in the discrimination context because of the human rights focus:

> [T]he principle that requires that the particular provisions of the Act must be read in the light of the statutory objects is of particular significance in the case of legislation which protects

---

59   *Waters*, 370 (Mason CJ & Gaudron J).
60   For example, *Secretary, Department of Foreign Affairs and Trade v Styles* (1989) 23 FCR 251, 263 (Bowen CJ & Gummow J).
61   Julius Stone, *Human Law and Human Justice* (Maitland Publications, 1965) 328. See also Chapter 9, this volume.
62   *Waters*, 379 (Brennan J), 383 (Deane J), 395–96 (Dawson & Toohey JJ), 410 (McHugh J).
63   *Waters*, 362 (Mason CJ & Gaudron J).

> or enforces human rights. In construing such legislation the courts
> have a special responsibility to take account of and give effect to
> the statutory purpose.[64]

This is a powerful sentiment, but it was soon nipped in the bud by the neoliberal turn. In subsequent cases, the court discarded the purposive approach in its interpretation of the legislation in favour of a narrow view that conformed with the orthodox and positivistic approach that had prevailed in the interpretation of antidiscrimination statutes in Australia.[65] The interpretative role seems to be directed towards contracting the human rights perspective in the name of efficiency or administrative convenience, the effect of which inevitably favours corporate respondents and frustrates legislative intent. The activism emerges not from a progressive approach to human rights legislation, as the detractors claim, but from a regressive approach, which relegates the broad aims of the legislation to the periphery or casts them off altogether. By way of illustration, I contrast *Waters* with *Purvis*, a disability case heard by the court 12 years later, which has been widely criticised.[66]

Purvis v New South Wales (Department of Education and Training) (2003) 217 CLR 92

Purvis involved a boy with intellectual disabilities who had been accepted into a mainstream high school. His violent behaviour led to several suspensions before he was excluded, whereupon his foster father lodged a complaint under the *Disability Discrimination Act 1992* (Cth) (*DDA*). At the initial hearing, the HREOC held that the behaviour of the boy, Daniel, arose from his disability.[67] This decision was overturned on appeal by a single judge of the Federal Court, who held that Daniel was excluded

---

64   *Waters*, 359.

65   Beth Gaze, 'Context and Interpretation in Anti-Discrimination law' (2002) 26 *Melbourne University Law Review* 325, 332.

66   Belinda Smith, 'From *Wardley to Purvis*: How Far Has Australian Anti-Discrimination Law Come in 30 Years?' (2008) 21 *Australian Journal of Labour Law* 3, doi.org/10.2139/ssrn.1005528; Colin D. Campbell, 'A Hard Case Making Bad Law: *Purvis v New South Wales* and the Role of the Comparator under the *Disability Discrimination Act 1992* (Cth)' (2007) 35(1) *Federal Law Review* 111, available from: journals.sagepub.com/doi/10.22145/flr.35.1.4; Jacob Campbell, 'Using Anti-Discrimination Law as a Tool of Exclusion: A Critical Analysis of the *Disability Discrimination Act 1992* and *Purvis v NSW*' (2005) 5 *Macquarie Law Journal* 201; Kate Rattigan, '*Purvis v New South Wales (Department of Education and Training)*: A Case for Amending the *Disability Discrimination Act 1992* (Cth)' (2004) 28 *Melbourne University Law Review* 532; Samantha Edwards, '*Purvis* in the High Court: Behaviour, Disability and the Meaning of Direct Discrimination' (2004) 26(4) *Sydney Law Review* 639.

67   *Purvis on behalf of Hoggan v New South Wales (Department of Education)* (2001) EOC ¶93–117 (HREOC).

because of his behaviour, not because of his disability.[68] Emmett J adopted a literal approach to the phrase 'in circumstances that are the same or not materially different' (*DDA* s. 5[1]), without regard to 'the scope and purpose of the Act' that had carried such weight in *Waters*. The narrow conceptualisation of disability, which severed the linkage between the disability and the behaviour, was upheld by the Full Court of the Federal Court[69] and then by a majority of the High Court.[70] McHugh and Kirby JJ (dissenting) held that Daniel's behaviour was a manifestation of his disability and formed part of his disability for the purposes of the *DDA*.

The severance of the linkage between the disability and the behaviour paved the way for the majority to conceptualise the appropriate comparator in direct discrimination complaints as a person without a disability who engages in the same conduct as a complainant with the disability.[71] They concluded that any other student who had behaved like Daniel would have been suspended and discrimination could be found only if the hypothetical student were not suspended. This narrow conceptualisation of equal treatment not only allowed the school to suspend Daniel to protect staff and other students, but also sloughed off the allegation that it had acted in a discriminatory manner by expelling him. In other words, the rationalisation of the action by the school relating to safety erased altogether the issue at the nub of the case—that is, the disability and the less favourable treatment that flowed from it. The approach pulled the rug from beneath the feet of complainants alleging direct discrimination (the basis of the preponderance of complaints), not only on the ground of disability,[72] but also potentially on other grounds,[73] including pregnancy[74] and age.[75] Sections 5(2) and 6(2) of the *DDA* have since been amended to enable the definition of discrimination to include a failure to make reasonable adjustments for a person with a disability.

McHugh and Kirby JJ (dissenting) held, following Commissioner Innes in the original HREOC decision, that Daniel's treatment by the school had to be compared with that of a student without a disability and

---

68   *New South Wales (Department of Education) v Human Rights and Equal Opportunity Commission* (2001) 186 ALR 69.
69   *Purvis v New South Wales (Department of Education and Training)* (2002) 117 FCR 237.
70   *Purvis* (Gleeson CJ, Gummow, Hayne, Heydon & Callinan JJ).
71   *Purvis*, 160 [220] (Gleeson CJ, Gummow, Hayne & Heydon JJ).
72   For example, *Zhang v University of Tasmania* (2009) FCAFC 35; *Collier v Austin Health* (2009) VCAT 565.
73   Smith (n. 66).
74   For example, *Dare v Hurley* (2005) EOC ¶93–405 (FMCA).
75   For example, *Virgin Blue Airlines P/L v Stewart* (2007) EOC ¶93–457 (SCQ).

without his disturbed behaviour.[76] This view is based firmly on established jurisprudence—Sir Ronald Wilson having made the same point some 15 years earlier:

> It would fatally frustrate the purposes of the Act if the matters which it expressly identifies as constituting unacceptable bases for differential treatment ... could be seized upon as rendering the overall circumstances materially different, with the result that the treatment could never be discriminatory within the meaning of the Act.[77]

The application of a strict equal treatment standard dilutes the provisions regarding accommodation of a disability. While the *DDA* did not impose positive duties on educational institutions at the time of *Purvis*, there was an implied recognition in the objects of the Act that such duties might be undertaken (*DDA* s. 3). The prospects of addressing discrimination and effecting rights to equality before the law for persons with disabilities could otherwise never be realised through recourse to the *DDA*. Consistent with their dissent, Justices Kirby and McHugh stress the remedial nature of the legislation:

> The international developments reflected in the Act have the high object of correcting centuries of neglect of, and discrimination and prejudice against, the disabled. It would be wrong and contrary to the purpose of the Act to construe its ameliorative provisions narrowly.[78]

These human rights aims were accorded short shrift by the majority of the High Court, who, like the judges of the Full Court of the Federal Court, were more concerned with economic rationality from a perpetrator perspective. They believed that a finding for the complainant would have 'draconian consequences' for the Department of Education. The 'activism' of the majority is thereby exposed in casting aside the legislative prescripts, as well as the formalistic canons of interpretation and respect for precedent, in the face of bureaucratic convenience and the cost for the respondent of accommodating a student with a disability.

---

76 *Purvis*, 112 [48].
77 *Sullivan v Department of Defence* (1992) EOC ¶92–421 (HREOC), cited in *Purvis* [119] (McHugh & Kirby JJ).
78 *Purvis*, 103 [18].

Where is the deference to the legislature in *Purvis* that Justice Heydon and the critics of judicial activism extol? Indeed, the narrow approach to comparability endangers the viability of the legislation.[79] If corporate convenience and cost had been invoked in *Waters* as the primary considerations, the inability to catch a tram without a conductor or scratch a ticket could have been held to be irrelevant and people with disabilities told to take taxis. The bad behaviour of the complainant in *Purvis*—kicking schoolbags, as well as a teacher's aide—was not only regarded as serious conduct, but also discussed by Chief Justice Gleeson in the context of criminality,[80] rather than as conduct explicable in terms of intellectual disability. Importing notions of potential criminality and health and safety into the definition of direct disability discrimination has no firm basis in law; the legislation includes no test of reasonableness or justifiability.[81]

To devise a new test involving the reading down of the comparator to mean a person without a disability but who evinced the same conduct, as opposed to a person without a disability *simpliciter*, entailed an overt act of judicial activism, which effectively vitiated the value of the *DDA*. As Jacob Campbell concludes, *Purvis*, in sharp contrast to *Waters*, gave little encouragement to people with disabilities: 'It carries a message of exclusion rather than inclusion, which undermines the usefulness of the Act as a mechanism for social change.'[82]

A common standard for statutory judicial activism in the US literature is the striking down of a statute but, as Cross and Lindquist suggest, interpreting a statute in a manner that is contrary to legislative intent may be an even more egregious form of activism: 'Instead of leaving a blank legislative slate (as in the case of invalidating a law), such a misinterpretation leaves in place a statute that means what the judges wish, not what the legislature wishes. This truly is judicial legislation.'[83]

An interpretation that has the effect of negating virtually any possibility of a complainant pursuing a remedy successfully under antidiscrimination legislation, as occurred with Daniel Hoggan, instantiated a new meaning. As mentioned, very few discrimination cases reach the High Court, but

---

79   C. Campbell (n. 66) 128.
80   *Purvis*, 98 [5].
81   Smith (n. 66).
82   J. Campbell (n. 66) 220.
83   Cross & Lindquist (n. 5).

those that are heard become important precedents not just for courts and tribunals below, but also for the conciliation arena, as the effect of decisions from the most authoritative level percolates down to the informal base of the dispute-resolution hierarchy, beyond which few complaints proceed.

Of course, the court can change the meaning it has accorded the comparator in the future, but few complainants have either the tenacity or the financial resources to persevere against powerful corporate respondents. Hence, what Cross and Lindquist refer to as 'judicial legislation'[84] may stand for some time. Indeed, the very idea that it exists is likely to have a chilling effect on prospective litigants not only because of the risk of having the ruling confirmed, but also because of the possibility of having to pay the respondent's costs as well as their own.

Purvis is not the only dubious instance of judicial activism in the field of discrimination since the court took a conservative turn. The favouring of corporate respondents over complainants in employment cases became a modus operandi, as illustrated in the following cases.

The inherent requirements of the job: Judges know best

The inherent requirements of a job may be invoked by a respondent as a defence to an allegation of unlawful discrimination, primarily because of disability. There are two decisions to which I turn where the conservative majority made law by determining the inherent requirement of employment in questionable ways—one dealing with age and the other with disability arising from HIV. In the process of actively deferring to employer prerogative, the majority judges again appear to frustrate the intention of antidiscrimination legislation.

Qantas Airways Ltd v Christie (1998) 193 CLR 280

The *Christie* litigation was initiated by a pilot who was dismissed on his sixtieth birthday but who wished to keep flying international aircraft. The relevant legislation was the *Industrial Relations Act 1988* (Cth) (s. 170DF), which rendered it unlawful to terminate employment because of age. (The action preceded passage of the *Age Discrimination Act 2004* [Cth].) The case did not turn on the actuarially greater likelihood of heart attack,

---

84   ibid.

stroke or other factor associated with age, as might be expected, although 'potential disability' lies at the heart of the case. Some countries to which Qantas flew precluded the flying of international passenger aircraft by pilots aged over 60, which meant the only overseas routes available were short-haul flights to Indonesia, New Zealand and Fiji. Because short flights were in limited supply, pilots had to bid for them to make up their rosters. Qantas claimed it could not accommodate all pilots who wished to continue to fly after reaching the age of 60; it argued that for a pilot to be under the age of 60 was an inherent requirement of the job.

The physical and mental skills and aptitudes necessary to perform a particular job are normally regarded as its inherent requirements, but the standing of operational requirements is uncertain.[85] A majority of the High Court (Brennan CJ, Gaudron, McHugh and Gummow JJ) was of the opinion that administrative convenience was an inherent requirement of the job of an airline pilot in that a pilot needed to be able to fly to a reasonable number of destinations.[86] Justice Gummow conceptualised the inherent requirement as the complainant being available for duty as required by Qantas in any part of the world[87]—a requirement that seems to possess only a tenuous connection with age, albeit arising from the contract of employment. Indeed, if the complainant were able to fly jumbo jets internationally to Denpasar, Fiji and New Zealand, it could not be said that age (as a proxy for the rostering system) was an inherent requirement of the job of being an international pilot, as the majority judges, Gray and Marshall JJ, had argued in the Industrial Relations Court.[88] Construing administrative convenience as an inherent requirement of a job is another example of activist judging, as it clearly transcends the core elements associated with the ability and aptitude to pilot jumbo jets internationally.

Kirby J, in dissent, would undoubtedly agree with this criticism, for he stressed the importance of a purposive approach when interpreting discrimination legislation to which various international conventions on discrimination were appended.[89] These instruments, he argued,

---

85   Peter Bailey, *The Human Rights Enterprise in Australia and Internationally* (LexisNexis, 2009) 560–64.
86   For a detailed analysis of the case and the various judgements, see Anna Chapman, 'Qantas Airways Ltd v Christie' (1998) 22 *Melbourne University Law Review* 743.
87   *Christie*, 319 [117].
88   *Christie v Qantas Airlines* (1995) 60 IR 17.
89   *Christie*, 332 [152].

must be given the same meaning as dedicated instruments proscribing discrimination.[90] Elevating 'operational issues' and administrative convenience to the status of the inherent requirement of a job, as he points out, means that such an exception could be perennially relied on in respect of sex, family responsibilities and pregnancy.[91] Elaborating on the point, Marshall J in the Full Bench decision hypothesised that Qantas could dismiss a female or gay pilot if one or more foreign countries refused the airline permission to fly into their airports.[92]

An inherent requirement of a job is a matter of fact to be determined by the relevant tribunal. However, as Ronald McCallum points out, the concept does not work well as the sole determinant of employability.[93] While the absence of legislative guidelines provides space for activism, the intention of the *DDA* is to prohibit discriminatory terminations unless continuation would require accommodation that was clearly unreasonable.[94] Extending the concept beyond the ability of a person to perform the job so as to include administrative convenience is always going to skew the outcome in the interests of the respondent employer. In *Christie*, therefore, we once again see a clear instance of the court making law by deferring to corporate convenience rather than to the relevant legislative and international instruments.

By elevating administrative convenience to the status of an inherent requirement, no space is left in which to manoeuvre; it operates as a form of rational discrimination that trumps the proscription of age discrimination. The activist approach to determining the inherent requirements of a job leaves the way open for ever more expansive interpretations in accordance with the revived notion of employer prerogative that prevailed because of radical reforms effected during the Howard years.[95] After *Wik*, the influence of neoliberalism could be clearly discerned within the court, although there is no bright line of demarcation, as several of the same judges sat on both *Waters* and *Christie*. Justice McHugh, in *Christie*, for example, acknowledged the importance of the prohibition against

---

90   ibid., 333 [152].
91   ibid., 343 [164].
92   *Christie v Qantas Airlines* (1996) 138 ALR 19, 39.
93   Ronald McCallum, 'Labour Law and the Inherent Requirement of the Job: *Qantas Airlines Ltd v Christie*—Destination the High Court of Australia—Boarding at Gate Seven' (1997) 19 *Sydney Law Review* 211, 217.
94   ibid.
95   Anthony Forsyth & Andrew Stewart (eds), *Fair Work: The New Workplace Laws and the Work Choices Legacy* (The Federation Press, 2009).

discrimination in the legislation, but was nevertheless prepared to cast aside its precepts in the context of 'a free enterprise system of industrial relations where employers and employees have considerable scope for defining their contractual rights and duties'.[96] This sentiment would seem to echo a rhetoric averring equality of bargaining power between management and individual workers that typified the nineteenth-century law of contract, where employer prerogative was all-important. In *Christie*, the definition of contractual rights by the employer authorised rational discrimination based on business convenience. After *Waters*, the values of neoliberalism had insidiously seeped into the court's adjudicative style to trump consistently the non-discrimination principle.

X v Commonwealth (1999) 200 CLR 177

A second case dealing with the inherent requirement of a job reveals an even more idiosyncratic manifestation of judicial activism on the part of the High Court. *X v Commonwealth* involved a soldier who was discharged from the army in accordance with Australian Defence Force (ADF) policy when found to be HIV-positive. He lodged a complaint of discrimination under the *DDA*. In its defence, the ADF relied on the inherent requirements of the job, expressly recognised by DDA s. 15(4). Under this section, discrimination is not unlawful if a person is unable to perform the job because of their disability and to employ them would 'impose unjustifiable hardship on the employer' in providing appropriate services and facilities. While physical capacity and knowledge of soldiering indubitably constitute inherent requirements, the question to be resolved, at the initiative of the respondent, was whether the ability to 'bleed safely' was also an 'inherent requirement'.

In the first instance, the complainant was found by the HREOC to be in excellent health, to be symptom-free and to be able to carry out the soldiering role for which he had been prepared.[97] An order of review was conducted before a single judge of the Federal Court and dismissed.[98] Relying on Mason CJ and Gaudron J in *Waters*, Cooper J stressed that *DDA* s. 15(4) was to be construed in light of the objectives of the Act. He acknowledged that the inherent requirements meant the ability or capacity consistent with the common law duty of care to avoid risk of loss or harm

---

96   *Christie*, 307 [79]–[80].
97   *X v Department of Defence* (1995) EOC ¶92–715 (HREOC).
98   *Commonwealth v Human Rights and Equal Opportunity Commission* (1996) 70 FCR 76.

to others. Nevertheless, it was not a finding of fact that 'bleeding safely' was an inherent requirement of the job of soldiering. This interpretation was rejected by the Full Bench of the Federal Court,[99] which held that an inherent requirement of employment as a soldier included the ability to 'bleed freely'. The court considered the view of the HREOC and the lower court to be too narrow: 'The inherent requirements of a particular employment are not to be limited to a mechanical performance of its tasks or skills.'[100] The issue of safety then became central, but from whose perspective is it to be assessed—that of the soldier, fellow employees or others? This was the question Mansfield J of the Full Bench of the Federal Court had perciently posed, which underscores the leeways of choice confronting judges. The High Court granted special leave to the complainant to appeal and upheld the Federal Court decision.

In *X v Commonwealth*, Gummow and Hayne JJ, with whom Gleeson CJ and Callinan J agreed, accepted the expansive construction of the inherent requirement articulated by the Federal Court. McHugh J also accepted the broad interpretation but expressed scepticism regarding the Commonwealth's insistence that the ability to bleed safely was the relevant inherent requirement.[101] He would have allowed the appeal and remitted the matter to the HREOC for a clear finding of fact regarding the precise nature of a soldier's employment. Curiously enough, the majority appears to have made their decision in the absence of sound evidence as to just what were the essential skills and aptitudes of soldiering. There seemed to be more concern with the prognosis for HIV. Gummow and Hayne JJ (Gleeson CJ and Callinan J agreeing) found that it leads to AIDS, which is fatal,[102] whereas McHugh J found that it *usually* leads to AIDS. While McHugh J was of the view that it was legitimate to have regard to the health and safety of others, he noted that the Commonwealth had not availed itself of *DDA* s. 48—an express exception pertaining to infectious diseases.[103]

In *X v Commonwealth*, we see stereotypical assumptions about health and safety in relation to someone who is HIV-positive being actively read into the interpretation of the inherent requirement of soldiering, just as

---

99 *Commonwealth v Human Rights and Equal Opportunity Commission* (1998) 76 FCR 513.
100 ibid., 519 (Burchett J).
101 *X v Commonwealth* 220 [72].
102 ibid., 206 [96].
103 ibid., 194 [52].

administrative convenience had been read into the inherent requirement of piloting international planes in *Christie*. As Cooper J pointed out, injury resulting in bleeding is by no means peculiar to soldiering.[104]

Kirby J (dissenting) believed there was no error of law on the part of the HREOC and the appeal should be allowed. He sought to restrict the inherent requirements of the job to those factors that are 'essential, permanent and intrinsic' to its performance.[105] He was the only judge to advert to the broader social role of the legislation and to the fact that, as remedial legislation, it should be construed beneficially. He specifically adverted to the way the typical discrimination complainant succeeds in the first instance, only to have victory subsequently snatched away as an error of law.[106] Yet again, we see how rational discrimination can be invoked to relegate the merits of a case and legislative intent to the periphery in the interests of a powerful respondent. In this case, it was the state itself that had embarked on a course that undermined its own legislation. This is a familiar scenario within the discrimination jurisdiction, as seen also in *Purvis*, *Amery* and *Schou*.[107]

Once the High Court has determined that the inherent requirement of a job is not limited to the skills and capacity associated with its performance, as occurred in *Christie*, it is difficult to contain, as Kirby J observed.[108] Carter C, in the initial HREOC hearing,[109] had drawn a useful distinction between the inherent requirements and the incidents of employment, but this did not win favour with the High Court, although the ability to bleed freely may have been characterised in that way.

It would be interesting to have Heydon's view on how this decision satisfied 'principles which are known or readily discoverable' and how the decision was 'drawn from existing and discoverable legal sources independently of the personal beliefs of the judge'.[110] While one can rarely uncover the judicial subjectivity at the heart of decision-making, since it is encased within the formal language of adjudication, there is a sense that homophobia and stereotypical assumptions about those who

---

104 *Commonwealth v HREOC* (n. 98) 91.
105 *X v Commonwealth*, 85.
106 ibid., 211 [114].
107 *Victoria v Schou* (2004) 8 VR 120 (VCA), discussed in Chapter 9, this volume.
108 *X v The Commonwealth*, 343.
109 *X v Department of Defence* (n. 97) 78377–78.
110 Heydon (n. 1) 108.

are HIV-positive could have played a role in the decision. Determining that the ability to bleed freely was an inherent requirement of the job of modern soldiering in the absence of sound evidence stands out as a dramatic manifestation of activist judging.

Homophobia or rules rationality?

IW v City of Perth (1997) 191 CLR 1 was another case involving HIV post *Wik*, albeit not in employment but in the provision of services, which I mention briefly for the sake of completion. The complainants, an incorporated association, People Living with AIDS (PLWA), applied unsuccessfully to a local council for permission to establish a daytime drop-in centre in a business district for people who were HIV-positive. There were objections from businesses, occupiers and residents to the City Town Planning Committee, which recommended to the council that the proposal be rejected. Five members of the council voted against the proposal because of what the Equal Opportunity Tribunal of Western Australia (EOTWA) found to be their ignorant and biased attitudes.[111] In other words, homophobia was found to be a causative factor that engendered discrimination on the ground of impairment. Although the minister for local government approved the application on appeal, PLWA proceeded with the discrimination complaint under the *Equal Opportunity Act 1984* (WA) (*WA EOA*). The complainants succeeded at the tribunal level[112] and in an appeal before a single judge of the WA Supreme Court,[113] but failed on technical grounds before both the Full Bench of the Supreme Court[114] and the High Court, which caused the question of homophobia to recede into the background.

In *IW*, Brennan CJ, with McHugh, Dawson and Gaudron JJ, held that the word 'service' was not wide enough to capture a statutory discretion, while Dawson and Gaudron JJ held that the appellant, although a member of the PLWA, was not an 'aggrieved person' for the purpose of the *WA EOA*. Brennan CJ and McHugh J, with the support of the *Interpretation Act 1984* (WA), reiterated the now familiar mantra that stressed the importance of a liberal construction of legislation intended

---

111 *DL (representing the Members of People Living with AIDS (WA) Inc.) v City of Perth* (1993) EOC ¶92–510 (WA EOT).

112 ibid., ¶92–422 (WA EOT).

113 *Perth City v DL* (1994) 88 LGREA 45; *City of Perth v DL, acting as representative of All Members of People Living with AIDS (WA)* (1992) EOC ¶92–466 (WASC).

114 *Perth v DL* (1996) 90 LGERA 178.

to be beneficial and remedial,[115] but accepted a rules rationality approach by way of justification—that is, a council may be acting as an arm of government rather than a provider of services for the purposes of the discrimination legislation.

Toohey and Kirby JJ, in separate dissenting judgements, took a broader view of the meaning of 'services'. The EOTWA had said that the granting of planning approval itself was a service, whereas Toohey J was of the view that it was too narrow an interpretation to find that the giving of the planning approval, not the consideration of the application, was the service.[116] Kirby J, again focusing on first principles, adverted to the aim of the *WA EOA*, which requires the elimination, as far as is possible, of discrimination on the ground of impairment; a narrow approach can only frustrate the purpose of the Act.[117] The ambiguity at the heart of the rule of law can accommodate both the narrow technical and the broad purposive interpretations so that the subjectivity of the judge is immunised from scrutiny. A reliance on rules rationality was able to occlude consideration of the discomfiting issue of homophobia at the High Court level, despite the clear finding of fact before the tribunal.

As Kirby J pointed out, the proceedings illustrate the difficulty of a complainant obtaining a successful outcome in a discrimination case even when there are relatively simple facts—that is, a finding by the tribunal of homophobia at the council meeting is transmuted into a rationalisation of discrimination by focusing on a restricted meaning of the word 'services', which is incompatible with the aims of the legislation.[118] What we see in *IW* is an example of excessive formalism at the expense of human rights, which enables a more subtle form of activist judging than seen in *X v Commonwealth*, although the effect is similar. Rather than an expansive interpretation of 'service' or 'aggrieved person', as we saw with the 'inherent requirement of the job', a narrow reading enables the judges to avoid confronting the issues of either homophobia or disability at the heart of the case.

---

115 *IW*, 12.
116 ibid., 28.
117 ibid., 58.
118 ibid., 73 (Kirby J).

An American example

The seeming attempts to eviscerate the *DDA* following the neoliberal turn resonate uncannily with the experience of the *Americans with Disabilities Act 1990* (US) (*ADA*) during Chief Justice William Rehnquist's leadership of the US Supreme Court. *Sutton v United Air Lines* is exemplary.[119] In this case, the court determined that severely myopic twin sisters who wished to become airline pilots were not substantially limited in one or more of life's activities in accordance with the terms of the statute because their vision could be corrected with glasses or other aids. Nevertheless, the sisters were denied employment as airline pilots *because* their uncorrected visual acuity was less than 20/100. The court's reasoning left the complainants bereft of a remedy. Justice Stevens, with whom Justice Breyer agreed, was scathing of the majority stance:

> Although vision is of critical importance for airline pilots, in most segments of the economy whether an employee wears glasses— or uses any of several other mitigating measures—it is a matter of complete indifference to employers. It is difficult to envision many situations in which a qualified employee who needs glasses to perform her job might be fired ... because ... she cannot see well without them. Such a proposition would be ridiculous in the garden-variety case.[120]

Like a majority of the Australian High Court in the latter constellation of discrimination cases discussed, a majority of the US Supreme Court was '[a]pparently unconcerned that the ADA (US) [was] a remedial statute that should be "construed broadly to effectuate its purposes"'.[121] The majority 'decided to ignore Congress's express instruction that the "purpose of [the *ADA* (US) is] to provide a clear and comprehensive national mandate for the elimination of discrimination against individuals with disabilities"'.[122] Justice Stevens, like Justice Kirby, exhorted a generous rather than a 'miserly' interpretation of the legislation in view of 'the remedial purposes of the Act'.[123]

---

119 *Sutton v United Air Lines* 527 US 471 (1999).
120 ibid., Stevens J at 510.
121 Andrew J. Imparato, 'The "Miserly" Approach to Disability Rights' in Herman Schwartz (ed.), *The Rehnquist Court: Judicial Activism on the Right* (Hill & Wang, 2002) 204.
122 ibid.
123 *Sutton* (n. 119) 495.

The effect of thwarting the aim of the *ADA* (US) for people with disabilities has been deplored by commentators. Imparato, for example, observes that the tendency of conservative courts to uphold the status quo by 'overblown deference to bureaucratic prerogatives means that disabled people will continue to experience unnecessary segregation and institutionalisation for many years to come'.[124] A commitment to formal equality treats everyone the same even if they are unequally situated, which only serves to exacerbate their inequality.

Conclusion

In the cases of *Purvis, Christie, X v Commonwealth* and *IW*, it is notable that there was no public outcry comparable to that which followed *Mabo* and *Wik*. The complainants had lost but were deemed undeserving— disfavoured Others who were aged, disabled, disadvantaged and, if HIV-positive, possibly also figures of abjection.[125] Women, too, could be added to this list (*Amery*). Had the complainants succeeded, there could have been cries of improper judicial activism, as occurred with *Mabo* and *Wik*, but, because they lost, the rule of law was deemed to have been upheld. In these cases, we see the way judicial activism can occur by stealth under the seemingly neutral cloak of the depersonalised techniques of legal formalism.

According to Heydon, the duty of the court is not to make law but to do justice according to law. While we would all like to believe that justice was the telos of lawmaking, I have suggested that there is little evidence of it, other than in a limited procedural sense, in the disability discrimination cases in the neoliberal climate post *Wik*. A majority of the High Court judges played an active role in subverting the intention of legislation that proscribes discrimination on grounds of disability to effect equality between all citizens. I have sought to demonstrate the proposition regarding the disability discrimination cases heard over a decade, all of which accord greater weight to employer prerogative and administrative convenience.

---

124 Imparato (n. 121) 211.
125 Julia Kristeva, *Powers of Horror: An Essay on Abjection*, translated by Leon S. Rondiez (Columbia University Press, 1982).

The favoured method of adjudication is narrow and formalistic. Despite the wealth of research and commentary that has emerged in respect of discrimination against older people and people with disabilities, including those who are HIV-positive, none of this literature is acknowledged by the majority judges of the High Court post *Wik*. 'Strict legalism' seems to mean self-referentialism, which enables judges to slough off not only all knowledge of discrimination as a social phenomenon, but also interdisciplinary perspectives and the non-discrimination aims of the legislation. Erasure of the problem means they then have no obligation to devise a remedy.

Dismantling the non-discrimination principle by stealth in deference to bureaucratic and corporate power destabilises the rule of law, for it sets dangerous precedents and encourages lower courts and tribunals to emulate the approach. The social liberal moment may have been fleeting, as a narrow approach is generally favoured by Australian courts in the adjudication of discrimination law.[126] It is therefore not the activist judges with a social conscience and a modest commitment to distributive justice who are corroding the rule of law, but those who, under a cloak of rationality, are construing antidiscrimination legislation in ways that accord with what has become neoliberal orthodoxy. These judges are fighting a rearguard action to sustain a version of the rule of law that constrains egalitarian human rights, while reviving the dominant values of a past age—a version that accords with benchmark masculinity, which it is well and truly past its use-by date.[127] Trammelling the interests of disfavoured Others, particularly people with disabilities, to achieve these ends constitutes an improper form of judicial activism.

---

126 Gaze (n. 65) 332; Glenn Patmore, 'The *Disability Discrimination Act* (Australia): Time for Change' (2003) 24 *Comparative Labor Law & Policy Journal* 62.
127 Hutchinson (n. 11).

11

'Otherness' on the Bench

Introduction

Even though the image of justice is feminised, the judge is invariably masculinised. He, not she, is the paradigmatic embodiment of wisdom and rationality in the Western legal tradition. This idealised figure is miraculously able to leave the particularity of his sex and other characteristics of identity, together with his life experiences, at the courtroom door to carry out the adjudicative role with impartiality. So complete is the bifurcation between the objectivity of the judicial role and the subjective persona of the judge that legal positivism avers that (he) does not make law but merely interprets it.[1] Depersonalisation and erasure of the self construct the judge as little more than a conduit for 'right' answers within the adjudicative process. While the objective/subjective split represents the nub of the existential dilemma at the heart of adjudication, concern tends to be raised only when the judge is a woman, although it may also emerge when the judge is black[2] or gay.[3] In such cases, the subjectivity of the embodied persona of the judge

1 As expounded by, for example, H.L.A. Hart, *The Concept of Law* (Clarendon, 1961); Hans Kelsen, *The Pure Theory of Law* (University of California Press, 1961); Joseph Raz, *The Authority of Law* (Oxford University Press, 1979); Tom D. Campbell, *The Legal Theory of Ethical Positivism* (Ashgate, 1996).

2 Former feminist Aboriginal magistrate Pat O'Shane faced complaints about her conduct on the bench after her appointment in 1986: see, for example, Imre Salusinszky, 'Fighting for Justice', *The Australian*, 31 January 2007, 11; 'Last Day in Court for Controversial Magistrate', *ABC News*, 25 January 2013, available from: www.abc.net.au/news/2013-01-25/controversial-nsw-magistrate-stands-down/ 4484636. An earlier controversy involved her quashing a charge of malicious damage against four women who defaced a billboard in which a woman was being sawn in half. Pat O'Shane, 'Launch of the Australian Feminist Law Journal: 29 August 1993' (1994) 2 *Australian Feminist Law Journal* 3.

3 For example, Leslie J. Moran, 'Judicial Diversity and the Challenge of Sexuality: Some Preliminary Findings' (2006) 28 *Sydney Law Review* 565; Margaret Thornton & Heather Roberts, 'Women Judges, Private Lives: (In)visibilities in Fact and Fiction (2017) 40(2) *University of New South Wales Law Journal* 761.

cannot be sloughed off. He or she is then indelibly marked as 'Other'—
an otherness that necessarily taints the adjudicative role and renders the
delivery of justice problematic.

The appointment of women as judges, on which I focus, is a significant
site of contestation in the narrative regarding the entry of women into the
public sphere. After more than a century of struggle to be 'let in' to the
legal profession, women now constitute 52 per cent of legal practitioners
in Australia[4]—a figure that is mirrored in other parts of the Western
world.[5] Nevertheless, once we peer behind the ostensibly progressivist
veneer of numerosity, a more complex story unfolds. The unruliness of
the feminine, it would seem, can be kept at bay if women are retained
in subordinate, managed or 'manned' positions. Indeed, women lawyers
are welcome when their services can be effectively deployed to satisfy
the needs of the global 'new knowledge economy' by facilitating capital
accumulation. Employed lawyers comport with the proletarianisation
theory of legal practice, which has been a corollary of the corporatisation
of law firms.[6] Lawyers are not identical to factory workers on a process
line, but the practice of assigning discrete segments of a case to clusters of
employed solicitors with limited autonomy under the control of a senior
partner underscores the aptness of the analogy.

The percentage of women exercising autonomy and independent
judgement in law remains disproportionately low. The equation is
a familiar one throughout the public sphere: the more authoritative
the position, the more men and the fewer women there are; the less
authoritative the position, the more women and the fewer men there
are. Partners in law firms,[7] barristers[8] and judges[9] are notable examples

---

4   Law Society of New South Wales, *2020 National Profile of Solicitors: Final* (Urbis, 2021) 8,
available from: www.lawsociety.com.au/sites/default/files/2021-07/2020%20National%20Profile%20
of%20Solicitors%20-%20Final%20-%201%20July%202021.pdf.

5   Ulrike Schultz, 'Introduction: Women in the World's Legal Professions—Overview and Synthesis'
in Ulrike Schultz & Gisela Shaw (eds), *Women in the World's Legal Professions* (Hart, 2003) xxxvi, xl.

6   Charles Derber, 'Managing Professionals: Ideological Proletarianization and Mental Labour' in
Charles Derber (ed.), *Professionals as Workers: Mental Labour in Advanced Capitalism* (G.K. Hall, 1982);
Joanne Bagust, 'The Legal Profession and the Business of Law' (2013) 35(1) *Sydney Law Review* 27.

7   In 2020, 25 to 30 per cent of partners in law firms in Australia were women. Hannah Wootton,
'Female Law Partners Break Through 30pc Barrier', *Australian Financial Review*, 10 December 2020,
available from: www.afr.com/companies/professional-services/women-partners-break-through-30pc-
barrier-20201130-p56j7u.

8   NSW figures: female barristers, 24 per cent; female senior counsel, 13 per cent. See NSW Bar
Association, *Statistics*, available from: nswbar.asn.au/the-bar-association/statistics.

9   Of all judges and magistrates in Australia, 38.8 per cent were women. Australian Institute of
Judicial Administration, *AIJA Judicial Gender Statistics: Number and Percentage of Women Judges and
Magistrates at 30 June 2020* (AIJA, 2020), available from: aija.org.au/wp-content/uploads/2020/07/
2020-JUDICIAL-GENDER-STATISTICS-v3.pdf.

of the more authoritative positions. Judging is seen as the apex of the organisational pyramid and it is the domain that has attracted the most critical commentary because of the conventionally problematic relationship between authority and the feminine, on which I elaborate.

The relationship between the legal profession and women as agents of legality has been historically fraught with difficulty. In the late nineteenth and early twentieth centuries, women struggled to enter the legal profession, meeting with sustained resistance, as shown in Chapter 1.[10] Reasoned argument, intellectual superiority and demonstrated ability on the part of women counted for little within a supposed sphere of rationality where masculinity had become the primary indicium of worth.[11] The modern liberal story of linear progress for women continues to stumble over positions involving the twin variables of authority and autonomy. It is only in the past few years that the inequitable profile of women in the judiciary has prompted progressive governments to respond, somewhat shame-facedly, to criticism and appoint more women to the bench. The liberal state requires the most egregious instances of discrimination to be addressed to maintain an appearance of fairness and legitimacy.[12]

In Australia, the primary catalyst for state intervention was the issue of 'gender bias in the judiciary', which received intense scrutiny when it was 'discovered' by the media in 1993.[13] The most notorious instance involved a remark in the course of a marital rape trial by Justice Bollen, then a judge of the South Australian Supreme Court, who expressed the view that 'a measure of rougher than usual handling' was acceptable on the part of a husband towards a wife who was less than willing to engage in sexual intercourse.[14] The ensuing furore compelled governments to review and justify their practices in making judicial appointments. The Australian Parliament conducted an inquiry that highlighted the lack of

---

10   See also Mary Jane Mossman, *The First Women Lawyers: A Comparative Study of Gender, Law and the Legal Professions* (Hart, 2006); Margaret Thornton, *Dissonance and Distrust: Women in the Legal Profession* (Oxford University Press, 1996).
11   Genevieve Lloyd, *The Man of Reason: 'Male' and 'Female' in Western Philosophy* (Macmillan, 1984) 138.
12   For example, E.P. Thompson, *Whigs and Hunters: The Origin of the Black Acts* (Penguin, 1975) 184.
13   For example, Liz Porter, 'Who Judges Our Judges?', *Sunday Age*, [Melbourne], 17 January 1993, 15; Karen Middleton, 'Some Judges Are Women Haters, Says Cook', *The Age*, [Melbourne], 13 May 1993, 5: Keith Gosman, 'Judges on Trial', *Sydney Morning Herald*, 14 May 1993, 9.
14   *R v Johns* (Unreported, Supreme Court of South Australia, Bollen J, 26 August 1992).

transparency in the process.[15] Some felt that appointment to the judiciary was too late to effect remediation and the focus should be directed to legal education.[16] Nevertheless, a practice of appointing more women to state and federal courts was one strategy that was initiated. What was possibly not anticipated by the reformers was the significant backlash the appointments would generate, particularly in Victoria and Queensland, where the changes were most marked.

Conservative governments favour affirmative action (AA) policies for 'benchmark men': the white, heterosexual, able-bodied, middle-class men who espouse mainstream Christian religious beliefs (if any) and right-of-centre political views, against whom women and Others are measured and invariably found wanting, for benchmark men are the normative agents of legality. Of course, such appointment practices are not labelled 'AA', as that term, with its pejorative gloss, is reserved for the appointment of women and Others, who are assumed to have been appointed by virtue of their sex or other characteristic of identity with scant regard to merit. It was the monopoly of benchmark men on the courts a century ago that enabled them to pronounce seriously and authoritatively that only men were 'persons' for the purpose of legal practice.[17] Their social power today permits them to continue to pronounce similarly that male judges are the 'best people' for the job, despite both the empirical evidence relating to women's achievements within the legal profession and the scientific evidence demonstrating that 'the mind has no sex'.[18] Nevertheless, a norm has no meaning without an Other.[19] Thus, years of diligent effort by feminist activists and their supporters to change the gendered constitution

15   For example, Australia, Parliament, Senate Standing Committee on Legal and Constitutional Affairs, *Gender Bias and the Judiciary* (Parliament of Australia, 1994): Australia, Attorney-General's Department, *Judicial Appointments: Procedure and Criteria* (Australian Government, 1993); Australian Law Reform Commission, *Equality Before the Law: Women's Equality* (Report No. 69, AGPS, 1994) Part II.

16   A government initiative involved the preparation of gender-sensitive teaching materials on citizenship, work and violence. The citizenship materials were prepared by Professor Sandra Berns, Paula Baron & Professor Marcia Neave, and the work and violence materials by Professor Regina Graycar and Associate Professor Jenny Morgan. The writer chaired the overseeing committee. See also Regina Graycar & Jenny Morgan, 'Legal Categories, Women's Lives and the Law Curriculum OR: Making Gender Examinable' (1996) 18 *Sydney Law Review* 431.

17   Albie Sachs & John Hoff Wilson, *Sexism and the Law: A Study of Male Beliefs and Judicial Bias in Britain and the United States* (Martin Robertson, 1978); see also Chapter 1, this volume.

18   Londa Schiebinger, *The Mind Has No Sex? Women in the Origins of Modern Science* (Harvard University Press, 1989).

19   Jean-François Lyotard, *The Postmodern Condition: A Report on Knowledge* (Manchester University Press, 1984).

of 'the judge' have been countered by the perennial need to reinscribe the normativity of benchmark masculinity and the otherness of the feminine within the social script.

Drawing on the Australian experiences of change, I consider three recent sites of contestation, all of which underscore the masculinist construction of merit within the adjudicative discourse. First, I consider the way the concept of merit assumed centre-stage in the case of the appointment of a woman judge, particularly at the most authoritative level; the second site of contestation relates to the assumption that merit had been subverted when a critical mass of women was appointed; the third scenario involves the resentment arising from the supposed disregard of the merit principle when a woman was appointed to a senior administrative position (chief magistrate), which culminated in her being (wrongfully) convicted and jailed.

These examples all received extensive attention in the Australian print media and show how negative representations of women judges circulate within popular discourse—both mirroring and constituting the woman judge in ways that entrench social stereotypes. These negative representations challenge not only the liberal accounts of progress and equal treatment, but also the feminist belief in gender justice. Such representations may also backlight the contentious view that women judges speak in a 'different voice'[20]—a complex issue that I do not propose to explore in this chapter.

Three sites of contest

'Woman "of merit" joins High Court'[21]

Mary Gaudron was the first woman appointed to the Australian High Court—a position she occupied from 1987 until 2003. When she resigned, it was anticipated that she would be replaced with another

---

20   Carol Gilligan, *In a Different Voice: Psychological Theory and Women's Development* (Harvard University Press, 1982). The question of whether women judges speak in a 'different voice' has given rise to an extensive literature. See, for example, Jennifer L. Peresie, 'Female Judges Matter: Gender and Collegial Decisionmaking in the Federal Appellate Courts' (2005) 114 *Yale Law Journal* 1759; Elaine Martin, 'Women on the Bench: A Different Voice?' (1993) 77 *Judicature* 126; Sue Davis, 'Do Women Judges Speak "In A Different Voice?": Carol Gilligan, Feminist Legal Theory, and the Ninth Circuit' (1992–93) 8 *Wisconsin Women's Law Journal* 143; Bertha Wilson, 'Will Women Judges Really Make a Difference?' (1990) 28 *Osgoode Hall Law Journal* 507; Carrie Menkel-Meadow, 'Portia in a Different Voice: Speculations on a Woman's Lawyering Process' (1985) 1 *Berkeley Women's Law Journal* 39.
21   Elizabeth Colman & Natasha Robinson, 'Woman "of Merit" Joins High Court', *The Australian*, 21 September 2005, 1.

woman, but this was not to be. At the time of the appointment of conservative male judge Dyson Heydon from New South Wales as her replacement, the media debate was concerned more with the question of state representation than the underrepresentation of women on the bench. However, Susan Crennan was appointed to the High Court in 2005, also by the conservative Coalition government of John Howard.

Justice Crennan had been appointed to the Federal Court 18 months earlier, having practised as a barrister for 26 years, mainly in the areas of commercial and civil law, and having played a role in several high-profile fraud cases. In addition, she was the first woman to be appointed chairman (her choice of title) of the Victorian Bar Council and the first woman to be appointed president of the male-dominated Australian Bar Association (not Women Lawyers, Women Barristers or Feminist Lawyers). A prominent role in professional associations assisted Justice Crennan in satisfying the informal criterion of 'being known'.[22] Justice Crennan's claim to merit was enhanced by being described as having a brilliant legal mind and a capacity for hard work, as well as being temperamentally suited to the task. In addition, these criteria were supplemented by descriptions of her as 'black letter', 'balanced', 'without baggage', 'fiercely independent' and 'not a feminist'.[23]

While Justice Crennan served as a Human Rights and Equal Opportunity Commissioner in the early 1990s and was personally described as supportive of individual women, the dominant media representation was of a woman who distanced herself from the feminine—and feminism— and positioned herself close to the masculinist norm, the power of which has enabled it to claim neutrality for itself. Indeed, the then attorney-general, Philip Ruddock, went so far as to deny that gender had been a factor in Cabinet's choice: 'I'm pleased to be able to appoint the best person for the job,' he said.[24] Eve Mahlab, a retired feminist lawyer, commented on the need for a woman judge to neutralise herself:

> If, as a woman, you want to get on, you devote yourself to the goals of your male colleagues and you don't rock the boat by asking, 'Is this fair to women?' … What I think Susan Crennan

22 Brenda Hale, 'Equality and the Judiciary: Why Should We Want More Women Judges?' (2001) *Public Law* 489, 492.

23 Colman & Robinson (n. 21).

24 Editorial, 'Caught in a Time Warp on Judicial Appointments', *The Age*, [Melbourne], 22 September 2005, 14.

always did, to her credit, was that she devoted herself to the goals
of the male society that makes up the profession of the bar. She
really contributed there and excelled.[25]

Karen Kissane elaborates on Crennan's stance, which, if not exactly
antifeminist (despite one newspaper headline),[26] could not be described
as supportive of those women who had experienced discrimination at the
hands of the legal profession: 'She has certainly rejected feminist rhetoric:
she says there is no evidence of gender bias in the law and that she has
never suffered discrimination at the bar, and she does not believe in
affirmative action.'[27]

Despite her best endeavours, however, Justice Crennan could not neutralise
herself entirely. Not only did the media pay disproportionate attention to
her gender, but also allusions to her age and possibly even her sexuality[28]
were made by referring to her status as a grandmother.[29] The connotations
of this grandmotherly image are that of a woman of mature years who is
safe and unthreatening because her 'manned' state is likely to mitigate the
dangerousness of the feminine in an unrestrained position of authority.

While a judge appointed to a superior court may feel that he or she is
free to exercise autonomy in a way that is impossible for an appointee to
a lower court, there was little in Justice Crennan's history to suggest that
she was likely to start speaking in 'a different voice'.[30] Justice Crennan's
appointment sought to guarantee, as far as possible, that there would be
no possibility of disorder emanating from an unleashing of the unruly
feminine. This is not to suggest that Justice Crennan lacked a sense of
justice, but the media representations of her conveyed the impression
that she would be joining the ranks of those women who had never
encountered sex discrimination themselves; it was always something that
happened to someone else.[31] These representations clearly placed pressure
on her to maintain this stance.

---

25   Karen Kissane, 'Welcome to the Club', *The Age*, [Melbourne], 5 November 2005, Insight 3.
26   Marcus Priest, 'Meet the High Court's Anti-Feminist', *Australian Financial Review*, 21 September 2005, 1.
27   Kissane (n. 25). Crennan's views on AA for women lawyers were reported as a reason for her having missed out on appointment to the position of Victorian chief justice. See Priest (n. 26).
28   Moran (n. 3, 580–81) points out that the married (male) norm was UK policy under Lord Chancellor Lord Hailsham in the 1970s and 1980s, supposedly because of the dangers of blackmail.
29   Michael Pelly, 'Ex-Teacher, Legal Dynamo and, Oh Yes, a Woman: Welcome to the High Court', *Sydney Morning Herald*, 21 September 2005, 1.
30   Gilligan (n. 20).
31   Rosemary Hunter, 'Talking Up Equality: Women Barristers and the Denial of Discrimination' (2002) 10 *Feminist Legal Studies* 113.

Lacking testosterone

In contrast to the cautious approach of his federal counterpart, the Victorian attorney-general Rob Hulls espoused a deliberate policy of appointing more women to the bench in the early years of the millennium to 'obliterate the so-called blokey culture of the courts'.[32] In seven years, he dramatically changed the gender profile of the Victorian justice system. Of a total of 80 appointees to the various state courts, 37, or nearly half, were women. Hulls appointed 16 female magistrates, from a total of 94 (including 16 new male magistrates); 15 of the 20 female County Court judges, from a total of 57 (including 13 new male judges); and five of the six female Supreme Court judges, out of a total of 34, while the sixth he promoted to chief justice (the court also included 11 new male judges). While well short of a majority, these numbers appear dramatic because of the very low base from which the appointments began.

The appointment of 'so many' women resulted in an undercurrent of disaffection and resentment on the part of male lawyers. One former member of the Bar Council was quoted as saying 'there is scope for criticism of the way in which some senior and eminently qualified people [read "men"] have been overlooked'.[33] The most notorious comment was attributed to Robert Richter QC, who reportedly said that it was an advantage for an appointee not to have testicles.[34] Other male lawyers described the appointments as 'queue jumping' and a divergence 'too far from merit',[35] which was 'undermining the intellectual rigour of the state judiciary'.[36]

The controversy surrounding the appointment of Justice Neave is illustrative. When Marcia Neave, a law professor and chair of the Victorian Law Reform Commission, was appointed to the Victorian Court of Appeal in 2006, she was criticised for never having practised law: 'You have to have trial experience to understand if a trial has miscarried,'

---

32 Katherine Towers, 'Hulls Takes On the Law's Old Guard', *Australian Financial Review*, 6 April 2006, 1.

33 Ian Munro & Fergus Shiel, 'The Two Sides of Rob', *The Age*, [Melbourne], 3 June 2006, Insight 3.

34 Richter later apologised to a senior woman barrister who walked out of the gathering. See Steve Butcher, 'Women and the Law: Top Silk Apologises Over Bias Comment', *The Age*, [Melbourne], 27 November 2003, 1.

35 Munro & Shiel (n. 33).

36 Towers (n. 32).

said one exasperated commercial QC.[37] This is despite the fact that an appellate court operates quite differently from a trial court and Neave had many years of experience teaching and writing about property, equity and family law, as well as taking responsibility for a vast array of references on the Law Reform Commission, including defences to homicide, sexual assault, intellectual disability and reproductive technologies. But then, Justice Neave was also attacked because of her law reform experience: 'Capable though she is, she has devoted much of her life to changing laws, not impartially administering them. To me, she seems more qualified as an activist than a judge.'[38]

In determining Justice Neave to be insufficiently respectful of the law as it is, we see not only a suggestion of the disorderly woman, but also a repetition of the positivist myth that the good judge does not make law, but merely interprets it.

As the percentage of women appointed crept towards 50 per cent and approximated the proportion of women law graduates and women practitioners, complaints about the sacrifice of merit and the evil of AA became more vociferous. Not only was there a concern on the part of male barristers that their settled expectations had been thwarted, but also there was a more insidious subtext relating to the feminisation of the judiciary and the possibility of disorder within the state.

Jailing a chief magistrate

Queensland chief magistrate Diane Fingleton was jailed in 2003 for having sent an email to a subordinate magistrate, Basil Gribbin, in which she was found to have threatened him, as she required him to show cause as to why he should stay in his position despite his disloyalty.[39] Gribbin had provided another magistrate, Anne Thacker, with an affidavit and lawfully given evidence in judicial proceedings when Thacker sought review of a decision that she be transferred. Fingleton was convicted of an offence under the Queensland Criminal Code[40] and sentenced to

---

37   ibid. In part, the antipathy displayed towards Justice Neave's appointment reflects the resistance to the appointment of academics as judges. It was only in the 1990s that law professors were first appointed—to the Federal Court and the NSW District Court.

38   Andrew Bolt, 'Law Wears a Dress', *Herald-Sun*, [Melbourne], 1 March 2006, 21.

39   Rosemary Hunter, 'Fear and Loathing in the Sunshine State' (2004) 19(44) *Australian Feminist Studies* 145, doi.org/10.1080/0816464042000226474.

40   *Criminal Code* 1899 (Qld), s. 119B.

12 months' imprisonment, reduced to six months on appeal.[41] After she had served her term, the High Court unanimously overturned the conviction, finding she was immune from prosecution when performing her duties.[42] Fingleton received backpay and was restored to the magistracy (but not to the position of chief magistrate).

Fingleton had been appointed to her position by a Labor attorney-general who, like his Victorian counterpart, felt that talented women had been overlooked for too long and something should be done about it. In Fingleton's case, her commitment to social justice and reform was the key reason for her appointment, not her gender.[43] Gender, however, undoubtedly played a role in her demise. Unlike her male predecessor, whose career was similarly terminated by a revolt over a transfer, Fingleton ended up in prison, while he was rewarded with a carefree life of fishing.[44]

Fingleton's promotion to chief magistrate angered some of her colleagues who considered themselves to be more experienced, although she had spent four years as a magistrate. Fingleton felt the antipathy towards her was exacerbated by her push for reform and her forthright manner.[45] In other words, she espoused a style that is regarded as authoritative in a male chief magistrate but unacceptable in a female chief. Ironically, however, had Fingleton occupied the docile and deferential subject position conventionally associated with the feminine, it is unlikely she would have been appointed to a position involving the management of more than 70 magistrates spread over a large geographical area with a brief to put the magistracy in order. She would probably have been found to lack forcefulness and authority.

An assertive woman (a feminist chief magistrate) who has offended the old guard can expect to be sanctioned more heavily than the comparable man. Nevertheless, such a savage attack on a woman occupying judicial office may be unprecedented, although there are instances of the scapegoating of women lawyers leading to the demise of their careers.[46]

---

41   *R v Fingleton* (2003) 140 A Crim R 216.
42   *Fingleton v The Queen* (2005) 216 ALR 474.
43   Hunter (n. 39) 146.
44   Leisa Scott & David Nason, 'Frying Fingleton', *The Australian*, 7 June 2003, 19.
45   Peter Wilmoth, 'A Life at Law Turned Inside Out', *Sunday Age*, [Melbourne], 25 September 2005, 15.
46   For example, Ann Daniel, *Scapegoats for a Profession: Uncovering Procedural Justice* (Harwood Academic Publishers, 1998).

Hunter refers to the 'terrorising effect' of the scapegoating of Fingleton, in that no other senior woman dared to speak out lest she became the next 'sacrificial victim'.[47]

The masculinity of merit

The definitional conundrum

Women figure prominently among the top students in law schools, and have done for several decades.[48] But, if this is the case, why is it that these women when subsequently being considered for senior positions are repeatedly found to be lacking in merit? There is something suspect about the concept since it is rarely defined. Indeed, merit seems to have entered political discourse only comparatively recently, 'its advent apparently coinciding with women's increasing pursuit of positions of influence within the public sphere'.[49]

Merit is an abstract term involving a claim to excellence, commendation or worth, but it has no meaning without reference to the social context in which it appears. Aristotle evinced a clear understanding of this issue 2,500 years ago,[50] but it is rarely subjected to scrutiny by modern decision-makers operating within a liberal meritocracy. It is assumed to be unproblematic that the 'best person' will be instantly discernible to all, as if by magic. In the case of judges, this process of instantaneous recognition is also deemed to occur even though, out of a pool of hundreds or even thousands, 'there is no way at the end of the day there is just one who is the best ... There will always be five or six names who are good enough to be appointed.'[51]

---

47   Hunter (n. 39) 153.
48   Jane H. Mathews. 'The Changing Profile of Women in the Law' (1982) 56 *Australian Law Journal* 634. Cf. Erika Rackley, 'Representations of the (Woman) Judge: Hercules, the Little Mermaid, and the Vain and Naked Emperor' (2002) 22(4) *Legal Studies* 602, doi.org/10.1111/j.1748-121x.2002. tb00671.x.
49   Rosemary Whip, '"Merit" and the Political Representation of Women' (2001) 20(2) *Social Alternatives* 41.
50   Aristotle, *Politics*, translated by John Warrington (Dent, 1959) §1283a.
51   Michael Lavarch, former federal attorney-general, quoted in Marcus Priest, 'Ruddock Appointee Joins Court Debate', *Australian Financial Review*, 15 November 2004, 3.

The 'best person for the job' is the person who, based on past performance, displays the greatest promise or potential. Hence, far from merit being an objective variable, there is always an element of uncertainty associated with it, because it involves making predictions about the future: if candidate A were to be appointed to a position she has never occupied before, how would she perform? Furthermore, there is an undeniable element of subjectivity in determining what factors are considered and how they are evaluated.[52] Despite this element of subjectivity, liberal individualism assumes that merit involves rational choice. Merit also encompasses the idea of desert, in the sense of entitlement: *after 20 years at the bar, he deserved to be appointed to the bench*. The two meanings of merit, excellence and desert, have become conflated, so that 'the best person for the job' is deemed to be the most deserving, as well as the most outstanding.

While there may be objective criteria enumerated for a position, such as certain qualifications, skills and experience, they mean little without the evaluative element.[53] Qualifications and abilities must be weighted in relation to other criteria and their relevance and standing compared with those of other candidates. Applying the merit principle to a selection process without any articulated criteria clearly presents something of a challenge, although this has historically been the method used in the selection of many prestigious positions, despite the insistent myth of objectivity. We are all caught up in the discourse of the 'best person' and want to believe in merit based on objective criteria, rather than extraneous factors, as the basis of appointment, but are at a loss to know how best to conduct the process of identification and evaluation.

It is a feminist truism that for a woman to succeed she has to be better than her male counterparts.[54] Perhaps this is why the merit of a particular judge is expressly raised only when the appointee is a woman: 'Every time a woman gets appointed there is noisy talk about the "merit" of the appointment, but whenever a man is appointed there is silence on the

---

52   Clare Burton, *Redefining Merit* (Affirmative Action Agency Monograph No. 2, Commonwealth of Australia, 1988); Margaret Thornton, 'Affirmative Action, Merit and the Liberal State' (1985) 2 *Australian Journal of Law and Society* 28.

53   Richard H. Fallon, 'To Each According to His Ability, from None According to His Race: The Concept of Merit in the Law of Antidiscrimination' (1980) 60 *Boston University Law Review* 815, 822.

54   For example, Mary Gaudron, 'Speech to launch Australian Women Lawyers', Melbourne, 19 September 1997, available from: www.hcourt.gov.au/assets/publications/speeches/former-justices/gaudronj/gaudronj_wlasp.htm.

question of merit.'[55] Try substituting 'Man "of merit" joins High Court' for 'Woman "of merit" joins High Court' in the case of the headline referred to above. It is virtually unimaginable.[56] Indeed, it would be tautologous because masculinity is already a tacit criterion of judicial merit.

When Queensland attorney-general Matt Foley appointed six women judges out of seven to the Supreme Court of that state in the late 1990s, like Rob Hulls in Victoria, he was accused of making appointments on the basis of gender rather than merit.[57] Indeed, he was officially asked under the protection of parliamentary privilege whether he would continue 'making appointments to judicial office on grounds other than judicial merit'.[58] Such asseverations do have an effect on public policy and it is notable that the appointment of women judges in Queensland slowed after the imbroglio involving Diane Fingleton.[59]

A graphic example of the way women and merit are treated as disjunctive within popular culture is encapsulated in an online poll at the time a replacement was being mooted for Mary Gaudron on the High Court, which asked participants, 'Should there be more women judges on the High Court?', and offered a choice of one of three answers: 'Yes', 'No' or 'Should Be Decided on Merit'.[60]

Deconstruction of the objectivity of merit in the context of judging, perhaps unsurprisingly, soon reveals it to be a masquerade as the process is characterised by an extraordinary opacity. When we look at the outcome for the Australian High Court, for example—six women,[61] one openly gay male judge and no Indigenous judges among 55 appointments

55 Kim Pettigrew, barrister, quoted in Fergus Shiel, 'Engendering a Legal Minefield', *The Age*, [Melbourne], 6 December 2003, 8.

56 This could change if the focus shifted to sexuality or some other suspect characteristic of identity. For example, former judge Michael Kirby speculates as to whether he would have been appointed to the Australian High Court had he 'come out' as a gay man before his appointment. See Moran (n. 3) 586, 596.

57 For example, Hedley Thomas, 'Selection Process is Judicious: Welford', *The Courier-Mail*, [Brisbane], 2 September 2004, 2; Terry Sweetman, 'Misjudged, Misguided Misogyny', *The Courier-Mail*, 15 February 2000, 15.

58 Hunter (n. 39) 153.

59 ibid.

60 Australian Broadcasting Corporation, *Public Record* (ABC, 2003), quoted in Rachel Davis & George Williams, 'Reform of the Judicial Appointments Process: Gender and the Bench of the High Court of Australia' (2003) 27 *Melbourne University Law Review* 819, 833. Davis & Williams record the outcome: 'Out of 983 votes, 56% voted "Yes"; 4% voted "No"; and 40% voted "Should Be Decided on Merit".'

61 Susan Kiefel, appointed to the court in 2007, became the first female chief justice in 2017.

in more than a century[62]—the myth of the objectivity of merit is exposed. Nevertheless, decision-makers and commentators endlessly reiterate reliance on the 'essential criterion of merit' as though it were unproblematic.[63]

Searching for criteria

Conventionally, an attorney-general makes a recommendation to Cabinet and the names are announced in due course. Even though the position may now be advertised in some jurisdictions, consultations with key individuals and professional bodies remain confidential. Governments in Australia retain an exclusive right to identify candidates for the bench and there is resistance to transferring this power to an unelected body, despite the benefits of independence.[64] While one can be critical of the highly politicised nature of the nomination hearings held for selection of US Supreme Court judges, the public process assists in making women's voices audible.[65]

The long history of appointing only benchmark men as judges has made it difficult to reimagine judicial merit in a non-gendered way. In other words, the fundamental or objective criterion associated with *hoi aristoi* ('the best people') has informally come to include maleness. Rosabeth Moss Kanter's description of the way social conformity is maintained within corporations can also illuminate our understanding of the constitution of judicial merit:

> The more closed the circle, the more difficult it is for 'outsiders' to break in. Their very difficulty in entering may be taken as a sign of incompetence, a sign that the insiders were right to close their ranks. The more closed the circle, the more difficult it is to share power when the time comes, as it inevitably must, that

62 'Justices of the High Court', *AustralianPolitics.com* (1995–2021), available from: australianpolitics.com/constitution/high-court/justices-of-the-high-court#.
63 For example, Davis & Williams (n. 60) 823; Samantha Maiden, 'High Court Decision Only On Merit, Says PM', *The Advertiser*, [Adelaide], 19 December 2002, 3.
64 The Australian Labor Party, when in government, reformed the procedure for appointing federal judges, but this was subsequently dismantled by Liberal attorney-general George Brandis when the Coalition assumed government. See Andrew Lynch, 'Australia is Lagging behind the World's Best on Judicial Appointments Reform', *The Conversation*, 13 August 2015, available from: theconversation.com/australia-is-lagging-behind-the-worlds-best-on-judicial-appointments-reform-45833.
65 Judith Resnik, 'Judicial Selection and Democratic Theory: Demand, Supply, and Life Tenure' (2005) 26 *Cardozo Law Review* 579, 635.

others challenge the control by just one kind. And the greater the tendency for a group of people to try to reproduce themselves, the more constraining becomes the emphasis on conformity.[66]

What is at work here is the phenomenon of homosocial reproduction whereby like favours like.[67] That is, benchmark men tend to appoint those who look most like themselves as a testament to their own worth and desert. Potential candidates may be inducted into the 'club' at an early stage of their careers. By means of what Dermot Feenan terms an 'epistemology of ignorance', lack of knowledge about criteria for appointment and networking operates to preserve privilege and ensures that women are excluded.[68] Feenan argues that ignorance is therefore a constitutive aspect of existing power relations. The lack of transparency surrounding the selection process can only serve to augment those power relations.

Some prominent men are nevertheless beginning to question conventional wisdom as a result of their experience with talented women lawyers. For example, Michael McHugh, in a speech shortly before his retirement from the High Court, expressly adverted to the masculinity of merit: '[Women] are at a disadvantage in competing on merit, as that term has been defined and understood in a male-dominated profession.'[69] The malleability of merit, the conservatism of the legal professional milieu and the virtually infinite criteria it embraces nevertheless authorise attacks on women judges for random deficiencies within legal and popular discourses as I have shown.

It is noteworthy that the higher one ascends in a hierarchy of prestigious positions in the public sphere, the greater is the emphasis on merit but, paradoxically, the more elusive and the less transparent are the criteria. As the descriptive variables become more slippery, the assertion of benchmark men to their right to occupy the most authoritative positions becomes more insistent. It can therefore be seen that merit serves an ideological role in assuaging concerns about the basis of societal allocations in the context of AA. It provides a distributive mechanism within liberalism that compels individuals to take responsibility for their

---

66   Rosabeth Moss Kanter, *Men and Women of the Corporation* (Basic Books, 1977) 68.

67   The 'homo' in homosocial is from the Greek *homoios* ('like'), not from the Latin *homo* ('man').

68   Dermot Feenan, 'Understanding Disadvantage Partly Through an Epistemology of Ignorance' (2007) 16(4) *Social & Legal Studies* 509, doi.org/10.1177/0964663907082733.

69   Michael McHugh, 'Women justices for the High Court: Speech delivered at the High Court Dinner hosted by the Western Australia Law Society, 27 October 1994', High Court of Australia, available from: www.hcourt.gov.au/assets/publications/speeches/former-justices/mchughj/mchughj_27oct04.html.

LAW AND THE QUEST FOR GENDER EQUALITY

success and non-success in life, regardless of countervailing realities such as the homosociality of the senior ranks of the bar, from where judges are generally drawn. The discourse of merit has thereby been able to sustain traditional power relations and conventional iterations of masculinity and femininity. In this way, merit operates as a central legitimating principle of the masculinist state.

While the transparency of selection criteria is clearly desirable, there is unlikely to be unanimity as to what the criteria should be, as former chief justice Murray Gleeson of the Australian High Court pointed out:

> There is plenty of room for argument about what constitutes merit in judicial selection. But, if it means nothing else, it must at least include the capacity to preside over adversarial litigation, conduct the proceedings with reasonable efficiency, and produce a well-reasoned judgment at the end.[70]

How does one assess the capacity to preside, conduct and produce? Surely, one can have the capacity to perform a task without having done it before. Would Justice Marcia Neave, who was attacked for not having conducted trials, satisfy the capacity requirement? 'Capacity' and 'merit', like 'integrity', 'skill' and 'experience', are constructed in such a way that the terms themselves have become gendered.

In 1993, then Australian attorney-general Michael Lavarch, in a discussion paper on judicial appointments, produced a longer list of criteria. He proposed a range of skills: legal, advocacy, administrative, oral and written communication, together with efficiency, as well as a range of personal qualities, including practicality and common sense, vision and a capability to uphold the rule of law and act in an independent manner. Finally, the appointee should contribute to the institution's fair reflection of society (consistent with merit).[71] Again, while most of the skills can probably be demonstrated, the personal criteria make little sense without explication, evaluation and reference to a particular context. Furthermore, one could always include a range of other desirable traits, such as knowledge of and sensitivity to diversity, contributions to the community and evidence of understanding and commitment to social justice. The point is that there can never be closure in the constitution

---

70   Murray Gleeson, 'Judicial Selection and Training: Two Sides of the One Coin' (2003) 77 *Australian Law Journal* 591, 592.
71   Lavarch (n. 51).

of merit because of the essential permeability and subjectivity of the evaluative element, which is going to differ in every context according to the candidate pool.

The rhetoric of affirmative action

A further means of denigrating women judges that enhances the construction of merit in conventional masculinist terms is to suggest they have been appointed because of affirmative action. AA is an open-ended concept that encompasses a range of proactive strategies designed to promote institutional diversity. These strategies might best be thought of as positions on a continuum. At one end are clustered minimalist strategies, or weak forms of AA, which might include encouraging women and minorities to apply or ensuring that the names of women and Others are included among the shortlisted candidates. At the other end of the continuum are stronger forms of AA, such as quotas and preferences—interventions designed to overcome the underrepresentation problem sooner rather than later. Quotas have been ordered by US courts from time to time to remedy instances of egregious discrimination, typically on the ground of race, in the workplace,[72] but they have never been ordered in Australia. In any case, it does not follow that quotas or preferences displace the merit principle, as the best-qualified candidates will be chosen when a choice must be made. Despite this commonsense view of the operation of quotas, the conservative swing engendered by neoliberalism has denounced anything other than a strict application of the equal treatment standard, which usually means retention of the status quo. The attack on an outcome-oriented approach resulted in the excision of the phrase 'affirmative action' from the official Australian Government lexicon in the late 1990s.[73] While it would be absurd to suggest that sex-based quotas were being used to appoint judges without regard to individual merit, this was the asseveration being made by those opposing the appointment of women judges in Victoria and Queensland.

---

72 For example, *RIOS v Enterprise Association Steamfitters Local 638* 501 F 2d 622 (2nd Cir, 1974); *United Steelworkers of America v Weber* 443 US 193 (1979).

73 Margaret Thornton, 'The Political Contingency of Sex Discrimination Legislation: The Case of Australia' (2015) 4 *Laws* 314, 325, doi.org/10.3390/laws4030314. Cf. Kate Malleson, 'Justifying Gender Equality on the Bench: Why Difference Won't Do' (2003) 11 *Feminist Legal Studies* 129.

By a certain sleight of hand, AA is construed by its detractors as being concerned with biology, not merit, thereby amounting to a form of reverse discrimination. AA, like merit, is another discourse in which gendered dualisms involving normativity and otherness circulate. The false antinomy between AA and merit is an insidious way of entrenching the idea that the beneficiaries of AA are unmeritorious, but it is one that is repeated endlessly within popular discourse, sometimes by women judges themselves[74]—the ultimate testament to its ideological force.

I.C.F. Spry depicts AA in judicial appointments as a misguided policy of the Left, spurred on by sectional interests:

> The matter of political appointments is now exacerbated by the current tendency of Labor governments to appoint unsuitable female judges, often at the instance [sic] of feminists ... Accordingly many of the female judges—there are some few exceptions—who sit in various Australian courts are there by reason of gender and lack the necessary abilities.[75]

It is a familiar tactic for conservatives to tag as 'political' all progressive judicial appointments to denigrate them, whereas they extol conservative appointments as 'meritorious'. A similar tactic is employed to denigrate women regardless of political persuasion. Spry would like the legal profession to adopt a stronger critical stance towards AA, considering what he claims to be the 'poorer quality of justice that is, with few exceptions, dispensed by female judges and law officers'.[76] He did not hesitate to attack the Victorian attorney-general for appointing a woman, Marilyn Warren, to the position of chief justice: '[Mr Hulls] claimed publicly that she was the most appropriate person to be appointed, a foolish claim because in fact there are various other available persons who are regarded as substantially more capable.'[77]

What is being played out here is the rhetoric of merit, which reveals itself to be a concept shaped by power. This power has traditionally been wielded by benchmark men and has largely gone unchallenged. Progressives

---

74 For example, Rosemary Balmford, 'Gender Equality in Courts and Tribunals' (1995) 94 *Victorian Bar News* 34, 36–37.

75 I.C.F. Spry, 'Affirmative Action for Judges', *National Observer*, [Melbourne], Summer 2004, 67.

76 ibid., 68.

77 ibid., 69. It is notable that Spry also did not hesitate to denigrate publicly Mary Gaudron when she announced her retirement from the High Court. See I.C.F. Spry, 'The Unlamented Departure of Justice Gaudron', *National Observer: Australia and World Affairs*, [Melbourne], Spring 2002, 68.

generally, not just feminist legal scholars, are questioning the power of benchmark men to determine behind closed doors what constitutes merit in judicial appointments. This has compelled gatekeepers to defend a position that has become increasingly untenable, or to specify criteria, when formerly there were none—other than benchmark masculinity and 'being known'.

These established characteristics of the judiciary and the clandestine nature of the appointments process have meant that women and Others have had no opportunity to contest and contribute to the construction of merit. I suggest that the disparagement of the feminine, which has been counterpoised with the masculinity of merit, is another rhetorical device that has served to sustain judging as a profoundly gendered activity. AA is one element of the arsenal of attack that has been useful to detractors in the case of the appointment of more than the single token woman, for it is assumed (or feared) that a critical mass of women will have some devastating (albeit unspecified) effect. A more open process may well mean more contestation, but the popular (mis)representations of women judicial candidates can then be publicly countered rather than being insidiously perpetuated.

The fictive feminine

Once women were 'let in' to the public sphere, it was assumed it would only be a matter of time before an egalitarian end state was reached in which equality between the sexes existed. When anomalies were pointed out, the rationality of liberalism would triumph and sex would have as much relevance as eye colour in appointment to public office.[78] As we know only too well, however, the liberal story does not comport with the gendered reality. Liberalism glosses over the animus towards the feminine because it encapsulates a premodern, nonrational element that sits uncomfortably with the rational humanism of liberal individualism. Nevertheless, misogyny remains a key subtext of the Western religious and cultural tradition, which constitutes women as 'others' to the masculinist norm.

---

78   Richard A. Wasserstrom, 'On Racism and Sexism' in Richard A. Wasserstrom (ed.), *Today's Moral Problems* (Macmillan, 3rd edn, 1985) 20–21.

For almost three millennia, all the influential theorists and jurisprudes were men, as were virtually the entire *dramatis personae* of the public sphere. These figures have possessed the power to write about the feminine in such a way that women were always the objects, never the subjects, of the authoritative social narratives. This lack of voice has allowed the category 'woman' and the concept of the feminine to be subjugated by power.

According to Aristotle, women were possessed of an imperfect deliberative faculty.[79] The view that the difference and inferiority of women are grounded in nature is entrenched within the Western intellectual tradition—an idea that has not evaporated with the cautious letting in of women associated with Second-Wave Feminism. Women's assignation to the private sphere, sexuality, affectivity, reproduction and care came to be associated with the essentialised feminine—or the fictive feminine, as I term it—denying all vestiges of individual subjectivity. This contrasts with the imagined masculine ideal that dominates the public sphere, encompassing the qualities of reason, impartiality, authoritativeness and decisiveness, which, coincidentally, go to make up merit in the constitution of the judge. The most pernicious strand of this mythical binarism is that the feminine has been constructed as a force that is dangerous to public office.

While caring for others would seem to be a positive characteristic for participation in public life, as it is closely connected to justice and mercy, it has also been constructed as the basis of the disorder of women. This thesis, which is elaborated on by Carole Pateman,[80] is based on the work of several canonical theorists, such as Rousseau and Freud, and avers that women are incapable of developing a sense of justice.[81] Their reasoning is that because women are preoccupied with the love and care of intimates, they can never transcend the particularity of the family in favour of the claimed universality associated with public sphere activity. Rousseau's idealised women, such as Sophy in *Émile*,[82] are confined to motherhood and subordination in the private sphere—the realm of the particular. The disability of particularity meant they could never be full citizens, let alone assume responsibility for judging or the running of the state. The fictional binary plays down the inevitable role of particularity in the public sphere,

---

79 Aristotle (n. 50) §1260a.

80 Carole Pateman, *The Disorder of Women: Democracy, Feminism and Political Theory* (Polity Press, 1989).

81 For example, Sigmund Freud, 'Some Psychical Consequences of the Anatomical Distinction between the Sexes' in James Strachey (ed.), *The Standard Edition of the Complete Psychological Works of Sigmund Freud. Volume XIX* (Hogarth Press, 1960) 257–58.

82 Jean-Jacques Rousseau, *Émile*, translated by Barbara Foxley (Dent, 1993).

such as the movement between the universal and the particular in the adjudicative process.[83] If women sought to think beyond the needs of their families, as male judges do, disorder would result: 'Love and justice are antagonistic virtues; the demands of love and of family bonds are particularistic and so in direct conflict with justice which demands that private interest is subordinated to the public (universal) good.'[84]

Classical liberalism was able to deal with the tensions between love and justice, as well as corporeality and reason, provided the feminised side of the set of dualisms associated with the public/private dichotomy was quarantined within the private sphere. This legitimated the domination of the public sphere by benchmark men, allowing them to mark as masculine, under the guise of universality, the values of reason, autonomy, authority and merit.

The disorder generated by female sexuality is a recurring leitmotif of the Western tradition. Female sexuality and eroticism were frequently adduced as a justification for refusing to admit women to the legal profession.[85] While this gendered binary plays down the sexuality, corporeality and affectivity of men—at least in the public domain—it continues to have currency in the rhetorical construction of judging.

Although there is a growing literature on women and judging, it has tended to steer away from engagement with the psychoanalytic effects of the dark and primordial facets of the feminine. The focus has been largely directed to overcoming structural hurdles that are perceived to be tractable to remediation, rather than addressing the discomfiting but pervasive fiction of the feminine as a disorderly force in the public realm, which transcends any simple blueprint for reform. This thesis possesses significant explanatory potential considering the latent hostility towards women judges that continues to circulate. The detractors of the appointment of women judges rarely go beyond endlessly repeating that the appointees are unmeritorious, as I have shown; they do not articulate just how disorder will manifest itself in the public sphere, but we are assured that it will.

---

83   Sandra Berns, *To Speak as a Judge: Difference, Voice and Power* (Ashgate, 1999) 193–94.
84   Pateman (n. 80) 21.
85   Thornton (n. 10) 45. Collier sets out to challenge the 'disavowal of men's corporeality' in law. See Richard Collier, '"Nutty Professors", "Men in Suits" and "New Entrepreneurs": Corporeality, Subjectivity and Change in the Law School and Legal Practice' (1998) 7(1) *Social & Legal Studies* 27, doi.org/10.1177/096466399800700103.

More insidious is the fear that a feminised judiciary will not be a fit and proper institution for men. Once the tipping point is reached, feminised occupations encourage male flight,[86] as with white flight (a phenomenon associated with the entry of Blacks and Hispanics into white, middle-class neighbourhoods in the United States). If an influx of women judges takes place, the crucial boundary between the masculinist norm and the feminised Other could similarly dissolve. Both the masculinity and the elitism of judging as an occupation would then be in jeopardy. Feminisation and male flight must therefore be resisted at all costs. Race, sexuality and religion (non-Christian) also worry benchmark men, but a critical mass of women, including one that is on course to reach the tipping point, as with the Victorian judicial appointments, is deeply destabilising because it hints at the real possibility of feminisation.

Conclusion

This chapter has sought to focus on the perception of women as judges rather than analyse modes of adjudication. The representational cameos I have presented challenge the objectivity of merit in both the selection process and the evaluation of judging. To allay any suspicion of disorder, the woman judge must suppress the feminine and assume the masquerade of Hercules.[87] She must position herself close to the masculine norm to ensure a semblance of authority. I have shown that the animus towards the feminine has not evaporated with the 'letting in' of women and the effluxion of time. A mere belief in liberal individualism cannot instantaneously erase the centuries of distrust that underpin liberal theory and are kept alive by public policy, legal discourse and popular culture. Faith in the idea that a critical mass will dilute the animus towards the feminine has not been borne out by the evidence. The attacks on women judges appointed in Queensland and Victoria attest to this. Once the FW2 ('first woman to …')[88] phenomenon lost its novelty, it was hoped that a critical mass would allay the fear of the feminine and pave the way for acceptance. While there is some evidence of tolerance of diversity, numerosity has simultaneously revived the fear of disorder and feminisation.

---

86   For example, Ann Game & Rosemary Pringle, *Gender at Work* (Allen & Unwin, 1983).
87   Rackley (n. 48).
88   Cheris Kramarae & Paula A. Treichler, *A Feminist Dictionary* (Pandora, 1985).

I suggest that the current political climate, in which there has been a notable swing away from social liberalism, has accentuated the resiling from progressive initiatives, such as the acknowledgement of group harms, whether based on gender, race, sexuality or other characteristic of identity. The turning away from the systemic character of sex discrimination towards an exclusive focus on the individual is one such example. The antinomy between AA and merit is a product of conservative discourse, underpinned by sexism, racism and a latent homophobia. Neoconservatism goes hand-in-glove with neoliberalism, giving rise to a revival of the discourse of 'the family', which has encouraged a move away from the subjectivity of the feminised self in favour of the objectified (masculinist) position. The feminised Other thereby becomes ineffable once more, which is why we see a marked tendency by women appointees to 'mainstream' and neutralise the feminine.

Aliotta suggests that it might take several cohorts of women moving through law school before the impact is felt in the judiciary.[89] While I would like to believe in this progressivist thesis, I reiterate the scepticism articulated at the outset. Rather than acceptance of increasing numbers of women in authoritative positions, the incidence of backlash may invite a more pronounced imperative on the part of women judges to govern the self and render mute what might be construed as a different voice. Nevertheless, the philosophical devaluation of the feminine underlines the quicksand nature of difference theory. It can be employed strategically, as Kate Malleson suggests, but it is a double-edged sword.[90] Law is more comfortable with sameness, but there is a danger that a focus on difference may entrench essentialism.

Undoubtedly, there is increased scope for diversity and dissent as the numbers of women on courts increase, but the unevenness of social change is apparent with a move towards a more conservative political milieu. Inevitably, the contemporary political imperatives will exert an impact on judging, rendering the process both more and less feminised. Some women judges will continue to perceive themselves as honorary men while there will be some at the other end of the spectrum who will perceive themselves as feminist judges. In between, there will be a range of perspectives. What we want is an acknowledgement of the subjectivity

---

89   Jilda M. Aliotta, Gender and judging: Some thoughts toward a theory (Paper presented at Annual Meeting of Midwest Political Science Association, Chicago, 3–6 April 2003) 10.
90   Malleson (n. 73) 1.

of women judges and a movement away from the notion that women are a homogeneous and undifferentiated mass—an assumption with which male judges rarely must deal.

If we come back to Richter's comment about women being appointed because they do not have testicles, we see something of the deep atavistic fear at the prospect of women—understood in biologistic and abject, as well as unmeritorious, terms—not just constituting a critical mass on the bench, but also dominating it. The objectified projection of corporeality carries the seeds of invidiousness with it, which inhibits the construction of individual subjectivity. One or two 'women of merit' can be tolerated when they position themselves close to the masculinist norm and suppress all vestiges of the feminine. They do not then threaten the crucial line of demarcation between the norm and the Other. Indeed, their very presence as exceptions to the rule serves to uphold it. To this end, individual women trailblazers in authoritative positions are frequently reminded of their outsider status.[91]

A predominantly masculinised institution that has historically sustained male power and privilege is not going to change overnight into a humane and caring one by the appointment of a few women when the feminine continues to be associated with disorder in public-sphere decision-making. In any case, legal institutions are more likely to change women than the converse.[92] The constraining factors that delimit autonomy, including public scrutiny and the possibility of being overruled, are undoubtedly stronger for women judges than for men.[93] Most significantly, benchmark men, who remain the primary decision-makers, prefer to appoint women who espouse values most like their own.[94] That is, they favour those who are white, able-bodied, heterosexual, middle class and politically right of centre.

91 Claire L'Heureux-Dubé, 'Outsiders on the Bench: The Continuing Struggle for Equality' (2001) 16 *Wisconsin Women's Law Journal* 15.
92 For example, Thornton (n. 10).
93 Heather Elliott, 'The Difference Women Judges Make: Stare Decisis, Norms of Collegiality, and "Feminine Jurisprudence"—A Research Proposal' (2001) 16 *Wisconsin Women's Law Journal* 41.
94 Patricia Yancey Martin, John R. Reynolds & Shelley Keith, 'Gender Bias and Feminist Consciousness among Judges and Attorneys: A Standpoint Theory Analysis' (2002) 27(3) *Signs* 665, doi.org/10.1086/337941.

Gilligan's theory,[95] or at least the way it has been represented, in associating a different morality with women, triggered a major debate about women and judging. However, I agree with Kathy Davis that insufficient attention has been paid to the rhetoric at the heart of the Gilligan debate,[96] which helps in understanding its contradictions and its circularity. That is, no definitive resolution is possible with different-voice theory because the aim is to persuade us to accept a particular way of thinking rather than making a truth claim.

The concept of merit exercises a similarly rhetorical role, as illuminated by Maria Drakopoulou, who explains how a particular episteme, or conceptualisation of knowledge, emerges during a given historical period, which, rather than being seen as 'a progressive unfolding of truth', is 'an integral part of a genealogy of feminist legal knowledge'.[97] Through the *querelle des femmes* of early seventeenth-century England, Drakopoulou suggests that women were able to create a discursive space in which to contest contemporary essentialised representations of female nature. Invoking this idea of the episteme, we can see how the 'different voice' struck a chord with feminist legal scholars, for it enabled the negative views of female nature within the Western intellectual tradition to be discursively contested.

In the end, what constitutes merit is always going to be contested. The claim to produce an objective 'best person' is a rhetorical one designed to maintain the judiciary as a gendered regime. If we conceptualise merit as a technology of disciplinary power that takes its colouration from the prevailing political climate, we can take advantage of its performative character. It can be unsettled by interrogation and exposure of its ambiguities and contradictions, as I have sought to do, and then reimagined. However, closure can never be attained. While both legal and popular discourses suggest that the meaning of merit is fixed, such a claim is based on no more than the rhetoricity of power.

---

95   Gilligan (n. 20).
96   Kathy Davis, 'Toward a Feminist Rhetoric: The Gilligan Debate Revisited' (1992) 15(2) *Women's Studies International Forum* 219.
97   Maria Drakopoulou, 'Women's Resolutions of Lawes Reconsidered: Epistemic Shifts and the Emergence of the Feminist Legal Discourse' (2000) 11 *Law & Critique* 47.

Part VI: Diversifying Legal Education

12

Wondering What to Do about Legal Education

Introduction: A university legal education

The university teaching of law is fraught with difficulties because of the need to satisfy simultaneously the demands of legal practice and the traditional values associated with the university. Engineering and medicine are vocational courses taught within the university in which the focus is on technical excellence; the concern has not been with the development of a critical, independent scholarship. In contradistinction, law has become riddled with self-doubt as to the primary aim of legal education. On the one hand, law, like engineering and medicine, wants to produce first-rate law graduates for practice who are respected and admired by other practitioners for their technical expertise. On the other hand, law wants respect within the academy as a legitimate academic discipline; it does not wish to be regarded as merely preparing graduates for a trade.[1] Technical analysis, however artful, cannot be equated with rigorous scholarly inquiry, for it is likely to lack intellectual depth and to be contingent on a predetermined standpoint. William Twining captured the polarity most graphically in his inaugural lecture, entitled 'Pericles and the Plumber',[2] in which he contrasted the visionary leader and law reformer, the product of

---

1   David Derham, 'An Overview of Legal Education in Australia' in Rosemary Balmford (ed.), *Legal Education in Australia: Proceedings of National Conference* (Australian Law Council Foundation, 1978) 14.
2   William Twining, 'Pericles and the Plumber' (1967) 83(3) *Law Quarterly Review* 396.

a liberal education, with the competent technocrat, the product of a skills-oriented training course. These conflicting values within contemporary legal education are in danger of engendering paralysis or divisiveness.[3]

However, when I allude to the contemporaneity of the problem, this is misleading. In fact, there has been a tension between the university teaching of law and practical training since law was first taught at the University of Bologna in about 1100 CE. Bologna and the other great universities that subsequently taught law, such as Oxford and Cambridge, taught it as a liberal art.[4] Their focus was on Roman law, canon law and jurisprudence, not the rules of practice. Would-be practitioners, who did not necessarily avail themselves of or have access to a liberal arts education, went off to the Inns of Court in London or a comparable site of local practice to learn the lawyerly art. In other words, the bifurcation of the scholarly and the skills dimensions averted potential tension. This separation was the favoured model for the education of lawyers throughout the Western world for hundreds of years. While the legal profession had control over admission to practice, its concern with legal education tended to be unsystematic and ad hoc, as future lawyers who acquired lawyering skills through apprenticeship could be vulnerable to the vagaries of individual masters.

This paradigm of legal education was characteristic also of Australian legal education until recently.[5] The first law faculties did not appear until the latter half of the nineteenth century. The establishment of the University of Sydney Law School, for example, was preceded by extensive debate on the 'propriety of establishing professional courses in a university'.[6] Generally speaking, lectures were given in the evening by practitioners, which meant a vocationally oriented standpoint was favoured. It is only since World War II that we find law schools staffed by full-time,

---

3   The tensions arising from an attempt to strike a balance between the theoretical and the practical are apparent in John Goldring, 'Babies and Bathwater: Tradition or Progress in Legal Scholarship and Legal Education' (1987) 17(2) *University of Western Australia Law Review* 216. For a critique, see Valerie Kerruish, 'Barefoot in the Kitchen: A Response to Jack Goldring' (1988) 18(1) *University of Western Australia Law Review* 167.

4   Helene Wieruszowski, *The Medieval University: Masters, Students, Learning* (Van Nostrand, 1966).

5   For example, David Weisbrot, *Australian Lawyers* (Longman Cheshire, 1990) 121; David Barker, *A History of Australian Legal Education* (The Federation Press, 2017); Susan Bartie, *Free Hands and Minds: Pioneering Australian Legal Scholars* (Hart, 2019), doi.org/10.5040/9781509922642.

6   Linda Martin, 'From Apprenticeship to Law School: A Social History of Legal Education in Nineteenth Century New South Wales' (1986) 9 *University of New South Wales Law Journal* 111, 127.

professional academics, because of which there has been a concerted endeavour to adopt a more scholarly approach towards the role of law within the academy.

Commendable though the increased scholarly focus might be, it has in one sense exacerbated the preexisting tension because deference to the legal profession is not just a political reality but also an integral dimension of university legal education. This is because an Australian LLB degree is accepted as a qualification for admission to practice. Admitting authorities in each state (the Supreme Court or a statutorily constituted authority in which senior members of the legal profession predominate) specify subjects or areas of knowledge that must be included within a law curriculum for the approval or accreditation of an LLB. Although prior accreditation is not strictly essential and has no effect on the academic worth of an LLB degree, no Australian university has deliberately chosen to ignore the professional prescripts—that is, to offer the law degree as a coherent course of study without prior accreditation, or at least without setting in train accrediting or endorsement procedures. In the United States, there is a bifurcation between the basic law degree (the Juris Doctor, JD, replaced the LLB) and admission, as graduates must undertake state bar examinations to be admitted to practice once they have completed the JD. Australian universities, particularly the newer ones, are timid about taking such a radical step because their graduates could be regarded as disadvantaged in the job market. It nevertheless might be noted that even US law schools, particularly the more recently established and less prestigious institutions, are extremely deferential to the perceived needs of legal vocationalism, despite the separate bar exam. Doctrinal exegesis is generally considered the best way to serve professional needs.

However, all practitioners, particularly members of the judiciary, do not consider the production of efficient technocrats to be in the best interests of the profession.[7] The power and status of the legal profession and of law itself within the community nevertheless enable legal vocationalism to shape the content of the law curriculum, regardless of whether this is formally required or not. It is in this way that the conflation of training and education has occurred.

---

7   Chief Justice Anthony Mason, 'Inauguration of the Faculty of Law: University of Wollongong' (Unpublished paper, 1991); Justice Richard McGarvie, 'The function of a degree: Core subjects' (Law Council of Australia Legal Education Conference, 13–16 February 1991).

The construction of legal knowledge

It is a myth of liberal legalism that the law is neutral and autonomous, just as it is a myth that the judiciary can divorce itself from the societal web within which it is enmeshed so that it can somehow miraculously hand down value-free decisions. Law is the central mechanism within our society for transmitting and legitimating societal values and, in every age, law has been shaped by the characteristics of the civilisation of which it is part.[8] The cloak of neutrality assumed by law operates to disguise its essentially ideological role in preserving social relations. We see that the law, far from being neutral, upholds the capitalist imperative and the dominance of white, Anglo-Celtic maleness. The techniques of legal positivism render challenge to the partiality of law difficult. I wish to show briefly how legal epistemology is constructed so that intellectual reflexivity is discouraged; society would rather not have law's carapace of neutrality disturbed.

The 11 compulsory subjects or areas of knowledge specified by the admitting authorities, known as the 'Priestley 11',[9] are those that tend to privilege property and profits in accordance with the capitalist imperative; they include property and land law, contracts, torts, criminal law, company law, equity and trusts. Family law, employment and trade union law, consumer law, welfare law, poverty law, discrimination and human rights law—the areas of practice generally associated with the less powerful sectors of society—are unlikely to appear on the compulsory list. The Victorian Council of Legal Education opted for the inclusion of company law rather than family law in a review of its required areas of knowledge in the early 1990s—a decision that was accepted by the Priestley Committee in the national model soon afterwards. Family law was rejected on the ground that the 'building block' components of family law were contract, property and trusts.[10] The fact that families sustain our affective lives, the legal regulation of which is extremely problematic, was ignored. The reduction of the site of affectivity, reproduction and nurturance to legal abstractions would seem to be a singularly unsatisfactory basis for the

---

8   Myron P. Gilmore, *Humanists and Jurists: Six Studies in the Renaissance* (Belknap Press, 1963), doi.org/10.4159/harvard.9780674281738.

9   After Justice Priestley, who chaired the Law Admissions Consultative Committee of State and Territory Law Admitting Authorities in 1992.

10   Council of Legal Education Victoria, *Report of Academic Course Appraisal Committee on Legal Knowledge Required for Admission to Practise* (Council of Legal Education Victoria, 1990) 12.

resolution of problems pertaining to incest or custody, for example, either in the particular case or in respect of the formulation of policy. Family law, together with the other subjects mentioned that are less concerned with the maintenance of the societal status quo than the compulsory subjects, may be offered as electives. However, their human-centredness and their peripheral status vis-a-vis the corporate culture have led to these subjects being characterised by students as 'soft' options in contradistinction to the 'hard' compulsories—the doctrinal and technocratic focus of which effectively disguises and reifies their political significance. The hierarchisation of subjects within the curriculum reflects the ordering of the legal professional market, which, in turn, reflects the dominant values of our society. Thus, the practice of corporate law and its facilitation of big business are accorded a much higher status than family law, as we see in the disproportionately high fees and salaries associated with the former compared with the latter. This distinction between 'hard' and 'soft' areas of endeavour within law also reflects the way in which the activities of the modern state are structured and conceived along patriarchal gender lines.[11] Accordingly, the favoured ordering of subjects may leave little space for elective or 'soft' subjects within the legal curriculum. For example, before the acceptance of the Priestley 11, admission to the Queensland Bar required completion of a massive 19 compulsory subjects, including the 'hard' cognate subjects of commercial law, securities and taxation, as well as company law. There was space for only one elective. A clear message as to what was important was conveyed to students by the emphasis on those areas that sustain the economy.

Even if subjects such as commercial law, taxation and securities are not specified as compulsory subjects, either by the admitting authorities or by the university, their privileged status within the constellation of favoured values will elevate them to the status of de facto compulsories. Those students who are ambitious to succeed in corporate legal practice believe that by doing as many commercially oriented subjects as possible, they will be making themselves more attractive in the job market.[12] Even if such subjects are not offered, the phenomenon of market drift manifests itself by students and prospective employers putting pressure on law schools to offer

---

11   Anna Yeatman, *Bureaucrats, Technocrats, Femocrats: Essays on the Contemporary Australian State* (Allen & Unwin, 1990).

12   The desire is rational as the evidence indicates that lawyers spend most time on business law, property law and civil litigation. See, for example, Jill Ewing, *Career Patterns of Law Graduates* (Law Institute of Victoria, 1990).

more subjects of this kind at the expense of subjects with a more humanistic and caring orientation. The favoured ordering seeks to draw a clear line of demarcation between public and private life—a dichotomy that privileges public life and the world of the market over private life in the eyes of the law. This public/private dichotomy is central to classical liberalism.[13] It is accepted as a fundamental premise of legal education that law belongs to the public side of the dualism. The dichotomy entails acceptance of the idea that most facets of private life are cordoned off, so they are placed beyond the limits of the law, unless they can be conceptualised within the established terms of legality, as with the contract, property or trusts focus of family law to which I have adverted. Hence, the social reality of violence, which characterises the lives (and deaths) of thousands of women within families and with which existing legal form is unable to grapple, receives scant attention because it tends to be perceived as a private-sphere phenomenon that cannot easily be subsumed within one of the subject compartments. The existence of predetermined divisions that may have the imprimatur of the legislature endows the chosen subjects with a rationality that forecloses serious challenge. Similarly, any questioning of the existing form of law is also likely to receive short shrift. The sex specificity of the harm arising from rape, for example, cannot be accommodated within the traditional criminal law paradigm.

Liberal legalism is ill at ease with corporeality, affectivity and desire—all of which have been relegated to the private sphere and deemed irrelevant to legality. It is therefore no surprise to find that the public/private dualism also coincides with masculinity and femininity. For example, the compulsory subjects emit a very clear message that the business dealings in which men engage within civil society are infinitely more important and valuable than what women have traditionally done within the home—that is, bear children and nurture them, care for the sick and elderly and perform essential household tasks *in order that* men might be free to engage in public-sphere activities. The inequities arising from this sexual division of labour within the private sphere have not been tractable to law reform despite the centrality of liberalism's commitment to formal equality. Conversely, legality has been resistant to the more human-centred and caring values associated with the private realm. I am referring not just to the ways in which the application of fine-sounding rhetoric extolling formal equality may permit grossly disproportionate outcomes

---

13   Stanley Benn & Gerald Gaus (eds), *Public and Private in Social Life* (Croom Helm, 1983).

for the poor, for Indigenous people and for differentiated others, but also to the uncaring nature of adversarialism. A combative style of cross-examination designed to elicit 'truth' as a predicate to securing 'justice' is one that displays little respect for the individual witness. It is this uncaring approach that has been frequently emulated within the pedagogic methods of legal education.[14] Its aggressive style has been frequently questioned by women students, who find both the style of pedagogy and the substantive sexual closures to be frustrating and alienating.[15] They long for a more personalised and relevant approach that takes cognisance of affectivity and caring.

Even more insidious than the separate spheres approach within the construction of legal knowledge is the fact that the legal standards that run through the common law are masculinist ones.[16] Thus, the 'reasonable man'—that pillar of the community forever consigned to riding on the Clapham omnibus—represents not a neutral abstraction, but a skewed standard against which the foibles of both men and women must be measured. This gendered partiality of law has long operated to the disadvantage of women, particularly within tort law and criminal law, but it is occluded by the unquestioned assumptions of neutrality and universality. Although there are pockets of feminist legal scholarship within Australian law schools and legal studies departments,[17] the more common uncritical doctrinal pedagogy subtly operates to maintain the hegemony of masculinity within our society by its tacit acceptance of the proposition that any challenge to legal form lies beyond the reaches of the law.

Just as an unmasking of the abstract standards of the law reveals the gendered nature of justice, a deconstruction exercise also reveals its partiality towards the dominant white, Anglo-Celtic, middle-class values of our society. The prevailing political rhetoric of racial and ethnic diversity has not been transposed into law because the one-dimensionality

---

14   Robert Kerry Wilkins, '"The Person You're Supposed to Become": The Politics of the Law School Experience' (1987) 45(1) *University of Toronto Faculty of Law Review* 98.

15   For example, Jenny Morgan, 'The Socratic Method: Silencing Cooperation' (1989) 1(2) *Legal Education Review* 151; K.C. Worden, 'Overshooting the Target: A Feminist Deconstruction of Legal Education' (1985) 34(4) *American University Law Review* 1141.

16   Ngaire Naffine, *Law and the Sexes: Explorations in Feminist Jurisprudence* (Allen & Unwin, 1990).

17   Regina Graycar & Jenny Morgan, *The Hidden Gender of Law* (The Federation Press, 1990); Judith Grbich, 'Feminist Jurisprudence as Women's Studies in Law: Australian Dialogues' in Andre-Jean Arnaud & Elizabeth Kingdom (eds), *Women's Rights and the Rights of Man* (Aberdeen University Press, 1990).

of liberal legalism cannot accommodate alterity.[18] The point is clearly illustrated in the case of the tardiness of the common law to recognise Indigenous claims to land and personhood over the past two centuries of white domination in Australia.[19]

There is a concern that challenges to the Austinian idea of law as the command of a sovereign might threaten authority and the stability of our society. In addition, the idea of the autonomy of law is embedded within Anglo-Australian legal positivism. While some law schools do attempt to address law within its social context, the prevailing deference to doctrine threatens to blanch that context of meaning, thereby reinforcing the myth that the rules are acontextual and value-free. Hence, legal vocationalism, in emphasising the internal logic of doctrine and *stare decisis*, plays a significant role in perpetuating the status quo.

At this point, I would like to interpolate a comment about the socioeconomic composition of law students. The evidence reveals that law schools cater to an elite group of students who attended prestigious private secondary schools and whose relatively affluent parents tend to have professional or managerial backgrounds.[20] This class background establishes a homology between law students, practising lawyers and business and professional people. Thus, law students are more likely than not to evince a predilection for subjects closely identified with their class interests.[21] Furthermore, it is no surprise to find that when the economy declines, there is a concomitant

18   Margaret Thornton, *The Liberal Promise: Anti-Discrimination Legislation in Australia* (Oxford University Press, 1990); Margaret Thornton & Ann Genovese, 'On *The Liberal Promise*: A Conversation' (2015) 41(1) *Australian Feminist Law Journal* 3, doi.org/10.1080/13200968.2015.1045113.

19   The two key cases that changed the common law were determined after this lecture was delivered. They were *Mabo v Queensland (No 2)* (1992) 175 CLR 1 and *Wik Peoples v Queensland* (1996) 187 CLR 1.

20   For example, William Twining, 'Access to Legal Education and the Legal Profession: A Commonwealth Perspective' in Rajeev Dharan, Neil Kibble & William Twining (eds), *Access to Legal Education and the Profession* (Butterworths, 1989); Weisbrot (n. 5) 79.

21   The Law Society of New South Wales adverted to the way admission to law school 'has resulted in law students becoming an elitist group unrepresentative of the community at large'. Law Society of New South Wales, *Undergraduate legal education and practical legal training* (Issues Paper, 1991) 5. The concern of the Law Society was the expected lack of provision of services for suburban and country clients as students of privileged status tended to favour highly paid positions in city firms. La Trobe University proposed to break the nexus between law school admission and the high aggregate entry mark for law by not admitting students into the LLB until after completion of at least two years of university study. The hope was that this would contribute to greater socioeconomic diversity, although it was suggested that no change in admission based on previous academic performance was likely to have a significant impact on the socioeconomic composition of law students. Dennis Pearce, 'Admission to law school' (Conference Paper, Law Council of Australia Legal Education Conference, 13–16 February 1991).

decline in interest in social justice and the more humanistic subjects on the part of law students whose future in the social hierarchy may no longer be assured. Social justice concerns are likely to be conveniently dismissed as passé—mere aberrations of the past. The contraction of the social welfare state also serves to reify the significance of the traditional commercial and property values associated with law.

Among the public generally, there is increasing cynicism as to law's ability to effect social change. Legal practice has come to be too strongly associated with attempts to legitimate questionable business deals and the generation of private profit to be seen as an unqualified social good. A technical focus on doctrinalism within legal education serves to occlude the partiality of practice and to ensure the transmission of formal legal knowledge as though it were unproblematic. This unwillingness to critique the sociopolitical reality of law within the modern state has the effect of exacerbating student cynicism, for it conveys the ethical message that obfuscation and duplicity are acceptable within legal practice.

The elusiveness of sociolegal scholarship

In the process of unmasking the partiality of justice, the hope is that understanding will pave the way to securing a fairer system in accordance with the ideal—an understanding aided by the insights of other disciplines. However, interdisciplinary or social science approaches to law are inchoate, even after almost 100 years of attempts to alter the substantive pedagogy.

A debt is owed to the American legal Realists of the 1920s and 1930s for demonstrating the ways in which legal knowledge is politically constructed. Central to Realist methodology was the idea that progressive law reform must be grounded in social scientific research.[22] The Realists were a disparate group of legal scholars reacting against what they saw as the sterile formalism of the 'law as science' approach developed by Langdell at Harvard University between 1870 and 1895. If legal rules were not value-free, they argued, the rules could have no predictive value. The Realist movement therefore brought about the end of the idea of law as an exact science.[23]

22　Note, ''Round and 'Round the Bramble Bush: From Legal Realism to Critical Legal Scholarship' (1982) 95(7) *Harvard Law Review* 1669, 1671, doi.org/10.2307/1340723.
23　Robert Stevens, 'Two Cheers for 1870: The American Law School' in Donald Fleming and Bernard Bailyn (eds), *Law in American History* (Little Brown & Co., 1971) 480.

In the 1920s, a faculty group at Columbia Law School in New York set out to design a curriculum that integrated law and the social sciences in accordance with prevailing functionalist philosophy. Even though the issue was taken seriously, with an outside chairperson engaged in 1926 and two years expended on the process, the enterprise had virtually collapsed by 1930. Conflict emerged between faculty members as to the role of the social sciences and the purpose of legal education. The uncertain value of the meaning of social science perspectives for the study of law led to questions being asked about Columbia's efficiency in producing practising lawyers.[24] Legal vocationalism's centripetal pull on the academy may again be observed, together with the idea that there is always a polarity, albeit latent, between law and other disciplines within the context of legal education.

In the 1930s, Yale became the centre of the Realist movement, where a greater commitment to the social sciences could be discerned.[25] Scholars from disciplines other than law, including economists, historians, psychiatrists and statisticians, appeared on the faculty. However, like the Columbia experiment, the functionalist reorganisation of courses that integrated law and the social sciences collapsed soon afterwards. In this case, the catalyst was the outbreak of World War II. This particular social context would seem to offer an important clue in analysing the reasons for Realism's collapse, as suggested by Laura Kalman:

> [The legal Realists'] ethical relativism seemed to mean that no Nazi barbarity could be justly branded as evil, while their identification of law with the actions of government officials gave even the most offensive Nazi edict the sanction of true law.[26]

It would seem that the idea of the rule of law as the neutral repository of justice affords a source of comfort that is not limited to times of acute crisis, such as the rise of totalitarianism or the experience of a post-crisis period when there is a need for stability and the appearance of clarity.[27] In modern society, which is characterised by an increasing sense of alienation and anomie for the individual arising from the loss of community, the rapidity of technological change and the increasing

---

24 ibid., 475.
25 Laura Kalman, *Legal Realism at Yale 1927–1960* (University of North Carolina Press, 1986) 76.
26 ibid., 121.
27 Cf. Eleanor M. Fox, 'The Good Law School, the Good Curriculum, and the Mind and the Heart' (1989) 39(4) *Journal of Legal Education* 473.

intrusiveness of bureaucratisation, the assumed certainty of neutral legal rules has an appeal beyond the reach of the presumptively value-laden social sciences.

Indeed, we see that post-Realist attempts to integrate law and the social sciences have not been able to demolish or even to lower the barrier between what continue to be understood as discrete disciplines. A concerted attempt was made by Lasswell and McDougal at Yale in the 1940s to train law students to be better policymakers. They built on legal Realism to make legal education more constructive through what they termed 'policy science'.[28] Lasswell and McDougal recognised that many law graduates became not lawyers in private practice but high-level government policymakers. It was this public destination they sought to encourage by their distinctive approach. Ironically, they were then criticised for not teaching 'law'—a familiar charge brought against those who have sought to broaden the curriculum, as occurred at Columbia. Indeed, the work of Lasswell and McDougal prompted an investigation of the Yale Law School by Yale University in 1948.[29]

Nevertheless, legal Realism did have an impact on US legal education, which had a flow-on effect in other parts of the Western world. Although no comparable movement seems to have occurred contemporaneously in either the United Kingdom or Australia, the work of the late Julius Stone, whom I was privileged to have as a teacher and who, in the early 1980s, was described as 'the last of the living Realists', constitutes an important legacy.[30] Generally speaking, however, interdisciplinarity and the development of sociolegal perspectives on law seem to have been located more within the realm of rhetoric than reality in Australia. The rhetoric first manifested itself with the establishment of the University of New South Wales Law School in 1971. Nevertheless, it is Macquarie University Law School, which opened its doors soon after the University of NSW, that consistently espoused a critical and interdisciplinary approach to the study of law, which set it apart in the history of legal education in Australia.

---

28 Harold D. Lasswell & Myres S. McDougal, 'Legal Education and Public Policy: Professional Training in the Public Interest' (1943) 52(2) *Yale Law Journal* 203, doi.org/10.2307/792244; Myres S. McDougal, 'The Law School of the Future: From Legal Realism to Policy Science in the World Community' (1947) 56(8) *Yale Law Journal* 1345, doi.org/10.2307/793069.
29 Kalman (n. 25) 184.
30 Julius Stone, *The Province and Function of Law: Law as Logic, Justice and Social Control—A Study in Jurisprudence* (Maitland, 1950); Julius Stone, *Legal System and Lawyers' Reasonings* (Maitland, 1964); Julius Stone, *Social Dimensions of Law and Justice* (Maitland, 1966).

However, the concept of interdisciplinarity is vague, be it at Macquarie or elsewhere. It has been sufficient that law is viewed through some disciplinary lens other than its own. However, an interdisciplinary approach requires a legal academic to be an expert in more than one discipline—an unrealistic expectation, particularly as the typical legal academic is primarily a generalist producing generalist lawyers.[31] The danger, as Valerie Kerruish warns, is that interdisciplinarity may amount to no more than a vacuous form of eclecticism: 'Legal theory tends to pick up baubles. Simplified versions of ideas and arguments, advanced in other disciplines in which the legal theorist takes a dilettante's interest, adorn its pages.'[32]

Several former members of staff at Macquarie were strong proponents of a critical approach because of what they regarded as the incoherence and manipulability of legal doctrine, as well as the traditional Anglo-Australian atheoretical legal pedagogy. Critical legal scholarship embraces a variety of philosophical and theoretical traditions, including feminist scholarship.[33] The approach averredly transcends that of a simplistic interdisciplinary eclecticism in favour of a new legal theory, which some saw in civic republicanism.[34] Other Macquarie academics were influenced by the US critical legal studies movement, the intellectual descendant of legal Realism, and by the European critical legal studies movement.

The agenda of critical legal scholarship is more radical than that of Realism in that it sets out not simply to reform the law within its existing framework but also to critique every facet of the legal order, including its ideologies, underlying philosophies and presuppositions. It is hoped to effect a transformation of society, not via revolutionary means, but via an intellectual process of critique and theorising. As with the Realists, critical legal scholars have been trenchantly attacked on account of the subversive nature of their inquiries, prompting the inevitable flash of déjà vu.[35] In particular, they have been attacked for engendering cynicism and nihilism by devoting inadequate attention to the processes of social

---

31 Cf. Stevens (n. 23).
32 Kerruish (n. 3) 169.
33 Carrie Menkel-Meadow, 'Feminist Legal Theory, Critical Legal Studies and Legal Education or "The Fem-Crits Go to Law School"' (1988) 38(1) *Journal of Legal Education* 61.
34 For example, Andrew Fraser, *The Spirit of the Laws* (University of Toronto Press, 1990).
35 David Fraser, 'What a Long, Strange Trip It's Been: Deconstructing Law from Legal Realism to Critical Legal Studies' (1988–89) 5 *Australian Journal of Law and Society* 35.

and legal change.[36] It would appear, however, that it is the deconstructive critique, which compellingly demonstrates that there are no right answers, that is so threatening to the legal establishment. The comparable experience of criticism to which Macquarie has been subjected,[37] viewed against the backdrop of initiatives over the past century, throws into high relief the inordinate difficulty involved in the task of succeeding with a different curriculum or pedagogy. The late James Crawford, a former dean of Sydney University Law School, described legal education in Australia as being 'universally of the same shade of grey'.[38] That is, the similarity of requirements by state authorities together with a common perception of how the 'compleat lawyer' should be produced have contributed to a depressing uniformity that has stifled imaginative and creative approaches and indeed all approaches that are in any way markedly *different* from the norm. So pervasive is the dominance of doctrinalism that difference is invariably equated with inferiority.

Educating the 'compleat lawyer'

There nevertheless resides an unresolved ambiguity even within the legal profession's own terms that law schools produce the 'compleat lawyer', for who or what is this archetype? The subjects and areas of knowledge specified for admission to practice have barely changed in a century, although the nature of practice has altered significantly. The favoured model of legal education arises from the assumption that law graduates are still going to become practitioners in traditional private practice. This does not accord with the reality, as somewhat less than 50 per cent of law

---

36 Paul D. Carrington, 'Of Law and the River' (1984) 34(2) *Journal of Legal Education* 222; Hilary Charlesworth, 'Critical Legal Education' (1988–89) 5 *Australian Journal of Law and Society* 27; Peter W. Martin, '"Of Law and the River," and of Nihilism and Academic Freedom' (1985) 35(1) *Journal of Legal Education* 1.

37 The attack culminated in a recommendation by the Pearce Committee that the Law School be either phased out or reconstituted. Dennis Pearce, Enid Campbell & Don Harding, *Australian Law Schools: A Discipline Assessment for the Commonwealth Tertiary Education Commission* (AGPS, 1987). For critiques of the *Pearce Report*, see Wojciech Sadurski, 'Research in Australian Law Schools' (1987) 11(3) *Bulletin of the Australian Society of Legal Philosophy* 144; Alice Erh-Soon Tay, 'Aimless Perspectives' (1987) 11(3) *Bulletin of the Australian Society of Legal Philosophy* 154; Klaus A. Ziegert, 'What Law Professors Know and What They Think They Know about the Performance of Law Schools' (1987) 11(3) *Bulletin of the Australian Society of Legal Philosophy* 127; Charles Sampford & David Wood, '"Theoretical Dimensions" of Legal Education: A Response to the Pearce Report' (1988) 62(1) *Australian Law Journal* 32.

38 James Crawford, 'The future of the public law schools' (Conference Paper, Law Council of Australia Legal Education Conference, 13–16 February 1991).

graduates enter and remain in private practice. Even then, a generalist legal education can in no way equip a graduate for the high degree of specialisation that is a characteristic of the contemporary Australian mega-firm. The degree of professional specialisation[39] also reflects the rapidity of substantive legal change that is currently effected through legislation. Thus, an approach that concentrates on doctrinal exegesis may well be obsolete by the time the student has graduated.

The 50 per cent of law graduates who do not venture into or remain in private practice enter a variety of fields, although some wish to never have anything more to do with law after their arid experience of legal education. For those who do, the public service, media, academia, politics, accountancy, legal aid, business and corporate inhouse legal offices are some of the multifarious areas for which a legal education is meant to equip graduates but is more likely to 'project an artificial and misshapen representation of legal reality'.[40] The question then arises as to the appropriateness of the current LLB to satisfy heterogeneous needs—a qualification that is increasingly being regarded as a generalist degree in the same way as a liberal arts degree.[41] Somewhat ironically, this would seem to represent a reversion to the earlier history of the teaching of law within universities when there was no particular attempt to accommodate the perceived needs of practice.

The noted English jurist Sir William Blackstone, on his election to the Vinerian Chair at Oxford in 1758, delivered a lecture—extraordinary for its time—extolling the virtues of a liberal university education for lawyers and decrying the practice orientation of contemporary legal training:

> If practice be the whole he is taught, practice must also be the whole he will ever know: if he be uninstructed in the elements and first principles upon which the rule of practice is founded, the least variation from established precedents will totally distract and bewilder him: *ita lex scripta est* is the utmost his knowledge

39 For example, Ian Dunn, 'Accreditation of specialists: The Victorian experience' (Conference Paper, Law Council of Australia Legal Education Conference, 13–16 February 1991); Michael Chesterman, 'Specialisation: The Victorian experience' (Conference Paper, Law Council of Australia Legal Education Conference, 13–16 February 1991).
40 Harry W. Arthurs, Richard Weisman & Frederick H. Zemans, 'Canadian Lawyers: A Peculiar Professionalism' in Richard L. Abel & Philip S.C. Lewis (eds), *Lawyers in Society: The Common Law World* (University of California Press, 1988) 149.
41 Pearce (n. 21).

will arrive at; he must never aspire to form, and seldom expect to comprehend, any arguments drawn *a priori*, from the spirit of the laws and the natural foundations of justice.[42]

Standing back from the profession is not synonymous with turning one's back on it. On the contrary, a space between the academy and the profession must redound to the benefit of the profession. As Blackstone recognised, an exclusive focus on prevailing doctrine is likely to induce a kind of intellectual myopia because it is designed only to facilitate an understanding of the law as it is now; it is not designed to produce an understanding of the underlying principles of a completely different statutory schema that may come into effect in a decade or two, for example. A semblance of independence and autonomy will permit the development of an essential critical space in which to question fundamental assumptions underpinning the law. This space permits the study of jurisprudence and legal philosophy so that graduates acquire 'a panoramic view of the law as an entire discipline rather than as a series of discrete and unrelated pigeonholes'.[43] The legal profession's concern for skills—technical excellence, advocacy, drafting, court procedures and negotiation—necessarily renders marginal the theoretical dimension. It is the omission of this dimension from Australian legal education of which the Pearce Committee was most critical.[44]

The analogy between law and theology has been noted before.[45] That is, it is assumed that the overpowering rightness of the basic legal presuppositions cannot be questioned within a positivist paradigm any more than could the existence of God within the medieval Christian universe. The questioning process—essential to academic life—is absent from legal education for it is perceived to be destabilising from the point of view of a profession that seeks to reproduce the profession as *it is*.

---

42   Gareth Jones (ed.), *The Sovereignty of the Law: Selections from Blackstone's Commentaries on the Law of England* (Macmillan, 1973) 22.

43   Mason (n. 7).

44   Pearce et al. (n. 37); see also Charles Sampford & David Wood, 'The Place of Legal Theory in the Law School' (1987) 11(2) *Bulletin of the Australian Society of Legal Philosophy* 98; Sampford and Wood (n. 37); Charles Sampford & David Wood, 'Legal Theory and Legal Education: The Next Step' (1989) 1(1) *Legal Education Review* 107, doi.org/10.53300/001c.5978; Charles Sampford, 'Rethinking the Core Curriculum' (1989) 12(1) *Adelaide Law Review* 38.

45   For example, Otto Kahn-Freund, 'Reflections on Legal Education' (1966) 29(2) *Modern Law Review* 121, doi.org/10.1111/j.1468-2230.1966.tb01109.x.

The poverty of legal education is a phenomenon of the Western legal world, both in common law and in civil law countries.[46] The same characteristics of conservatism and formalism are found everywhere so that lawyers are reproduced in the traditional mould. In Germany, the final oral examinations have been described as a 'conformity test' to see whether the candidate's thought processes fit the appropriate pattern of 'perceiving, thinking and judging'.[47] Duncan Kennedy, a Harvard critical legal scholar, shows how the process of acculturation is developed through every aspect of legal education to conduce to an overall homogeneous self-image of what it is to be a lawyer within a hierarchical system.[48]

The subordination of the scholarly to the more pedestrian facets of the doctrinal has necessitated sacrificing what should be law's preeminent role in university education:

> University legal education could so easily be the paradigm of university education. Law is at the intersection of the ideal and the real, of metaphysics and magic, of the actual and the possible, of ideas and power, of fact and value, of is and ought, of the past and the future, of the individual and the social, of economics and politics. With the power to communicate so much, we choose instead to have the students learn law as if it had the intellectual, spiritual and moral content of knitting-patterns.[49]

Given the striking degree of uniformity characteristic of legal education and the extraordinary degree of institutional deference towards the professional mainstream, it would be naive to think that either the substance or the style of pedagogy could be instantaneously revolutionised. *Stare decisis* is not just a hermeneutic principle. By association, it has become an implicit quality of law. Change within the framework of legality can therefore be only ad hoc and marginal. As Eleanor Fox put it when discussing the experiment at Queen's College in the City University of New York: '[O]ne of the predictable ironies of life is that tradition ousts

---

46   For example, Abel & Lewis (n. 40); John Henry Schlegel, 'Review: Langdell's Legacy or, The Case of the Empty Envelope' (1984) 36(6) *Stanford Law Review* 1517, doi.org/10.2307/1228676.

47   Erhard Blankenburg & Ulrike Schultz, 'German Advocates: A Highly Regulated Profession' in Richard L. Abel & Philip S.C. Lewis (eds), *Lawyers in Society: The Civil Law World* (University of California Press, 1988) 131.

48   Duncan Kennedy, 'Legal Education as Training for Hierarchy' in David Kairys (ed.), *The Politics of Law: A Progressive Critique* (Pantheon, 1982). Cf. Richard L. Abel, *American Lawyers* (Oxford, 1989) 212 ff.

49   Philip Allott, 'Glum Law', *The Times Higher Education Supplement*, [London], 21 August 1987.

inspiration.'[50] Thus, a law school that developed a humane, interrelated curriculum was subjected to violent attack because the graduates did not know exactly what the bar examiners expected them to know; they knew much more.

However, as various illustrious legal educators have noted, learning the law as information is a waste of time,[51] an occupation for fools,[52] which can produce only 'plumbers' mates'.[53] Locating law within the dynamic landscape of the Western intellectual tradition necessitates cognisance of the historical forces and philosophical trends that have influenced it. Legal studies have benefited from the insights of the more recent disciplines of sociology, anthropology, political science and economics to enhance our understanding and to imagine what a utopian vision might look like— an ideal society in which justice, fairness and the nondiscrimination principle are normative. The study of law in an intellectual vacuum stifles the imaginative impulse.

Conclusion: Towards transdisciplinarity

Feminist scholars have sought to develop a transdisciplinary approach to the study of gender in society. Centuries of exclusion of women's experiences have rendered traditional disciplinary approaches inadequate. To overcome this history of exclusion and to develop new theoretical perspectives, women's studies has eschewed the favouring of one disciplinary approach over another. I would like to suggest, therefore, that the only way in which a truly integrated sociolegal approach towards the study of law and the legal order could develop would be by adopting this transcendent insight from feminist scholarship.

The Department of Legal Studies at La Trobe University has attempted to do this since its inception in 1972. That is, it rejected the methodology of legal doctrinalism in favour of a more expansive and creative critique of the legal order that was not contingent on a predetermined standpoint. However, legal studies subjects were included as part of a Bachelor of Arts program, not as part of a Bachelor of Laws. The greater challenge

---

50   Fox (n. 27).
51   Karl N. Llewellyn, *The Bramble Bush: On Our Law and its Study* (Oceana Publications, 1960) 93.
52   Kahn-Freund (n. 45) 133.
53   Twining (n. 2) 422.

is to develop a transdisciplinary approach to the study of law within the Bachelor of Laws program that is not distorted by doctrinalism and a naive belief in 'right' answers. Without a thoroughly integrated approach between law, history, philosophy and the social sciences, the historical experiences of failure in North America are likely to be repeated. Effort therefore needs to be expended on developing coherence and a clear sense of direction within law curricula: 'Heroic, but random efforts to integrate "law" and "the other social sciences" fail through lack of clarity about what is being integrated, and how, and for what purposes.'[54]

I recognise that it is difficult to argue against vocationalism in an age committed to efficiency, productivity and economic rationality. The Pearce Committee's report arose because of the attempt by the state to harness the higher education sector in the 'national interest'.[55] In addition, there is a demand for legal education places in Australia that exceeds that of other disciplines. The resourcing of legal education is assessed at the base rate, predicated on a questionable lecture model in which large groups of students passively imbibe predigested knowledge. Australian universities have responded with alacrity to meet the demand for law places, attracted by the prestige of a professional degree and its low cost to teach. With deference accorded the prescripts of the state, little thought has been directed to the question of the nature or quality of the new law programs. Experimentation in the pursuit of knowledge is not valued in the modern age: 'According to Lyotard's musings on post-modernity the social system can only tolerate experimentation to the extent that it enhances its performativity, that is, its efficiency, its ability to produce a result.'[56]

Scholarship that cannot be compressed within the contemporary value matrix is therefore likely to receive short shrift.

Nevertheless, La Trobe took a step towards the development of a genuine sociolegal approach to the study of law by locating the LLB within the School of Social Sciences. The conventional model, which locates law

---

54   Lasswell & McDougal (n. 28) 204.
55   Gill H. Boehringer, 'Resisting Pearce: The Significance of the Review of Macquarie Law School—The Role of Macquarie's Progressives' (1988–89) 5 *Australian Journal of Law and Society* 93; Ian Duncanson, 'Legal Education, Social Justice and the Study of Legality' (1990) 10(1) *University of Tasmania Law Review* 16.
56   Costas Douzinas, Shaun McVeigh & Ronnie Warrington, 'Postlegality: After Education in the Law' (1990) 1 *Law and Critique* 81, 95, doi.org/10.1007/bf02439607.

in a separate school or faculty, symbolically reinforces the idea of the autonomy of law, artificially cordoned off from any consideration of the social forces that inform it. This isolationist policy was an undeniable factor in the failure of sociolegal scholarship in the past.

The second important development at La Trobe was the preponderance of students who would receive joint degrees within the same school— that is, the School of Social Sciences. While joint degree programs are now the norm within Australian law schools, the law degree is not integrated with a degree in arts, economics or science, even if undertaken concurrently rather than sequentially. Any benefits accruing from the intended interdisciplinary approach are entirely accidental. The bifurcation underscores the secondary nature of 'non-law' knowledge and enhances the focus on doctrinalism. If history, philosophy and politics are studied elsewhere, it is averred, legal academics do not need to trouble their heads with the insights of these disciplines for law. The context of law is thereby quickly shed. However, there is also the very real problem of 'legal scholar as dilettante' to which I have adverted. At La Trobe, it was hoped to obviate this problem by organising teaching teams, as far as practicable, on a multidisciplinary basis.[57] It was envisaged that historians, philosophers, sociologists and economists would participate in the teaching of the traditional areas of knowledge required for admission to practice, in addition to teaching a range of options with creative and critical perspectives on law and the legal order within the Bachelor of Arts, the Bachelor of Legal Studies as well as the Bachelor of Laws programs.

Hence, the hope was that the social context would not be relegated to the periphery or rendered irrelevant and that a variety of disciplinary and philosophical standpoints would enrich the educational experience for law students in a trailblazing way within the contours of Australian legal education. From these new roots would spring changed meanings of legal knowledge. It was also hoped that bringing imaginative transdisciplinary critiques and theoretical insights to bear on legal practice would enable the new incarnation of Portia as enlightened legal practitioner, judge, academic, lawmaker, law reformer and citizen, to implement her vision of a more diverse and more caring jurisprudential community appropriate for the twenty-first century.

---

57   Cf. Peter d'Errico, Stephen Arons & Janet Rifkin, 'Humanistic Legal Studies at the University of Massachusetts at Amherst' (1976) 28(1) *Journal of Legal Education* 18.

13

Why the Gender and Colour of Law Remain the Same

Marcuse before Habermas, and Weber before Marcuse, identified as the most ominous feature of a fully 'disenchanted age' not an immaculate nihilism but a form of nihilism in which 'technical reason' (Marcuse), 'means-end rationality' (Habermas), or 'instrumental rationality' (Weber) becomes the dominant and unchallengeable discourse framing and ultimately suffusing all social practices.[1]

Introduction: The technocentric imperative

I use the term 'technocentrism' to capture the way in which rules rationality exercises a centripetal pull within legality to disqualify other forms of knowledge. Regarding legal education, I seek to show how technical legal rules, with their appearance of neutrality and objectivity, effectively mask the partiality and the power of law, despite contemporary moves to alter law's masculinist and racialised partiality. Far from being neutral, the technical is in fact highly political, as Herbert Marcuse argued.[2] Although dominant interests are not temporally fixed, law continues to favour the interests of 'benchmark men'—that is, those who are white, Anglo-Celtic, heterosexual, able-bodied and middle class, and who support a mainstream

---

1   Wendy Brown, *States of Injury: Power and Freedom in Late Modernity* (Princeton University Press, 1995) 33.
2   Herbert Marcuse, *One-Dimensional Man: Studies in the Ideology of Advanced Industrial Society* (Beacon, 1964) xvi, 168.

religion and a right-of-centre politics. Benchmark masculinity asserts its normativity by reproducing itself through legal and other discourses as the invariable standard against which 'otherness' is measured.

Law can be imagined as a transparency that is placed over prevailing dominant interests so that it absorbs and reflects those interests. The movement at the edges of the transparency provides some scope for change in the configuration of dominant interests, but not very much. Michel Foucault's circulatory theory of power[3] acknowledges the discursive effects of the challenges that occur at the edges, or in the 'capillaries'. Foucault shows how the traditional notion of sovereign, or juridical, power is supported by and interwoven with mechanisms of disciplinary power because they can disguise and deflect attention from the formal sites of authority and their exercise of power. I show how dominant interests are served by sites and techniques within both legal education and legal practice, together with the way in which they are imbricated with each other. I also suggest that the fragmented nature of contemporary corporatism, or the 'new economy',[4] has required recourse to more technocratic modes of control, leaving even less space for alterity.

The changes that occurred in the wake of the restructuring of the global economy have included the dismantling of the Keynesian welfare state—a neoliberal phenomenon that has occurred in many parts of the world.[5] Neoconservatism, deregulation and the privatisation of public enterprises are notable facets of the restructuring that industrial economies have confronted. Massive restructuring has been facilitated through a proliferation of rational mechanisms to satisfy the 'means–end calculus'.[6]

The technocratic approach to law has been supported by modernist legal theory, particularly legal positivism, which pays scant attention to power within the shifts and turns of national and global socioeconomic movements. While the modernist jurisprudential vision has averredly been ruptured by dynamic new discourses, including feminist legal

---

3   Michel Foucault, *Power/Knowledge: Selected Interviews and Other Writings, 1972–1977*, edited & translated by Colin Gordon (Harvester Wheatsheaf, 1980) 98.

4   Harry W. Arthurs & Robert Kreklewich, 'Law, Legal Institutions, and the Legal Profession in the New Economy' (1996) 34 *Osgoode Hall Law Journal* 1.

5   For example, ibid., 8; Pierre Guislan, *The Privatization Challenge: A Strategic, Legal and Institutional Analysis of International Experience* (The World Bank, 1997); Philip Morgan (ed.), *Privatization and the Welfare State: Implications for Consumers and the Workforce* (Dartmouth, 1995); Jane Kelsey, *Rolling Back the State: Privatization of Power in Aotearoa/New Zealand* (Bridget Williams, 1993).

6   Max Weber, *Economy and Society: An Outline of Interpretive Sociology. Volume 2*, edited by Guenter Roth & Claus Wittich, translated by E. Fischoff (University of California Press, 1978) 1002.

theory, legal positivism continues to be central to legal education within law schools, because it is preeminently concerned with law as a system of rules—a notion central to 'learning the law'. Legal positivism assumes that law is a self-referential system that can produce 'right' answers. While there are many shades of positivism, its characteristics, as summarised by H.L.A. Hart, one of its most influential exponents, include the ideas that law is autonomous and that there are discernible boundaries between law and morality, law and politics, and law and other disciplines.[7] While legal positivism legitimates economic rationality in the interests of capitalism, it fails to capture the pragmatic, the instrumental, the institutional and the bureaucratic elements that shape the law in action. Technocentrism goes further in, first, emphasising the way that *techné* (technical knowledge) is privileged perennially over 'non-legal' forms of knowledge. Second, the word *techné* makes clear that law cannot lay claim to a scientific status, but is a human artefact, and that legal truths are created, crafted and produced. Third, *techné* also conveys something of the legal bias towards humanism and intellectualism.[8] Fourth, *techné* captures the idea of the lawyer as the knower or all-knowing technocrat who possesses privileged knowledge and who exercises power because of that knowledge. Indeed, as agents of legality, lawyers are the '*par excellence* institutional inventors'[9] who spend their time devising ways to circumvent regulation for corporate clients. Accordingly, lawyers are also primary producers of legal knowledge, although jurisprudence—feminist and postmodern, as well as traditional—pays more attention to adjudication as the primary source of legal knowledge.[10] The adjudicative bias is grounded in the law school case method, which privileges appellate decisions in which detailed written reasons are produced. The high level of abstraction associated with superior appellate courts facilitates a propositional approach, relegating the merits and particularity of cases to the background. The pedagogical practice, which focuses primarily on formal rules, creates a law school environment in which the technocratic is normalised, thereby facilitating the connection between the means and the end.

---

7   H.L.A. Hart, *The Concept of Law* (Clarendon, 1994) 302. See also Charles J.G. Sampford, *The Disorder of Law: A Critique of Legal Theory* (Basil Blackwell, 1989) 24 ff.

8   Cf. David O. Friedrichs, 'Narrative Jurisprudence and Other Heresies: Legal Education at the Margins' (1990) 40 *Journal of Legal Education* 3, 14.

9   Maureen Cain, 'The Symbol Traders' in Maureen Cain & Christine B. Harrington (eds), *Lawyers in a Postmodern World: Translation and Transgression* (New York University Press, 1994) 15, 31.

10   Cf. Robert W. Gordon & William S. Simon, 'The Redemption of Professionalism?' in Robert L. Nelson, David M. Trubek & Rayman L. Solomon (eds), *Lawyers' Ideals/Lawyers' Practices: Transformations in the American Legal Profession* (Cornell University Press, 1992) 230, 238.

The specification of subjects and areas of law by admitting authorities encourages the teaching of law as unproblematic categories of finite technical knowledge. The reduction of social problems to predetermined legal formulae permits what then passes for bona fide *legal* knowledge to be cordoned off from the affective, the corporeal and the intuitive. The substance of the 'core' legal curriculum is remarkably similar within Western liberal democratic countries, not only within common law jurisdictions,[11] but also within civil law jurisdictions.[12] Indeed, the 'core' curriculum has witnessed comparatively few major changes of substance over the past half-century, apart from the tendency to make more similarly oriented subjects compulsory. This is the phenomenon of the 'creeping core' to which William Twining has referred in the English context.[13] Even within new law schools, curricular consistency is a notable characteristic. The subjects that are specified as essential prerequisites for admission to legal practice pertain to private property, individual rights and profits, thereby reflecting the dominant capitalist imperatives, even though modes of capital accumulation may have altered. Accordingly, it is no surprise to find that the foundational subjects include contract, property, torts and company law—subjects that tend to be preoccupied with technical rules and are known as 'hard' law, thereby also signifying their phallocentric orientation. Such subjects facilitate the free market, corporatism and private property ownership, and are invariably treated as compulsory within the law curriculum—as prerequisites for the award of a law degree and/or for admission to the practice of law.

Commercially oriented subjects may be contrasted with subjects that involve the intimate aspects of people's lives, which are not easily commodified. This cluster of subjects includes family law, human rights and discrimination law—the averredly 'soft' or feminised subjects that are primarily concerned with women and children, as well as racialised, ethnicised and sexualised Others, rather than the benchmark man of law. Because of the unruliness of the social and its resistance to being compressed within legal form, it could be suggested that subjects involving the affective and the conventionally private are not 'real' law,

11   Richard L. Abel & Philip S.C. Lewis (eds), *Lawyers in Society: The Common Law World. Volume 1* (University of California Press, 1988).
12   Richard L. Abel & Philip S.C. Lewis (eds), *Lawyers in Society: The Civil Law World. Volume 2* (University of California Press, 1988).
13   William L. Twining, *Blackstone's Tower: The English Law School* (Stevens & Sons/Sweet & Maxwell, 1994) 163.

so that teachers of 'soft' subjects sometimes set out to harden them by teaching them primarily as propositional and rules-based. In such a case, the centripetal pull of rules rationality may be compared with the way in which some women and Others are attracted to masculinised subject positions to secure approval and legitimacy.

In an endeavour to discourage reflexivity, technocentrism purports to slough off the theoretical, the critical and the contextual but, as Ian Duncanson reminds us, law always *does* have a context.[14] The 1970s imperative that law be taught 'in context' instantiates the myth that technocratic law is taught as though it were neutral and acontextual—as though it were engaged in the pursuit of objective justice, rather than primarily facilitating the interests of wealthy corporations and benchmark men. Perhaps unsurprisingly, liberal legalism prefers any conscious advertence to context to be anodyne. Critical perspectives, with their subversive potential, and 'soft' subjects, with their partial and humanistic orientation, are likely to be treated as optional or peripheral to the project of creating the 'compleat lawyer'.

The seeming neutrality and objectivity of legal doctrinalism effectively legitimate curricular cleavages between the compulsory contract/tort/crime/commercial clustering and the optional family/human rights/theoretical clustering so that such cleavages are assumed to be rational. The divisions mirror the separation between public and private spheres of life that are assumed to be rational and 'natural' and are legitimised by law. In fact, the public/private dichotomy is a convenient and malleable mechanism that has been constituted so that it shifts according to the political demands of the moment. Nevertheless, this separation operates to maintain iterations of masculinity and femininity, and of heterosexuality and homosexuality. If law wishes to avert its eyes from nuptial contracts, for example, it will characterise them as private, because they lack the technical requirements of intent and consideration.[15] In contrast, a court will have no problem with a contract between strangers engaging in a profitmaking transaction; it is unlikely even to expend time

---

14 Ian Duncanson, 'The Ends of Legal Studies' (1997) 3 *Web Journal of Current Legal Issues* 1, available from: www.bailii.org/uk/other/journals/WebJCLI/1997/issue3/duncan3.html.
15 For example, *Balfour v Balfour* [1919] 2 KB 571. For critique, see Michael Freeman, 'Contracting in the Haven: Balfour v Balfour Revisited' in Roger Halson (ed.), *Exploring the Boundaries of Contract* (Dartmouth, 1996); Margaret Thornton, 'Intention to Contract: Public Act or Private Sentiment' in Ngaire Naffine, Rosemary Owens & John Williams (eds), *Intention in Law and Philosophy* (Ashgate, 2001).

LAW AND THE QUEST FOR GENDER EQUALITY

on the threshold question of whether there was a contract or not. Separate spheres are thereby constructed through law, and the activities of the market are legitimised and privileged over those characterised as private qua domestic, such as housework and childcare—activities performed for love, not money. However, a feminist preoccupation with the gendered symbiosis between private and public life-worlds can deflect attention from the dramatic changes being effected within the public sphere qua government regarding the deregulation and privatisation of education and welfare, and other heretofore 'public' goods.

For all intents and purposes, a merger has been effected between so-called private enterprise and the public sphere of government.[16] This is the 'new corporatism' that emerged in political theory in the 1970s to describe the distinctive organisation of economic and political interests within the capitalist state.[17] Deregulation and privatisation, together with the declining role of unions, have significantly altered the corporatist character of the state. Nevertheless, the idea that there is a clear boundary between public and private life continues to be pervasive. Through the play on difference, or what Jacques Derrida refers to as *différance*,[18] law is able to 'oil the wheels of capitalism' in a way that appears unproblematic and even natural.[19] Furthermore, the consistent devaluation of the private qua domestic and affective side of life continues to have significant ramifications for the construction of masculinity and femininity, and of heterosexuality and homosexuality, despite the ongoing efforts of feminist and queer legal scholars to remove the cloak enshrouding the private. Indeed, corporatism is predicated on and sustained by law's constitution and retention of separate spheres, cleverly concealed beneath a technocratic carapace. The accord between the public sphere qua government, civil society and the economy is possible only with the unacknowledged contributions of women in the private qua domestic sphere. The lopsided efforts of legislation to effect equal opportunity in the public sphere perpetuate this inequity no less than other, ostensibly neutral, regimes.

---

16 For example, Charles A. Reich, *Opposing the System* (Crown, 1995) 169.
17 Peter J. Williamson, *Corporatism in Perspective: An Introductory Guide to Corporatist Theory* (Sage, 1989); Alan Cawson, *Corporatism and Political Theory* (Blackwell, 1986).
18 Peggy Kamuf (ed.), *A Derrida Reader: Between the Blinds* (Columbia University Press, 1991) 63.
19 For a thoroughgoing critique of the way capitalist economic society is presented as 'natural', see Jürgen Habermas, *Legitimation Crisis*, translated by Thomas McCarthy (Beacon, 1975).

Techné in the law school

To ensure retention of the privileged status of *techné*, there is an expectation of docility from law students so they might be transformed through the experience of legal education. The docile student is one who is teachable (from the Latin *docere*: 'to teach'). Foucault defines the docile body as one that may be 'subjected, used, transformed and improved'.[20] In the context of legal education, the process of transformation is likely to be facilitated with the law student's consent; students cannot be said to be oppressed in the sense that Paulo Freire speaks of pedagogical oppression.[21] Indeed, so great is their desire to conform that within a few weeks of commencing law school, law students sound like fully fledged lawyers with a proficient command of the grammar of law. The lure of professionalism is a powerful factor in effecting the transformative project. Furthermore, most law students in traditional law schools are generally not social outsiders. Private school background and family connections mean there is already an acceptance of the correlation between white ruling class, masculinity and legality[22]—a homology that facilitates acceptance of corporatism.

While the image of 'the lawyer' has been constructed in terms of benchmark man, the desire on the part of some law students from diverse class and cultural backgrounds to be assimilated as soon as possible cannot be discounted. To some extent, they act as the agents of their own transformation. They go to law school because they wish to make a successful career in law and to erase any memory of perceived disadvantage as quickly as possible. They evince an ever-present desire to move close to the norm—that is, the privileged position occupied by benchmark man, to merge with him and to become indistinguishable from him. Some students are aided and abetted in the normalising project by upwardly mobile parents who may have experienced disadvantage and lack of opportunity themselves. Law school rankings[23] can induce anxiety in students in lesser-ranked schools, which they seek to overcome by

---

20   Michel Foucault, *Discipline and Punish: The Birth of the Prison*, translated by Alan Sheridan (Vintage, 1995) 136.

21   Paulo Freire, *Pedagogy of the Oppressed: 30th Anniversary Edition* (Continuum Press, 2005) 33.

22   Alex Ziegert, 'Social Structure, Educational Attainment and Admission to Law School' (1992) 3(2) *Legal Education Review* 155, doi.org/10.53300/001c.5996.

23   For example, Times Higher Education, *World University Rankings* (2021), available from: www.timeshighereducation.com/world-university-rankings; *QS World University Rankings 2022*, available from: www.topuniversities.com/university-rankings/world-university-rankings/2022.

establishing their command of *techné* as early as possible. The centripetal pull of *techné* thereby operates to slough off diversity and radicalism in legal education.

Not all students accept the docile subject position expected of them and they may find themselves responding with anger, anxiety or dismay at what they perceive to be the intellectually stultifying and personally transformative experience of legal education.[24] Chris Goodrich has written insightfully about his year as a student at Yale Law School, undertaking a special master's degree for journalists. He enrolled for a collection of subjects typical of first-year law students, including constitutional law, torts, contract and civil procedure. Goodrich describes his fear of being seduced by legal training, 'which doesn't create selfish, aggressive people—but it does provide the intellectual equipment with which recipients can justify and give force to beliefs and actions most people would wholeheartedly condemn'.[25] He proceeds to describe the subtle process in which the law school engaged to 'steal his soul'. Being taught to 'think like a lawyer' involved inducing a massive sense of insecurity in the first instance:

> [I]t seemed impossible for anyone to go through a single day of law school without sensing that he or she didn't measure up— that the ability to think like a lawyer was demonstrably different, and better, than the ability to think as one once did, like an ordinary person.

This sense of insecurity may be magnified on the part of those women and racialised Others who endeavour to resist the mesmerising effects of the norm.[26]

What does it mean to 'think like a lawyer'? Is it qualitatively different from thinking like any intelligent human? The answer is probably not. The law student learns the principles of legal reasoning and legal method: how to identify material facts, how to characterise the issues for resolution, how to select an authoritative precedent to be applied to the instant case, how to determine the *ratio decidendi* of a case and how to interpret

24 Cf. Rick Abel, *American Lawyers* (Oxford University Press, 1989) 213.
25 Chris Goodrich, *Anarchy and Elegance: Confessions of a Journalist at Yale Law School* (Little, Brown, 1991) 4.
26 Catherine Weiss & Louise Melling, 'The Legal Education of Twenty Women' (1988) 40(5) *Stanford Law Review* 1299, 1314, doi.org/10.2307/1228867.

a statute,[27] as well as deference to hierarchy.[28] The successful acculturation of the law student into accepting automatically legal form facilitates the process of rendering substantive justice incidental. The outcome of a dispute is then treated as analogous to the outcome of a sporting contest; it does not matter who wins, provided the rules are fair. Technocratic law cloaks the partiality of justice to disguise its masculinist, classist, racist, heterosexual and corporatist predilections. As Goodrich observes, the legal system's rules about justice may ensure that justice is not done.[29] There is, therefore, a political dimension to learning to think like a lawyer; the process is directed not only to improving the quality, precision and clarity of thinking,[30] but also to the rationalisation of outcomes. It is this unstated political dimension that constitutes the distinctive element of 'thinking like a lawyer'.

The political underpinnings of law are further occluded by a 'submersion or denial of self' within legal discourse.[31] The distance between the legal knower—the creator of knowledge—and the knowledge itself is collapsed, so that the knowledge appears to be objective. A familiar technique in legal writing—and one that students are encouraged to emulate—is the use of the third person. The norm of depersonalisation is breaking down in law review articles, where the subjective voice has acquired a semblance of legitimacy because of the impact of feminism and postmodernism, and the correlative denunciation of essentialism. Depersonalisation, however, remains the norm in judicial discourse. The technique operates to deny the 'leeways of choice' encountered at every step of the adjudicative process.[32] The positivist myth that the judge lacks agency and is no more than a conduit through which objective knowledge is received has contributed to the erasure of the subjectivity of law.

The form of law is a key technocratic device for delimiting the ambit of law that quickly takes on an appearance of normalcy and naturalness to the neophyte law student. I have noted the limits of law as a remedial

---

27 Mary Jane Mossman, 'Feminism and Legal Method: The Difference It Makes' (1986) 3 *Australian Journal of Law and Society* 30.
28 Duncan Kennedy, 'Legal Education as Training for Hierarchy' in David Kairys (ed.), *The Politics of Law: A Progressive Critique* (Pantheon, 1982) 40.
29 Goodrich (n. 25) 260.
30 John O. Mudd, 'Thinking Critically about "Thinking Like a Lawyer"' (1983) 33 *Journal of Legal Education* 704.
31 Friedrichs (n. 8) 12.
32 Julius Stone, *Legal Systems and Lawyers' Reasonings* (Stanford University Press, 1964).

tool in addressing complaints of systemic discrimination.[33] The sexism, racism and homophobia giving rise to discriminatory acts are buried deep within the social fabric, but a formal complaint requires a complainant to identify a particular wrongdoer and to prove a causative nexus between the wrongdoer and the impugned conduct. The social harms of sexism, racism and homophobia are not legal harms unless they conform to the procedural requirements of a formal complaint of discrimination. The probative burden that the individual complainant must bear is onerous, particularly in the case of employment complaints where the employer invariably adduces a rational explanation for the impugned conduct. The disparity in power and resources between an individual complainant and a respondent make it almost impossible for, say, an Indigenous woman to succeed in *proving* employment discrimination according to the requisite standard against, say, a mining corporation. To endure a hearing and then fail to satisfy the burden according to legal form may legitimise racism and sexism because the discriminator has been exonerated by a seemingly fair and neutral process in which it is assumed that complainant and respondent are engaged in a contest on a 'level playing field' because both 'sides' are legally represented. This is the myth of equality before the law. The form of law privileges corporatism, as well as masculinity and racism, for respondents in sex and race discrimination suits are invariably powerful institutional players with significant resources. Arthurs and Kreklewich suggest that the privileging of corporatism in legal disputes is likely to become more overt with the propulsion towards deregulation and privatisation.[34]

When we focus a little more closely on approaches to teaching in a professional program, technocentrism permits the development of what Derber calls 'ideological desensitisation'.[35] The focus on technical knowledge enables professional workers to deny the real significance of the work in which they are engaged. This concept is particularly pertinent to law as it facilitates an understanding of the way in which legal

---

33   Margaret Thornton, *The Liberal Promise: Anti-Discrimination Legislation in Australia* (Oxford University Press, 1990); Margaret Thornton & Ann Genovese, 'On *The Liberal Promise*: A Conversation' (2015) 41(1) *Australian Feminist Law Journal* 3, doi.org/10.1080/13200968.2015.1045113. See also Dominique Allen, 'A Reflection on *The Liberal Promise* on its 30th Birthday' (2020) 45(4) *Alternative Law Journal* 300, doi.org/10.1177/1037969x20946906.

34   Arthurs & Kreklewich (n. 4) 27.

35   Charles Derber, 'Managing Professionals: Ideological Proletarianisation and Mental Labour' in Charles Derber (ed.), *Professionals as Workers: Mental Labour in Advanced Capitalism* (G.K. Hall, 1982) 167, 180.

practitioners can absolve themselves of ethical responsibility when serving dubious interests, such as defending the racist and sexist behaviour of a mining company towards an Indigenous woman. The predominant ethical interest is loyalty to one's client—a principle upheld by the adversarialism of the common law and the 'cab rank' rule. Broader issues of ethical practice and justice are likely to be given short shrift and treated as subordinate to the mastery of rules. The technocentric imperative is underpinned by the fact that professional ethics are rarely accorded even the status of an optional subject within the law curriculum, although admitting authorities may require a few hours of lectures pertaining to the rules of professional conduct in terms of 'unreflective conformity'.[36] The 'good' lawyer is one who sets out to win the case for the client, regardless of the social ramifications.

The ethical dilemmas are complicated by the fickleness of corporate clients in the postmodern world, for they no longer feel obliged to remain loyal to a particular law firm but are likely to shop around for one prepared to do their bidding at the best price.[37] Hence, the corporate client can exert pressure on maverick law firms to refashion professional ethics—always located in a shadowy terrain behind *techné*. Law and the facilitation of corporatism thereby become imbricated with one another so that what might elsewhere pass for unethical behaviour becomes normalised. Students are quickly acculturated into accepting this mode of thought. Derber reports that studies involving first-year students in a wide range of professions, including law, reveal a rapid shift from a predominantly moral orientation to a technocratic one.[38] The phenomenon of law students demanding to know 'the law'—understood in applied terms—and resisting theoretical and critical material is a familiar one to teachers of first-year law students, particularly those teaching non-technocratic courses, such as history and philosophy of law or introductory jurisprudence. The metamorphosis of the neophyte law student concerned with social justice into graduate obsessed with status and money has joined the stock figures that populate anti-lawyer jokes.[39]

36　Gordon & Simon (n. 10) 236.
37　See Elizabeth Nosworthy, 'Ethics and Large Law Firms' in Stephen Parker & Charles Sampford (eds), *Legal Ethics and Legal Practice: Contemporary Issues* (Clarendon, 1995) 57, doi.org/10.1093/acprof:oso/9780198259459.003.0004. See also Gordon & Simon (n. 10) 257.
38　Derber (n. 35) 182.
39　For example, The Rodent, *Explaining the Inexplicable: The Rodent's Guide to Lawyers* (Pocket Books, 1995).

The pedagogical methods of law school assist in embedding the technocratic approach and the moral neutering of the law student.[40] The so-called Socratic method—widely attacked because of the scarifying experiences to which students have been subjected[41]—has had a narrowing effect because law teachers, unlike Socrates himself, all too often assume that there *is* a right answer. Even more constraining is the lecture method. Financial pressure on public universities has caused a reversion to large lectures where the interchange between lecturer and student is minimal and the student passively imbibes predigested knowledge. The pressure to teach more students means that research essays, which provide at least a modicum of scope for imagination and critique, are likely to be discouraged, because they take longer to assess than examination scripts. Economic rationality aids in reining in knowledge boundaries so that students understand that they are expected to regurgitate aspects of the doctrinal exegesis that made up the substance of lectures—in a limited time and according to a predetermined formula. Freire's metaphor of banking aptly describes this pedagogy in which students are treated as passive receptacles who receive knowledge from a 'knower' because they know nothing.[42] The banking notion of legal consciousness is one in which the lecturer regulates the way in which the legal world 'enters into' law students.[43] The process contributes to the dehumanisation and objectification of legal knowledge, neutralises the agency of students and ensures reproduction of that which is 'knowable':

> The more students work at storing the deposits entrusted to them, the less they develop the critical consciousness which would result from their intervention in the world as transformers of that world. The more completely they accept the passive role imposed on them, the more they tend simply to adapt to the world as it is and to the fragmented view of reality deposited in them.[44]

Technocentric legal knowledge disqualifies the life-world knowledge students bring with them to law school, as well as the nonlegal knowledge they acquire elsewhere within the academy. Attempts to alter the gender and colour of law from within the law school are limited, other than in

---

40   See Walt Bachman, *Law v. Life: What Lawyers Are Afraid to Say about the Legal Profession* (Four Directions, 1995) 57.

41   For example, Jenny Morgan, 'The Socratic Method: Silencing Cooperation' (1989) 1 *Legal Education Review* 151.

42   Freire (n. 21) 53.

43   Cf. ibid., 57.

44   ibid., 54.

a simplistic additive sense. The micropolitical sites of power that operate within the substance and pedagogy of legal education are underpinned by the multifaceted character of corporatism.

The power of corporate law

Corporate law firms, where practice is likely to take the most technocratic and specialised form in the interests of clients, exert a disproportionate impact on the legal culture.[45] Corporate law firms are a primary destination of law school graduates, particularly for those from the older, elite institutions. As corporate lawyers are an important source of alumni donations, their expectations cannot be ignored in designing the curriculum. Law schools are also anxious that corporate firms employ their graduates and sponsor recruiting visits by them. By not promoting alternative forms of legal practice, such as public-interest law, law schools subtly discourage it.

Many law graduates themselves find it difficult to resist the lure of the big corporate firms. The first-year salaries offered to associates in these firms are often staggering compared with typical starting salaries. In New York City, the starting salary in 2021 was US$136,000.[46] The myth that the conjunction of money and power means corporate legal work is the most intellectually challenging also encourages many bright students to gravitate to the big firms with their often-narrow specialisations. In addition, the contraction of the public sector, including the move to abolish or privatise public instrumentalities, has meant there are fewer public sector jobs for altruistically minded graduates. Significant debts accumulated in the process of higher education also make the financial offers of the big firms harder to resist. Once ensnared, associates are kept captive by the firm and its corporate clients during a lengthy and insecure period of associateship as they work feverishly for the great rewards flowing from elevation to partnership, including a salary as much as 10 times their present salary: 'Thus, the long and painful apprenticeship in the law firm teaches the associate that extraordinary rewards will be granted by those

---

45   Anthony T. Kronman, *The Lost Lawyer: Failing Ideals of the Legal Profession* (Belknap, 1993) 273.
46   'First Year Associate Salaries in New York City, NY, United States', *Glassdoor*, 18 June 2021, available from: www.glassdoor.com.au/Salaries/new-york-city-first-year-associate-salary-SRCH_IL.0, 13_IM615_KO14,34.htm.

in absolute power to some of those who display total obedience and work compulsively.'[47] The intense competition stifles creativity, other than how best to serve the interests of the firm and its corporate clients.

The increase in the time it takes to become a partner and the decrease in the number of equity partnerships available in global firms are also important technologies of power through which knowledge boundaries are circumscribed. Furthermore, partners in corporate law firms do not have the same degree of security as in the past, for a lacklustre performance can result in a partner being dismissed. In addition, economies of scale dictate depersonalisation and a high level of generality. National and international law firms are stratified, bureaucratised, top-down organisations that bear little relationship to the typical law firm of the past.[48] The direct ad hoc control of day-to-day operations by a small group of partners has been replaced with a specialised division of powers between professional administrators, long-range planners and departmental heads. The term 'the law factory' first appeared in the 1930s to capture the growth in scale that had already occurred in US law firms.[49] Arthurs and Kreklewich refer to the 'Fordist law firm' to continue the industrial analogy into today's world and to argue that lawyers' lives are being altered by the new economy in ways that parallel the working lives of blue-collar workers.[50]

Within the new milieu, the legal associate is transformed and rendered docile by bureaucratisation and the desire to win approval in a way that is like the subjection of the law student. Lawyers employed in the contemporary mega-firm are subject to surveillance through a plethora of bureaucratic devices, including the phenomenon of billable hours. Foucault draws attention to the regulation of the day as a key disciplinary technology of power.[51] If the day of lawyers is divided into six-minute slots, for which they are accountable, there is no time for reflexivity or critique. They must focus on being skilled technocrats, whether advising wealthy corporate clients or 'bread and butter' family law clients. The corporatisation of contemporary legal practice is therefore able to accommodate increased numbers of women and diverse Others, if they

---

47   Abel (n. 24) 222.
48   For the classic study of status and institutional rigidity that accompany bureaucratic ordering, see Weber (n. 6).
49   Marc Galanter & Thomas Palay, *Tournament of Lawyers: The Transformation of the Big Firm* (University of Chicago Press, 1991) 16–17.
50   Arthurs & Kreklewich (n. 4) 44.
51   Foucault (n. 20) 149.

are docile and accept legal orthodoxy. The universalising tendencies of technocentrism effectively erase advertence to the sexed, racialised and sexualised identities of the agents of legality.

The absorption of increased numbers of women, Indigenous people and differentiated Others into law has coincided with the period of economic growth in common law countries since the 1960s and 1970s. The global economy 'needed' more skilled personnel to accommodate changes in the delivery of legal services. The expansion led to the rise of mega-firms in Europe, North America and Oceania, with highly centralised and bureaucratised administrative structures designed to adapt quickly to rapidly changing market conditions. Reflecting the character of legal technocentrism in the way that it deals with personnel within an abstract, rule-bound system, bureaucratisation sheds the social, the subjective and the affective. Thus, corporate workplaces may be prepared to adopt procedures for 'dealing with' what are perceived to be largely gender-specific problems, such as sexual harassment, because of the fear of adverse publicity. However, bureaucratisation and formalism do not necessarily mean that such workplaces are any more accommodating of gender issues than small workplaces that lack a human resources department, as is apparent in the tardiness to make reasonable accommodation for lawyer-parents. In fact, small firms may be more amenable to flexible work.

Indeed, the corporatisation of law firms has resulted in a mirroring of the gendered configurations that typify bureaucracies. Hierarchical ordering within bureaucracies results in superordinate positions becoming masculinised, while subordinate positions remain feminised, racialised and ethnicised. The characteristics of control create the conditions of feminisation that cause male flight. Thus, the lower echelons of the legal profession, including contractualised and casualised positions, are carried out by proportionally more women than men, as is the case elsewhere. 'Feminisation' therefore does not mean that the increased numbers of women are evenly distributed across the profession or within hierarchies, but that women preponderate within the pyramidal base of professional legal hierarchies. Although gender, racial and social exclusiveness may have been reduced or even swept away at the recruitment level, these characteristics remain significant within the inner sanctums of elite firms. It is preferred that women and 'Others' who threaten the calculus of the technical should occupy subordinate positions where they will be subject to surveillance so that any possibility of disorder can be kept at bay.

The nexus between the practice of law and corporate capital is facilitated by the depersonalised focus on procedural rules. As Freeman points out, it is not that corporate legal practice itself oppresses poor people, but that it has the potential to commit ever-increasing legal resources to corporate struggles.[52] The 'winner' in such a case emerges after a virtual war that may go on for months, with lawyers working insane hours. Despite the myth that corporate practice represents the apex of lawyerly ability, ultimately, resources, not expertise, secure the victory. Hence, the system of corporate lawyering renders it virtually impossible to effect substantive change in the lives of those deemed peripheral to corporate interests, such as those with few resources. In focusing on the technocratic rules of procedure, the merits or justice of a case are soon sloughed off. In the case of intercorporate contests, extensive public resources—in the form of judicial infrastructure—are expended in the pursuit of victories designed to privilege corporate interests above others. Camouflaged by technocentrism, these contests reify the conjunction of status, power, money and benchmark masculinity in obeisance to the corporate imperative. When it is understood that the overwhelming preponderance of litigation within courts of general jurisdiction is dominated by corporate litigants whose lawyers are inventive technocrats, it can be appreciated that the scope for altering the gender and colour through litigation is limited.

Pedagogical politics

In Australia, there has been a dramatic expansion in legal education in recent years, with the number of law schools increasing from 11 to 40 over 30 years but, contrary to what the casual observer might have expected, the evidence of curricular diversity is limited. This increase occurred because of the shift from free higher education to a user-pays system and the decision of government to devolve programming responsibility to universities. The offering of law programs was a popular choice among vice-chancellors because of the high demand, the calibre of law students, the prestige of a professional degree and the comparatively low cost of teaching law (based on the large-lecture method, now supplemented by, or replaced with, online teaching). However, the expansion in legal education coincided with the introduction of Uniform Admission Rules (UAR) for

---

52　Alan Freeman, 'A Critical Look at Corporate Practice' (1987) 37 *Journal of Legal Education* 315, 319.

legal practitioners in Australian states and territories in 1994. Thus, at the crucial moment of realising the possibility of diversification in law schools, the impetus was nipped in the bud by the rationality of uniform rules in a federal system. There are 11 prescribed areas of knowledge that must be studied for admission.[53] As already pointed out, the 'core' subjects and their technical orientation exercise immense influence on the law curriculum in the common law world, despite ongoing attempts to diversify the 'legal canon' by including feminist, postcolonial and law and humanities perspectives. However, some of the new law schools have favoured an approach that is even more conservative than that of the established schools in the belief that traditionally educated graduates will be able to compete more effectively for positions in prestigious corporate law firms. Technocentric orthodoxy is thereby clinched via the legal labour market.

In the current conservative and economically rationalist environment, the intellectual parameters of the law discipline are contracting even further. Some law schools sloughed off, or at least contained, their earlier commitment to diversity and sociolegal scholarship. The case of La Trobe University is salutary. For 20 years, legal studies programs were taught within the School of Social Sciences, which did not qualify graduates for admission to legal practice. The school was therefore not theoretically constrained in directing its critical and scholarly gaze towards any facet or perspective of law. Indeed, it was one of only a handful of institutions in the English-speaking common law world to focus exclusively on this project. I took up a chair in legal studies at La Trobe in 1990 when the question of offering an LLB, in addition to the existing programs, was being mooted. I was excited at the prospect of being involved in an innovative law and legal studies program within the School of Social Sciences. While the social sciences do not necessarily eschew a positivistic approach, they can provide a critical standpoint, the possibility of which may be denied by an overly close relationship with legal professionalism, which can occur in the case of the more conventional law schools. In my inaugural lecture (Chapter 12, this volume), I considered past endeavours to integrate law with the social sciences, such as the attempts by the US legal Realists

---

53   The areas of knowledge were revised slightly in 2019. Law Admissions Consultative Committee (LACC), *Prescribed Areas of Knowledge: Administrative Law, Civil Dispute Resolution, Constitutional Law, Contract, Corporations Law, Criminal Law and Procedure, Equity and Trusts, Ethics and Professional Responsibility, Evidence, Property and Torts: Law Admissions Consultative Committee* (LACC, 2019), available from: legalservicescouncil.org.au.

at Columbia Law School in the 1920s[54] and at Yale Law School in the 1930s,[55] all of which were unsuccessful. Indeed, both Columbia and Yale universities instituted inquiries into why their law schools were not teaching 'law'. I hoped that by developing a transdisciplinary approach, comparable with that adopted by women's studies, there would be a possibility of at least experimenting with the integration of law and the social sciences at La Trobe. The rigidity of disciplinary borders would then be collapsed, allowing space for a reflexive sociolegal approach.[56]

The possibility of developing a sociolegal orientation was enhanced by the diverse disciplinary composition of the school: of the 40 full-time academic staff, 20 were legally qualified, while 20 regarded themselves as primarily historians, economists, political scientists, philosophers or sociologists/criminologists. In a further attempt to discourage legal professionalism from disqualifying alternative sources of knowledge, applicants for the LLB program were required to have completed at least two years of a university degree other than law. Generally, in Australia, students undertake an LLB concurrently with another undergraduate program, but the experience of combined programs has been that law tends to disqualify non-legal knowledge. In the La Trobe case, it was hoped that the students, most of whom were mature graduates, would be equipped with the necessary arsenal to resist legal technocentrism but, as was the case in North America, this was not to be.

The erosion of the sociolegal orientation of the law degree began to occur even before the first students had enrolled as it did not accord with what university management deemed 'appropriate' for a law school. A list of the 'law' subjects to be offered was circulated, all of which sounded very traditional and very familiar (albeit that the UAR had not then been devised): contracts, torts, property, criminal law, equity and trusts, and so on. While these subjects do not have to be taught conventionally, there was pressure to hire doctrinally oriented legal academics, rather than sociolegal scholars, to teach what were perceived to be 'black-letter law' subjects, which immediately disturbed the disciplinary balance among the staff.

---

54 Robert Stevens, 'Two Cheers for 1870: The American Law School' in Don Fleming & Bernard Bailyn (eds), *Perspectives in American History: Law in American History. Volume 5* (Charles Warren Center for Studies in American History, Harvard University, 1971).
55 Laura Kalman, *Legal Realism at Yale 1927–1960* (University of North Carolina Press, 1986).
56 Duncanson (n. 14); Peter Goodrich, 'Sleeping with the Enemy: An Essay on the Politics of Critical Legal Studies in America' in Jerry D. Leonard (ed.), *Legal Studies as Cultural Studies: A Reader in (Post)modern Critical Theory* (State University of New York, 1995) 299.

It was assumed that 'to be authentic, an understanding of law must be from a lawyer's point of view'.[57] University management was concerned that the critical and theoretical approaches favoured by incumbent staff would not be approved by the state admitting authorities. Indeed, the suspicion of a legal studies orientation did attract unprecedented scrutiny of the new programs to be offered by La Trobe and Deakin University (another Victorian institution with a reputation for innovation). The Academic Course Appraisal Committee wanted details about the pedagogical methods, forms of assessment and number of hours to be devoted to the various topics within each subject area. The result was that sociolegal perspectives were largely blanched from the subjects specified for admission to practice, although completion of the 'core' subjects was not initially necessary for the award of the LLB at La Trobe, but it was rare for a student to opt to not undertake them—'just in case' they decided to be admitted later, or 'to keep their options open'. Once again, it can be seen how the legal labour market plays a powerful role in securing institutional conformity within the legal academy.

The law students initially shared optional subjects with humanities students, but a schism manifested itself at an early stage: 'We want more *law* subjects,' chorused many of the law students. What they wanted was more technocratic law, for they put in petitions for advanced contracts, trade practices and mainstream taxation (eschewing the critical feminist tax course on offer). The profile of the school began to change as more mainstream lawyers were appointed and the sociolegal scholars departed, or their contracts were not renewed. The culture was rapidly transformed from a sociolegal studies environment to that of a conventional law school.

Friedrichs has written about the way in which those who study the legal system may be marginalised within the legal culture if they adopt an interdisciplinary, critical and humanistic approach.[58] Unquestioning deference to the dominant legal culture is all-important, as law students soon realise that it is dangerous for a lawyer to look in the mirror. As Collier has noted, 'methodological reflexivity … in law … remains …

---

57   Ian Duncanson, 'Degrees of Law: Interdisciplinarity in the Law Discipline' (1996) 5 *Griffith Law Review* 77, 80.
58   Friedrichs (n. 8). Cf. Lawrence M. Friedman, 'The Law and Society Movement' (1986) 38(3) *Stanford Law Review* 763, doi.org/10.2307/1228563.

akin to heresy'.[59] Thus, La Trobe staff, as well as students, sought to secure their futures and to legitimate their intellectual positions by disowning critique or by dissociating themselves from legal studies altogether.

Government policy also played a role in narrowing the curricular canvas. After a conservative (Liberal–National Coalition) government came into office in 1996 at the federal level, it reduced expenditure on higher education. As a result, La Trobe University determined that more law and fewer humanities students would be enrolled in what was no longer a Faculty of Social Science, but a Faculty of Law and Management, which clearly signalled the new economic turn. Gone was the requirement that LLB applicants have at least two years of university education and law was costed at a higher rate than arts, so that BA and LLB students could no longer take the same subjects; the schism had been set in concrete. Subjects such as feminist legal theory, postcolonial studies and critical criminology were rationalised, while new subjects 'more appropriate' for law students were introduced. They involved more of the technocratic law for which the students had lobbied, while legal studies students were left with the remnants of the critical, the interdisciplinary and the theoretical subjects perceived to be dispensable—a point made more poignant by encouraging staff who taught in these areas to take redundancy packages or early retirement. In this way, the 'social' was contained so that the voices of women and Others were muted or silenced altogether within an abstract and universalised discourse designed to privilege mainstream corporate interests. While academics still theoretically had a space in which to articulate critical ideas, the Damoclean sword of downsizing induced a remarkable quiescence regarding changes to the academy, including the demise of legal studies. Ian Duncanson put forth a persuasive case for the retention of legal studies, which, he argued, must necessarily 'operate at some remove from the traditional vocational priorities of the law discipline',[60] but this argument did not prevail.

It might be noted that the academy more generally was also in the process of sloughing off its long-cherished norms of collegiality in favour of bureaucratised, top-down, managerialist forms of governance, reflecting the 'Fordism' that has transformed law firms. Clark and Tsamenyi refer

---

59   Richard Collier, 'Masculinism, Law and Law Teaching' (1991) 19 *International Journal of the Sociology of Law* 427, 434.

60   Duncanson (n. 14) 12.

to this phenomenon as 'creeping corporatism',[61] whereby academics have become workers whose tenure is no longer assured and who are likely to be subjected to multifarious disciplinary technologies of surveillance. Deans and unit heads who were responsible for the policing of staff were now appointed rather than elected and likely to be subject to supervision by an additional layer of control, comprising 'mega-deans' and pro-vice-chancellors. Reflecting the gendered pyramidal structure of the law firm, the apex became more overtly masculinised, while the pyramidal base, comprising support staff and academics employed on a casual basis or short-term contracts, remained feminised and ethnicised.

With the example of Law and Legal Studies at La Trobe University and the changes that have occurred in the funding of Australian universities, I have sought to show that corporatist and masculinist forms of power flow through whatever sites are available, including any that might arise out of opportunities created by the new economy. The dominant is thereby subtly able to continue to shape the law school environment to better serve the interests of the powerful, while simultaneously limiting the possibility of critique. Thus, the launching of a radical project from within a law school is a risky enterprise. As Goodrich has observed: 'The dice are loaded against a politically radical critical legal studies.'[62]

Conclusion

Feminist scholarship has sought assiduously to alter the landscape of legal education over recent decades. Indeed, there has been a marked broadening of issues in course curricula and textbooks, together with a notable change in the content and character of mainstream law journals, as well as special issues and journals dedicated to feminist legal scholarship. Feminism has also exerted an effect on legal theory, as has critical race theory and queer theory. However, critical legal theory of whatever kind is marginal to the facilitative and technocratic project of the law school. The marginality of subjects such as 'Feminist Legal Theory', 'Indigenous Peoples and the Law', 'Sexuality and the Law', 'Law and Literature', 'Law and Culture', and so on, is secured through their optional and 'add-on' status. The message

---

61   Eugene Clark & Martin Tsamenyi, 'Legal Education in the Twenty-First Century: A Time of Challenge' in Peter Birks (ed.), *Pressing Problems in the Law: What Are Law Schools For? Volume 2* (Oxford University Press, 1996) 43.
62   Goodrich (n. 56) 323.

of optionality affirms the peripheral status to the calculus of the technical of all critical and theoretical subjects, which are dispensable at times of economic rationalisation. Thus, despite the effort expended, critical theory generally has exerted surprisingly little impact on the mainstream curriculum. Indeed, as I have argued, it is the role of technocentrism to resist such destabilising incursions because what we are witnessing is the attempt to reabsorb the study of law into mainstream intellectual life. Such a project necessarily represents a further site of contest because few practitioners are prepared to recognise the desire of legal academics to be accepted primarily as bona fide scholars and intellectuals within the academic community.

While the discursive attempts to alter the gender and colour of law are not insignificant, they are unable to displace the potency of technocentrism. The role of technical reason is crucial in decentring and diffusing power— a phenomenon that Brown refers to as 'centrifugation',[63] which is the converse of the centripetal effect on competing knowledges. Nevertheless, there is a symbiosis between these twin movements—the centrifugation of power and the centripetal effect of the technocratic (technocentrism)— as they move in opposite directions to confuse and diffuse the loci of corporate and masculinist power. This fragmentation suggests a more complicated phenomenon than a simple dominance theory.

I have argued that moves towards the new economy, including the global phenomenon of large corporate law firms and the privatisation of public goods, have been facilitated by the magnetic, albeit numbing, effects of technocentrism to which law students quickly succumb. The law school culture, including modes of assessment, the pressure to be accepted as a high-class professional and the lure of the legal labour market, serve to neutralise student resistance, even if the partiality of *techné* is glimpsed through the fog that is induced by studying countless cases and statutes. To prevent the possibility of insurgency in legal practice, I have also argued that the bureaucratised corporate law firm itself constitutes another disciplinary regime. Government and university changes reveal there are in fact 'polymorphous disciplinary mechanisms' in operation that underpin and normalise (corporate) power.[64] In seeking to project an image of itself as value-free and neutral, law can accommodate— chameleon-like—divergent interests, including those perceived to be in

---

63   Brown (n. 1) 34.
64   Foucault (n. 3) 106.

vogue at a particular moment, such as gender, postcolonialism or sexuality. The commitment is parlous, however, and may be jettisoned if education programs must be economically rationalised.

The insidious way that law operates was percipiently remarked on by de Tocqueville 150 years ago:

> The lawyers [of the United States] form a party which is but little feared and scarcely perceived, which has no badge peculiar to itself, which adapts itself with great flexibility to the exigencies of the time, and accommodates itself without resistance to all the movements of the social body. But this party extends over the whole community, and penetrates into all the classes which compose it; it acts upon the country imperceptibly, but finally fashions it to suit its own purposes.[65]

The 'deification of technicality'[66] is denounced from time to time but few legal critics are prepared to confront the full import of de Tocqueville's words—that is, that dominant interests are complicit in fashioning law in their own image. Le Brun and Johnstone, for example, acknowledge the impoverishment of a rule-oriented approach to legal education and the reluctance to change.[67] While they identify several endogenous factors as to why law schools perpetuate a rule-based image of law, including convention and deference to hierarchy,[68] they tend to disregard factors such as the prevailing socioeconomic trends and the growth of corporatism. On the other hand, numerous legal scholars have expressed concern about the increasing commercialisation of legal practice and the decline of professionalism,[69] and about the malaise besetting the legal profession, including the profound dissatisfaction and cynicism regarding the teaching and practice of law.[70] Goldsmith acknowledges that while the practice of

---

65   Alexis de Tocqueville, *Democracy in America*, translated by Henry Reeve (Sever & Francis, 1862) 358.
66   L. Maurice Wormser, *The True Function of Schools of Law* (Bronx County Bar Association, 1923) 17. Cf. Marcuse (n. 2).
67   Marlene Le Brun & Richard Johnstone, *The Quiet Revolution: Improving Student Learning in Law* (Law Book, 1994).
68   ibid., 28–38.
69   For example, Paula Baron & Lilian Corbin, *Ethics and Legal Professionalism in Australia* (Oxford University Press, 3rd edn, 2020); Joanne Bagust, 'The Legal Profession and the Business of Law' (2013) 35 *Sydney Law Review* 27.
70   Mary Ann Glendon, *A Nation Under Lawyers: How the Crisis in the Legal Profession is Transforming American Society* (Farrar, Straus & Giroux, 1994); Kronman (n. 45).

law is increasingly dominated by concern for efficiency and profitability, a transformation of the curriculum can be effected by a pedagogy that combines theoretical, experiential and technical knowledge.[71]

The tension between the life of the scholar and the practice of law is longstanding,[72] but the schism has become more pronounced. Conservative scholar Anthony Kronman went so far as to suggest that the tension in the case of US legal education could be described as pathological[73]—a condition for which he holds antiprudential movements, such as critical legal studies, responsible. Kronman evinces an idealised longing for the past when the 'lawyer-statesman' was committed to serving the public good. Far from idealising the benchmark masculinity of the past, feminist, critical race and LGBTIQ+ legal scholars focus on the future in their endeavours to envision the way things might be. Many have rejected legal practice as a subject of study in favour of more arcane and esoteric areas of scholarship and remain deeply suspicious of the sexism, racism and homophobia that typify legal practice. This reflexivity and the interrogation of power have rendered impossible a return to the modernist methodologies of the past, despite institutional pressures to do so. Has it become the fate of postmodern intellectuals, then, as Peter Goodrich asks, to be tied to a specific institution and its practice, while diverting their gaze elsewhere?[74]

Although not optimistic about changing the gender and colour of law because of the way the exigencies of the new economy within a neoliberal context have neutralised past gains, I do not wish to suggest that the legal system is totally closed. As Foucault has demonstrated, power is never totalising; it always generates a resistance that creates instability.[75] Thus, some law students, especially those who carry the seeds of 'otherness' with them, will not accept the power of orthodoxy. Their questioning unsettles law's claims to truth, neutrality and universality. In addition, critical legal scholarship of all kinds endeavours to resist the tentacles of technocentrism. As I have suggested, law journals are overflowing with

71　For example, Andrew Goldsmith, 'Heroes or Technicians? The Moral Capacities of Tomorrow's Lawyers' (1996) 14 *Journal of Professional Legal Education* 1.

72　For example, Twining (n. 13) 53; Albert Venn Dicey, *Can English Law be Taught at the Universities? (Inaugural Lecture Delivered at All Souls College, Oxford, 21 April 1883)* (Macmillan, 1883) 29; William Blackstone, *An Analysis of the Laws of England* (Clarendon, 3rd edn, 1758) 37.

73　Kronman (n. 45).

74　Goodrich (n. 56) 317.

75　Michel Foucault, *The History of Sexuality, An Introduction. Volume 1*, translated by R. Hurley (Random House, 1978) 114.

articles that explore alternative forms of knowledge emanating from areas such as law and feminism, critical race theory, LGBTIQ+ studies, and law and literature. However, while the dynamism of postmodern scholarship can be intellectually exciting, its impact has been limited, not only because of the technocratic imperative, but also because it tends to evince only the most marginal relationship with policy and the academic discipline of law.[76] At the barriers of legitimate legal knowledge, technocentrism either resists what is threatening or assimilates a few anodyne notions. The homologous relationship between the core subjects of the law degree and corporate practice must be understood as a site of ongoing contest that demands eternal scholarly vigilance. The new corporatism is not just another modernist narrative that has passed its use-by date.

---

76   Goodrich (n. 56) 304.

Part VII:
The Corporatised Academy

14

Universities Upside-Down

Introduction

A large advertisement in an Australian newspaper caught my eye in late 2008. It was headed: 'Entire University Campus for Lease: QUT Carseldine Campus, Queensland.'[1] The fully equipped campus property of 45 hectares was described as a desirable piece of real estate that was available for up to 25 years. However, what was not mentioned was of more interest to me. This was the fact that the campus, which had formerly housed the Faculty of Arts at the Queensland University of Technology (QUT), had been closed following a decision by university management. I had been a speaker at the faculty's 'Last Post' colloquium in late 2007 when it was hoped a change of federal government might win a reprieve, but this was not to be.

To replace the Faculty of Arts, the university had established a new Faculty of Creative Industries, which its website promised would offer 'diverse and rewarding career opportunities'—presumably unlike the Faculty of Arts. Now, there is nothing wrong with creative industries, which include visual and performing arts, but where was the space to study the liberal arts: history, philosophy, classics, feminism or Indigenous studies? There was none.[2] The fate of QUT's Faculty of Arts is a graphic illustration of my thesis.

---

1   *Australian Financial Review*, 15 September 2008, 36.
2   Rather than a university, the QUT has been described as now verging on a technical college. See Howard Guille, 'The Last Post: Humanities at QUT—Introduction' (2008) 5 *Journal of the Public University*, available from: web.archive.org/web/20110219041122/http://www.publicuni.org/journal/volume/5/JPU5_Introduction.pdf.

For centuries, the university has been viewed as the custodian of culture, the seat of higher learning and the paradigmatic site of free inquiry. These lofty aims have been turned upside-down by a constellation of values emanating from the interstices of neoliberalism, the new knowledge economy and globalisation. The result is that the university as a key knowledge producer is now regarded primarily as a source of wealth creation to be exploited. As the market enters the soul of the university, it has caused the commitment to traditional values to contract.

This transformation first began within the context of a notable swing to the right in global politics. Whereas social liberalism paid at least a modicum of attention to the idea of the public good, equality and distributive justice, neoliberalism shifted the focus from civil society to the market, with a correlative fixation on the interests of the individual and the accumulation of private wealth. To this extent, neoliberalism has revived some of the tenets of classical liberalism, while endorsing a more positive conception of state power.[3] It might be noted that Friedrich Hayek, who has been described as the father of neoliberalism, emphasised the importance of knowledge as the key to economic growth in the 1930s and 1940s.[4] However, it has taken the technological revolution for the significance of knowledge as a commodity to be realised, causing a shift away from land and physical resources.[5] The new knowledge economy nevertheless engenders risks that 'haunt'[6] entrepreneurialism in ways that have not previously been known, as the GFC and, more recently, Covid-19 have reminded us. To abate the risk, it is believed that new knowledge must possess use value in the market.

In this chapter, I provide an overview of the trajectory of change, from the emergence of the modern university and the contestation over the claim to the universality of knowledge by feminist scholars. As a touchstone in this respect, I refer to a 1984 publication edited by Ursula Franklin,

---

3   Mark Olssen & Michael A. Peters, 'Neoliberalism, Higher Education and the Knowledge Economy: From the Free Market to Knowledge Capitalism' (2005) 20(3) *Journal of Education Policy* 313, 315, doi.org/10.1080/02680930500108718.

4   Friedrich Hayek, 'Economics and Knowledge' (1937) 4 *Economica* 33; Friedrich Hayek, 'The Use of Knowledge in Society' (1945) 35(4) *American Economic Review* 519.

5   Lyotard observed almost 40 years ago that knowledge had replaced land, raw materials and cheap labour in the struggle for power among nation-states. See Jean-François Lyotard, *The Postmodern Condition: A Report on Knowledge* (Manchester University Press, 1984).

6   Jane Kenway, Elizabeth Bullen & Johannah Fahey, with Simon Robb, *Haunting the Knowledge Economy* (Routledge, 2006), doi.org/10.4324/9780203030493. For the classic study of risk, see Ulrich Beck, *Risk Society: Towards a New Modernity*, translated by M. Ritter (Sage, 1992).

entitled *Knowledge Reconsidered: A Feminist Overview.*[7] I then consider the paradigm shift in the academy arising from the emergence of the new knowledge economy and its ramifications for feminist knowledge. I suggest the new knowledge economy is facilitating the remasculinisation of the academy behind a facade of rationality, technocentrism and marketisation.

The *idea* of the university

The inception of the modern university is marked by Wilhelm von Humboldt's establishment of the University of Berlin in 1810. Even though this new iteration of the university was to be state-funded and charged with safeguarding the culture of the nation-state, the freedom of the individual was to be maximised.[8] The modern university was concerned with the erudition, learning and refinement of the emerging bourgeoisie rather than with medieval scholasticism or aristocratic *noblesse oblige*. Bourgeois revolutionary education was rational, universal, secular and enlightened—values that came to represent the essence of a liberal university education.[9] Cardinal Newman eloquently captures the *idea* of the university,[10] the passing of which many rue, even though Newman's famous treatise is directed towards the education of a small, elite sector of society, viz., Irish-Catholic gentlemen:

> If then a practical end must be assigned to a University course, I say it is that of training good members of society. Its art is the art of social life, and its end is fitness for the world. It neither confines its views to particular professions on the one hand, nor creates heroes or inspires genius on the other ... But a University training is the great ordinary means to a great but ordinary end; it aims at raising the intellectual tone of society, at cultivating the public mind, at purifying the national taste, at supplying true principles to popular enthusiasm and fixed aims to popular

7   Ursula Martius Franklin, Michèle Jean, Sylvia van Kirk, Andrea Levowitz, Meg Luxton, Susan Sherwin & Dorothy E. Smith, *Knowledge Reconsidered: A Feminist Overview* (Canadian Research Institute for the Advancement of Women, 1984).

8   Wilhelm von Humboldt, *The Limits of State Action*, edited & translated by J.W. Burrow (Cambridge University Press, 1969) 54.

9   Masao Miyoshi, 'The University in the Global Economy' in Kevin Robins & Frank Webster (eds), *The Virtual University? Knowledge, Markets and Management* (Oxford University Press, 2002) 52.

10   John Henry Newman, *The Idea of a University*, edited & introduced by I.T. Ker (Clarendon, 1976 [1852]).

aspiration, at giving enlargement and sobriety to the ideas of the age, at facilitating the exercise of political power, and refining the intercourse of private life.[11]

The kernel of the *idea* was that the university constituted a site of free inquiry, hence its liberal descriptor. Thus, according to Newman, the university was not constrained by particular presuppositions, vocationalism or practical skills. Even within a religious context, Newman considered the role of the university to be intellectual rather than moral. Most significantly, knowledge should be pursued for its own sake, not for instrumental reasons. Thus, the end of knowledge was knowledge itself. Newman identified the attributes of liberal education as 'freedom, equitableness, calmness, moderation, and wisdom'.[12] Academic freedom as articulated by Newman was to become the leitmotif of the liberal incarnation of the university, which, at least in the abstract, allowed a thousand flowers to bloom.

While knowledge for its own sake has connotations of the ivory tower that serves no functional purpose, the crucial role of the modern university in preserving the culture of the nation-state reveals that it serves several multifaceted functions. First, the liberal ideal was a political tool for the creation of good liberal citizens,[13] which is an idea Newman himself supported.[14] The study of the humanities and the natural sciences was believed to fashion character, although I reiterate that it was only the character of upper-class and bourgeois men that was of concern. Indeed, the elitism of the university was effectively deployed in the nineteenth century to exclude women and racialised Others, as well as to suppress democratic moves by the working class. This cultural elitism was invoked by European nations overseas to promote notions of superiority over colonised peoples. Hence, the university supported imperialism and global capitalism, as well as nationalism.

Other instances of instrumentality are also discernible, such as the centrality of basic and applied science to the German university from the second half of the nineteenth century. Von Humboldt, unlike Newman, believed in the linkage of teaching and research in the modern

---

11   ibid., 154.
12   ibid., 96.
13   This idea was particularly strong in the United States. See Alan Ryan, *Liberal Anxieties and Liberal Education* (Hill & Wang, 1998) 95.
14   Newman (n. 10) 154.

university.[15] However, he believed that knowledge was not stagnant but constantly revived by new knowledge. In addition, the nexus between the national defence system and the university in the United States in the mid twentieth century shows the importance of the applied research model, which was to become the linchpin of academic capitalism.[16]

Nostalgia for an idealised notion of the university in an age of overt functionality should not cause us to lose sight of the reality. The assumption that the university, as a site of liberal education, was formerly class-free, unrestricted, self-motivated and unbiased is a persistent myth.[17] Nevertheless, First-Wave feminists—inspired by the idealised vision of universality, neutrality and objectivity—agitated to be let into this masculinised, class-based world. The emancipist focus was directed towards treating women as rational and fully human.[18]

Knowledge reconsidered

By the late twentieth century, feminist acceptance of the claim to the universality of knowledge had lost some of its allure. Second-Wave feminists were no longer content with merely being 'let into' the academy as it was but, instead, sought to transform the nature of knowledge and the structures of power. The knowledge that had been assiduously safeguarded throughout the Western intellectual tradition and transmitted in the belief that it was objective, neutral and true began to be dissected and its biases exposed by feminist scholars.

The feminist critique challenged the very presuppositions that had sustained the Western intellectual tradition. This is even though the interrogation of known knowledge underpinned the notion of free inquiry that is central to the liberal university.[19] Unsurprisingly, what was

---

15 Marianne Cowan (trans. & ed.), *Humanist without Portfolio: An Anthology of Writings of Wilhelm von Humboldt. Volume X* (Wayne State University Press, 1963) 134.

16 Gerard Delanty, 'The University and Modernity: A History of the Present' in Kevin Robins & Frank Webster (eds), *The Virtual University? Knowledge, Markets, and Management* (Oxford University Press, 2002) 37.

17 Miyoshi (n. 9) 53.

18 Pat Fitgerald, 'A Woman Knows These Things: Women's Knowledge and Liberal Education' in Bob Brecher, Otakar Fleischmann & Jo Halliday (eds), *The University in a Liberal State* (Aldershot, 1996) 39.

19 Paul Axelrod, Paul Anisef & Zeng Lin, 'Against All Odds? The Enduring Value of Liberal Education in Universities, Professions, and the Labour Market' (2001) 31(2) *Canadian Journal of Higher Education* 47, 52.

perceived to be an epistemological assault on foundational knowledge was highly contentious. There was clearly a limit to critical thinking, which included challenging the dominant tradition of moral philosophy and culture that instructed women to be silent in the presence of men.[20] This truism resulted in not just the devaluation of women's voices and ideas, but also the difficulty of accepting women as authoritative knowers. The new feminist knowledge signalled a paradigm shift in the academic social order.

Across the disciplines, feminist scholars systematically revealed how the denigration of women's activities operated to augment male power and cohesion.[21] Despite the resentment and antipathy, the new forms of knowledge gradually began to influence what is known and what is knowable,[22] although masculinist sceptics remained unconvinced. The work of Canadian feminist theorists such as sociologist Dorothy Smith[23] and philosopher Lorraine Code[24] were influential in developing new understandings of knowledge that drew on feminist subjectivities. The interdisciplinarity of women's studies was also a crucial aspect of the distinctiveness of feminist knowledge.

Nevertheless, any notion that the discourse of women's studies might have denoted a universal 'woman' was soon scuttled. 'She' was criticised for the insularity of her white, middle-class orientation. She lost her credibility because indigenous women, women from non–English-speaking backgrounds, lesbians, women with disabilities and working-class women felt marginalised. The implosion of the category 'woman' coincided with the postmodern turn. French theorists such as Michel Foucault, Jacques Derrida, Jean-François Lyotard and Jacques Lacan all similarly challenged the notions of universality and truth that had for so long been associated with the idea of the university, albeit from a masculinist perspective.

---

20   Nannerl O. Keohane, 'Speaking from Silence: Women and the Science of Politics' in Elizabeth Langland & Walter Gove (eds), *A Feminist Perspective in the Academy: The Difference It Makes* (University of Chicago Press, 1983) 92.

21   Cynthia Fuchs Epstein, 'Women in Sociological Analysis: New Scholarship Versus Old Paradigms' in Elizabeth Langland & Walter Gove (eds), *A Feminist Perspective in the Academy: The Difference It Makes* (University of Chicago Press, 1983) 151.

22   'Editors' Notes', in Elizabeth Langland & Walter Gove (eds), *A Feminist Perspective in the Academy: The Difference It Makes* (University of Chicago Press, 1983) 2.

23   Dorothy E. Smith, *The Everyday World as Problematic: A Feminist Sociology* (Open University Press, 1988); Dorothy E. Smith, *Texts, Facts, and Femininity: Exploring the Relations of Ruling* (Routledge, 1990).

24   Lorraine Code, *What Can She Know: Feminist Theory and the Construction of Knowledge* (Cornell University Press, 1991), doi.org/10.7591/9781501735738.

The ensuing culture wars highlighted the contestation over the authority of the incumbents and their right to map out the territory vis-a-vis feminist, postcolonial, postmodern and cultural theory contenders.

The gatekeepers, however, claimed that the challengers lacked rigour and were 'too political'. They had an ideological standpoint, unlike the benchmark men of the academy who were presumably perched on an Archimedean pinpoint in their claim to universality and neutrality. The courses of the newcomers were denigrated, closed or made more anodyne and less threatening. In many institutions, women's studies disappeared in favour of more acceptable, de-gendered nomenclatures, such as 'diversity studies'.

Were these attacks crude manifestations of the backlash and ploys to safeguard the preserve of benchmark men or did they represent a new epistemic moment that signalled a shift away from the category 'woman'? While 'she' had served a useful political and legal purpose, was she now past her prime? Did the widespread disappointment in her also herald the shift away from one-dimensionality in favour of interrogating masculinity as well as indigeneity, sexuality and postcoloniality? While some feminist scholars embraced postmodernism, acknowledging the one-dimensionality of the universal woman, others felt the postmodern attack was a manifestation of a backlash that emerged just when women began speaking up for themselves.[25] It is difficult to disentangle the elements of backlash that seem to be a perennial counterpoint to the struggle by women and Others for acceptance within the academy. Despite the crisis of legitimation that postmodernism highlighted, a tsunami of far greater magnitude was about to envelope the university and change it irretrievably. Its potential for harm was also commensurably far greater and, as I will suggest, more insidious.

Knowledge capitalism

The corporate university

What may be termed the third revolutionary phase in the history of the university, after modernisation and feminisation, is that of corporatisation, which has emanated from the new knowledge economy. This phase has

---

25   Carol Nicholson, 'Postmodern Feminisms' in Michael Peters (ed.), *Education and the Postmodern Condition* (Bergin & Garvey, 1995) 80.

365

produced a string of new terms that only a short while ago would have been viewed as dissonant and disjunctive, such as 'academic capitalism'[26] and 'the enterprise university'.[27] Regardless of the descriptor invoked, the reality is that the university is now the preeminent site of knowledge production deployed by contemporary nation-states to generate wealth.

Alan Burton-Jones suggests that the change in favour of the new knowledge economy is as profound as the Industrial Revolution.[28] He explains that new knowledge is a form of capitalism with the same distinctive features as traditional capitalism: 'Capitalism as we know it, and emerging Knowledge Capitalism, both thrive on capital accumulation, open market competition, free trade, the power of the individual, and the survival of the fittest.'[29]

All capitalist economies now wish to exploit knowledge as an untapped source of wealth. The phenomenon has gathered momentum all over the world, not just in the West, but also in China and Eastern Europe. Indeed, it is notable that nation-states seeking to enhance their standing as new knowledge economies have the support of significant international bodies—the Organisation for Economic Co-operation and Development (OECD),[30] the International Monetary Fund[31] and the World Bank[32]—which are concerned to maximise productivity by fostering scientific and technological innovation.[33] The global spread of the logic of the market renders the chances of resistance virtually impossible.

'New knowledge' is not knowledge in the sense of the accumulated fruit of wisdom referred to by Newman or knowledge that is associated with the transformative power of feminist knowledge envisaged by Ursula Franklin's *Knowledge Reconsidered*.[34] New knowledge is a term of art that refers to useful knowledge (know-how as opposed to know-what) that may

---

26   Sheila Slaughter & Larry L. Leslie, *Academic Capitalism: Politics, Policies, and the Entrepreneurial University* (Johns Hopkins University Press, 1997).

27   Simon Marginson & Mark Considine, *The Enterprise University: Power, Governance and Reinvention in Australia* (Cambridge University Press, 2000).

28   Alan Burton-Jones, *Knowledge Capitalism: Business, Work, and Learning in the New Economy* (Oxford University Press, 1999) 3.

29   ibid., 20.

30   Brian Kahim & Dominique Foray (eds), *Advancing Knowledge and the Knowledge Economy* (MIT Press, 2006).

31   The International Monetary Fund and World Bank Group hosted a major expo in 1998, entitled 'The Knowledge Economy', available from: www.imf.org/external/am/1998/expo.htm.

32   The World Bank, *Higher Education: The Lessons of Experience* (World Bank, 1994).

33   The United Nations is also responsible for producing a Global Knowledge Index. See United Nations Development Programme, *Global Knowledge Index* (UNDP, 2020).

34   Franklin et al. (n. 7).

be utilised to impart skills to future knowledge workers in the expectation that they will generate wealth. The notion of applied knowledge captures the slippage that has occurred between 'knowledge' and 'information'. The philosophical conditions for knowledge as traditionally understood—belief, truth and justification—are not satisfied by information, which is defined as 'data transmitted from a "sender" to a "receiver"'.[35] Perhaps the most significant manifestation of the dystopian effect of the knowledge society is that knowledge is no longer viewed as wisdom but as data.[36] Instead of the intellectual passion for ideas associated with scholastic and Enlightenment knowledge, there is now what has been described by Dominique Foray as a 'wild passion for private property in the realm of knowledge creation'.[37] This understanding has contributed to the manner in which bureaucratic and market discourses now invariably trump academic discourse.[38]

The introduction of business principles into the university is not a new phenomenon. The influential US theorist Thorstein Veblen, who, like Newman, believed the university was for the pursuit of knowledge for its own sake, identified the deleterious effects of business on universities more than a century ago.[39] Nevertheless, the new managerialism that is orchestrated by a nation-state,[40] or a group of states,[41] is infinitely more far-reaching in its endeavours to deploy the new knowledge produced by universities for profit. Despite its potentially devastating effects for

---

35   Michael Peters, 'Universities, Globalisation and the Knowledge Economy' (2002) 35(2) *Southern Review* 16, 27.

36   Helga Nowotny, Peter Scott & Michael Gibbons, *Re-Thinking Science: Knowledge and the Public in an Age of Uncertainty* (Polity, 2001) 12. The other elements of the 'knowledge society' that the authors identify as dystopian are the promotion of inequality between the knowledge-rich and the knowledge-poor; the dissolution of traditional canons of art, ideas and artefact; and the fact that it proliferates environmental, ethical and intellectual risks.

37   Dominique Foray, 'Optimising the Use of Knowledge' in Kahim & Foray (n. 30) 13.

38   Readings' discussion of the way the concept of excellence has become a vacuous marketing and bureaucratic tool illustrates the point. See Bill Readings, *The University in Ruins* (Harvard University Press, 1996) 21.

39   Thorstein Veblen, *The Higher Learning in America: A Memorandum on the Conduct of Universities by Business Men* (Academic Reprints 1954 [1918]) 135.

40   For example, United Kingdom, Department for Education and Skills, *The Future of Higher Education* (The Crown, 2003).

41   Europe and its member states formulated the goal of making Europe one of the strongest knowledge societies in the world when 29 European countries pledged in 1999 to reform and effect convergence of their structures of higher education. Confederation of EU Rectors' Conferences & Association of European Universities, *The Bologna Declaration on the European Space for Higher Education: An Explanation*, available from: iehost.net/pdf/bologna.pdf. See *The Role of the Universities in the Europe of Knowledge: Communication from the Commission* (2004) 36(2) *European Education* 5, doi.org/10.1080/10564934.2001.11042352.

the future of the academy, the transformation of the university has been accepted with remarkable rapidity by faculty, students and society at large,[42] which has enabled the academic capitalist discourse to be normalised. The evisceration of academic authority in favour of top-down managerial power, underpinned by manifold technologies of audit, has ensured that academics have quickly learned to adapt to the new environment. In fact, this third paradigm shift attests to the effectiveness of managerial compliance mechanisms that have largely displaced academic debate.[43]

However, the public university is no longer certain about what it is for, as its orientation shifts from civil society to the market. Those parts of the university that are unable to demonstrate profitability face an uncertain future, as indicated at the outset with the example of the demise of QUT's Faculty of Arts. A similar pressure is confronting humanities and social sciences faculties elsewhere, particularly as a result of Covid-19.[44] They are beset with an anxiety to disprove any suggestion of 'use-less-ness' and reports regularly appear endeavouring to prove their value.[45] Even the United States, where higher education is diverse in both its orientation and its funding models compared with most other countries, has been profoundly affected by the intensity of change, particularly in a post–Covid-19 environment.[46] Teaching and research have both been transformed by this academic capitalist environment but in very distinctive ways.

Students as customers

Massification and privatisation are the twin characteristics of the education revolution as the neoliberal state resiles from responsibility for the funding of public universities. The shift from elite to mass was symbolically effected in Australia in 1988 and in the United Kingdom

---

42 Miyoshi (n. 9) 52.

43 Stephen Rowland, *The Enquiring University: Compliance and Contestation in Higher Education* (Society for Research into Higher Education & Open University Press, 2006) 14.

44 For example, Sarah Lansdown, 'Humanities Courses Could Be Cut at Regional Universities', *The Canberra Times*, 17 June 2021, available from: www.canberratimes.com.au/story/7299649/humanities-courses-in-firing-line-at-regional-universities/.

45 For example, Deloitte Access Economics, *The Value of the Humanities* (Macquarie University, 2018); Academy of the Social Sciences in Australia, *State of the Social Sciences 2021* (ASSA, 2021), available from: socialsciences.org.au/publications/state-of-the-social-sciences-2021/.

46 For example, Katya Schwenk, '"They're Running it Like a Business": As More Cuts Loom, UVM Faculty Debate the Mission', *VT Digger* [Montpelier, VT], 12 January 2021, available from: vtdigger.org/2021/01/12/theyre-running-it-like-a-business-as-more-cuts-loom-uvm-faculty-debate-the-mission/.

in 1990 by converting colleges of advanced education and polytechnics, respectively, into universities. The vastly increased numbers of students attending the new universities were not expected to be the beneficiaries of a liberal university education but, rather, were expected to be trained as productive workers who would augment the new knowledge economy. In fact, they would be more likely to have their horizons narrowed than broadened by their university experience to prepare them for the world of productive work. This phenomenon, which is by no means restricted to the new universities, has been aptly described as 'vocationalising the curriculum'.[47] It is distinguishable from embarking on a specific vocational specialisation, such as engineering. The effect of vocationalism has been to skew courses across the entire spectrum of the university towards applied fields and the acquisition of skills.

The trend towards 'privatising the public university' emerges from treating education as a commodity.[48] Again, Australia is a dramatic example since free higher education was an initiative of the Whitlam government in 1974. However, Australia is now a leading exponent of a user-pays system. As fees are ratcheted up and students assume responsibility for an increasing proportion of the cost of their education, they have morphed into customers, while universities have been relegated to 'course providers'. Universities must not only satisfy the demands of the student body to maximise the institution's income, but also avoid student complaints lest the institutional brand name be damaged, which could affect its market share.

Students/customers, too, are more likely to be interested in credentialism than the pursuit of a liberal education because they have one eye on ballooning education debt and the other on an assured career path in an uncertain world that has reified the swing towards vocationalism. Commodification has encouraged a sloughing off or a dilution of a liberal curriculum—a phenomenon that is notable in the case of law, as discussed in Chapter 13.[49] Regardless of discipline, including the humanities, the emphasis is now on marketable skills.[50] Instrumentalism encourages a less

---

47   Ann Bousfield, 'The Voice of Liberal Learning: Is There Still Room for the "Idea of a University" in 1996?', in Brecher et al. (n. 18) 72.

48   Margaret Thornton, *Privatising the Public University: The Case of Law* (Routledge, 2012).

49   Cf. Harry W. Arthurs, 'The Political Economy of Canadian Legal Education' (1998) 25(1) *Journal of Law and Society* 14.

50   For example, Chloe Lane, 'Is It Worth Studying a Humanities Subject?', *TopUniversities.com*, 25 February 2021, available from: www.topuniversities.com/courses/arts-humanities/it-worth-studying-humanities-subject.

reflexive, theoretical and critical approach to the knowledge transmitted. The idea of an applied focus is designed to appeal to prospective employers, thereby strengthening the conveyor belt between universities and business.

Not only are business courses the most popular in the contemporary vocational university, but also higher education itself has become a business, signifying its changed conceptualisation in terms of the market. In Australia before the Covid-19 pandemic, higher education was the third biggest export earner after coal and iron, adding A$140 billion to the economy.[51] Once again, it is business that embodies the international language of communication, which is most sought after by international students. As the new knowledge economy has become essential to nation-states, they have a personal stake in a regime that privileges the transmission of applied knowledge over critical and theoretical knowledge.

The pressure in favour of job-readiness became much more overt because of Covid-19 in 2020 when the international student market collapsed. In an endeavour to replenish lost income, legislation was passed to encourage the enrolment of domestic students in applied areas of study to ensure 'job-readiness' on graduation, as is apparent from the title of the legislation: Higher Education Support Amendment (Job-Ready Graduates and Supporting Regional and Remote Students) Act 2020 (Cth). The Act provides incentives for students to enrol in areas designated as national priorities—namely, STEM (science, technology, engineering and mathematics), together with nursing and teaching. The financial contributions made by students in these areas have been reduced, while the government contributions have been increased. In contrast, students proposing to enrol in law, accounting, economics, communications or society and culture (humanities and social sciences) are charged more and the government contribution is reduced.[52]

---

51   Universities Australia, *Data Snapshot 2019* (Universities Australia, 2019) 4.

52   The maximum student contribution for a government-supported place in the now less-favoured disciplines of law, accounting, economics, commerce, communication, and society and culture from 1 January 2021 was increased to A$14,500 per annum, while the Commonwealth contribution was reduced to A$1,200 (7 per cent). This contrasts with a government-supported place in one of the favoured disciplines (education, clinical psychology, English, mathematics or statistics) for which the cost to the student is proportionally lower (A$3,950) and the Commonwealth contribution is proportionally higher (A$13,250) (77 per cent).

We can therefore see how government is engineering a focus on applied knowledge and job-readiness according to discipline by varying the cost of degrees. However, it remains to be seen what effect this intervention will have on student choice, as the Higher Education Contribution Scheme–Higher Education Loan Program (HECS-HELP) still exists with what Jayasuriya terms its 'submerged privatization' of fees,[53] which are not repayable until the graduate secures a certain income threshold.

Knowledge transfer

While the neoliberal state might have resiled from its fiscal responsibility for public universities, it continues to micromanage them, thereby acting as the driver of the new knowledge economy. It is notable that it has not only orchestrated research to maximise wealth production, but also permitted the benefits of that wealth to be privatised. In the process, the state has ceded significant control over knowledge production to the private sector. It is paradoxical that the resources of public universities are now being used for the private good of corporations, which signifies just how dramatic is the shift away from the values of social liberalism. Claire Polster has observed that the enhanced role of industry in research has had disastrous results for the social sciences and the humanities in Canada because of the way it skewed research towards industrially related knowledge.[54]

Technology transfer is the key to academic capitalism as far as research is concerned. This means the outcomes of research cannot be permitted to lie fallow (knowledge for its own sake) within the academy but must be made to serve a useful purpose, such as being deployed to resolve practical problems or generate wealth. The transfer of knowledge to corporations with the capacity to exploit its potential is therefore seen as highly desirable.

In the United States and the United Kingdom during the terms of Ronald Reagan and Margaret Thatcher, respectively, the use of public resources for the benefit of private enterprise rapidly gained in popularity in accordance with the neoliberal agenda.[55] The 1980 *Bayh–Dole Act* in the United States

---

53   Kanishka Jayasuriya, 'COVID-19, Markets and the Crisis of the Higher Education Regulatory State: The Case of Australia' (2020) 18(4) *Globalizations*, doi.org/10.1080/14747731.2020.1815461.
54   Claire Polster, 'Dismantling the Liberal University: The State's New Approach to Academic Research' in Brecher et al. (n. 18) 106. See also Axelrod et al. (n. 19).
55   Miyoshi (n. 9) 60.

allowed universities themselves to commercialise inventions developed through federally funded research programs.[56] As a result, universities are intent on forming partnerships with industry to secure research funding in anticipation of future collaboration and commercialisation.

Entrepreneurialism, commercialisation and technology transfer have become primary aims of contemporary universities everywhere.[57] These characteristics have been elevated to the same status as the traditional university's missions of teaching and research. The focus on profitmaking has been sharpened as governments expect universities to do more while providing them with less public funding.[58] In response, universities such as the University of Queensland, are embedding entrepreneurial learning across all disciplines.[59]

Thus, it is in the interstices of the technocratic and the profitable that at least a partial explanation for the resiling from feminist scholarship can be found, about which Ursula Franklin made a similar observation in *Knowledge Reconsidered* 40 years ago.[60]

Academic capitalism and the remasculinisation of the academy

I have already noted that the new knowledge society is concerned more with the transmission of data than the pursuit of wisdom ('know-how' rather than 'know-what'). Understanding and critiquing new knowledge are not dimensions of the present agenda, and the undervaluation of the humanities and dispensing with the social have invariably contracted the traditional spaces for critique. Critique is not only deemed to lack use value in the market, but also likely to be discomfiting to corporations

---

56   *Bayh–Dole Act*, 35 USC 200–12.

57   European Commission & Organisation for Economic Co-operation and Development, *A Guiding Framework for Entrepreneurial Universities* (OECD, 2012), available from: web.archive.org/web/2013 1126104948/http:/www.oecd.org/site/cfecpr/EC-OECD%20Entrepreneurial%20Universities%20 Framework.pdf.

58   Shuiyun Liu & Peter C. van der Sijde, 'Towards the Entrepreneurial University 2.0: Reaffirming the Responsibility of Universities in the Era of Accountability' (2021) 13 *Sustainability* 3073, available from: scholar.archive.org/work/akvdvrts4naqjmuex2mfazfe4e.

59   The University of Queensland, *Entrepreneurship Strategy 2018–2022* (UQ Ventures, 2019), available from: ventures.uq.edu.au/files/3440/EntrepreneurshipStrategy.pdf.

60   Franklin et al. (n. 7). See also Ursula Martius Franklin, *Will women change technology or will technology change women?* (CRIAW Papers, CRIAW/ICREF, 1985), available from: www.criaw-icref. ca/publications/will-women-change-technology-or-will-technology-change-women/.

that would prefer not to have their business practices exposed. Thus, the critical pursuit of knowledge for its own sake is out of favour, not only because it is regarded as unprofitable in terms of knowledge transfer but also because neoliberals are suspicious of its very raison d'être. Law and business are notable examples of the shift away from the prudential towards the applied in their curricular orientation—a factor that is not without significance at a time of large-scale corporate collapse and executive greed, as illustrated by the GFC of 2008–09.[61]

I would also suggest the new knowledge economy is deeply gendered and racialised, despite its best endeavours to present a neutral facade to the world. In one sense, capitalism has little incentive either to eradicate or to encourage sexism or racism,[62] unless gender and race can be deployed by the market for profit.[63] However, there is a concealed manifestation of antifeminism lurking beneath the surface of the new knowledge economy and embedded within its technologies of power.[64] Ursula Franklin noted insightfully in 1985 how technology was grafted on to traditional masculinist notions of power that replaced the old social order. In this regard, it is not so much the gender or race of the social actors that drives the present climate as the new ideologies.[65]

In their description of the academic subject, Kenway et al. capture the subtle incarnation of gender that emerges as 'technopreneurial', which refers to the way the favoured techno-scientific knowledge is combined with business acumen.[66] The technopreneur works alone, taking risks and promoting the self, unconcerned about collegiality and the collective good, since the intensification of the economic function of knowledge has come at the expense of the social function.[67]

---

61 Mevlüt Tatliyer, 'The 2008–2009 Financial Crisis in Historical Context' in Ümit Hacioğlu & Hasan Dinçer (eds), *Global Financial Crisis and its Ramifications on Capital Markets* (Springer, 2017).
62 Miyoshi (n. 9) 74.
63 The phenomenon of 'girl power', which focuses on sexy fashions for young women, is one example of this. See, for example, Shelley Budgeon, 'The Contradictions of Successful Femininity: Third-Wave Feminism, Postfeminism and "New" Femininities' in Rosaline Gill & Christina Scharff (eds), *New Femininities: Postfeminism, Neoliberalism and Subjectivity* (Palgrave Macmillan, 2011), doi.org/10.1057/9780230294523_19; Angela McRobbie, 'Top Girls?' (2007) 21(4) *Cultural Studies* 718; Chilla Bulbeck, 'Explaining the Generation Debate: Envy, History or Feminism's Victories?' (2006) 15 *Lilith* 35.
64 Franklin (n. 60) 83.
65 Magda Lewis, 'More Than Meets the Eye: The Under Side of the Corporate Culture of Higher Education and Possibilities for a New Feminist Critique' (2005) 2(1) *Journal of Curriculum Theorizing* 7, 10.
66 Kenway et al. (n. 6) 42.
67 ibid.

Picking up on the masculinised character of the technopreneur, Henry Giroux goes somewhat further by graphically describing the American university post-9/11 as a 'militarised knowledge factory'.[68] He suggests the hatred of democracy and dissent in an authoritarian neoliberal environment has given rise to a politics of 'militarised masculinity', associated particularly with the war in Iraq[69] and the domestic War on Terror, which marked the return of the 'warrior male', whose paranoia is endlessly stoked by the existence of a feminised culture of critical thinking, a gay subculture and a liberal ideology that exhibits a disrespect for top-down order and unquestioned authority and discipline.[70]

Universities as 'militarised knowledge factories' are not involved in producing conventional soldiers so much as producing graduates with a uniform habit of mind that is clearly gendered. More is at stake here than simply affirming the stereotypical conjunction between militarism and masculinity. The denigration of the feminine emerged with the populist neoconservative attacks on tertiary educated 'elites' who were concerned about social justice, rights for indigenous peoples, same-sex relationships and welfare rights.[71] It is perhaps unsurprising that this populist form of antifeminism first emerged in the United States and later surfaced in new guises in other Anglophone countries, such as Canada and Australia.[72]

To reclaim 'authentic manliness' through technocratic new knowledge, the act of critique, which is the essence of liberal academic life within these new 'knowledge factories', is currently depicted as undervalued, dispensable and feminised. It is assumed that technocratic and applied knowledge, delivered as information, does not need to be interpreted; it speaks for itself. The most effective way of dispensing with critique is to contract the space that enables it, which is disastrous for projects such as feminism, which is necessarily a critical project. The evisceration of this space has enabled antifeminism to be revived within the new knowledge

---

68 Henry A. Giroux, 'The Militarization of US Higher Education after 9/11' (2008) 25 *Theory Culture Society* 56. Cf. John Armitage, 'Beyond Hypermodern Militarized Knowledge Factories' (2005) 27(3) *Review of Education, Pedagogy, and Cultural Studies* 219, doi.org/10.1080/10714410500228884.

69 The United States spearheaded both the 2003–11 Iraq War and the War in Afghanistan (2001–21).

70 Giroux (n. 68) 61.

71 See Damien Cahill, 'New-Class Discourse and the Construction of Left-Wing Elites' in Marian Sawer & Barry Hindess (eds), *Us and Them: Anti-Elitism in Australia* (API Network/Curtin University of Technology, 2004).

72 Marian Sawer, 'Populism and Public Choice in Australia and Canada: Turning Equality Seekers into "Special Interests"' in Marian Sawer & Barry Hindess (eds), *Us and Them: Anti-Elitism in Australia* (API Network/Curtin University of Technology, 2004).

scripts of the academy even though, as Magda Lewis points out, terms such as patriarchy and sexism have become anachronistic because of the ideological shifts that have occurred.[73] However, gender does not go away. As Dorothy Smith observed 40 years ago, it remains integral to social relations: 'The apparently neutral and impersonal rationality of the ruling apparatus is, in fact, organised by gender. The male subtext concealed beneath its apparently impersonal forms is integral, not accidental.'[74]

It is therefore unsurprising that the gendered subtext of the new knowledge economy has adapted to the new circumstances and new ideologies. New knowledge is the ostensibly neutral apparatus that enables the production of a new manifestation of gender, despite its technocratic veneer of gender neutrality. Thus, while the gendered identity of academic subjects no longer counts as much as their productivity, the gendered subtext of the new knowledge economy is subtly reified. Competition policy and the logic of the market necessarily produce inequality, not equality, and it is notable that there has been a resiling from the language of equality and equality of opportunity in the academy as well as in public policy more generally.[75] The legitimation of inequality tilts the scales permanently in favour of the status quo. In addition, neoliberalism has seen an erosion of progressive public-interest policies in favour of individualism, which has impacted disproportionately on women.[76] Promotion of the self through neoliberal rationality has effectively displaced a collective commitment to gender politics in the academy, which has spilled over into the constitution of new knowledge.

Conclusion

The transformation of the university through the targeting of funds for commercial research, privatisation and corporatisation has not only exerted a profound effect on what is taught, what is researched and what

---

73 Lewis (n. 65) 11.

74 Dorothy Smith, 'The Renaissance of Women', in Franklin et al. (n. 7) 7.

75 Janine Brodie, 'We Are All Equal Now: Contemporary Gender Politics in Canada' (2008) 9(2) *Feminist Theory* 145, doi.org/10.1177/1464700108090408; Margaret Thornton, 'The Political Contingency of Sex Discrimination Legislation: The Case of Australia' (2015) 4 *Laws* 314, 326–28, doi.org/10.3390/laws4030314.

76 Anne Summers, *The End of Equality: Work, Babies and Women's Choices in 21st Century Australia* (Random House, 2003); Marian Sawer, 'From Women's Interests to Special Interests: Reframing Equality Claims' in Louise Chappel & Lisa Hill (eds), *The Politics of Women's Interests* (Routledge, 2006).

is valued; it has been suggested that it is also causing the disintegration of the university.[77] Xiaoying Wang suggests the university will soon 'cease to be an institution informed by intellectual autonomy; instead, it will become an appendage of corporations … tailored to the needs of industry and commerce'.[78] In the United States, there is already a proliferation of corporate universities run by multinationals, such as McDonald's and Motorola. These giant functionaries are paradigmatic transmitters of new knowledge that are dedicated to serving corporate interests, with no interest in critique or the questioning of orthodoxy. As German philosopher Karl Jaspers showed in *The Idea of the University*, which he wrote in 1923 and revised almost 40 years later, the primary role of the university in seeking truth is endangered if it ends up in the 'functionalism of giant institutions'.[79]

How did academics come to accept the new regime with so little resistance? It is not just a question of being directed from above but that academics themselves have become 'active subjects' in the new regime.[80] This entails academics managing themselves so that they are ever more productive in ways that best suit the new knowledge economy: 'The fact that immaterial labor produces subjectivity and economic value at the same time demonstrates how capitalist production has invaded our lives and has broken down all the oppositions among economy, power, and knowledge.'[81]

The web of governmentality in which academic subjects are enmeshed ensures compliance, for they inhabit an audit culture that requires constant demonstration of their productivity. Resistance may invite disapprobation, disciplinary action and even retrenchment—all of which are salutary disincentives for would-be dissidents. The fact that more than 40,000 Australian academics lost their jobs because of Covid-19 in 2020–21 rendered tenure increasingly parlous.[82] As a dimension of governmentality, conformity, rather than difference or distinctiveness,

---

77   Slaughter & Leslie (n. 26) 243; cf. Xiaoying Wang, 'Farewell to the Humanities' 17(4) (2005) *Rethinking Marxism* 537.

78   Wang (n. 77) 533.

79   Karl Jaspers, *The Idea of the University*, edited by Karl Deutsch, translated by H.A.T. Reiche & H.F. Vanderschmidt (Peter Owen, 1960 [1946]).

80   Maurizio Lazzarato, 'Immaterial Labor' in Paolo Virno & Michael Hardt (eds), *Radical Thought in Italy: A Potential Politics* (University of Minnesota Press, 1996) 134.

81   ibid., 142.

82   Karen MacGregor, 'Study Finds 40,000 Tertiary Jobs Lost during Pandemic', *University World News*, 17 September 2021.

typifies the corporatised university, which has profound implications for academic freedom. It is predicted that the struggle over the meaning and value of knowledge will continue to be a feature of the 'education wars'.[83] The corporatisation of the university and academic capitalism mean the struggle over knowledge is no longer solely an intellectual debate, as the struggle between university management and academics over resources has moved to centre-stage to create a new iteration of knowledge.

It is unimaginable that things might revert to the way they were because the higher education sector has come to rely on the wealth generated through academic capitalism. The disinvestment by neoliberal governments in public universities has ensured compliance with the commercial imperative. As the nation-state has turned away from sustaining universities as public goods, institutions have felt they have no option but to enter the market. This has enabled the state to justify the creation of new universities, the expansion of student numbers, the prioritisation of 'job-readiness', fee hikes and liaisons with industry on the ground of necessity, assuaging public criticism with a handful of scholarships and tokenistic gestures in support of the humanities and social sciences. Students then become enmeshed in what one may liken to a system of infeudation where everyone is caught in a web of responsibility—both to those above and to those below—from which there is no escape. Hence, I agree with Michael Peters that, far from being able to end the liaison between public education and business, it is likely to become even stronger:

> In the age of knowledge capitalism, we can expect governments in the West to further ease themselves out of the public provision of education as they begin in earnest to privatise the means of knowledge production and experiment with new businesses and public education at all levels.[84]

All the signs—including the facilitative roles of multinational corporations and supranational bodies such as the OECD and the World Bank—point in this direction, which has clearly been boosted by the impact of Covid-19. New knowledge and capital have become so thoroughly entwined within the 'knowledge economy' that they cannot be disentangled. After an inordinately fleeting time, feminist knowledge, in all its guises, appears to have become a shadowy presence within the academy once more. Considering the way women's voices were formerly systematically erased

---

83 Olssen & Peters (n. 3) 340.
84 Peters (n. 35) 165.

within the Western intellectual tradition, Dorothy Smith anticipated the likelihood of a further period of erasure if an institutional base were not secured for feminist scholarship: 'Without access to this institutional process, we will see again what we have seen in the past: the disappearance of a knowledge of women from the public social discourse.'[85]

Although women have secured an institutional base in the academy as both students and academics, this has not been enough to safeguard the place of feminism in the academy, for it is primarily as neoliberal subjects that they are now valued. In this capacity, feminist scholars, like academics generally, are expected to serve the new knowledge economy as teachers and technopreneurs rather than critique it.

Feminist studies was abolished at QUT when the Faculty of Arts was closed because the humanistic and the social were no longer viewed as valuable. Ironically, the replacement Faculty of Creative Industries was reported to have experienced similar difficulties to those of the former faculty.[86] Its teaching program acquired a deficit, there was a high attrition rate and it had difficulty meeting its marketing promise of preparing graduates for the 'forefront of entrepreneurial, cultural and creative developments'.[87] Trying to transmute the humanities into an industry in the interest of profitmaking can only do further damage to what is left of the idea of the university.

It is imperative that feminist and progressive scholars continue to exercise the vital academic role of 'critic and conscience of society',[88] rather than acceding to being mere pawns in the operation of the new knowledge economy. Acquiescence in the corporatised role of neoliberal subjects is not only hastening the conversion of universities into giant technological and profitmaking institutions in the interests of the state, but also encouraging a reversion to their masculinisation.

---

85 Smith (n. 74) 11.
86 The Faculty of Creative Arts was subsequently expanded to include education and social justice.
87 QUT, *Creative Industries Faculty Review (Final Report)*, 2–5 April 2007, 14, cited in Guille (n. 2).
88 The express role of the university, which is included in the *Education Act 1989* (NZ), s. 5(4)(a)(v).

15

The Mirage of Merit

Introduction: 'Just a matter of time'

There is a plethora of literature on the masculinity of the academy and its seemingly implacable resistance to the feminine in respect of authoritative positions. While 47 per cent of full-time and fractional academic staff in Australian universities in 2021 were women, 54 of the top 74 jobs (chancellor and vice-chancellor) were held by men—that is, 73 per cent.[1] The liberal progressivist response has long been that numerosity will magically provide the solution and that it is 'just a matter of time' before women are proportionately represented throughout the academy. Indeed, women are now more likely than men to have a bachelor's degree as well as postgraduate qualifications.[2] I suggest, however, that far from numerosity providing a solution to gender inequality, it may point to the very reason for the ongoing resistance to the feminine in senior positions. This appears to arise from an atavistic fear that the academy as a former bastion of masculinity is in the process of becoming feminised, thereby signalling a decline in its status. This was the experience with secretarial work and bank telling—once both masculinised areas of endeavour. After women were 'let in' to these occupations, their numbers rapidly increased, which resulted in a decline in pay and prestige that caused men to flee.[3]

---

1   Marcia Devlin, 'No Change at the Top for University Leaders as Men Outnumber Women 3 to 1', *The Conversation*, 8 March 2021, available from: theconversation.com/no-change-at-the-top-for-university-leaders-as-men-outnumber-women-3-to-1-154556.
2   Australian Bureau of Statistics, *Gender Indicators, Australia* (ABS, 2020), available from: www.abs.gov.au/statistics/people/people-and-communities/gender-indicators-australia/latest-release.
3   Ann Game & Rosemary Pringle, *Gender at Work* (George Allen & Unwin, 1983).

The typical equation is that the more prestigious an area of endeavour, the greater is the resistance to the feminine. Law was also once a masculinist preserve but, as discussed in previous chapters, women now make up more than 50 per cent of practising lawyers.[4] Feminisation, however, has not caused male flight—a fate that has been averted by a hardening of the line of demarcation between the apex and the base of the organisational pyramid. As women entered legal practice, they found themselves increasingly relegated to the managed or 'manned' positions at the base, leaving relatively untouched the male domination of the apex—that is, the positions associated with autonomy and authority. I argue that a similar phenomenon is occurring in higher education.

Although the traditional gender pyramid has been destabilised by feminist critiques and equity initiatives, it has been reaffirmed by a growing divergence between research and teaching,[5] with research consistently privileged over teaching, as is apparent in the increasing stratification of universities. The emergence of an underclass of precarious workers to assume responsibility for the preponderance of teaching throughout the sector is a by-product of academic capitalism, on which I elaborate. It has also boosted the thesis that the pyramidal base is the appropriate site for the feminine.

It is well documented that it is conventionally more difficult for women to be appointed to authoritative positions in the academy and promotion invariably takes longer.[6] While the evidence reveals that women's research

4   Law Society of New South Wales, *2020 National Profile of Solicitors: Final* (Urbis, 2021) 7, available from: www.lawsociety.com.au/sites/default/files/2021-07/2020%20National%20Profile%20of%20Solicitors%20-%20Final%20-%201%20July%202021.pdf.
5   Jill Blackmore & Judyth Sachs, *Performing and Reforming Leaders: Gender, Educational Restructuring, and Organizational Change* (State University of New York Press, 2007) 130; Tanya Fitzgerald & Jane Wilkinson, *Travelling towards a Mirage? Gender, Leadership and Higher Education* (Post Pressed, 2010).
6   Margaret Thornton, 'The First and Last (?) Feminist Law Professors in Australia' in Ulrike Schultz, Gisela Shaw, Margaret Thornton & Rosemary Auchmuty (eds), *Gender and Careers in the Legal Academy* (Hart Publishing, 2021), doi.org/10.5040/9781509923144.ch-025; Belinda Probert, '"I Just Couldn't Fit It In": Gender and Unequal Outcomes in Academic Careers' (2005) 12(1) *Gender, Work and Organization* 50, 58, doi.org/10.1111/j.1468-0432.2005.00262.x; Erica Halvorsen, 'Female Academics in a Knowledge Production Society' (2002) 56(4) *Higher Education Quarterly* 347, 352, doi.org/10.1111/1468-2273.00224; Barbara Bagilhole & Jackie Goode, 'The Contradiction of the Myth of Individual Merit, and the Reality of a Patriarchal Support System in Academic Careers: A Feminist Investigation' (2001) 8(2) *European Journal of Women's Studies* 161, 162, doi.org/10.1177/135050680100800203; Christine Heward, 'Academic Snakes and Merit Ladders: Reconceptualising the "Glass Ceiling"' (1994) 6(3) *Gender and Education* 249, doi.org/10.1080/0954025940060302.

outputs are marginally less than those of men,[7] women take greater responsibility for administration and pastoral care, as well as teaching— all of which are accorded less weight than research, entrepreneurialism and leadership.

Despite years of feminist activism, an incipient understanding of the non-discrimination principle within universities, the development of equal opportunity (EO) and the acceptance of more fluid identities, I suggest the ideal academic continues to be constituted in the image of the benchmark man—the normative standard that favours those who are white, heterosexual, able-bodied and middle class and who espouse a right-of-centre politics and a nominal mainstream religion, if any. When the achievements of women and racialised Others are measured against benchmark men, they are invariably found wanting.

Despite the permeability of the postmodern new knowledge economy, which renders seeming absolutes passé, the modernist hierarchical and gendered values associated with the academy are not easily sloughed off but remain powerful cultural subtexts. I suggest that the fear of feminisation has been staunched and the masculinity of the ideal academic injected with new life with the neoliberal turn, the corporatisation of the university and the embrace of academic capitalism. I also consider why equity initiatives have been unable to withstand the academic capitalist imperative.

I begin by deconstructing the concept of merit, which has received comparatively little scholarly attention in recent years, even though it lies at the heart of the intractable gendered binary within the academy. Merit provides the key to understanding how the ideal academic and its less-than-ideal counterpart are constituted as gendered creations.

The mystique of merit

It is an essential tenet of modern liberal democratic governance that positions are allocated on merit rather than status, patronage, seniority, gender, race or other facet of identity. It is believed that if candidates openly compete for positions, the best person for the job should be appointed according to his or her abilities and achievements without regard to status

---

7   Fitzgerald & Wilkinson (n. 5) 65.

or identity.[8] The secondary meaning of merit associated with desert is also relevant in that it is assumed that the 'best person for the job' *deserved* to be appointed.[9] The notion of desert is deemed to satisfy the imperatives of justice and fairness.

Appointment to the public service on the basis of merit rather than patronage in the late nineteenth century was regarded as an important sign of modernisation, although merit was formally recognised as a secondary consideration to gender.[10] The history of what purports to be merit selection in the academy is even shorter than that of the public service, as Boyle et al. point out that public advertising for academic positions became the norm in Australia only in the 1970s.[11] Despite the unmasking of gender in the constitution of merit, which has revealed it to be a concept infected with bias, our society continues to place unparalleled confidence in it as an egalitarian, rational and fair means of allocating scarce resources.

Faith in the idea of an unequivocal 'best person' arises from the belief that merit is a neutral and apolitical variable, although the evaluative dimension is central as merit comprises an amalgam of objective and subjective elements. The objective element comprises factors such as a candidate's qualifications, employment history, success in grant applications, publications, teaching undertaken, PhD supervisions and completions. This is the type of information appearing on an academic's CV, but a literal approach to a list of achievements makes no sense without evaluation. From which institution were the qualifications obtained? What is the standing of that institution? Is the candidate's work history relevant? Are the publications refereed? What is the reputation of the journals in which they appeared or, in the case of books, the publishing houses that published them? How significant is the body of research? How original and creative is it? What impact has the candidate's scholarship had in the field? And so on.

---

8   Clare Burton, *Redefining Merit* (Monograph No. 2, Affirmative Action Agency, 1988) 5.
9   Margaret Thornton, 'Affirmative Action, Merit and the Liberal State' (1985) 2(2) *Australian Journal of Law and Society* 28, 29–20.
10   Linda Colley, 'Merit is in the Eye of the Beholder: Barriers to Female Employment in the Queensland Public Service from 1859–1959' (2004) 9(1) *Journal of Interdisciplinary Gender Studies* 62.
11   Gregory J. Boyle, John J. Furedy, David L. Newmann, H. Rae Wesbury & Magnus Reistad, 'Balance between Merit and Equity in Academic Hiring Decisions: Judgemental Content Analysis Applied to the Phraseology of Australian Tenure-Stream Advertisements in Comparison with Canadian Advertisements' (2010) 52(2) *Australian Universities Review* 49.

Any data are meaningless without an evaluative component, but they cannot be weighed up in a test-tube. The task must be undertaken by fallible humans who are acculturated into ways of thinking about the normative construction of 'the best person for the job' in a particular context. In view of the long history of the exclusion of women from the academy, it is unsurprising that merit has come to be imbricated with benchmark masculinity, as is apparent in complaints of sex discrimination against universities.[12] Unsurprisingly, gender bias is reflective of the standpoint of decision-makers, who are invariably benchmark men themselves or 'safe' women who endorse benchmark masculinity.

I was first struck by the malleability of merit from my experience of sitting on university selection committees. On one not atypical occasion, several well-credentialled women were bypassed in the compilation of a short list in favour of an objectively less-distinguished male candidate who was supported strongly by the chair of the committee. Although the chair conceded that the candidate's record was less than outstanding, what the favoured candidate had to make up for his shortcomings, the chair assured us, was 'potential'. Now, while potential, like merit, is another category of indeterminate reference, projections about the future must be based on past performance. In this case, the candidate's potential was something that could be discerned by the chair but eluded the rest of us. What was it that the candidate had potential for? The construction of the best person did not require this to be spelled out. The committee members were expected to understand intuitively what it meant and that it was necessarily imagined in terms of benchmark masculinity, which trumped the objective merit markers evinced by the superior women candidates. Nevertheless, most members of the committee accepted the chair's recommendation.

This incident, which first prompted me to write about merit,[13] shows how homosocial reproduction[14]—the replacement of like with like—is unproblematically performed on a regular basis with a little help from an authoritative decision-maker. The visible signs of identity may create

---

12   Katherine A. Lindsay, 'A Critique of the Culture of Complaint: Trends in Complaints of Sex Discrimination in University Employment' (1996) 1 *Australia & New Zealand Journal of Law & Education* 99.
13   Thornton (n. 9).
14   Jean Lipman-Blumen, 'Toward a Homosocial Theory of Sex Roles: An Explanation of the Sex Segregation of Social Institutions' in Martha Blaxall & Barbara Reagan (eds), *Women and the Workplace* (University of Chicago Press, 1976).

a presumption in favour of appointability and 'fitting in',[15] although the presumption is rebuttable. Nevertheless, the burden of proof in formally challenging a decision is likely to be onerous.

Homosocial reproduction also means that the ideal academic's career trajectory is likely to emulate that of the paradigmatic male decision-maker: an honours undergraduate degree, an *international* postgraduate degree, an *international* postdoctoral fellowship, followed by an unbroken academic career focusing on research rather than teaching, regular attendance at *international* conferences, *international* institutional visitorships, as well as a string of grants, publications, awards, honours and prizes. I stress here that the international is invariably privileged above the domestic to the advantage of male candidates, as women have found it difficult to be supported for overseas scholarships in the past, although this is undoubtedly changing.

The status of referees—a euphemism for patrons—is considered essential for the purposes of legitimation of the candidate's scholarship and is the seemingly neutral means of effecting homosocial reproduction and sustaining benchmark masculinity. The credentials of the candidate will be gauged by considering the international standing of the referee whose voice will carry most weight in the evaluation of scholarship. Teaching is less likely to attract patrons.[16] If service is adverted to, it is more likely to be managerial experience, which is interpreted as leadership.

The fact that merit is perceived as an apolitical and value-neutral criterion is the key to its force and moral persuasiveness. The ostensible neutrality of merit in high-status appointments continues to be endlessly reiterated while the conjunction of merit and benchmark masculinity is subtly retained. This was aptly illustrated by a front-page headline in a national newspaper announcing the appointment of Susan Crennan to the High Court of Australia in 2005: 'Woman "of Merit" Joins High Court.'[17] As suggested in Chapter 11, it would have been unimaginable to have read, 'Man "of Merit" Joins High Court'. In assuring readers that Justice Crennan possessed the requisite degree of merit, she had to be presented as an exceptional woman and 'letting in' women did not pose a threat to the masculinity of judicial power. Despite the progressivist thesis that

---

15   Burton (n. 8) 5.
16   Heward (n. 6) 259.
17   Elizabeth Colman & Natasha Robinson, 'Woman "of Merit" Joins High Court', *The Australian*, 21 September 2005, 1.

sex discrimination is passé, the exceptionality subtext implies that merit and the feminine remain prima facie disjunctive while the notion that there is a symbiotic relationship between benchmark masculinity and merit lingers.

The ideal academic as technopreneur

The status of universities as key knowledge producers has been enhanced on the world stage as new knowledge economies replace agriculture and manufacturing with alternative sources of capital accumulation. Alan Burton-Jones suggests the change in favour of new knowledge is as profound as the Industrial Revolution.[18] Such a major transformation is inevitably going to affect the constitution of the ideal academic.

Instead of being regarded as a public good, higher education has become a commodity. Within the new 'higher education industry', students have become customers who purchase a product from service providers. The marketisation of higher education has signalled a change in all the familiar discourses of the academy. So effortlessly has the idea of education as a commodity been absorbed and naturalised that universities may now even relish defining themselves in economic terms.[19]

Nevertheless, the transition is not all smooth sailing for universities. As business entities, they are inescapably subjected to the full force of the 'risk society'.[20] Indeed, every aspect of entrepreneurialism is 'haunted' by risk.[21] Notable examples have included the GFC, fluctuations in the dollar, huge investment by China (a major market) in higher education that is now in jeopardy, attacks on Indian students and, most recently, the impact of Covid-19. The global context is a crucial dimension of the changed environment in which university education has become a major export earner for Australia and other OECD countries. By means of a policy of persistent underfunding over more than three decades, governments

---

18   Alan Burton-Jones, *Knowledge Capitalism: Business, Work, and Learning in the New Economy* (Oxford University Press, 1999) 3.

19   Henry A. Giroux, 'Beyond the Swindle of the Corporate University' in Michael Bailey & Des Freedman (eds), *The Assault on Universities: A Manifesto for Resistance* (Pluto Press, 2011) 147, doi.org/10.2307/j.ctt183p22h.16.

20   Ulrich Beck, *Risk Society: Towards a New Modernity*, translated by Mark Ritter (Sage, 1992 [1986]).

21   Jane Kenway, Elizabeth Bullen & Johannah Fahey, with Simon Robb, *Haunting the Knowledge Economy* (Routledge, 2006), doi.org/10.4324/9780203030493.

have been able to maintain the pressure on universities to generate income through the export of higher education and other entrepreneurial activities.[22] Although markets in higher education are fragile and volatile, they are the mainstay of Australian universities as international students pay higher tuition fees than domestic ones. The closure of borders because of the outbreak of Covid-19 in 2020 proved to be financially disastrous for the sector, with a predicted revenue loss of billions of dollars.[23]

Competition rather than collaboration is the raison d'être of the market, which affects all facets of the university. League tables—virtually unheard of before the millennial turn—are a startling manifestation of the way competition policy is retained at the forefront of the institutional academic agenda. They entail universities competing with one another for rankings at the national and international levels, based on a range of reputational factors, which invariably privilege research over teaching.

The economic significance of the transformation of universities for the nation-state has aided in muting dissent and marginalising the gender agenda in an environment that extols promotion of the self; to quote one Viennese professor, 'academics are people who make a career out of *outdoing others*'.[24] The difference now is that the academy is no longer conceptualised as a site for exemplary individual achievement, as the discourses of performativity are directed to the acquisition of institutional capitalism. Academics are expected to be economically productive and to enhance the brand of the university through entrepreneurial activities. While knowledge creation is a central aim of the university, the new culture exerts pressure on academics to create knowledge—not for its own sake, à la Newman, but for its use value in the market. The research findings of individual academics can no longer be permitted to lie fallow but must be exploited; this is the raison d'être of knowledge transfer. 'Enterprise' now represents the radical nub of the once public university. De Sousa Santos refers to the conflict between the production of high culture, critical thinking and exemplary scientific and humanistic knowledge, on the one hand, and instrumental knowledge demanded for

22   Margaret Thornton, *Privatising the Public University: The Case of Law* (Routledge, 2012).
23   Hazel Ferguson & Susan Love, 'The Impact of COVID-19 on Australian Higher Education and Overseas Students: What Do the Numbers Say?', *FlagPost*, [Parliamentary Library Blog], 12 August 2020, available from: apo.org.au/node/307462.
24   Beate Krais, 'Academia as a Profession and the Hierarchy of the Sexes: Paths Out of Research in German Universities' (2002) 56(4) *Higher Education Quarterly* 407, 414, doi.org/10.1111/1468-2273.00227.

capitalist development, on the other, as the 'crisis of hegemony'.[25] Thus, the very essence of the university—the pursuit of knowledge for its own sake—has been trumped by instrumentalism.

What does the 'crisis of hegemony' say about the conventional construction of the ideal academic? Not only do we encounter the questionable commodification of the fruits of research, but also academic capitalism exercises an incidental gender effect. Can we not immediately discern the masculinist character of the academic entrepreneur who, like the rogue explorer of yore, sloughs off personal ties and wanders for years in search of new lands to secure fame and glory? Women were notably absent from this scenario, other than as sexual companions. Of course, the modern variation of entrepreneurialism is replete with contradictions as more women embrace academic capitalism, but there is persistent evidence that women scientists and engineers produce fewer patents and engage less in commercialisation than their male counterparts.[26]

Gaze and Stevens attribute the potential inequity of knowledge transfer for women academics to their overrepresentation in insecure positions, which means they are less likely to be able to focus on higher-impact knowledge transfer.[27] Gaze and Stevens exhort that attention be paid to the issue of gender bias as well as the disproportionate impact of knowledge transfer on disciplines that are feminised, such as humanities and the creative arts. However, I am dubious that the new knowledge economy will be mindful of this exhortation because of the intense pressure in favour of competition policy and capital accumulation. Indeed, Metcalf and Slaughter observe in the US context that even in heavily male-dominated fields of endeavour, men appear to have moved to resource-rich centres and institutes where they can focus on patenting and industrial partnerships.[28]

25   Boaventura de Sousa Santos, 'The University in the 21st Century: Toward a Democratic and Emancipatory University Reform' in R. Rhoads & C.A. Torres (eds), *The University, State, and Market: The Political Economy of Globalization in the Americas* (Stanford University Press, 2006) 60, doi.org/10.1515/9780804767729-006.
26   Amy Scott Metcalfe & Sheila Slaughter, 'The Differential Effects of Academic Capitalism on Women in the Academy' in Judith Glazer-Raymo (ed.), *Unfinished Agenda: New and Continuing Gender Challenges in Higher Education* (Johns Hopkins University Press, 2008).
27   Beth Gaze & Carolyn Stevens, 'Running Risks of Gender Inequity: Knowledge Transfer Policy in Australian Higher Education' (2011) 26(5) *Journal of Education Policy* 621, 634, doi.org/10.1080/02680939.2010.514362.
28   Metcalfe & Slaughter (n. 26) 95.

In the new volatile and competitive environment, academics must not only be productive; they must be *seen* to be productive. Hence, performativity and productivity are the twin variables through which excellence is established, the demands of which are relentless and insatiable. One can never do enough—a proposition that the neoliberal academic subject quickly internalises. An audit culture has emerged as a corollary of corporatisation to ensure visibility and accountability. Drawing on Lyotard, Stephen Ball has written of the 'terrors of performativity'[29] to capture the nightmarish technology of surveillance and control now set in place to compel academics to do more and more. The relentless need to perform and promote the self has become an inescapable dimension of governmentality in the postmodern university. Everything that is done must be calculable through auditing regimes. If there is no 'output', the activity is discounted. Thinking is the example to which Bill Readings draws attention;[30] it no longer counts because there is no tickable box for it. The same could be said for the pastoral care of students, the mentoring of junior colleagues or the reviewing of books. Of course, book reviews do have a tangible output that is valuable to academics within a discipline, but they are discounted by the university because they do not represent original knowledge.

To be calculable, the work must be capable of generating funds and enhancing the institution's positional goods. Publishing means *international* refereed journals or *international* book publishers of high repute. Even an Australianist must be willing to reinvent the self and publish in international rather than Australian journals if that comports with the latest Excellence in Research for Australia (ERA) criteria. Ideal academics must be single-minded and ruthless in the pursuit of excellence—however defined at a particular moment—to assist in ensuring the top rating for their discipline.

Choosing one's own area of research was once a fundamental manifestation of academic freedom, but that has been compromised by market imperatives, particularly if an esoteric area of study is unlikely to be remunerative. The loss of academic freedom is rued by academic researchers who generally evince less-than-wholehearted support for

29   Stephen Ball, 'The Teacher's Soul and the Terrors of Performativity' (2003) 18(2) *Journal of Education Policy* 215.
30   Bill Readings, *The University in Ruins* (Harvard University Press, 1996) 175.

corporatisation from within the academy.[31] Perhaps for this reason, the empirical evidence tracked by Goedegebuure et al.[32] suggests that technology transfer is undertaken by less than one-fifth of all Australian academic staff,[33] although the authors do not consider the gender breakdown of this figure. The masculinist domination of the sciences, engineering and biotechnology, which receive the preponderance of grant moneys, nevertheless attests to the gender disproportionality. In contrast, arts and social sciences—feminised disciplines with large numbers of students and limited opportunities for academic capitalism—are perennially vulnerable to cuts and redundancies.

The ideal academic must be prepared to transmute him/herself from being a preeminent teacher (the nineteenth-century Newmanite ideal), to being a preeminent teacher and researcher (the twentieth-century ideal), to being a preeminent researcher and academic capitalist (the twenty-first-century ideal). While teaching has been relegated to the second order in the corporatised university, it must still be 'excellent' to enhance the university's brand and appeal to the student market.

Despite the prevailing rhetoric of teaching excellence and the proliferation of awards, teaching has increasingly become the preserve of the less-than-ideal academic in the contemporary academy. Less time is now likely to be devoted to teaching by all full-time academics, apart from those in teaching-only positions. An empirical study of the reported activities of Australian academics in 2007 compared with earlier studies concluded that the average number of hours dedicated to teaching had already decreased by five hours a week, while the hours for research had increased by about three hours and for administration and service by about 2.5 hours a week.[34] Today, the ideal academic is likely to undertake very little teaching at all to focus on securing the competitive grants and research outcomes that are most highly valued by the market. Martínez Alemán characterises teaching as a dimension of the *reproductive economy*, in which knowledge is given as a gift, in contrast to the *productive economy*, which is associated

31 'Academic Freedom's Precarious Future' (2021) 63(1)[SI] *Australian Universities Review* 7. This Special Issue was prompted by a government report authored by former High Court chief justice Robert French, *Report of the Independent Review of Freedom of Speech in Australian Higher Education Providers* (Department of Education and Training, 2019), available from: www.dese.gov.au/higher-education-publications/resources/report-independent-review-freedom-speech-australian-higher-education-providers-march-2019.
32 Leo Goedegebuure, Hamish Coates, Jeannet van der Lee & V. Lynn Meek, 'Diversity in Australian Higher Education: An Empirical Analysis' (2009) 51(2) *Australian Universities Review* 58.
33 ibid., 49, 54–56.
34 ibid.

with academic capitalism.[35] Despite the moral worth of the educational mission of the university—the reproduction of culture—it is necessarily trumped by market capitalism: the productive aspect.

Service, or being a good academic citizen, no longer comports with prevailing notions of excellence in the productive economy either. Its significance is underplayed compared with research and publication.[36] Once again, there is a gendered subtext as women are expected to assume responsibility for a disproportionate amount of routine administration, which deflects attention from scholarship.[37] Auditing templates are unlikely to contain a performative box to be ticked simply for serving on a committee, for the ideal academic is expected to be a leader, not a follower.

While the discourse of managerialism has generally replaced that of administration or service in an endeavour to enhance the roles of line managers (from heads of departments to deans to pro and deputy vice-chancellors to vice-chancellors and presidents), academics are still the ones who are expected to provide academic leadership in the corporatised academy. The distinction between management and leadership is articulated by a UK study of academic leadership by Bolden et al.: '"Academic management" is mostly concerned with *alignment*, "academic leadership" is mostly concerned with *commitment*, and *direction* is enacted through a process of "self-leadership".'[38]

Although academic leadership is nebulous and indeterminate, it is apparent that academics do not generally look to university managers for inspiration and vision. The UK study revealed the 'tension, ambiguity and scepticism' on the part of many of the 350 academic respondents regarding the possibility of effecting a balance between these roles within a corporatised environment.

---

35   Ana M. Martínez Alemán, 'Faculty Productivity and the Gender Question' in Judith Glazer-Raymo (ed.), *Unfinished Agenda: New and Continuing Gender Challenges in Higher Education* (Johns Hopkins University Press, 2008) 157.
36   Clare McBeath, 'Professional Activities and Community Service' in Robert H. Cantwell & Jill J. Scevak (eds), *An Academic Life: A Handbook for New Academics* (ACER Press, 2010) 150.
37   Aimee Lapointe Terosky, Tamsyn Phifer & Anna Newmann, 'Shattering Plexiglas: Continuing Challenges for Women Professors in Research Universities' in Judith Glazer-Raymo (ed.), *Unfinished Agenda: New and Continuing Gender Challenges in Higher Education* (Johns Hopkins University Press, 2008).
38   Richard Bolden, Jonathan Gosling, Anne O'Brien, Kim Peters, Michelle Ryan & Alex Haslam, with Luz Longsworth, Anna Davidovic & Kathrin Winklemann, *Academic Leadership: Changing Conceptions, Identities and Experiences in UK Higher Education* (Research and Development Series 3: Publication 4, Leadership Foundation for Higher Education, University of Exeter, 2012) 36. Emphasis in original.

University managers similarly look to academics for academic leadership, but they are more interested in the material fruits of research, which is why universities are prepared to buy international 'stars'—the ideal academics of the twenty-first century. The domination of a field, a dazzling array of publications and/or discoveries, prizes and honours shape the construction of the ideal academic. The reconstituted ideal must comport with what Kenway et al. refer to as a 'technopreneur'—a neologism that refers to the way 'techno-scientific knowledge is combined with business acumen'.[39] The technopreneur is prepared to take risks with knowledge capitalism and to promote the self for the greater good—that is, for the institution, the community, the nation-state and humankind more broadly. Thus, if a cure for cancer could be patented and commercialised, it would enhance the brand of the institution and the financial rewards would be immeasurable. The ideal academic, then, is expected to engage in 'a sort of business politics'[40] by promoting the self and exercising something akin to a marketing role. In the process, s/he can slough off responsibility for students and the feminised emotional labour associated with teaching and pastoral care. Even though a flat salary system operates in Australia, where academics, including those deemed to be closest to the market (such as business and management), are paid approximately the same as those deemed to be furthest away (such as philosophy and creative arts), an exception is made for international 'stars'. Most particularly, the gendered subtext of technopreneurialism enables the revival of 'authentic manliness'—presently under threat from the feminisation of the academy.

The creation of the less-than-ideal academic

Paralleling technopreneurialism, which is subtly contributing to the remasculinisation of the ideal academic, is the casualisation of teaching that is entrenching the feminisation of the less-than-ideal academic. Contract researchers, most of whom are women, are more likely to be working on someone else's project, which deprives them of any real authority.[41] The result is an increasing gulf between academic labour and academic

---

39   Kenway et al. (n. 21) 42.
40   Olil-Helena Ylijoki, 'Entangled in Academic Capitalism? A Case-Study on Changing Ideals and Practices of University Research (2003) 45 *Higher Education* 307, 315.
41   Valerie Hey, 'The Construction of Academic Time: Sub/Contracting Academic Labour in Research' (2001) 16(1) *Journal of Education Policy* 67, 72, doi.org/10.1080/02680930010009831.

capital.[42] This reconfiguration of the academy in which subordinate workers, mainly women, service those who generate academic capital, mainly men, reveals how insidiously the remasculinisation of the academy is occurring as a corollary of numerical feminisation.

Casualisation—euphemistically referred to as 'numerical flexibility' in the labour market literature[43]—entrenches the bifurcation of the academic workforce along gender lines by distinguishing between core and peripheral workers.[44] The core workers are the stable component in the workforce; they are regarded as valuable assets as they possess unique skills, while peripheral workers are dispensable.[45]

The subservience of women to the needs of others has conventionally assisted in the construction of the masculinist ideal. Joan Williams' thesis is that employers believe they are entitled to workers who are immune to family responsibilities—an immunity that has come to be an implicit characteristic of the ideal worker.[46] Although no longer relegated to the home 1950s style, there is still a cultural expectation that women take primary responsibility for caring and housework, which sustains the ideology of the ideal worker. In its neotraditional formation, the heterosexual nuclear family remains the norm with the male partner as the primary breadwinner. The difference now is that the female partner is expected to engage in paid work. However, this is only as far as her domestic and caring obligations allow, which may necessitate working restricted hours to coincide with the length of the school day, for example. The growth in casualisation together with the correlative decline in full-time and tenurable positions dovetail with the neotraditional family model, which is a marked manifestation of the neoliberal turn.[47]

---

42 Diane Reay, 'Cultural Capitalists and Academic Habitus: Classed and Gendered Labour in UK Higher Education' (2004) 27(1) *Women's Studies International Forum* 31, 34, doi.org/10.1016/j.wsif.2003.12.006.

43 For example, Hazel Conley, 'Modernisation or Casualisation? Numerical Flexibility in Public Services' (2006) 30(2) *Capital & Class* 31, doi.org/10.1177/030981680608900102.

44 'Numerical flexibility' is not to be confused with 'temporal flexibility' (flexible work) where workers are able to control the timing of their work. See Forrest Briscoe, 'From Iron Cage to Iron Shield? How Bureaucracy Enables Temporal Flexibility for Professional Service Workers' (2007) 18(2) *Organization Science* 297, doi.org/10.1287/orsc.1060.0226.

45 Conley (n. 43) 53.

46 Joan C. Williams, *Unbending Gender: Why Family and Work Conflict and What to Do About It* (Oxford University Press, 2000) 20.

47 Cf. Judith Glazer-Raymo, 'The Feminist Agenda: A Work in Progress' in Judith Glazer-Raymo (ed.), *Unfinished Agendas: New and Continuing Gender Challenges in Higher Education* (Johns Hopkins University Press, 2008) 5–9.

The neotraditional family model allows women to be regarded as the ideal incumbents of casualised academic positions in the academy, which are now computed at approximately 45 per cent overall and as much as 70 per cent in some universities.[48] The casualisation of teaching not only saves on staffing costs, it also enables more attention to be paid to research by the technopreneurial core.

The 'good mother' discourse associated with the neotraditional family model conflicts directly with that of the ideal or 'successful' academic.[49] Gratitude for being allowed to keep one foot in the door contributes to the construction of women as the ideal academic subclass. Casualisation also avoids the subject position of the 'difficult woman' who questions policy because precarious workers do not have time for faculty meetings,[50] or they are ineligible to attend. As renewal of a contract invariably depends on pleasing a person in authority, casual teachers appeal to management as they do not complain or ask for additional resources, but diligently perform their teaching obligations and quietly leave when no longer required.

Precarious work fits in with the conventional social stereotype that women with young children have jobs rather than careers. However, after a few years spent raising children, academic women want to resume their careers, but find it difficult. Despite a decade or more of loyal teaching service, they may find that a 'broken career pattern' with an erratic research and publication record falls short of that expected of the ideal academic who has maintained a linear career trajectory and has been able to promote (him)self on the global academic stage. These 'good mothers' may then be considered suitable for teaching-only positions.[51] Neoconservative assumptions about parenting therefore operate to sustain the gendered research/teaching, core/periphery binaries of the enterprise university.

---

48 Damien Cahill, 'Wage Theft and Casual Work Are Built into University Business Models', *The Conversation*, 27 October 2020, available from: theconversation.com/wage-theft-and-casual-work-are-built-into-university-business-models-147555.

49 Arwen Raddon, 'Mothers in the Academy: Positioned and Positioning within Discourses of the "Successful Academic" and the "Good Mother"' (2002) 27(4) *Studies in Higher Education* 387, doi.org/10.1080/0307507022000011516.

50 Kathleen M. Shaw, M. Kate Callahan & Kimberly Lechasseur, 'Female Faculty in the Community College: Approaching Equity in a Low-Status Sector' in Judith Glazer-Raymo (ed.), *Unfinished Agendas: New and Continuing Gender Challenges in Higher Education* (Johns Hopkins University Press, 2008).

51 Blackmore & Sachs (n. 5) 206 ff.

What help equity?

The passage of sex discrimination legislation and the inclusion of universities in affirmative action legislation were important symbolic steps in the struggle for gender equity. Why were these measures unable to resist the gendering of academic capitalism?[52]

The favoured model of antidiscrimination legislation, as exemplified by the federal *SDA 1984*, places responsibility squarely on an individual complainant to prove she was discriminated against—typically, that she was treated less favourably than another in the same or similar circumstances by virtue of her sex. This is an onerous burden in any workplace situation, and few cases proceed to formal hearing in the context of the corporatised university.[53] The gender bias of technopreneurialism lies buried deep within the social psyche, which makes it impossible for a complainant to disinter the appropriate evidence and *prove* that a respondent university *caused* the act of discrimination. In an appointment scenario, the university would undoubtedly argue that merit was the sole criterion for appointment and that candidate X was more meritorious than the complainant. Furthermore, it could now be argued that entrepreneurialism was a bona fide consideration in the construction of merit. Its acceptance by universities around the world would be likely to immunise the respondent university. Antidiscrimination legislation can deal only with acts of discrimination close to the surface, not systemic discrimination.[54] An unbroken causal thread must link the respondent to the discriminatory act. The long history of benchmark masculinity in the academy and its contribution to the subtle moulding of merit according to prevailing norms are bound to militate against success by an individual complainant.

Another notable instance of the myth of the objectivity of merit is illustrated by the former *AA Act*—ostensibly proactive legislation that was intended to foreclose the burden on individual complainants. However, the legislation was weak, requiring corporations, including universities,

---

52   For a more comprehensive analysis of this question, see Margaret Thornton, 'The Evisceration of Equal Employment Opportunity in Higher Education' (2008) 50(2) *Australian Universities Review* 59.
53   *Chen v Monash University* (2015) EOC ¶93–760 (FCA) involved 53 allegations of sex discrimination and sexual harassment, which the complainant was unable to prove.
54   Margaret Thornton, *The Liberal Promise: Anti-Discrimination Legislation in Australia* (Oxford University Press, 1990) 7–8.

to do little more than lodge annual reports regarding progress on equal opportunity in their organisations. The sole condition was that women be employed on merit, which was designed to allay fears that 'forward estimates' might be construed as quotas based on biology alone. After complaints from the Business Council of Australia about compliance costs, the legislation was re-enacted in 1999 in even weaker form, as the *Equal Opportunity for Women in the Workplace Act 1999* (Cth), followed by the present Act, the gender-neutral *Workplace Gender Equality Act 2012* (Cth).

Universities were initially anxious to be seen to be remedying gender inequalities by appointing EO officers and by developing active recruitment policies, which included advertising themselves as 'Employers of Choice for Women'. However, the initiatives lasted for a mere nanosecond before they fell out of favour. The problem, as Blackmore and Sachs point out,[55] was that 'EO was not embedded into the cultural practices of universities', which made it easy for them either to minimise its impact or to resile from it altogether. Hence, the academic culture continued to be one of benchmark masculinity, which endorsed a skewed notion of merit, as I have suggested.

Furthermore, at the very moment EO initiatives were implemented, they were under stress from the effects of the Dawkins reforms of 1988. The dramatic increase in the number of universities—from 18 to 34 in four years[56]—soon destabilised the commitment to gender equity. Redundancies, casualisation, managerialism and entrepreneurialism contributed further to a cooling of interest. EO either disappeared from the agenda altogether or was diluted when EO units lost their quasi-independent status by being incorporated within established areas such as human resources.[57] Equity did not sit well with academic capitalism or the new managerialism with its harsh top-down style. Thus, as suggested, it was not a concept that was compatible with the maximisation of profits or an institution's standing on league tables. In an environment where

---

55   Blackmore & Sachs (n. 5) 235.
56   Simon Marginson & Mark Considine, *The Enterprise University: Power, Governance and Reinvention in Australia* (Cambridge University Press, 2000) 29.
57   Andrea North-Samardzic, 'Looking Back to Move Forward: The (D)evolution of Australia's EEO Regulatory Framework' (2009) 20(1) *The Economic and Labour Relations Review* 59, 71, doi.org/10.1177/103530460902000105.

competition policy prevailed, *in*equality, not equality, was the raison d'être. As Blackmore puts it, academic equity agendas became 'too difficult, too expensive, and too dangerous'.[58]

Rather than disappearing altogether, equity agendas took on a new life by being shifted from staff to students.[59] As prospective customers in the commodified academy, students had to be wooed. Gender equity in the academy was now passé; if there was minimal compliance with the *WGEA*, nothing more needed to be done. After all, an equity policy did nothing for an institution's ranking on league tables. As an EEO manager interviewed by Blackmore and Sachs drily remarked: 'If a university judges itself as a research institution, they are not going to care if they are good at affirmative action.'[60]

When affirmative action was unceremoniously dropped from the official discourse in 1999 with the repeal of the *AA Act*, the language of both equity and equal opportunity also began to recede as these terms, too, came to be seen as incompatible with the neoliberal agenda. This language insidiously began to be replaced with the discourse of diversity.[61] The new anodyne discourse effectively neutralised and depoliticised the dangerous antonyms of *in*equality, *in*equity, exclusion and discrimination against women, as well as racialised and sexualised Others,[62] which underpinned equity, equality and EO. The repetition of these terms in the face of failure induced an element of 'equity fatigue'.[63] EO, and its cognate terms, came to be viewed, perhaps conveniently, as passé. Accordingly, it had to be discarded. Diversity was presented as more 'fluid and positive' than the 'inflexible and punitive' discourse of EO.[64] Diversity was a vague umbrella

58   Jill Blackmore, 'Globalisation and the Restructuring of Higher Education for New Knowledge Economies: New Dangers or Old Habits Troubling Gender Equity Work in Universities?' (2002) 56(4) *Higher Education Quarterly* 419, 428, doi.org/10.1111/1468-2273.00228.
59   Rosemary Deem & Louise Morley, 'Diversity in the Academy? Staff Perceptions of Equality Policies in Six Contemporary Higher Education Institutions' (2006) 4(2) *Policy Futures in Education*, doi.org/10.2304/pfie.2006.4.2.185.
60   Blackmore & Sachs (n. 5) 234.
61   Sara Ahmed, 'Doing Diversity Work in Higher Education in Australia' (2006) 38(6) *Educational Philosophy and Theory* 745, doi.org/10.1111/j.1469-5812.2006.00228.x; Blackmore & Sachs (n. 5); Jane Wilkinson, 'A Tale of Two Women Leaders: Diversity Policies and Practices in Enterprise Universities' (2009) 36(2) *The Australian Educational Researcher* 39, doi.org/10.1007/bf03216898; Carol Bacchi, 'The Seesaw Effect: Down Goes Affirmative Action, Up Comes Managing Diversity' (2000) 5(2) *Journal of Interdisciplinary Gender Studies* 64.
62   Sexual orientation, gender identity and intersex status were included as new grounds in the *SDA* in 2013.
63   Ahmed (n. 61) 747.
64   Blackmore & Sachs (n. 5) 227.

term that meant that sexism, racism and homophobia largely disappeared from view, along with a commitment to redistributive justice.[65] Boyle et al. analyse the merit and equity markers that appeared in newspaper advertisements for tenure-stream positions between 1970 and 2003.[66] They treat the merit and equity markers as though they were disjunctive, which is somewhat problematic, but one suspects that a contemporary focus would reveal not only a shift away from the language of equity in favour of merit, but also a shift to a particular kind of merit marker that accommodated entrepreneurialism.

The gender-neutral language of the *WGEA* signalled a turning away from 'women' to gender neutrality as a key constituency in government policy. Instead of relying entirely on the good graces of employers to improve the gender profile of their workplace, the Workplace Gender Equality Agency is expected to play a more active role than its predecessors.[67] Perhaps, the main hope for universities is that employees and employee organisations have an opportunity to comment formally on their university's report, which could help them reclaim a small political space for advocacy. However, I am sceptical that a transformation is likely to occur, despite retention of the word 'equality' in the title. Not only is there a long history of legislative timidity in the face of corporate power, but also the privileging of academic capitalism over gender equality is underscored by the inclusion of 'productivity and competitiveness' as express objects of the *WGEA* itself. A reported loss of at least 40,000 academic jobs in Australia in 2020–21 because of the collapse of the international student market due to the Covid-19 pandemic, with further shortfalls predicted, is not a propitious time for the ideal academic to undergo a sex change.

Conclusion

In concluding, I suggest that the ideal academic is a fiction. Instead of the stable values associated with the modernist university, the risky and ephemeral nature of competition policy at the institutional, national and global levels have disrupted the traditional notion of the ideal. In the current global hypercompetitive environment, the ideal academic,

---

65   Ahmed (n. 61) 746.
66   Boyle et al. (n. 11).
67   Carolyn Sutherland, 'Reframing the Quest for Equality: The Equal Opportunity for Women in the Workplace Amendment Act 2012 (Cth)' (2013) 26(1) *Australian Journal of Labour Law* 102.

or 'post-academic', is a high-flying technopreneur dedicated to his or her career—that is, an international superstar with business acumen who can generate capital through knowledge transfer. While benchmark masculinity may not expressly be the primary criterion of appointment, it continues to be inextricably intertwined with the prevailing construction of merit, just as it has always been.

The ideal academic does not have time for work–life balance; work–work is what is expected. If this paragon has children, their care is assigned to someone else, such as a dependent partner who is prepared to work part-time or casually. In the workplace, an army of support staff—administrators, casual teachers and research assistants, who are overwhelmingly women—cushion the life of the ideal academic. Thus, despite the dramatic change in the gender profile of the graduating class adverted to at the outset, the simplistic recitation of these data says little without further investigation. The gains that women have made are associated with 'public good knowledge' rather than the 'resource-rich academic capitalist knowledge/learning'.[68] In this context, Metcalfe and Slaughter pose a telling question: '[D]o men in roughly gender-balanced fields support women, or do they seek to re-establish dominance?'[69] While not denying support for individual women from time to time, I have suggested that the fear of feminisation remains an ever-present subtext of the contemporary academy that academic capitalism has sought to assuage.

Thus, the 'ideal academic' has not assumed a more feminised hue despite the changed gender demographic. Rather, the ideal has been reconfigured in masculinised terms while the 'less-than-ideal academic' has become even more unequivocally feminised. The instantiation of the two distinct subject positions has served to reinscribe the familiar gendered binary on the academy despite sustained efforts to destabilise it.

---

68 Metcalf & Slaughter (n. 26) 100.
69 ibid., 102.

Postscript

At the time of assembling this collection of essays in 2021–22, several incidents occurred that were salutary reminders that women are still far from equal in our society and the struggle is ongoing. These incidents also show how parlous are any ostensibly positive reforms, as well as rebutting the central tenet of liberal progressivism that things are always getting better.

First, I note the ballooning incidence of sexual harassment, although the increase might be partly attributable to a 'perception paradox' arising from a higher rate of reportage. Since the phrase 'sexual harassment' was first coined in the 1970s,[1] it has attracted notoriety because of 'celebrity scandals' involving high-profile men such as superior court judges.[2] Of most significance was the scandal involving Hollywood movie mogul Harvey Weinstein,[3] which reverberated around the world and crystallised into the #MeToo movement.[4] This encouraged countless women who had been silenced for so long to speak out, and it led to the initiation of multiple lawsuits, inquiries and reports.[5] In 2018, the Australian

---

1   For example, Catharine MacKinnon, *Sexual Harassment of Working Women* (Yale University Press, 1979).

2   For example, Clarence Thomas, Brett Kavanaugh and Dyson Heydon. Justin Worland, 'Supreme Court Justice Clarence Thomas Denies Groping Accusation', *TIME*, 27 October 2016, available from: time.com/4548119/clarence-thomas-sexual-harassment/; Haley Sweetland Edwards, 'How Christine Blasey Ford's Testimony Changed America', *TIME*, 4 October 2018, available from: time.com/5415027/christine-blasey-ford-testimony/; Kate McClymont and Jacqueline Maley, 'High Court Inquiry Finds Former Justice Dyson Heydon Sexually Harassed Associates', *Sydney Morning Herald*, 22 June 2020, available from: www.smh.com.au/national/high-court-inquiry-finds-former-justice-dyson-heydon-sexually-harassed-associates-20200622-p5550w.html.

3   'Harvey Weinstein Timeline: How the Scandal Unfolded', *BBC News*, 7 April 2021, available from: www.bbc.com/news/entertainment-arts-41594672.

4   Jessica Haynes, 'What is the #MeToo Campaign?', *ABC News*, 16 October 2017, available from: www.abc.net.au/news/2017-10-16/what-is-the-metoo-campaign/9055926.

5   For example, Kieran Pender, *Us Too? Bullying and Sexual Harassment in the Legal Profession* (International Bar Association, 2019).

Human Rights Commission undertook a national inquiry that resulted in a substantial, 1,000-page report, *Respect@Work*.[6] The extent of harassment exposed by this study was startling: of the 10,000 respondents, 71 per cent (85 per cent of women and 56 per cent of men) reported having been subjected to sexual harassment at work.

The Australian Government was tardy in responding to the *Respect@ Work* report and rejected some of its recommendations[7]—most notably, a requirement that employers develop a proactive approach to inhibit the extent of sexual harassment at work. This underscores the point made in the Introduction about the resistance to prophylactic action by the state, particularly in the case of harms allegedly associated with male sex right. The state, which is still overwhelmingly masculinist in orientation, would prefer to leave remediation to the chance action of individual victims. While it is unlikely that discrimination can ever be 'eliminated' in accordance with the aspiration contained in the wording of the CEDAW,[8] the prevalence of sexual harassment can undoubtedly be inhibited by sustained public scrutiny of the kind generated by the #MeToo movement, multiple law reform bodies and the judiciary, particularly women on the bench.[9]

The second issue I note is related to the first. It involved a series of incidents in Parliament House, Canberra, in 2020 that included the rape of a staffer and its alleged coverup by senior parliamentarians.[10] These incidents were compounded by an allegation of historical rape against then attorney-general Christian Porter, which could not be pursued because of the death of the accuser, and was further complicated by Porter instituting defamation proceedings against a journalist.[11] The irony

---

6   Australian Human Rights Commission, *Respect@Work: Sexual Harassment National Inquiry Report* (AHRC, 2020), available from: humanrights.gov.au/our-work/sex-discrimination/publications/respectwork-sexual-harassment-national-inquiry-report-2020.

7   *Sex Discrimination and Fair Work (Respect at Work) Amendment Act 2021* (Cth).

8   *Convention on the Elimination of all Forms of Discrimination against Women*, Article 11.

9   For example, *Richardson v Oracle Corporation Australia Pty Limited (No 2)* [2013] FCA 359. For detailed commentary, see Madeleine Castles, Tom Hvala & Kieran Pender, 'Rethinking *Richardson*: Sexual Harassment Damages in the #Me Too Era' (2021) 49(2) *Federal Law Review*, doi.org/10.1177/0067205X21993146.

10   James Glenday, Andrew Probyn & Matthew Doran, 'The Big Questions Left Unanswered about the Alleged Rape of Brittany Higgins at Parliament House', *ABC News*, 21 February 2021, available from: www.abc.net.au/news/2021-02-21/heres-what-we-know-and-dont-about-brittany-higgins-alleged-rape/13173526.

11   ibid.; Australian Associated Press, 'Christian Porter Tries to Prevent Publication of Unredacted ABC Defamation Defence', *The Guardian*, [Australia], 18 August 2021, available from: www.theguardian.com/australia-news/2021/aug/18/christian-porter-tries-to-prevent-publication-of-unredacted-abc-defamation-defence.

was that the attorney-general was the most senior legal officer of the Commonwealth, who was charged with overseeing the operation of human rights, antidiscrimination legislation and federal law reform generally. It became apparent that the incidents in Parliament House were underpinned by a culture of sexism and misogyny, as revealed by a major investigation undertaken by the Sex Discrimination Commissioner and the publication of a detailed report, *Set the Standard*.[12] The report exposed a culture in which bullying, sexual harassment and sexual assault were rife, in stark contrast to the government's official rhetoric of a commitment to equality and the non-discrimination principle.

Although the lives and careers of multiple women have been damaged by bullying, sexual harassment and sexual assault in the workplace, the Morrison government was sensitive to the exposure of the extent of the abuse and absence of procedural regularity within Parliament House, particularly in the eyes of the international community. Soon after *Set the Standard* was released, the government responded with alacrity. On the first sitting day of parliament in 2022, a Statement of Acknowledgement was issued on behalf of the Cross-Party Leadership Taskforce[13] and the government undertook to implement all 28 recommendations contained in the review.[14]

While the willingness of the government to remedy the culture of Parliament House is commendable, the seeds of invidiousness associated with implicit bias in elite workplaces of this kind are buried deep within the social psyche, making them difficult to eradicate. They may be fostered in single-sex boys' private schools, where boys have little opportunity to relate to girls as peers. These private schools—curiously described as 'public' in the English tradition—are a hangover from a colonial past. They tend to exercise an adverse effect on gender equality in the workplace, as the benchmark homosociality fostered between students facilitates links with more senior men in public life, so that homosocial reproduction

---

12 Australian Human Rights Commission, *Set the Standard: Report on the Independent Review into Commonwealth Parliamentary Workplaces* (AHRC, 2021), available from: humanrights.gov.au/set-standard-2021.

13 Parliament of Australia, 'Statement of Acknowledgement', 8 February 2022, available from: www.aph.gov.au/News_and_Events/Joint_statements_by_the_Presiding_Officers/Statement_of_Acknowledgement_20220208.

14 Senator the Hon. Simon Birmingham, Minister for Finance, 'Jenkins report recommendations', Media Release, 4 February 2022, available from: www.financeminister.gov.au/media-release/2022/02/04/jenkins-report-recommendations.

assumes a central role in the constitution of merit. The counterpoint is an implicit bias against women, racialised Others and those from a working-class background.

Prestigious men-only clubs are another anachronistic hangover from an imperial past, which are more suited to the era of Blackstone and the eighteenth century than a modern, ostensibly equal-opportunity society, but many male parliamentarians and senior bureaucrats belong to such clubs. Indeed, it is notable that the Australia Club, one of the oldest and most prestigious of such clubs, voted as recently as 2021 to retain its exclusive men-only status,[15] just when the drama in Parliament House was unfolding. Through the fostering of private single-sex institutions, such as elite boys' schools and men's clubs, women, racialised Others, gender-diverse and working-class people are treated with suspicion, if not permanently excluded from the community of equals and authoritative positions, although they may be the preferred incumbents of subordinate positions. They may also be regarded as being sexually available by powerful men, as the Parliament House scandals revealed, thereby echoing the notion of male sex right of an earlier age.

The third issue that has long been on the feminist reform agenda is that of abortion. While procuring a miscarriage was a criminal offence in the nineteenth and much of the twentieth centuries, Second-Wave Feminism struggled to decriminalise and legalise abortion on the basis that control over reproductive rights was an issue of personal autonomy for an individual woman in consultation with her doctor; it was not an issue for patriarchal states or male judges. While most jurisdictions accept the right to an abortion until a foetus is viable, although the time is variable, trenchant anti-abortion campaigns are periodically mounted by right-to-life activists. A dramatic example occurred in the United States in mid 2022 when the US Supreme Court overruled its 1973 decision of *Roe v Wade*[16] in a case that arose from a restrictive Texan law that banned abortion after a foetal heartbeat is detected—a ban that applied even in the case of rape and incest.[17]

---

15   Tita Smith & Kevin Airs, 'Australia's Oldest and Most Secret Gentlemen's Club—Which Boasts John Howard, Malcolm Turnbull and James Packer as Members—Votes AGAINST Allowing Women to Join', *Daily Mail Australia*, 15 June 2021, available from: www.dailymail.co.uk/news/article-9687107/Australias-oldest-secretive-mens-club-votes-AGAINST-women-joining.html.
16   410 US 113 (1973).
17   *Dobbs v Jackson Women's Health Association* (US Supreme Court, 24 June 2022).

The conservative anti-abortion lobby was anxious for the matter to be referred to the US Supreme Court while it was dominated by conservative judges, three of whom were appointed by former Republican president Donald Trump. In the majority opinion, Justice Samuel Alito found *Roe v Wade* to be 'egregiously wrong' because the Constitution contained 'no inherent right of privacy or personal autonomy'; abortion was a matter to be decided by states or voters in the states. The three dissenting judges (Judges Stephen Breyer, Sonia Sotomayor and Elena Kagan) stated that 'young women today will come of age with fewer rights than their mothers and grandmothers'.[18] The decision could have wide ramifications for gender equality in other parts of the world.

The fourth contemporary event that is exerting a deleterious impact on gender equality is Covid-19. Not only was the arrival of the pandemic totally unexpected, it also exerted a dramatic effect everywhere due to the high incidence of contagion, illness and death. It has disproportionately impacted women, so much so that it has been described as having effected a 'backlash against women's rights'.[19] Empirical studies have shown that because of the injunction to work at home, women have continued to assume responsibility for the preponderance of domestic labour, as well as the supervision of home schooling, while simultaneously coping with paid work, even if a male partner is present;[20] institutional childcare has also been unavailable. The evidence indicates that the situation has deteriorated further for many women because of increased levels of domestic violence during lockdowns.[21] Being confined to a small, shared space from which there is no escape can clearly exacerbate tensions in an already fraught relationship. So marked has been the increase in domestic violence during the pandemic that it has been referred to as 'the shadow pandemic'.[22] At the same time, the overwhelming preponderance of healthcare workers responsible for sustaining life during the pandemic are women, who are

---

18   Nina Totenberg & Sarah McCammon, 'Supreme Court Overturns Roe v. Wade, Ending Right to Abortion Upheld for Decades', *All Things Considered*, NPR, 24 June 2022, available from: www.npr.org/2022/06/24/1102305878/supreme-court-abortion-roe-v-wade-decision-overturn.

19   Gaby Hinsliff, 'The Coronavirus Backlash: How the Pandemic is Destroying Women's Rights', *The Guardian*, 23 June 2020, available from: www.theguardian.com/lifeandstyle/2020/jun/23/the-coronavirus-backlash-how-the-pandemic-is-destroying-womens-rights.

20   For example, Margaret Thornton, 'Coronavirus and the Colonisation of Private Life' (2021) 1(1) *Legalities* 44, doi.org/10.3366/legal.2021.0006.

21   United Nations, *Policy Brief: The Impact of COVID-19 on Women* (UN, 2020), available from: www.un.org/sexualviolenceinconflict/wp-content/uploads/2020/06/report/policy-brief-the-impact-of-covid-19-on-women/policy-brief-the-impact-of-covid-19-on-women-en-1.pdf.

22   ibid.

either working in a voluntary capacity or are significantly underpaid as aged care workers and nurses, thereby reflecting both the feminisation and the undervaluation of caring in our society—a factor that is central to gender inequality.

The fifth issue that is frustrating the realisation of equality to which I draw attention is the profound impact of the pandemic on higher education.[23] Not only does this augur badly for the future of women in the academy, it also does not bode well for the relative status of women and creative thinking generally. The loss of revenue from international students during the pandemic has been disastrous in the United States,[24] the United Kingdom[25] and Australia[26]—countries where there has been substantial disinvestment in public education because of the neoliberal turn. For example, by 2021, 40,000 full-time academic positions were lost in Australia, 61 per cent of which were held by women.[27] Universities sought to make up the financial deficit by increasing domestic enrolments, as well as by introducing austerity measures and increasing teaching loads—factors that are more likely to affect women because of the feminisation of teaching, as I have argued. Federal legislation was enacted to encourage more job-ready graduates in favoured areas, such as STEMM (science, technology, engineering, mathematics and medicine), while increasing the financial burden on those proposing to enrol in law and society and culture[28]—areas that include the humanities and the social sciences, and which are likely to impact women disproportionately. Such changes are also likely to contribute to the remasculinisation of the academy, as discussed in Chapters 14 and 15.

---

23   Andreas Schleicher, *The Impact of COVID-19 on Education: Insights from Education at a Glance 2020* (OECD, 2020), available from: www.oecd.org/education/the-impact-of-covid-19-on-education-insights-education-at-a-glance-2020.pdf.

24   Chris Mackie, 'The Pandemic Drives Unprecedented Decline in International Students', *WENR World Education News + Reviews*, 24 November 2020, available from: wenr.wes.org/2020/11/the-pandemic-drives-unprecedented-decline-in-international-students.

25   Peter Dolton, 'The COVID-19 Pandemic is Causing a Crisis in the UK Universities', *Vox EU*, 31 May 2020, available from: voxeu.org/article/covid-19-pandemic-causing-crisis-uk-universities.

26   Hazel Ferguson & Susan Love, 'The Impact of COVID-19 on Australian Higher Education and Overseas Students—What Do the Numbers Say?', *FlagPost*, [Parliamentary Library Blog], Parliament of Australia, 12 August 2020, available from: apo.org.au/node/307462.

27   Karen MacGregor, 'Study Finds 40,000 Tertiary Jobs Lost during Pandemic', *University World News*, 17 September 2021, available from: www.universityworldnews.com/post.php?story=202109 17061003607.

28   *Higher Education Support Amendment (Job-Ready Graduates and Supporting Regional and Remote Students) Act 2020* (Cth).

The essays in this collection have sought to show that the quest for gender equality remains a work in progress. The patriarchal heritage that has infused iterations of liberal legalism for centuries cannot be sloughed off instantaneously, for the philosophical values of the past continue to be influential in key areas, such as the way the public is privileged over private life, the individual over group rights and formal equality over substantive equality. Just when it appears that a semblance of gender equality might be realisable, this hope is likely to be thrown into disarray by a dramatic instance of sexual abuse, femicide or the resurgence of opposition to women's rights, as occurred with the repeal of *Roe v Wade* by the US Supreme Court. Such events are a reminder that we cannot rely on a simplistic liberal progressivist thesis that things are always getting better; nor can we rely solely on legislatures and policymakers to effect social change. It is incumbent on all of us to do what we can to make the world a fairer and more equitable place, by speaking out and challenging the instances of sexism, racism and homophobia that we encounter in our everyday lives.

www.ingramcontent.com/pod-product-compliance
Lightning Source LLC
Chambersburg PA
CBHW050806270326
41926CB00026B/4567